Neurodiversity-Affirming Occupational Therapy

of related interest

I Will Die On This Hill
Autistic Adults, Autism Parents, and the Children Who Deserve a Better World
Meghan Ashburn and Jules Edwards
Illustrated by Nathan McConnell
Foreword by Morénike Giwa Onaiwu
ISBN 978 1 83997 168 6
eISBN 978 1 83997 169 3
Audio ISBN 978 1 39981 203 0

Occupational Therapy, Disability Activism, and Me
Challenging Ableism in Healthcare
Georgia Vine
ISBN 978 1 83997 667 4
eISBN 978 1 83997 668 1

Antiracist Occupational Therapy
Unsettling the Status Quo
Edited by Musharrat J. Ahmed-Landeryou
Foreword by Professor Elelwani Ramugondo
ISBN 978 1 83997 574 5
eISBN 978 1 83997 575 2

Occupational Therapy Disruptors
What Global OT Practice Can Teach Us About Innovation, Culture, and Community
Sheela Roy Ivlev
Foreword by Juman Simaan
ISBN 978 1 83997 665 0
eISBN 978 1 83997 666 7

Occupational Identity
Journeys of Minoritized Occupational Therapists Across Race, Religion, and Culture
Alaa Abou-Arab and Erica V. Herrera with the Coalition of Occupational Therapy Advocates for Diversity
ISBN 978 1 83997 820 3
eISBN 978 1 83997 821 0

Neurodiversity-Affirming Occupational Therapy

Empowering Approaches to Foster Neurodivergent Participation

Edited by Bryden Carlson-Giving, OTD, OTR/L

Foreword by Winnie Dunn

Jessica Kingsley Publishers
London and Philadelphia

First published in Great Britain in 2026 by Jessica Kingsley Publishers
An imprint of John Murray Press

4

A CIP catalogue record for this title is available from the British Library and the Library of Congress

ISBN 978 1 80501 407 2
eISBN 978 1 80501 408 9

Printed and bound by CPI Group (UK) Ltd, Croydon, CR0 4YY

Jessica Kingsley Publishers' policy is to use papers that are natural, renewable and recyclable products and made from wood grown in sustainable forests. The logging and manufacturing processes are expected to conform to the environmental regulations of the country of origin.

Jessica Kingsley Publishers
Carmelite House
50 Victoria Embankment
London EC4Y 0DZ

www.jkp.com

John Murray Press
Part of Hodder & Stoughton Ltd
An Hachette Company

The authorised representative in the EEA is Hachette Ireland, 8 Castlecourt Centre, Dublin 15, D15 XTP3, Ireland (email: info@hbgi.ie)

To the courageous Neurodivergent individuals, whose resilience ignited the neurodiversity movement into the heart of occupational therapy—this work is for you. Thank you for reminding me about the power of community.

We are not a raindrop but a torrential downpour. We are carving a new future in a world that longs for change, a dream that can no longer be ignored.

A cascade is approaching, and the Neurodivergent future awaits.

Going Beyond Land Acknowledgement

This book's formulation was conducted on the ancestral land of the Dakota people, currently occupied by the municipality of Buffalo, Minnesota (Mni Sota Makoce). The editor lives on Dakota land and acknowledges the oppressive forces that have impacted and continue to impact Indigenous people. The editor recognizes the colonial influences remaining within today's society, which this editor benefits from as a white individual. Colonialism isn't an abstract metaphor; it is deeply embedded in our systems, practices, and daily lives, including occupational therapy and occupational science. This author aims to move beyond land acknowledgement* and optical allyship by advocating against Indigenous oppression, supporting decolonizing efforts, and amplifying Indigenous occupations within Western-focused occupational frameworks. Sections of this book highlight Indigenous perspectives and provide recommendations on how to support Indigenous occupations and advance decolonization in occupational therapy. The editor is committed to continuing to support for Land Back efforts, and a portion of the book's income will be donated to Indigenous organizations.

* Consider examining the Indigenous land you reside on by visiting https://native-land.ca and reflect on how you can advocate beyond land acknowledgements at https://nativegov.org/news/beyond-land-acknowledgment-guide

Contents

Part II: Application

Co-Authors and Contributors

Musharrat J. Ahmed-Landeryou, PhD
Associate Professor of Occupational Therapy
London South Bank University
London, UK

Haley Biddanda, EdD, NCSP
School Psychologist
Montgomery County Public Schools
Rockville, MD, USA

Greg Boheler, MS, OTR/L
Chief Operating Officer, School-Based Transition Facilitator
B3 Coffee and Carrboro High School
Carrboro, NC, USA

Jacklyn Boheler, MS, OTR/L
Executive Director, Co-Founder
B3 Coffee, OTs for Neurodiversity
Carrboro, NC, USA

Maya Brandsen
Nail Technician
Altoona, IA, USA

Sam Brandsen, PhD
Independent Contractor (Autism Researcher)
Cambridge, Ontario, Canada

Amy Coopersmith, OTD, OTR/L; MA ED FAOTA
Director
Self-Determined Kids
Montgomery, NY, USA

Aaron R. Dallman, PhD, OTR/L
Assistant Professor
Rutgers Health
Newark, NJ, USA

Elizabeth Duffy, MS, OTR/L
Occupational Therapist and Co-Owner and Co-Founder, President
Roots and Wings Therapeutic Services LLC, Minnesota Neurodivergent Education Advocacy and Therapy Services (MnNEAT)
Twin Cities, MN, USA

Christopher D. Edwards, OTD
Co-Host of Unmasked Podcast
New Haven, CT, USA

Meg Ferrell, MS, OTR/L
Occupational Therapist and Founder
Learn Play Thrive, LLC
Asheville, NC, USA

LaVonne Fox, PhD, MOTR/L
Youth Outreach Specialist—Project Director—NDTHRIVES
Health Disparities Specialist—MPATTC
Training and Implementation Specialist—CMHIS
University of North Dakota
Dunseith, ND, USA

Aster Gallus, OTD, OTR/L (He/They)
Occupational Therapist, Roots and Wings Therapeutic Services, Owner of Empower Occupational Therapy Services
Minneapolis, MN, USA

Sofi Ghassaei
Student, I-ASC Nonspeaking
Leadership Council
Seattle, WA, USA

Isaiah Tien Grewal
Trainee Fellow
Leadership Education in
Neurodevelopmental Disabilities
Program, Stony Brook University
School of Social Welfare
Toronto, Ontario, Canada

Bri Guerra
Student and Advocate
CT, USA

Razan Hamad, PhD, OTR/L, FAOTA
Associate Professor and Associate Director
Columbia University
New York, NY, USA

Kathryn L. Hansen, PhD, OTR/L
Associate Professor of Occupational Therapy
University of North Carolina at Pembroke
Raeford, NC, USA

Mary Katherine Howell, PhD
Licensed Psychologist
State of Maryland
Washington, DC, USA

Khalilah R. Johnson, PhD, MS, OTR/L, FAOTA
Assistant Research Professor
University of North Carolina at Chapel Hill
Chapel Hill, NC, USA

Shayda Kafai, PhD
Associate Professor
California State Polytechnic University
Pomona, CA, USA

Amy Laurent, PhD, OTR/L
Developmental Psychologist and
Occupational Therapist, Co-Director
Autism Level UP!
North Kingstown, RI, USA

Ryan Lavalley, PhD, OTR/L
Assistant Professor
University of North Carolina at Chapel Hill
Chapel Hill, NC, USA

Amy K. Lynch, PhD, OTR/L, FAOTA, TBRI® Educator, SCFES
Occupational Therapist, Associate Professor
Temple University
Philadelphia, PA, USA

Kelly Mahler, OTD, OTR/L
Occupational Therapist and Owner
Mahler Occupational Therapy
Hershey, PA, USA

Lisa Marnell, OTD, MBA
Faculty, Boston University
Founder, Kids Master Skills LLC
Thousand Oaks, CA, USA

Kavitha Murthi, PhD, OTR, FHEA
Post-Doctoral Research Fellow
New York, NY, USA

Devlynn Neu, MS, OTR/L, CSOT (They/He)
Occupational Therapist,
Assistant Professor, Creator
The Rainbow OT
Ithaca, NY, USA

Janet Njelesani, PhD, OTR/L, FAOTA
Associate Professor
New York University
New York, NY, USA

Katie O'Day, MOT, OTD, OTR/L
Occupational Therapist, Creator
of Visual Activity Sort
Portland Public Schools, Providence
Health and Services
Portland, OR, USA

Kelsie Olds, OTR/L
Occupational Therapist
"The Occuplaytional Therapist"
Geelong, Victoria, Australia

Stephanie Olszewski, OTR/L, CASDCS
Occupational Therapist, Co-Founder
Diverge Community Services
Flat Rock, MI, USA

Kristie K. Patten, PhD, OT/L, FAOTA
Professor, Department of OT NYU
Steinhardt, Counselor to the President, NYU
New York University
New York, NY, USA

Robert B. Pereira, PhD (Social Inclusion), BOccThy (Hons), Reg OT
Director and Occupational Therapist, Adjunct Associate Professor
Pear Tree Occupational Therapy, University of Canberra
Geelong, Victoria, Australia

Diamond Rashad, OTD, MHS, OTR/L (She/Her)
Occupational Therapist, Owner of A Dime of OT, LLC
South College
Savannah, GA, USA

Kelsie Reed, PhD, NCSP
School Psychologist, Founder
Prince George's County Public Schools, Strengths-Based Collective
Silver Spring, MD, USA

Rachel Robertson, MOT, OTR/L, CBIS
Occupational Therapist, Co-Founder
Diverge Community Services
Ann Arbor, MI, USA

Breea M. Rosas, EdS, NCSP, LEP
School Psychologist, Founder
ND Affirming School Psychologist, LLC
Los Angeles, CA, USA

Toni Saia, PhD, CRC
Assistant Professor
San Diego State University
San Diego, CA, USA

Sarah Selvaggi Hernandez, MOT, OTR/L
Owner of Living Sensory and The Autistic OT
Enfield, CT, USA

Lucio Serio, MS, LEP, NCSP
Licensed Educational Psychologist, Sexuality Educator, Owner
Bookworm Educational and Psychological Services Inc., Club 21 Learning and Resource Center for Individuals with Down Syndrome
Los Angeles, CA, USA

Alisa Jordan Sheth, PhD, OTR/L
Assistant Professor, Doctoral Capstone Coordinator
Pacific University
Hillsboro, Oregon, USA

Julia Sterman, PhD, OTR
Senior Lecturer in Occupational Therapy, Course Coordinator
Australian Catholic University
Canberra, ACT, Australia

Laura VanPuymbrouck, PhD, OTR/L, FAOTA
Associate Professor
Rush University
Chicago, IL, USA

Lori Vaughn, OT, MSOT, OTD, OTR
Professor of Occupational Therapy
Springfield College
Springfield, MA, USA

Georgia Vine
Occupational Therapist, Disabled Activist
University of Huddersfield
Sheffield, UK

Melanie E. Wright, OTD, OTR/L
Occupational Therapist
Brick Township Public Schools, Abilities in Action Pediatric Therapy
Brick, NJ, USA

Daryl Patrick Yao, PhD (cand.), MS(OT), OTRP
Graduate Student (PhD in Disability Studies); Research Assistant
University of Illinois—Chicago
Chicago, IL, USA; Cebu, Philippines

Foreword

I think I know... until I know more.

In my lifetime...

Girls didn't get to play sports.

Children with high support needs didn't get to go to school.

Sometimes, in our day-to-day professional lives, we feel frustrated that things are not improving. Yet, across time, tiny, incremental changes lead to substantial, consequential shifts in expectations and opportunities.

One parent decided to advocate for his daughter to play sports.

Families spoke up about their children's access to education.

Today we see women's sports on the same streaming services as men's sports. We are stunned at the idea that a child would be denied educational services and supports at their neighborhood locations. These "leaps" actually occurred in the everyday courageous actions of many people who could imagine a better way.

In my lifetime...

We used words like "deficit"; we acted like detectives to find what was "wrong" so we could make a plan to "fix it." As I developed relationships with families, educators, Neurodivergent individuals, I saw that factors other than "fixing the problem" mattered to outcomes. And when I reported about my research with Neurodivergent individuals such as those who are Autistic, ADHDers, or who have schizophrenia, audience members would tell me "my husband, neighbor, friend does this too!" It became clear to me that **everyone's humanity** was reflected in my findings. Neurodivergent individuals were actually showing the rest of us the way to understanding ourselves. How could we continue to think of these characteristics as a problem? We could not; we had to find a better way.

Neurodiversity-Affirming Occupational Therapy, edited by Bryden Carlson-Giving, marks the next moment in time when we get to see a contemporary shift in expectations and opportunities. We have matured as a discipline; we recognize the work of other disciplines to inform our evolution. We have access to the voices of Neurodivergent individuals and communities to gain insights about how it feels to live with a complex matrix of identities. We get to hear what is actually helpful, being reminded that self-determination drives everyone's life choices.

At each of these reflection points, I am reminded that the core tenets of occupational therapy are already aligned with neurodiversity-affirming practices, even though some of our strategies fall short of this goal. It is hard to change our ways of implementing practices. Luckily, the authors of *Neurodiversity-Affirming Occupational Therapy* are showing us what, why, and how to affirm neurodiversity in our work. They answer questions such as: "How does it feel to read/hear what professionals write/say about us?" "What does it take for people to feel heard/seen for their identities?" "What are ALL the ways to accomplish that participation goal?" Applying their recommendations means we must trust ourselves to see therapeutic opportunities in whatever stories, approaches, and goals people share with us.

We don't yet know how deeply neurodiversity-affirming practices will expand our understanding—but we know the journey is ongoing. Let's stay curious and ready for the next waves of awareness, insights, and growth moments to come.

I am grateful to these authors for showing us the way.

Winnie Dunn, PhD, OTR, FAOTA
Distinguished Professor
Department of Occupational Therapy Education
College of Health Sciences
University of Missouri
Certified Positive Psychology Coach

Preface

Occupational therapy is a profession rooted in possibility. What is more powerful than supporting individuals to *be*, *do*, and *live* in ways that are truly meaningful to them? At its best, it has the potential to honor the full spectrum of human experience and support liberation, but only if we can confront the ableism and inequities woven into our foundations. Few ideas illuminate this conflict more clearly than the axiom of equality. When I first discovered the axiom of equality, it shook me to my core. The axiom of equality asserts that a number (let's call it "x") has an intrinsic uniqueness that does not change, making it always equal to itself; x = x.[1]

Even if you try to reduce the number to its most basic components or present the number in a different way, its fundamental essence will not change.

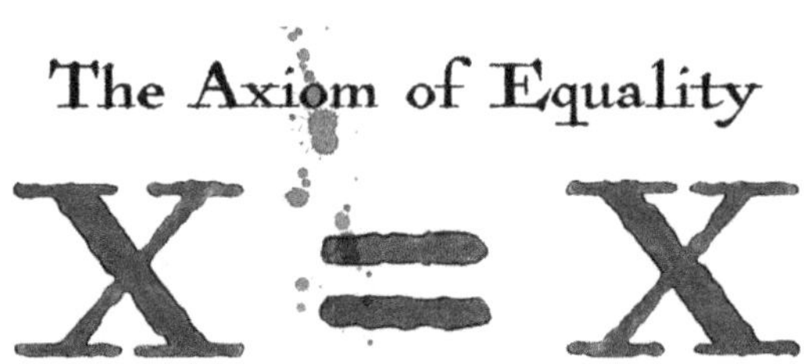

It sounds very straightforward, but this theorem has profound implications when you think about the occupational therapy profession. The axiom of equality illuminates a hard but necessary truth that has forever shaped my understanding of the profession: no matter how we try to make an ableist practice more neurodiversity-affirming, it remains ableist at its core. And perhaps an even harder realization is that ableism permeates every aspect of our field. From our research, our education, professional leadership, all the way down to even the very assessment tools and intervention methods we use with clients, ableism informs our work. The axiom of equality reminds us that true inclusive and affirming practice requires more than just surface-level adjustments. We need a complete dismantling and rebuilding of everything we have known about occupational therapy...

I know, it sounds overwhelming right? But this journey of being an anti-ableist and neurodiversity-affirming practitioner isn't impossible, and you don't have to do it alone. This book was created as a guide and journey companion to help you navigate, unpack, and transform your practice into one that fully embraces neurodiversity and supports Neurodivergent participation.

Though I am Queer and multiply Neurodivergent, I am also white, a cis-gender male, and can pass as non-disabled, and with that comes significant privilege and a deep responsibility as an editor on a subject that requires intersectionality and disability justice to be at its heart. Neurodiversity is rich with complexity, and it was essential to me to maximize the representation of experiences throughout this book. This book represents a collective undertaking, involving friends and colleagues from around the world, all united in the belief that occupational therapy can make this change and align with the neurodiversity movement. The radical insights shared within these pages are not new; they reflect the long-standing advocacy of Marginalized communities that have been and continue to be overlooked by our profession. This book isn't intended to be the definitive resource on neurodiversity-affirming occupational therapy but introduce readers to key messages championed by Neurodivergent individuals and be a helpful step forward to fostering anti-ableist practice.

A neurodiversity-affirming approach is more than just a shift in mindset—it's a lifelong commitment to learning, unlearning, and growth. Becoming anti-ableist is challenging because it asks us to question and undo much of what we've been taught and what we've always known. It's not a linear path, but rather a continuous journey that requires patience, reflection, and above all grace with yourself. Some or even many concepts may be new to you, and as you read this book, remember it's okay to be uncomfortable. This work is hard, *so* hard! Even for those of us who have been on this journey for some time, navigating the complexities of ableism and injustice is still messy and humbling (I am still unpacking my internalized ableism every day). But it's in these moments of discomfort and challenge that true growth happens. Neurodivergent people can't do this on our own, and as I write this in the spring of 2025, the need for allies has never been more dire.

Being an ally—whether neurotypical or Neurodivergent—means learning how to navigate the nuanced balance of knowing when to speak up while also respecting the need to listen and create space for those voices to be heard.[2] To be an ally involves grappling with the discomfort of potentially (and likely) saying the wrong thing, understanding that mistakes will be made along the journey of allyship, but continuing to engage within the process regardless.

Just as a forest thrives through cycles of growth and renewal, give yourself the grace to make mistakes and reflect (the abundance of nature inspiration in the illustrations is no coincidence). The path to becoming an anti-ableist practitioner isn't about achieving perfection—it's about showing up with intention, with care, and with a willingness to learn and adapt. By embracing this journey, you're not only empowering your clients but also contributing to a broader movement toward justice and inclusion within occupational therapy. The co-authors, contributors, and I all believe in you—let's take this journey forward, together.

With love and unwavering solidarity,

Bryden Carlson-Giving, Editor
Neurodivergent Nexus

Endnotes

1 Yanagihara, H. (2015). *A little life*. Doubleday.
2 Reid, N. (2022). *The good ally*. HQ.

Key Notes About the Book

Roadmap of the Book

The book is organized into two main sections, with the first half exploring foundations necessary for neurodiversity-affirming practice.

- *Chapter 1* opens with a vibrant introduction to neurodiversity and the neurodiversity multiverse.
- *Chapter 2* offers an overview of various models of disability, helping readers reframe their perceptions and understanding of disability.
- *Chapter 3* explores Neurodivergent perspectives of occupation, encouraging readers to expand their views of what occupational participation can look like.
- *Chapter 4* introduces Sins Invalid's principles of disability justice, featuring an activist perspective for each principle and concluding with an exploration of Indigenous perspectives of disability and neurodiversity.
- *Chapter 5* delves into trauma-informed and interoception-based approaches.
- *Chapter 6* presents a candid discussion of racism within the profession and practical guidance on how readers can support antiracism efforts with their clients.
- *Chapter 7* provides strengths-based approaches to practice and higher education.

The second half of the book focuses on applying the neurodiversity framework into occupational therapy practice through a sequential process.

- *Chapter 8* introduces critical reflexivity, offering practical tools on how readers can reflect on their biases when working with Neurodivergent clients.
- *Chapter 9* provides a holistic overview of how to conduct neurodiversity-affirming evaluations, including a neurodiversity-affirming evaluation

process, recommended assessment tools, strengths-based documentation, goal-writing, and more.
- *Chapter 10* explores neurodiversity-affirming services and supports, offering concrete examples of how to become an affirming practitioner and support occupations from a neurodiversity-affirming perspective.
- *Chapter 11* focuses on advocacy, presenting the Disability Allyship Framework and actionable strategies to promote neurodiversity across various settings.
- The final chapter, *Chapter 12*, introduces the EMPOWER model, a neurodiversity-focused occupational therapy framework designed to help readers apply principles of neurodiversity-affirming practice throughout the therapeutic process.

Throughout this book, *Spotlights* are featurettes that highlight the experiences and perspectives of the most marginalized within the neurodiversity community—such as Nonspeaking and Trans individuals, or those with intellectual and developmental disabilities (IDD).

Other Notes

- The authors and contributors of this book have a combined representation of Neurodivergent and neurotypical neurotypes, with collective experiences across settings (e.g. clinical environments, academia, advocacy) and identities.

- Throughout the book, occupational therapy practitioner (OTP) and occupational therapist (OT) will be used depending on the context and location of the co-authors. Countries designate these terms differently. Whenever OT or OTP are used, this includes all occupational therapy professionals including certified occupational therapy assistants (COTAs).

- An online Vault exists with over 100 pages of supplemental content that you can download and can access here: https://neurodivergentnexus.com/neurodiversityaffirmingotbook. Password: Neurodiversityot123. Material throughout the book marked by means it can be downloaded from the Vault. Much of the additional content is meant to help readers apply this content into practice, such as the EMPOWER model action plan, a neurodiversity-affirming evaluation template, the Cultural Identity Assessment, and a resource on supporting Neurodivergent students in higher education.

- Illustrations note—I had the joy of creating all the illustrations and most of the figures throughout this book; I hope you are a fan of dark watercolor. Additionally, a downloadable resource containing all figures as plain text is also available.

- To support your reflections and learning from this book, and to help you translate this knowledge into practice, three appendices are included at the back:
  - **Appendix A: Reflections for Change**—A helpful tool to guide your ongoing reflections after each chapter and throughout your journey with this book.
  - **Appendix B: Matrices for Action**—A practical companion offering additional ideas to help you implement many of the concepts explored within the book into practice.
  - **Appendix C: Downloads and Resources**—A list of supplementary materials and resources available from the Vault.

- In this book, we have chosen to capitalize words relating to historically excluded communities such as Neurodivergent, Autistic, Nonspeaking, Black, and Indigenous. These capitalizations reflect the conventions of each individual culture and acknowledge these descriptors as essential aspects of an individual's identity. In commitment to social justice and to decenter neurotypicality and whiteness from the book's explorations on Marginalized experiences, terms relating to the dominant cultural norms (e.g. "neurotypical," "white") will be in lowercase.

PART I

Foundations

CHAPTER 1

Introduction to Neurodiversity

LORI VAUGHN, CHRISTOPHER D. EDWARDS, AND SARAH SELVAGGI HERNANDEZ

Introduction

Neurodiversity is a biological fact, involving naturally occurring variations in neurocognitive functioning. Neurodivergent advocates have likened neurodiversity to other forms of diversity such as ethnicity, gender, race, and culture. As there is no one right or superior way of being, so too is there no one "'normal' or 'healthy' type of brain or mind, or one 'right' style of neurocognitive functioning."[1] Informed by this knowledge, Neurodivergent advocates sought to create a framework for how to support and affirm neurodiversity in society. This is known as the neurodiversity paradigm. The neurodiversity paradigm is the "how" to support and affirm neurodiversity in society. The creation and acceptance of this paradigm helped spark a social justice movement that "seeks civil rights, equality, respect, and full societal inclusion for the neurodivergent," known as the neurodiversity movement.[2] Indeed, the authors of this book recognize that there is beauty in racial, ethnic, gender, and other areas of diversity that provide a richness to the diverse tapestry of humankind; and so there is a beauty and richness in neurodiversity as well. The neurodiversity movement recognizes, values, and celebrates this diversity and the natural brain variations that influence how an individual thinks, learns, communicates, interacts, processes sensory information, and perceives their world as a part of human diversity.

> The term neurodiversity can be literally translated as "neurological variation"; the prefix "neuro" relates to the nervous system and the word "diversity" means variety.[3] Central to the concept of neurodiversity is the belief that differences in neurology are not differences in need of "fixing," but instead are unique expressions of an individual's humanness, and Neurodivergent individuals should be recognized for the strengths they possess.[4]

It is essential for society not only to accommodate neurocognitive diversity, but to celebrate it as part of the human spectrum.[5] While initially associated with autism, neurodiversity has come to encompass any differences in brain function from what is considered neurotypical, including ADHD, dyslexia, dyscalculia, specific learning differences, anxiety and depression, intellectual disabilities, Down syndrome, and many others.[6,7] Although conceptually associated with medical diagnoses, current understanding of neurodivergence extends beyond the diagnosis and neurological presentation to also include the social and societal factors and practices that exist at any given period of time.[8] For example, the understanding of and treatment for Down syndrome has changed over time; children who once may have been institutionalized are now affirmed as vibrant members of society, participating in school, work, and the community. While many neurotypes are labeled as disabilities, it is important to view this from an ecological perspective; disability includes biological factors as well as societal factors that evolve throughout a person's lifetime.[9] When providing interventions, as will be discussed throughout this book, social, medical, educational, and therapeutic interventions are all important for supporting Neurodivergent individuals; however, it is essential that all interventions respect and promote an individual's personal agency and autonomy.[10] This is consistent with the primary tenets of occupational therapy practice.

This chapter includes the above introduction to neurodiversity; an overview of the types of neurodivergence; an exploration of the evolution of the neurodiversity movement; a discussion and examples of radical inclusion; a brief look at the characteristics within the neurodiversity multiverse; a discussion of the Neurodivergent brain; and strategies for flipping the narrative in language and practice. In addition, the authors introduce the readers to intersectionality, neurodivergence, neuroqueering, and neurodiversity and privilege. Finally, the authors will discuss strategies for the profession of occupational therapy moving forward. To help the reader with some of the terminology used in this chapter, a brief glossary of terms is available for download in the book's Vault.

Types of Neurodiversity

Neurodiversity means all brains belong, and everyone gets to be their authentic self without changing who they are to fit societal definitions or molds of "normal." Neurodiversity encompasses all brains and the wide range of ways they work. This includes not only neurotypes like autism, ADHD, and dyslexia but also intellectual disabilities, psychiatric disabilities celebrated through movements like Mad Pride, and even cultural identities such as Deaf culture. Mad Pride, an activist movement of current and former consumers of mental health services, challenges mental health stigma by reclaiming language like "mad" and celebrating the resilience and contributions of those with psychiatric disabilities.[11] Similarly, Deaf culture highlights the richness of sign languages and the shared experiences of being Deaf as a cultural identity rather than a deficit. Neurodiversity invites us to embrace the full spectrum of human brains and celebrate the unique strengths, cultures, and perspectives they bring to our world.

A person is Neurodivergent if their neurocognitive experiences differ from societal norms of what neurocognitive experiences "should" be. Originally coined by Kassiane Asasumasu in 2000, being Neurodivergent is neither intrinsically positive or negative; the experience of the impact of neurodivergence is left up to the Neurodivergent individual to decide. Asasumasu was intentional about creating a term that was inclusive for all, and it is essential to remember that neurodivergence is a socio-political term and not a medical term. Indeed, the term neurodivergent resists the idea that diverging from neuronormativity is bad or disordered.

Although commonly discussed forms of neurodivergence use diagnostic labels (e.g. autism, depression, schizophrenia), neurodivergence expands to *any* difference in neurocognitive experiences and functioning. Examples include:[12]

- **Developmental and genetic neurotypes** (e.g. autism, ADHD, learning differences, developmental disabilities).
- **Contextual and acquired neurodivergence** (e.g. TBI, PTSD, brain changes from chronic stress, stroke, "burnout brain" from sustained masking or overadaptation).
- **Psychiatric disabilities** (e.g. depression, anxiety, bipolar disorder, OCD).
- **Altered states and perceptions** (e.g. sensory processing differences, synesthesia, schizophrenia).
- **Non-normative behaviors and experiences** (e.g. stigmatized support needs, attentional differences, heavy psychedelic use, communication differences, neurocognitive differences as a result of COVID).

The neurodiversity movement also does not oppose treatment or cures for neurodivergence if that is what the Neurodivergent person chooses; what the movement does oppose is placing neuronormativity as a benchmark for functioning and not supporting the Neurodivergent individual's autonomy to make such choices.[13] As practitioners, we must support the needs of everyone, promote Neurodivergent participation, and embrace the uniqueness of all brains. This commitment to inclusiveness and empowerment was the catalyst for the neurodiversity movement.

The Evolution of a Movement

The neurodiversity movement is a social justice initiative focused on human rights and committed to acceptance, inclusion, and the end of oppression for Neurodivergent individuals.[14,15] It is believed to have its origin in the early 1990s and is associated with the removal of social barriers of exclusion for Autistic individuals and an increase in access to the internet. The ability to access and interact in a text-based format was empowering and provided a vehicle for connection, sharing, and ultimately a catalyst for activism.[16] Social media platforms amplified Marginalized voices, increasing knowledge and awareness regarding social inequities, and a global movement for all Neurodivergent individuals was born.[17] The term "neurodiversity" has been widely attributed to Judy Singer, an Australian sociologist, who used the term in her master's honors thesis. There is much debate over the origin of both the term and the concept of neurodiversity, with some attributing both to Singer. Much evidence points to the origins of the concept developing through the online community/email group of Autistic activists and allies called Independent Living (InLv), which was managed by Martijn Dekker and of which Judy Singer was a member for the purpose of completing her thesis.[18] Evidence indicates the term "neurological diversity" was in use prior to the publication of Singer's thesis and the concept of neurodiversity relative to the collective lived experiences of Neurodivergent individuals was a lively topic of discussion within this group as early as October 1996.[19] In 1997 the term "neurological diversity" and in 1998 the term "neurodiversity" were included in the work of journalist Harvey Blume, who has also been associated with the origin of the phrase, although he himself has attributed its origin to the online community of InLv.[20] Singer herself has stated she never claimed to originate the concept of neurodiversity, but rather was the first to describe it in her work and through her role as a "participant observer."[21] The general belief of the collective origin of the concept of neurodiversity within the online community has been corroborated by individuals who were active participants of the group at the time, and some believe the foundation for the movement began even earlier in Autism Network International, founded in 1992 and comprised of Autistic and disability activists.[22] Some researchers suggest using a decolonial viewpoint when considering the ideological origin of neurodiversity as a concept and extend our awareness beyond the Global North, which is the locus of much of the published literature, to also include Global Southern philosophies and knowledge systems that include Indigenous communities. Examining knowledge and evidence precolonization reveals that neurodiversity is not purely a white Northern concept and actually existed in the Global South prior to and aligned with Northern scholarship. The Global Southern viewpoint of disability acknowledged the reciprocal relationship between ability and the community and was centered on spiritual, physical, and mental well-being using a holistic, non-reductionist approach. Without the contribution of Global Southern and Indigenous intellect, knowledge, and scholarship, much of what is known and published by Global Northern scholars would not have been possible.[23]

While foolproof evidence of the origin of the term may never be retrieved, there is little dispute regarding the evolution of the concept and its expansion beyond the online community of InLv. Throughout the 1990s and 2000s, the dialogue expanded as social media grew and neurodiversity branched out from the Autistic community to the neurodiversity multiverse. As previously mentioned, this expansion included the coining of the terms "Neurodivergent" and "neurodivergence" by Kassiane Asasumasu and the broadening of the concept in theoretical, social science, and research arenas.[24,25] In the mid- and late 2000s, the concept expanded to include a range of Neurodivergent neurotypes and shifted from a curative focus to embracing the strengths of Neurodivergent individuals. The concept also expanded to the workplace in the 2010s with the advent of hiring policies and practices to support Neurodivergent workers.[26] While progress has been made, there is still a long way to go toward acceptance, inclusion, and personal agency. Practitioners have a responsibility to recognize and appreciate the humanness of Neurodivergent individuals and respect the rights and autonomy of all. One strategy for recognizing and appreciating neurodivergence is through radical inclusion.

Radical Inclusion

Radical inclusion is the unwavering commitment to ensuring that everyone belongs, without exception. Within the neurodiversity paradigm, this means not only recognizing and valuing all variations in brain function but actively creating spaces where all individuals, regardless of support needs, communication styles, or perceived ability, are welcomed and celebrated. Radical inclusion challenges us to shift from tokenistic accommodations (superficial accommodations that give the appearance of meeting an individual's needs, but are more appearance than substance), to transformative practices that center lived experiences and honor Neurodivergent voices.[27] Practically, this involves amplifying Marginalized perspectives, redesigning systems to eliminate barriers, and embracing accessibility as a baseline rather than an afterthought. Moving toward a neurodiversity-affirming paradigm means adopting flexible approaches to participation, rethinking success and productivity through a Neurodivergent lens, and fostering environments where every person is seen, heard, and respected. Radical inclusion is not just a value—it is a daily practice of dismantling exclusion and building a world where belonging is unconditional. In practice and life, this can take many forms, including hiring practices; work and community environments that are accommodating and supportive of diverse needs; work, home, and community spaces that are flexible and sensory sensitive; policies that are supportive and collaborative of Neurodivergent needs; training in neurodiversity issues at all levels; and identifying strengths-based roles for neurodiverse individuals.[28] In the community, an example of radical inclusion might be a sporting event, such as a hockey game, that includes a tailored experience for Neurodivergent individuals. This might include modifications to the sensory aspects of the games, such as ensuring access to noise-cancelling headphones or sunglasses, and other sensory experiences, as well as quiet spaces away from the game that include activities to allow for self-regulation and sensory organization. In the workplace, radical inclusion might include flexible working hours or virtual options for some aspects of the job, policies that are supportive but that do not require documentation of a diagnosis, and environments that respect the sensory and safety needs of the worker. Radical inclusion is about honoring the individual as they are, where they are, and with pure and profound acceptance that recognizes and values all.[29] Acceptance requires understanding the many facets of Neurodivergent expression within the multiverse.

The Neurodiversity Multiverse

Each neurodivergence has its own culture and universe of experiences, all coming together to form the neurodiversity multiverse (Figure I.1). Each universe has vibrant galaxies and nebulae that reflect an intertwining array of abilities, strengths, and experiences. The galaxies and nebulae interact and respond within different contexts, celebrating the dynamic nature of Neurodivergent experiences.

Even when people have different neurotypes, there's often a lot of overlap in Neurodivergent experiences and characteristics, which can create strong points of connection and mutual understanding. For instance, both ADHDers and Autistic individuals experience social participation differently. Autistic individuals have shared that they navigate through the world differently for many reasons, especially for differences in social communication and sensory processing experiences. ADHDers often engage with attention and spontaneity in ways that diverge from societal expectations. Though challenges may arise for Autistic and ADHDer individuals, we assume it is because of their neurotypes. In actuality, it is not always from these differences themselves, but from the mismatch between their ways of being and neuronormative environments that exist within our systems. And even though there are shared cultural differences between Autistics and ADHDers, both communities experience shared marginalization.

This shared experience of marginalization creates a sense of solidarity among Neurodivergent people, even across neurotypes (or you could say, universes). It is also essential to recognize that neurodivergence rarely exists in isolation—many individuals navigate multiple intersections, including being BIPOC (Black, Indigenous, or people of color), living with trauma, or facing systemic barriers. Understanding this complexity reminds us that while shared experiences unite us, the nuances of individual identities and intersections must always be honored. One area contributing to our individual identities and Neurodivergent expression is the brain.

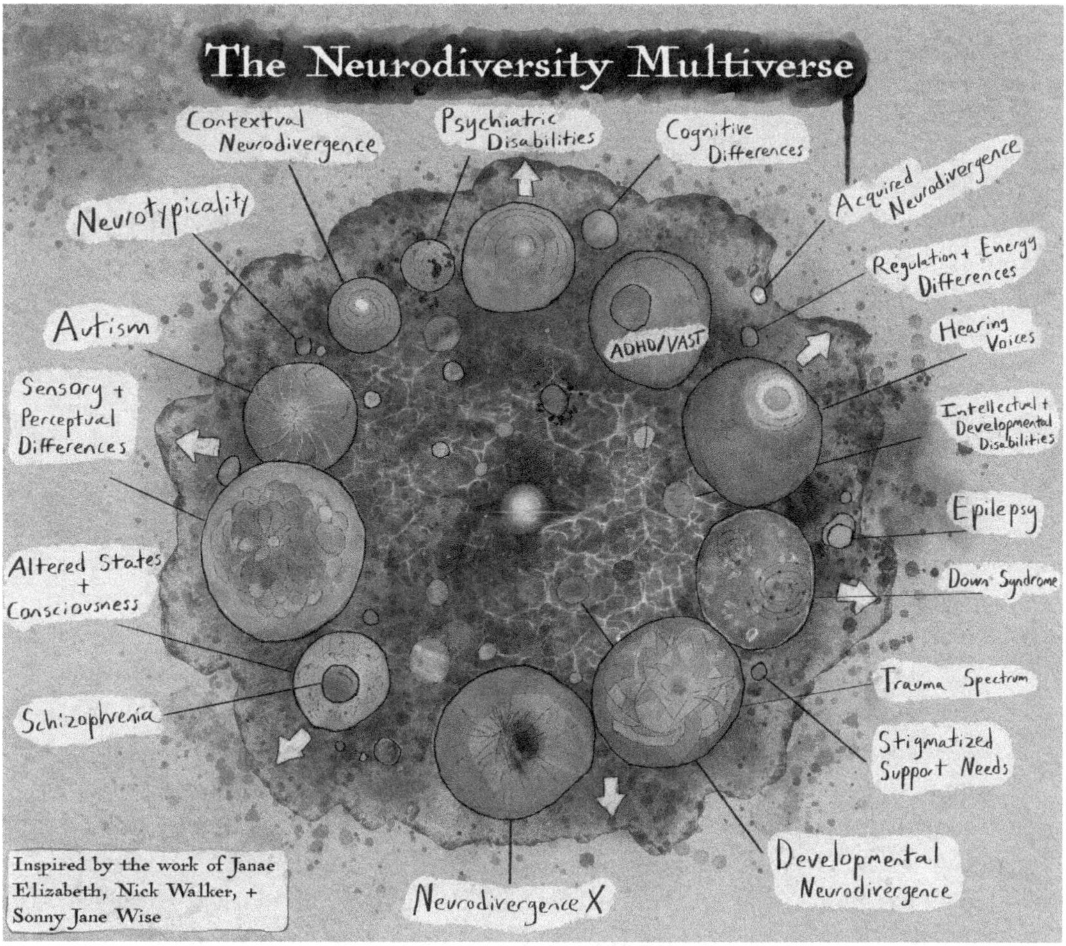

Figure 1.1—The Neurodiversity Multiverse

Note. This is a non-exhaustive list. For further details on the neurodiversity multiverse, see Carlson-Giving.[30]

The Neurodivergent Brain

As has been highlighted throughout this chapter, neurodivergence encompasses more than just differences in the brain and is shaped also by lived experience, social context, and culture. We cannot ignore the evidence of brain-based diversity to affirm that these ways of being are not imagined or pathological, but real and meaningful aspects of the human experience. Neuroimaging studies have been conducted and highlight differences in brain structure and function that influence how a person thinks, learns, processes information, regulates emotions, and perceives and experiences the world.[31] These variations in human neuroanatomy and neurophysiology are considered the brain signature. Functional MRI studies have been conducted to explore differences in neuroanatomy and neurophysiology between neurotypes and have shown distinct neural signatures associated with neurodivergence, and statistically significant differences between the neural signatures of Neurodivergent and neurotypical individuals.[32] Research also indicates neuroanatomy and neurophysiology differ from person to person naturally regardless of neurotype or identity; therefore it is logical to assume that due to differences in the characteristics of the brain, how the brain works or functions would also vary from person to person.

Similar to individual fingerprints with differences in whorls, loops, and arches, all human brains are unique with individual differences in skills, preferences, and perception of the world around us. It is essential that we embrace and honor these differences rather than pathologize and view them as deficits that need to be fixed. Neurodivergent brains are beautifully complex and have strengths in many areas, such as music, logic, and reasoning, that are not always captured or identified through traditional cognitive testing.[33]

Whether you consider yourself Neurodivergent or not, we encourage you to explore Sonny Jane Wise's Neurodiversity Smorgasbord on their resources page.[34] Sonny created the Neurodiversity Smorgasbord as an alternative framework for understanding neurocognitive differences outside of diagnostic labels, and to ultimately support self-discovery and self-understanding of neurodiversity beyond the DSM. The Neurodiversity Smorgasbord visualizes various characteristics, such as stimming, emotions, memory, sleep, altered states, voice hearing, and time perception with descriptions to help readers identify how much they resonate with that characteristic. To really support this exploration of Neurodivergent identity, they have a Neurodivergent Spectrum Chart (also on their resources page) where you can color in the impact of how your differences diverge from neuronormativity, and create your own unique profile. Exploring the Neurodiversity Smorgasbord and the Neurodivergent Spectrum Chart can deepen our appreciation for the incredible multiverse of human neurocognitive experiences. As we embrace our neurocognitive profiles, it becomes even more clear how we talk about these differences shapes how they are understood.

As practitioners, we must normalize the acceptance of differences and eliminate deficit-based, non-affirming language by flipping the narrative.

Flipping the Narrative

While acknowledging there are differences in brain structure and function that can help shed light to better understand neurodivergence, as occupational therapy practitioners (OTPs), the underlying reason for neurodivergence is secondary to acknowledging the unique needs and strengths of Neurodivergent individuals. One way to do this is to "flip the narrative" and consider how the words we use may promote the "neurotypical ideal." Let's consider a question posed by American psycholinguist Viorica Marian in her book *The Power of Language: How the Codes We Use to Think, Speak, and Live Transform Our Minds*. Marian asks if our perceptions of the world influence how we speak about the world, or does how we speak about the world influence our perceptions? Marian concludes her opening chapter by stating, "the labels we use matter. Something as simple as changing the labels we use to refer to someone makes an immediate difference in how we mentally represent those we are speaking about."[35] Throughout this book, the authors will strive to guide our readers toward using more neurodiverse-affirming, identity-first and/or person-first language to help readers promote a more inclusive community.

The first step to flipping the narrative is understanding the differences between deficit-based language, person-first language, and identity-first language. Deficit-based language is ableist in nature and assumes that a person is "suffering" or "afflicted" by neurodivergence. Furthermore, deficit-based adjectives do not always depict one's ability accurately. One example includes the tendency for neurotypical individuals to refer to Nonspeaking individuals as non-verbal. As Cole Sorenson and Jordyn Zimmerman point out,

> "using the term 'nonverbal' (can be) harmful because it suggests that the person has no language and thus can't benefit from language-based AAC [augmentative and alternative communication devices], instead of simply conveying that they cannot speak. Because speech is a motor function and language is a cognitive function, there is no reason to assume that a hearing person who cannot speak has a language disability."[36]

Because of this, and as a general rule, the neurodiversity community rejects deficit-based language and prefers person-first or identity-first language. Some disability communities prefer identity-first language, such as ADHDers, Autistic individuals, or Deaf individuals. Other disability communities have advocated for person-first language, secondary to their neurodivergence not being central to their identity, such as those with Down syndrome or those with depression. It is important to note that it is very likely for a Neurodivergent individual to have compounding neurotypes and identities but refer to these compounding neurotypes and identities differently. For example, a person diagnosed with autism and depression may want others to use identity-first language when describing their autism (i.e. they are Autistic) but not when describing their depression. Instead, they may prefer person-first language (i.e. they are living with depression) when talking about their depression because it is not central to their identity whereas being Autistic is a core part of who they are. Neuro-affirmative practitioners are and should always be curious about the people they serve and find out, in any way possible, how their clients identify. For example, we should never assume that a person living with autism is going to identify as an "Autistic person."

Another step to flipping the narrative is to be cognizant of deficit-based terms commonly used and the neuro-affirmative alternatives that are available. Throughout this book, readers will come across a variety of neuro-affirmative language and terms to add to their toolbox for future reference. Table 1.1 offers examples of deficit-based terminology and neuro-affirming alternatives.[37]

Table 1.1—Flipping the Narrative: From Deficit-Based to Neuro-Affirming Language

Instead of using these terms...	Try using these terms...
Suffering from	Living with, experiencing, navigating
Poor eye contact	Comfort with minimal eye contact
Low/high-functioning	Low/high support needs (be specific about the support needs)
Unable to/can't	Can with alternative strategies, prefers alternative approaches
Challenged	Experiences barriers, facing obstacles
Impulsive	Spontaneous/enthusiastic
Non-verbal	Nonspeaking, uses alternative communication
Poor speech	Use of varied multimodal communication
Hyperactive	Excited, passionate, energetic
Abnormal intensity of focus	Outstanding focus, hyperfocused
Inattentive	Variable attention, attention fluctuates pending on interest
Lazy	Purposeful
Socially incompetent/awkward	Authentic

Dependent	Interdependent
Repetitive, non-purposeful actions	Self-regulatory behaviors, purposeful for regulation
Sensory disorders	Variations in how individuals process sensory information; sensory processing differences
Perseverations, restrictive interests	Topics or activities that bring joy and deep engagement; deeply focused; passion-driven; highly interested in...; monotropic interests
Tendency to monologue	Excitement to share information
Black and white thinking	Categorical thinking
Intolerance to change / unwavering routine	Preference for sameness
Slow processing speed	Thoughtful
Appearing to act normal	Masking

Using these language strategies and adjusting the terms we use can help practitioners change how they think, feel, interact with, and advocate with Neurodivergent individuals. It is important to note that this is not an exhaustive list. Furthermore, language will still, forever and always, continue to evolve. Language is meant to be dynamic, progressive, and active. As we collectively move forward to radical inclusion of neurodiversity, it is important to center Neurodivergent empowerment and self-determination in creating the terms and definitions that reflect the lived experiences of Neurodivergent individuals and use affirming language that empowers rather than pathologizes. Remember this, too—client, culture, and familial preferences matter, and the best strategy to use to understand the preferences and identities of those we work with is to ask. In addition to being mindful of the language we use, we must also be mindful of and consider the complex and multifaceted identities of our clients.

The third step to flipping the narrative is rejecting neurotypical standards of occupation and embracing Neurodivergent ways of living. Table 1.2 is adapted from an in-progress article by Dr. Carlson-Giving and gives examples of common neurotypical standards and their neurodiversity-affirming alternatives to guide occupational therapy practice.

Table 1.2—Deficit-Based Versus Affirming Views of Neurodivergent Characteristics[38]

Neurodivergent Neurotype Characteristic	Deficit-Based View	Neurodiversity-Affirming Perspective
Hearing voices and auditory hallucinations *(Common for those with schizophrenia, bipolar disorder, and depression)*	Society views hearing voices as a negative experience and often treats it in such a way that it eliminates the ability to hear voices versus understand them. The hearing of voices is viewed as inherently negative and a flaw of the central nervous system.	Voice hearers have shared that engaging with their voices provides insight into their lives, is a source of companionship, and is seen as a positive aspect of their identity.[39] Hearing voices is not in itself a sign of negative mental health. OTPs can create a safe space and engage in open dialogue where clients can explore the meanings behind their voices, and see if clients would like to practice using their hearing of voices as a regulatory tool. By doing so, you are amplifying voice-hearing culture. While honoring the affirming aspects of voice hearing, it remains essential for occupational therapists to be responsive to the individual's interpretation of their hearing of voices (e.g. if they are negatively impacting their life).[40]
Attentional differences *(Common for ADHDers, Autistic individuals, and anxiety)*	Society holds a pretty narrow view of what attention should look like, and in educational and workplace environments, sustained attention and linear productivity are prioritized. There is an assumption that maintaining focus for long periods of time without interruption or "whole body listening" are components of ideal engagement.	Attentional differences are not deficits of executive functioning or attention span. Instead (for example with ADHDers), ADHDers have a completely different sense of time. Depending on how interesting the activity is, time perception is either slowed or sped up. OTPs can cultivate their differences in time perception by supporting flexible time management strategies, incorporating sensory or movement breaks and executive functioning supports, and empowering individuals to self-advocate for their needs and preferences. Many individuals with attentional differences thrive on structured and yet dynamic tasks that accommodate fluctuations in attention and allow switching between tasks.[41]

Executive functioning differences *(Common for those with intellectual and developmental disabilities [IDD], such as Down syndrome, cerebral palsy, and fetal alcohol spectrum disorders)*	Neurotypical standards establish cognitive benchmarks that define success as independence in daily living skills, and social participation norms that prioritize speaking communication.	Contrary to popular beliefs, many individuals with IDD share that they have a strong sense of identity, and purpose, and want to have more of a voice in making decisions about their lives.[42] The role of siblings, family members, and caregivers is a significant part of the empowerment narrative for those with IDD, making meaningful relationships an important aspect of IDD culture.[43] OTPs can promote interdependence, support access to robust communication methods (e.g. not trying to maximize speech communication prior to considering assistive technology), support the individuals in understanding their rights, and focus on the individual's aspirations instead of conventional norms and milestones.

The information provided in this section is only a portion of the strategies that will be outlined throughout this book. The bottom line is that we, as OTPs, have a duty and moral imperative to flip the narrative surrounding our Neurodivergent clients that put their trust in us to advocate for their well-being and support occupational justice. Occupational justice also requires consideration of intersectionality, neurodivergence, and the practice of neuroqueering.

Intersectionality, Neurodivergence, and the Practice of Neuroqueering

Intersectionality is a term coined by Kimberlé Crenshaw in 1989 to challenge the assumption that discrimination and subordination occur "along a single categorical line" and that, in truth, individuals who belong to multiple Marginalized groups experience compounding prejudices.[44] In other words, as Crenshaw alludes to, Black women do not experience prejudice for being Black OR for being a woman. They experience prejudice for being Black AND for being a woman. With this argument, Crenshaw started a discourse on how different identities intersect to help "tell the stories of who we are individually and collectively based upon specific social, historical, and cultural contexts."[45]

In this book, we are going to look at intersectionality from a broader perspective to help practitioners better understand the complex stories that impact the experiences of the Neurodivergent individuals who walk through life beside us as friends, colleagues, or clients. Within the neurodiversity paradigm, we must consider the intersection between all identities, including gender, race, ethnicity, socioeconomic status, sexual orientation, and disability status/neurotype.[46] We will discuss how Neurodivergent individuals may face compounding stigmas/

stereotypes and related traumas, and how to help Neurodivergent individuals navigate through these traumas to improve quality of life and build self-esteem.

It is important to note that these authors are not redefining intersectionality, nor do we intend to discredit the context in which Kimberlé Crenshaw crafted her hallmark dissertation. We only intend to further an important discourse so that we, as practitioners, can be better informed to make client-centered decisions. In fact, Crenshaw herself provides room for expansion and states that we must "embrace the complexities of compoundedness (and adopt a) top-down approach to discrimination [to address] the needs and problems of those who are most disadvantaged [and recenter] discrimination discourse at the intersection [to] facilitate the inclusion of Marginalized groups."[47] In other words, "we must understand [the] differences within Marginalized communities if we wish to effectively engage in" meaningful and transformative advocacy.[48]

Indeed, the neurodiversity movement, as originally envisioned, was meant to advocate for neurodiversity as a recognizable and intersecting identity, and a framework for client-centered practice.[49] In fact, within the neurodiversity paradigm exists the theory of neuroqueering, which was first coined by Nick Walker while he was in graduate school during the late 2000s. Walker defines neuroqueer as both a verb and an adjective to describe "any individual whose identity, selfhood, gender performance, and/or neurocognitive style have in some way been shaped by their engagement in practices of neuroqueering, regardless of what gender, sexual orientation, or style of neurocognitive functioning they may have been born with." In other words, according to Walker, one can be Neurodivergent and/or Queer, but not identify as neuroqueer, and vice versa. In this way, neuroqueering is viewed as a life practice/lifestyle in which the engager subverts, defies, disrupts, or "liberates themselves from neuronormativity and heteronormativity simultaneously."[50]

Throughout this book, we will continue exploring the intersectionality of multiple identities as it is crucial to upholding our code of ethics and understanding the diverse experiences faced by Neurodivergent individuals. In doing so, we also honor Kimberlé Crenshaw's foundational work on intersectionality as we expand the conversation to include the unique narratives within the neurodiversity paradigm. By doing so, we empower practitioners to engage in more informed, empathetic, and client-centered advocacy, ultimately fostering a more inclusive and equitable society. Inclusivity and equity must also include consideration of the intersection of neurodiversity and privilege.

Neurodiversity and Privilege

You cannot hold a discourse on intersectionality without discussing privilege. Privilege can come in many forms: race, class, educational, gender, sexuality, and disability identity exist in our culture. It is important to understand privilege and its relationship to intersectionality and neurodiversity. As mentioned in Dr. Carlson-Giving's introduction, the authors and editors of this book are diverse in their experiences and identities and span the gamut of the neurodiversity multiverse; however, as authors and editors, we are privileged to have the educational knowledge, background, and opportunity to write this book. That is, we understand the responsibility we have to speak truthfully in these pages as we attempt to communicate for those who do not have the privilege to tell their individual stories to a broader audience.

The relationship between neurodiversity and privilege is complex. Many Neurodivergent individuals experience differences in cognition, sensory processing, motor coordination, or a combination of these. These differences can present challenges to Neurodivergent individuals to engage fully in many of their occupations, including activities of daily living, instrumental activities of daily living, health management, work and play, rest and sleep, social participation, leisure, and education. Due to ableist assumptions, Neurodivergents are therefore discriminated against for their disability and are assumed to be inferior to what is considered the pinnacle of normalcy in any given society.[51] As described previously, when other Marginalized identities intersect, this discrimination is compounded. This is articulated by sociologists Chantelle Jessica Lewis and Jason Arday who discuss being Black Neurodivergent scholars within the present context of British academia and how these intersecting identities create a "double jeopardy" as the authors are forced to "negotiate racialization and neurotypical hegemony, both of which have an impact on the construction of the ideal scholar."[52] As alluded to previously, the neurodiversity movement advocates against such ableism and racism by arguing that all neurotypes should be accepted and respected.

We also cannot talk about neurodiversity-affirming care without recognizing that the lived experiences of Neurodivergent individuals are diverse and complex. Some individuals require ongoing, intensive support across many domains of daily life. Because of ableist systems that fail to provide adequate resources, this can place emotional, financial, and physical strain on families and caregivers. The neurodiversity-affirming framework recognizes caregiver stress as a reflection of structural barriers—such as underfunded services, lack of inclusive programming, inaccessible environments, and insufficient respite care. The goal should not be to diminish the identity or humanity of those with high support needs, but to fight for better systems that uplift them and those who care for them. Caregiver well-being matters—not as a justification for viewing Neurodivergent people through a deficit lens, but as a call to action for increased funding, community-based support, and policies that affirm both the rights and the needs of people across the spectrum of support. It is also important to recognize that for some Neurodivergent individuals, they may want to remediate their Neurodivergent characteristics, and we need to support their decision! It is important to note that the neurodiversity movement does create space for families and individuals who may not feel empowered by their disability and lived experiences, and emphasizes the need for individualized support, accessible resources, and systematic change to ensure that all Neurodivergent people—regardless of their level of support needs—receive the care and accommodations necessary to improve their well-being and quality of life on their terms.

The concept of privilege will be explored throughout the book; however, the bottom line is that, as neuro-affirmative practitioners, we have an obligation to be cognizant of ableism within and beyond the Neurodivergent community and help advocate for better resources and better care for Neurodivergent individuals and their caregivers to break down barriers and promote equitable care and health management education.

We have presented a broad overview of neurodiversity, some concepts of which will be more fully explored throughout this text. The authors of this chapter feel we would be remiss in not including our thoughts about how the profession of occupational therapy, as well as individual practitioners, can foster neurodiversity in practice.

Moving Forward

As a profession, occupational therapy has expressed a commitment to neurodiversity-affirming practice. It is impossible to utilize a client-centered approach without being identity-affirming. Affirming practice has been identified as a valuable framework for practice to support all neurotypes across the lifespan. Practitioners must understand that neurodiversity is human diversity, and must move away from pathologizing neurodivergence in an attempt to "fix" the individual or behavior, and provide evaluations and interventions that respect the humanity, autonomy, and dignity of Neurodivergent individuals. In occupational therapy, practitioners must work toward reducing the systemic barriers impacting the ability to provide and receive services that are respectful, affirming, and empowering. Treatment should not attempt to reduce or replace behavior that is not harmful, cause trauma, or attempt to force neurotypicality. Using a strengths-based approach, goals should focus on intrinsically meaningful participation in ways that are comfortable and natural to the individual. Occupational therapy must promote self-advocacy, autonomy, and amplify Neurodivergent voices. Neurodivergent ways of being must be supported and promoted in all areas of practice. Practitioners, researchers, educators, and all members of the occupational therapy profession must work in a collaborative manner and center Neurodivergent voices in research, policy development, and practice. With a commitment to client-centered practice, autonomy, and dignity, occupational therapy is well-equipped to champion the neurodiversity movement today, tomorrow, and for the future.

Endnotes

1 Walker, N. (2021). *Neuroqueer heresies: Notes on the neurodiversity paradigm, autistic empowerment, and postnormal possibilities.* Autonomous Press.
2 ibid.
3 Goldberg, H. (2023). Unraveling neurodiversity: Insights from neuroscientific perspectives. *Encyclopedia, 3*, 972–980. https://doi.org/10.3390/encyclopedia3030070
4 Sharma, M. (2020). Neurodiversity in education celebrating differences and embracing strengths. *Global International Research Thoughts, 8*(1), 16–19. https://girt.shodhsagar.com/index.php/j/article/view/39
5 ibid.
6 Goldberg, H. (2023). Unraveling neurodiversity: Insights from neuroscientific perspectives. *Encyclopedia, 3*, 972–980. https://doi.org/10.3390/encyclopedia3030070
7 Neurodiversity Next. (2024, March 3). *Neurodiversity advocacy: A short timeline and history.* https://neurodiversitynext.com/about/what-is-neurodiversity
8 Sharma, M. (2020). Neurodiversity in education celebrating differences and embracing strengths. *Global International Research Thoughts, 8*(1), 16–19. https://girt.shodhsagar.com/index.php/j/article/view/39
9 Dawson, C. (2023). Neurodiversity is human diversity, an equity imperative for education. *International Journal for Talent Development and Creativity, 10*(1–2), 217–229. https://doi.org/10.7202/1099954ar
10 ibid.
11 Mental Health Matters. (2024). *Mad pride.* https://mental-health-matters.org/2024/07/11/what-is-mad-pride
12 Elizabeth, J. (2025). *Let's talk about the original definition of neurodivergence.* Facebook – Trauma Geek.
13 Walker, N. (2021). *Neuroqueer heresies: Notes on the neurodiversity paradigm, autistic empowerment, and postnormal possibilities.* Autonomous Press.
14 Goldberg, H. (2023). Unraveling neurodiversity: Insights from neuroscientific perspectives. *Encyclopedia, 3*, 972–980. https://doi.org/10.3390/encyclopedia3030070
15 Roberts, J. (2023). The neurodiversity movement: An overview for autism service providers. *Speech Pathology.* www.speechpathology.com/articles/neurodiversity-movement-overview-for-autism020554
16 ibid.
17 Goldberg, H. (2023). Unraveling neurodiversity: Insights from neuroscientific perspectives. *Encyclopedia, 3*, 972–980. https://doi.org/10.3390/encyclopedia3030070
18 Botha, M., Chapman, R., Giwa Onaiwu, M., Kapp, S. K., Stannard Ashley, A., & Walker, N. (2024). The neurodiversity concept was developed collectively: An overdue correction on the origins of neurodiversity theory. *Autism: The International Journal of Research and Practice, 28*(6), 1591–1594. https://doi.org/10.1177/13623613241237871
19 ibid.
20 ibid.
21 Singer, J. (2023, November 7). *Reflections on neurodiversity blog: My response to Martijn Dekker's libels.* https://neurodiversity2.blogspot.com/2023/10/a-factual-response-to-martijn-kekkers.html
22 Botha, M., Chapman, R., Giwa Onaiwu, M., Kapp, S. K., Stannard Ashley, A., & Walker, N. (2024). The neurodiversity concept was developed collectively: An overdue correction on the origins of neurodiversity theory. *Autism: The International Journal of Research and Practice, 28*(6), 1591–1594. https://doi.org/10.1177/13623613241237871
23 Nair, V. K., Farah, W., & Boveda, M. (2024). Is neurodiversity a Global Northern white paradigm? *Autism: The International Journal of Research and Practice*, 13623613241280835. https://doi.org/10.1177/13623613241280835
24 Neurodiversity Next. (2024, March 3). *Neurodiversity advocacy: A short timeline and history.* https://neurodiversitynext.com/about/what-is-neurodiversity
25 Botha, M., Chapman, R., Giwa Onaiwu, M., Kapp, S. K., Stannard Ashley, A., & Walker, N. (2024). The neurodiversity concept was developed collectively: An overdue correction on the origins of neurodiversity theory. *Autism: The International Journal of Research and Practice, 28*(6), 1591–1594. https://doi.org/10.1177/13623613241237871
26 Neurodiversity Next. (2024, March 3). *Neurodiversity advocacy: A short timeline and history.* https://neurodiversitynext.com/about/what-is-neurodiversity
27 Majid, U. (2020). The dimensions of tokenism in patient and family engagement: A concept analysis of the literature. *Journal of Patient Experience, 7*(6), 1610–1620. https://doi.org/10.1177/2374373520925268
28 Borrett, A. (2024, December 19). Employers seek to tap Neurodivergent workers. Labour market. Recruitment businesses wake up to value of growing social group hitherto shunned in hiring practices. *Financial Times, 2.* Gale General OneFile, link.gale.com/apps/doc/A820427227/ITOF?u=mlin_w_sprcol&sid=bookmark-ITOF&xid=e503854b
29 Boren, R. (2024, March 21). *Radical inclusivity.* Stimpunks Foundation. https://stimpunks.org/glossary/radical-inclusivity
30 Carlson-Giving, B. (2024). *The neurodiversity multiverse.* Neurodivergent Nexus. https://Neurodivergentnexus.com/neurodiversitymultiverse

31 Hernandez, L. M., Rudie, J. D., Green, S. A., Bookheimer, S., & Dapretto, M. (2015). Neural signatures of autism spectrum disorders: Insights into brain network dynamics. *Neuropsychopharmacology, 40*(1), 171–189. https://doi.org/10.1038/npp.2014.172

32 Alves, C. L., Martinelli, T., Sallum, L. F., Rodrigues, F. A., Toutain, T. G. L. de O., Porto, J. A. M., Thielemann, C., Aguiar, P. M. de C., & Moeckel, M. (2024). Multiclass classification of autism spectrum disorder, attention deficit hyperactivity disorder, and typically developed individuals using fMRI functional connectivity analysis. *PloS One, 19*(10), e0305630. https://doi.org/10.1371/journal.pone.0305630

33 Robertshaw, S. (2024, May 21). *There's no such thing as a "slow" or "lazy" brain*. www.additudemag.com/Neurodivergent-brain-embracing-differences-adhd

34 Sonny Jane Wise. (n.d.). *Resources*. The Lived Experience Educator. https://www.livedexperienceeducator.com/resources

35 Marian, V. (2023). *The power of language: How the codes we use to think, speak, and live transform our minds*. Penguin Publishing Group.

36 Sorenson, C., & Zimmerman, J. (2021). *This is not about me: A story about growing up Nonspeaking*. https://thisisnotaboutme.film/wp-content/uploads/2021/10/CommunicationFirst-This-Is-Not-About-Me-Toolkit.pdf

37 Marnell, L. (2023, April 18). *An end to ableism: Adopting neurodiversity-affirming and strengths-based approaches for pediatric Autistic clients* [Conference session]. American Occupational Therapy Association Conference, Kansas City, MO.

38 Carlson-Giving, B. (2025). (in press). The EMPOWER model: A framework for fostering neurodivergent occupational participation and supporting neurodiversity-affirming occupational therapy practice. *Open Journal of Occupational Therapy.*

39 Marquis, N., Maignan, A., & Daelman, C. (2024). Voice-hearers and highly sensitive people reversing the stigma of madness. In N. Marquis (Ed.), *Education, parenting, and mental health care in Europe: The contradictions of building autonomous individuals* (pp. 237–253). Routledge. https://doi.org/10.4324/9781003377207-1

40 National Hearing Voices Network. (n.d.). National hearing voices network: Lots of people hear voices or see visions. Let's talk about it. National Hearing Voices Network. https://www.hearing-voices.org/wp-content/uploads/2019/06/HVN-Intro-Booklet_webshare.pdf

41 Ali, M., Grabarski, M. K., & Baker, M. (2024). An exploratory study of benefits and challenges of Neurodivergent employees: Roles of knowing Neurodivergents and neurodiversity practices. *Equality Diversity and Inclusion: An International Journal, 43*(2), 243–267. https://doi.org/10.1108/edi-03-2023-0092

42 Midjo, T., & Aune, K. E. (2018). Identity constructions and transition to adulthood for young people with mild intellectual disabilities. *Journal of Intellectual Disabilities: JOID, 22*(1), 33–48. https://doi.org/10.1177/1744629516674066

43 McMahon, M., Bowring, D. L., & Hatton, C. (2019). Not such an ordinary life: A comparison of employment, marital status and housing profiles of adults with and without intellectual disabilities. *Tizard Learning Disability Review, 24*(4), 213–221. https://doi.org/10.1108/tldr-03-2019-0014

44 Crenshaw, K. (1989). Demarginalizing the intersection of race and sex: A Black feminist critique of antidiscrimination doctrine, feminist theory and antiracist politics. *University of Chicago Legal Forum, 1989*(1). https://chicagounbound.uchicago.edu/uclf/vol1989/iss1/8/?utm_source=chicagounbound.uchicago.edu

45 Botha, M., & Gillespie-Lynch, K. (2022). Come as you are: Examining Autistic identity development and the neurodiversity movement through an intersectional lens. *Human Development, 66*(2), 93–112. https://doi.org/10.1159/000524123

46 Roberts, J. (2023). The neurodiversity movement: An overview for autism service providers. *Speech Pathology*. www.speechpathology.com/articles/neurodiversity-movement-overview-for-autism020554

47 Crenshaw, K. (1989). Demarginalizing the intersection of race and sex: A Black feminist critique of antidiscrimination doctrine, feminist theory and antiracist politics. *University of Chicago Legal Forum, 1989*(1). https://chicagounbound.uchicago.edu/uclf/vol1989/iss1/8/?utm_source=chicagounbound.uchicago.edu

48 Botha, M., & Gillespie-Lynch, K. (2022). Come as you are: Examining Autistic identity development and the neurodiversity movement through an intersectional lens. *Human Development, 66*(2), 93–112. https://doi.org/10.1159/000524123

49 ibid.

50 Walker, N. (2021). *Neuroqueer: An introduction*. https://neuroqueer.com/neuroqueer-an-introduction

51 Dunn, D. S. (2021). *Understanding ableism and negative reactions to disability*. American Psychological Association. www.apa.org/ed/precollege/psychology-teacher-network/introductory-psychology/ableism-negative-reactions-disability

52 Lewis, C. J., & Arday, J. (2023). We'll see things they'll never see: Sociological reflections on race, neurodiversity and higher education. *The Sociological Review, 71*(6), 1299–1321. https://doi.org/10.1177/00380261231184357

SPOTLIGHT

How Neurodivergence and Transness Have Brought Me Home

ASTER GALLUS

My sense of gender and neurodivergence are inextricably tied together. I could not have found one without the other. At 28 years old (at the time of writing this I am 30) I finally got my autism and ADHD diagnoses, and through unmasking as a Neurodivergent, I gained access to my queerness and transness.

ADHD was not a surprise to me. I constantly felt the drive of my creativity and like my current reality could deal with a little more pizzazz, like I was leaping across thoughts and ideas and sometimes they would come so fast that processing them (for me and other people) felt like drinking out of a fire hose. Autism was more of a surprise for me, but when the psychologist told me I was Autistic, and why she came to that conclusion after testing and talking to me, I cried.

I cried because for so long I felt like communicating with some people (now who I realize were largely neurotypical) was often painful, and there were so many mismatches in what we were trying to say to each other that eventually we would just give up. I love thoughtful patterns and order and organization, so I know what is needed from me so I can feel safe in my environment. I love getting lost in something fascinating, like space or writing or cats or queerness or something else that resonates with my soul. And I love what other people enjoy getting lost in or what makes them excited, and when I find people with overlapping special interests, we have boundless joy from that! I cried because I finally felt like I wasn't broken. I'm Autistic. And despite what people have tried to tell me, being Autistic does not mean being broken.

I bought *Unmasking Autism* by Dr. Devon Price to celebrate the gift of my diagnosis. I drank up his words about unmasking and letting go of neurotypical expectations. Soon after my diagnosis, I let myself look wherever I wanted to at my hospital job instead of constantly forcing eye contact. I came home with so much more energy! It felt so good!

Unmasking was an incredibly powerful process for me. The way I talked, walked, moved, and how I chose to spend my time radically shifted. Stimming felt so good, and as it turns out with many of us, I was already surrounded by other Autistics and Neurodivergents! We got closer and closer and felt so seen and loved by each other. Our communication deepened as we shared a new language to talk about our everyday experiences.

And then something beautiful began emerging. My queerness got louder. And louder. And LOUDER! In unmasking neurotypical traits that I had been conditioned into, I also found gender and sexual norms falling away at a rate that shook the foundations my life had been built on. My now ex-husband and I looked at each other and knew I could not be the full version of myself in our relationship. I spent time listening to my body and realized I had been feeling intense dysphoria (a painful, dizzying, and cruel mismatch between a Queer person's felt sense of self and who society tries to tell them they are) for a long time but had never had words for it. The more I unmasked and listened to myself instead of other people, the more I found my queerness and neurodivergence taking me somewhere I had always wanted to go but had never been before!

I had been identifying as non-binary (neither male nor female but instead something magical) for about nine months before I received my diagnoses, and while "non-binary" had felt more resonant, I still felt like I was holding back on my expression to preserve my marriage and the orderliness of my life. Once I was surrounded by enough safe and kind Neurodivergent and Queer people, I kept unmasking, and I found more of myself. My people-pleasing habits of hypervigilance lessened. I asked for what I wanted, not just what I thought other people wanted. I found myself performing less and less, less acting how a "woman in a marriage" was supposed to act, and with decreased performance what was left of the shell of my previously constructed identity kept falling away. I finally felt safe to reach for and take hold of my transness. It was time for button-downs. It was time for beards. It was time for magic. And no one could stop me from feeling safe in my skin and being in love with who I am most deeply anymore.

My queerness and neurodivergence continue to amplify each other, and as I lean into them more and more, my life grows into one that feels so good for me. I ended up leaving my hospital job and moving from the southern state I lived in at the time to the much safer and affirming state of Minnesota. It's colder, but I love who I have found here!

> My chosen family astounds me every day with their beauty, courage, and resilience. So much of the world was not made with us in mind, and we are making a new home here for ourselves where we feel safe, bold, and full of joy.

I love my life and the community I am building. And I can access it because of the other beautiful Neurodivergent and Queer folk that have loved me into existence. The way I see the world may be different than how many other people see it, but there is so much we can learn from each other when we are allowed to be fully who we are.

So, my fellow OTPs, as you encounter Queer and Neurodivergent folk, celebrate us! Join us in this beautiful world we are making, because there is a place for you in it, too!

Practical Implications for Occupational Therapy

- The Queers are having more fun than you, I guarantee it, because we choose ourselves and each other over any other ideology, creed, or law. What are ways you could choose yourself and prioritize your intuition over other demands (for example, maybe you should try those Oxford shoes!)? How often do you compromise your own desires to follow the "rules" of societal expectations? How could prioritizing your inner voice change how you practice?

- A lot of us Queer folks DREAD medical appointments because we are not seen or heard, are misgendered and invalidated. To decrease our emotional labor, consider engaging with some of our creative work! Some wonderful resources to read and listen to include *Seeing Gender* by Iris Gottlieb, *How to Understand Your Gender* by Alex Iantaffi and Meg-John Barker, and the *Transgenda* and *Gender Stories* podcasts are two works that eventually inspired my own gender journey. I also have my own work on my journey as a Queer and Neurodivergent occupational therapist at *Aster in Space* on Substack.

Where to Follow Aster

Website: https://astergallus.substack.com

CHAPTER 2

Disability and Ableism

Models, Perspectives, and Implications for Occupational Therapy

ALISA JORDAN SHETH AND LAURA VANPUYMBROUCK

Throughout its history and evolution as a healthcare and rehabilitation profession, occupational therapy (OT) has been influenced by the societal and cultural contexts in which it exists, including other fields of study. One such influence has been disability studies, broadly defined as the "socio-political-cultural examination of disability."[1] This interdisciplinary field has its roots in larger disability rights and disability justice movements and has influenced occupational therapy practitioners (OTPs), educators, and researchers for several decades.[2] Importantly, disability studies recommend the OT profession explore how OTPs might examine and develop interventions focused on systemic and environmental factors versus only person factors as solutions to disability.[3] To date there have been two special issues in the *American Journal of Occupational Therapy* centered around disability studies[4] and other scholarship, particularly published outside of the United States, that challenge occupational therapy to examine its perpetuation of oppressive and discriminatory practices in the current health and rehabilitation landscape.

A disability studies frame of reference raises the important question of "Why do we need to define disability?" In this chapter, a variety of models of disablement will be presented and discussed, as there is a myriad of ways to conceptualize disability impacted by context and perspective. Legal definitions define disability, as well as influence the application of laws and protections of rights. Programmatic and clinical definitions may determine who qualifies for or is excluded from specific services and how these services are billed or reimbursed. In research, defining disability can determine who is eligible to participate in studies and how those studies receive funding. This then impacts what types of knowledge are created, disseminated, and incorporated into evidence-based practice. In all of the above examples, disability is often defined by professional diagnosis and rigid criteria. This can leave out much more personal definitions of disability, including self-diagnosis.[5] For some, disability is a central part of their identity and daily experience, while for others it may feel like a more fluid experience or heavily context-dependent.[6] OTPs must engage in this theoretical conversation of models of disablement because it directly influences the effectiveness of supports and, more importantly, validates the very real and complex challenges Neurodivergent and Disabled clients experience every day.

The Medical Model of Disability

Connected to how we define disability is how we conceptualize or frame this term. Historically, health and rehabilitation services including OT have been heavily rooted in the medical model of disability.[7] In this conceptualization, disability is quantified into diagnoses at an individual level, with the goal of intervention often being to correct impairments and treat someone so they function within non-disabled norms. Connected to this medicalized view is the tragedy model of disability, which views disability as an individual or familial misfortune and the Disabled individual as defective in some way.[8] These models often co-exist together in framing disability as something to be overcome through medical treatment that relies on the expertise of clinicians and professionals.

The medical and tragedy models of disability also have strong connections to the charity model of disability, which has been highly influential in disability services in the United States. In this model, Disabled people are seen as deserving of support and services, but only if those services and related organizations are predominantly controlled by non-disabled people. This model is at the core of fundraising efforts and appeals based on pity, fear, and inspiration narratives. Efforts are often concentrating on finding cures for or eliminating certain diagnoses or conditions, and the model conceptualizes Disabled people as dependent on non-disabled people for survival and participation in society. All of these models have a common feature across them. They each directly target what the individual is not able to do, whether it be work, education, speech, or mobility, and all other considerations for being able to function as part of society in "normal" ways. This concept is the foundation for rehabilitation practices, including occupational therapy. Figure 2.1 illustrates examples of the medical model of disability within occupational therapy practice, and Table 2.1 provides a brief overview of medicalized models of disability.

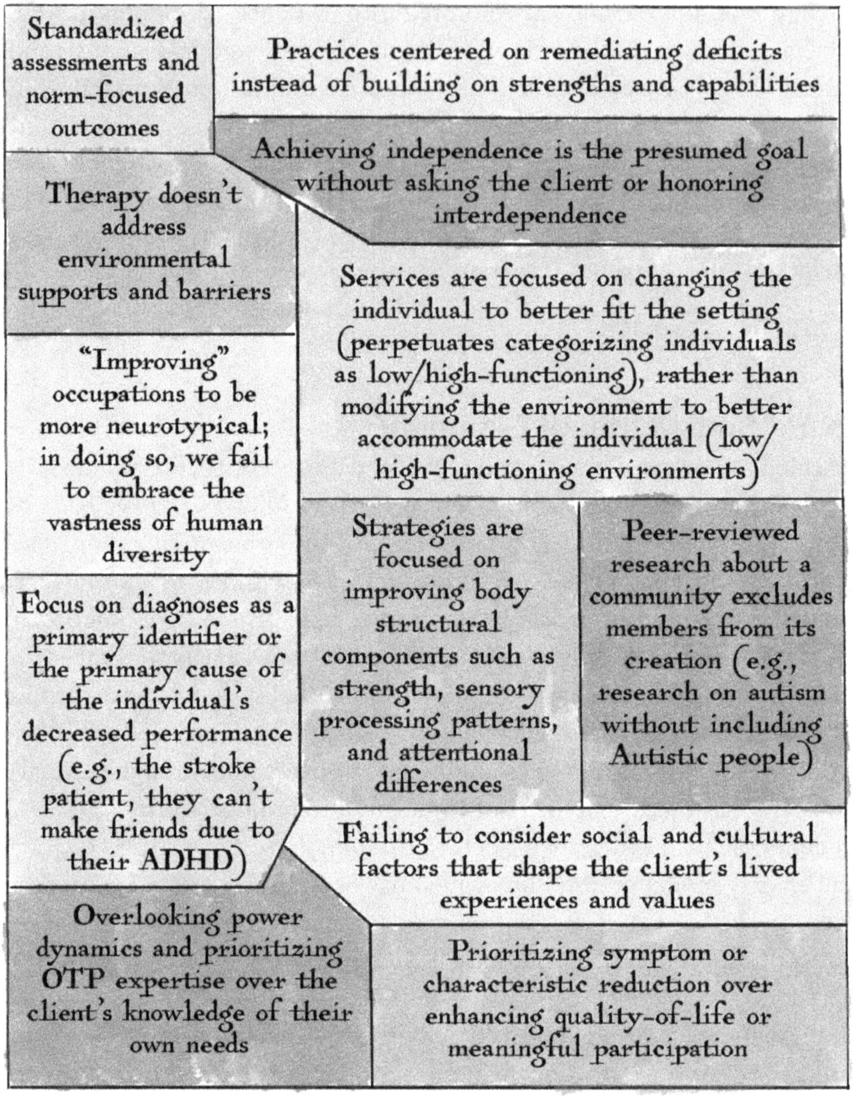

Figure 2.1—The Medical Model in Occupational Therapy Practice and Research

Table 2.1—Medicalized Models of Disability

Model of Disability	**Key Components**	**Practice Example**
Medical	• Disability is an individual deficit and deviation from normal. • Intervention focuses on curing or fixing impairments. • Professional expertise is centered.	Working to reduce Neurodivergent characteristics so a client will present as neurotypical.

Tragedy	• Disability is devastating for an individual and family. • Disability should be feared. • Popular media depicts Disabled people as disturbing, pitiful, or inspirational.	Describing a client's experience as overcoming their disability or being successful in spite of their disability.
Charity	• Disability is distressing, and Disabled people are helpless. • Assistance needs to come from non-disabled people. • Funding is gained through pity rather than rights or justice.	Working in an organization with a mission to serve people with disabilities, and only non-disabled leadership have input into priorities. Services rely on fundraising campaigns that portray Disabled people as needy, vulnerable, and powerless (e.g. Autism Speaks).

Curative Practices

In the earliest years of occupational therapy practice, individuals engaged clients they worked with in occupations because they recognized the positive impact that engaging in meaningful occupations had on clients' health and well-being.[9] However, within a relatively short period, the medical model's influence shifted the focus of the profession to fixing impairments, limitations, or any individual factor that was determined to be different or abnormal, based on standards of neurotypical and non-disabled social activity and productivity.[10] Despite a paradigm shift to return to a more holistic view that examines socially constructed barriers to engagement,[11] most OTPs, other healthcare professionals, and society continue to perceive that occupational therapy's role is to overcome individual impairment.[12]

In Research

As a part of the medical model's influence on occupational therapy's development, there were critiques from other healthcare professions that OT lacked theoretical as well as scientific evidence that engaging in occupations did in fact positively influence health and well-being.[13] An outgrowth of these critiques was the emergence of a focus on individual pathology and abnormalities as the root cause of occupational dysfunction, resulting in research focused on eliminating or reducing individual deficits.[14] As mentioned earlier, this problematically turned our professional lens away from societal barriers to exclusion while simultaneously strengthening the influence of ableism from the medical model within our profession's culture and frameworks, and our practices with the broader community. Contemporary critiques from within and outside the profession argue for recognition of the limitations and inadequacies of an occupational therapy influenced by the medical model, with recommendations including research exploring ableism's impact on occupational dysfunction, as well as on how professional research lacks representation of experts by experience of occupation disenfranchisement, exclusion, marginalization, and discrimination.[15]

The Social Model of Disability

In an effort to challenge the individualistic, disempowering, and discriminatory impacts of the medical model of disability, disability rights activists, building on the work of civil rights activists, began developing what is commonly referred to as the social model of disability. Activists from the United Kingdom created the Union of the Physically Impaired Against Segregation (UPIAS) in 1974 and outlined the differences between impairment and disability. Impairment resides within the individual, while disability is defined by the disadvantages or activity restrictions imposed by how systems and structures are established within society.[16] As most robustly developed by Michael Oliver,[17] the social model of disability views environments and contexts as disabling, rather than individual impairments. This view challenges the discriminatory attitudes toward disability and societal barriers of disability as issues to be addressed at the environmental rather than individual level.

Looking Beyond the Social Model

While the social model has been a significant influence in disability studies and many other fields, it has not been without critique, including calls for the model to evolve to reflect a more nuanced and expansive experience of disability. Much of the critique of these earlier conceptualizations of disability centers on the limited binary of impairment versus disability that the medical and social models of disability suggest. For example, the normalization model[18] has been proposed as a replacement for the medical model of disability, acknowledging that seeking out medical care is not inherently bad and sometimes very necessary, but the problem lies within another binary—that of abnormal versus normal.

Development of the political economy of disability[19] came out of the critique that the social model of disability often focused too much on individual environments and that zooming out to examine larger economic forces was essential to understanding disability. This frame of reference examines how economic systems, such as capitalism, work to "build and maintain disability as a multi-billion-dollar business,"[20] and how Disabled people are viewed in relation to their contributions to the economy, whether through work or as consumers of products and services, including occupational therapy. The political economy of disability also provides a model to better understand differences in the disability experience around the world, where national or regional economic factors dictate access to care and basic human needs.

In the cultural model of disability,[21] impairment and disability are intentionally not viewed as distinct phenomena but rather connected factors that are both impacted by larger cultural forces. The cultural model asserts that impairment and disability are both subjective and viewed through a contextual lens, recognizing that how societies define non-disabled is essential in understanding how disability is viewed. It places disability as central to understanding how a culture views and categorizes people and how this evolves over time.[22] In OT practice, implicit or explicit definitions of non-disabled can present in definitions of maladaptive and adaptive behavior, norm-references, evaluation, and individual or cultural perceptions of typical functioning and performance.

Kafer's political-relational model also challenges the impairment/disability binary central to the social model of disability. This model "neither opposes nor valorized medical intervention"[23] and recognizes that, for many, impairment, whether in the form of pain, fatigue, or other symptoms, can be very disabling. The political-relational model of disability considers how health and rehabilitation services do not exist outside of political and ideological contexts and the experience of disability is connected to relationships with others, including therapeutic relationships. Here, disability is not only a personal identity but also a political one impacted by power differentials and structural inequities. Indebted to intersectional disability justice movements, the political-relational model of disability examines how multiple Marginalized identities impact Disabled people and the societies in which they live. Table 2.2 highlights anti-ableist models of disability, and Figure 2.2 illustrates examples of anti-ableism in occupational therapy practice.

Table 2.2—Anti-Ableist Models of Disability

Model of Disability	Key Components	Practice Examples
Social	• Impairment is part of natural human diversity. • Disability occurs because of barriers presented by a society designed for non-disabled people. • The lived experience and expertise of Disabled people are centered.	Evaluating and addressing environmental barriers to participation and engagement.
Political Economy	• Disability is influenced by economic systems and contexts. • In many economies, disability is valued based on the profits people make off of related services and goods. • Systems that frame disability related to economic contributions are harmful.	Advocating for policy changes that prohibit profiteering of Disabled people and services.

cont.

Model of Disability	Key Components	Practice Examples
Cultural	• Disability is central to understanding cultural groupings of people. • Experiences of impairment and disability are impacted by cultural contexts. • Cultural definitions of non-disabled inform views of disability.	Discussing cultural understandings of disability with clients and how these may be impacting their experiences.
Political-Relational	• Disability is a political identity impacted by social norms and built environments. • Both impairment and disability are socially constructed. • Healthcare and services are not separate from culture and ideology.	Collaborating and supporting disability justice work to create a more equitable, inclusive, and accessible future.

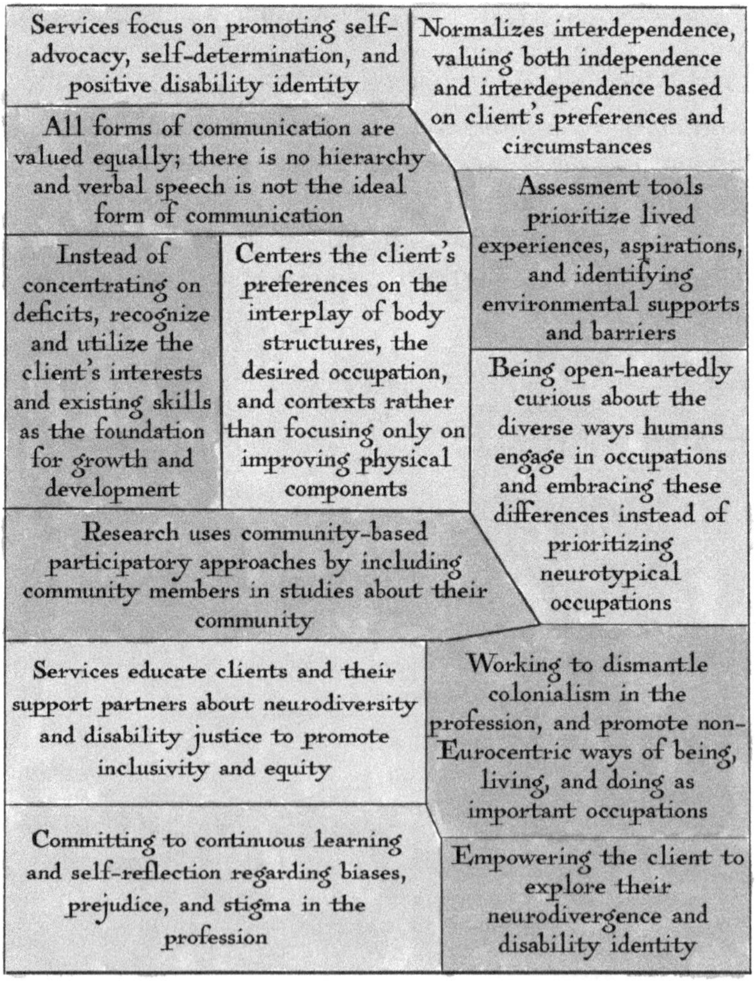

Figure 2.2—Anti-Ableism in Occupational Therapy Practice and Research

Connections to Neurodiversity

A neurodiversity model can be viewed as a frame of reference that also challenges the binary medical model versus social model of disability. Neurodivergent individuals may identify strongly with a diagnosis and the use of medicalized assessment or evaluation tools. Ongoing debates around the validity of self-diagnosis versus professional diagnosis and the value many find in medical interventions like medications highlight the value that can be found in identifying impairments.[24] However, there is also recognition of how systems can gatekeep access to diagnosis to legitimize medical professional power and authority, and recognition that society is largely set up in ways that promote curative or fixing behaviors and Neurodivergent characteristics, rather than supporting a variety of human neurological variation.[25] This nuance may also be captured by Neurodivergent individuals seeking services to adapt to and cope with more neurotypical environments that allow them to engage in meaningful roles and occupations.

Cultural, political, and economic models of disability have been applied to neurodiversity, such as through the articulation of the autism industrial complex.[26] The autism industrial complex helps highlight the powerful systemic forces at play that have turned autism into a commodity through pathologizing Autistic traits and behaviors that generate money through vast diagnostic, educational, and therapeutic services, often with a focus on curative or neuro-normalizing approaches. OTPs must consider how they benefit from the autism industrial complex and how individuals, families, and communities may be exploited in the process.

Ableism: An Introduction

No matter the conceptual approach or frame of reference being used to explain and explore the nature of disability, the shared feature common to all is Disabled people's experiences of oppression and exclusion that result from living in a normatively constructed world and the dichotomy between Disabled and non-disabled people. Understanding these experiences requires exploring the deeply embedded social, structural, and institutional disability prejudice known as ableism. A common definition of ableism is that it is a form of social oppression, similar to other "isms" like racism, grounded in the devalued and inferior status and capacities of Disabled people.[27] Importantly, ableism weaves within and intersects with racism, sexism, ageism, and the many "isms" in complex ways,[28] in diagnosis as well as inequitable access to services and supports.

The historical evolution of the term "ableism" as a concept emerged from social rights movements within the disability community.[29] Ableism imposes a corporeal standard of normalcy, normalization, and humanness, enforcing compulsory non-disability and neurotypicality.[30] Importantly, ableism is not just discrimination against Disabled people but illuminates society's preferences for non-disabled traits and how non-disabled perspectives are privileged, and perpetuates unequal and unfair treatment of Disabled people across all of society.[31] Ableism frames abilities and inabilities. Ableism impacts daily routines, interactions, speculations, and, significantly, imagination. All people are affected by ableism, just as all people are affected by racism, but ableist practices impact Disabled and non-disabled people very differently. Some individuals impacted by ableist practices actually benefit from ableism.[32] For example, everyday encounters of "fitting in" and acceptance are highly associated with normative appearance and behaviors.[33] In contrast, it can be the subtle nuances of non-Autistic behavior and Autistic behavior and societal expectations that create negative experiences. For example, ableism prioritizes specific ways to play and engage in leisure, encouraging OTPs to target Autistic play styles and skills to be more "normal." Ableism's impact stems from attitudes and the social constructions that result in negative interactions that take place between a person with an impairment/condition/state and their social environment. The impairment/condition/state is part of the negative interaction but not the cause of disability.[34]

Importantly, at an individual level, ableism develops over time, manifests differently, and functions differently whether it is conscious (explicit) or unconscious (implicit).[35] Explicit biases are conscious attitudes that inform decisions on choices and behaviors. Explicit attitudes can be markedly influenced by knowledge the person has of the socially and culturally appropriate behaviors toward a person during encounters or when making choices. These are typically measured by using self-report surveys or questionnaires.[36] In contrast, implicit biases are unconscious attitudes and beliefs that inform behaviors, especially when there is little time for reflection, choices and decisions. Implicit biases are harder to measure and most often done by using automatic responses, the method used by the Implicit Association Test.[37] Of interest is that many people's implicit and explicit biases don't often align with each other.

Looking at the combinations of both of these attitudes provides some insight into how they might inform how a person reacts to interactions and the behavior(s) they may have toward a Disabled person. Figure 2.3 provides the four different categories of combinations of ableist attitudes toward Disabled people: symbolic, aversive, principled conservative, and truly low prejudiced.[38] One of the categories, principled conservative, has a high explicit but low implicit bias toward Disabled people. This category is the least common and less is understood about how people who are principled conservatives behave. They commonly hold strong conservative ideas and value social tradition but may apply or abandon their values based on a person's group membership.[39] In contrast, people with low explicit and high implicit bias are aversive ableists and consciously believe they are not prejudiced, but unconsciously they are. This mismatch can produce anxiety and awkward behaviors that actually reinforce ableism and are influenced by the normalization of disability prejudices and stereotypes.[40] Symbolic ableists have high biases explicitly and implicitly. Symbolic ableists have strong beliefs grounded in individualism, believing that Disabled people are a drain on society and support a "pick yourself up by the bootstraps" approach to society.[41]

		Implicit Attitude	
		Low	High
Explicit Attitude	Low	Truly low prejudiced	Aversive ableist
	High	Principled conservative	Symbolic ableist

Figure 2.3—Forms of Ableist Expression
Note. From Friedman;[42] utilized with permission.

In rehabilitation and occupational therapy practice, these categories of ableism can inform interactions with our clients as well as clinical decision-making and can produce significant power dynamics. To explore examples of how these might manifest in the profession, see Figure 2.4.

Other forms, descriptions, definitions, and experiences of ableism have been described. For example, Nario-Redmond et al.[43] describe common ways ableism is experienced from the perspectives of a diverse group of Disabled people. These researchers identified paternalistic ableism, inspirational or benevolent, hostile or angry forms of ableism, envious ableism, objectifying, and fear-based forms of ableism. It is clear Disabled people experience stereotyping, prejudices, marginalization, and discrimination due to deeply embedded stigmas that are perpetuated at individual and institutional levels in society based on ableism.

Within healthcare and rehabilitation, deeply embedded and internalized societal and individual ableism supports/reinforces medicalization within rehabilitation practices. To be clear, many Disabled people acknowledge the medical model's value to their own lives.[44] However, healthcare providers' including occupational therapists' biased attitudes of ableism and disability inform not only behaviors but also clinical decision-making, and these have been linked to disparities in healthcare access and health outcomes.[45]

For example, a non-disabled occupational therapist may be considered the expert on community living as a Disabled person versus the person themselves, which in itself is a manifestation of ableism. Similarly, a non-autistic OTP acquires the Certified Autism Specialist (CAS) credential and views themselves as an authority on autism, rather than recognizing Autistic individuals as the true experts of their lived experiences. This positioning can have serious negative consequences as the OTP often has the power to determine if the individual is "safe enough" to return to living at home in the community versus an institutional setting.[46] Exploring how an OTP might practice is informed by how their own biases of ableism might influence decisions, and understanding the influences of models such as the medical or tragedy models can be one way to achieve true client-centeredness and focus instead on a client's strengths and environmental barriers to participation.[47]

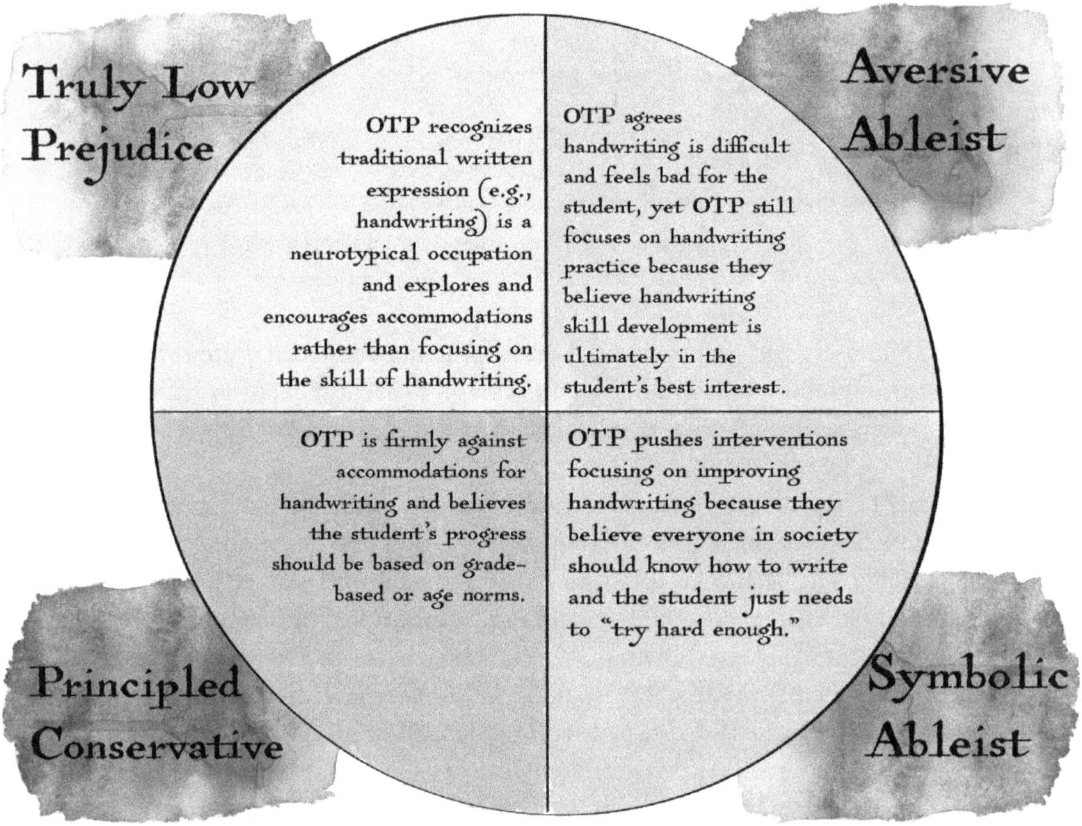

Figure 2.4—Example of Ableist Expressions for OT Scenario
Note. Scenario—An OTP supporting a student's handwriting.

Toward an Anti-Ableist Approach in Occupational Therapy

An OTP informed by their knowledge of how ableism might influence their clinical decision-making and behaviors can turn toward more of a neurodiversity, cultural, or social model lens. As a result, this knowledge works to address the many barriers to participation that isolate, marginalize, exclude, and discriminate against the disability community broadly as well as at individual levels. An OTP can use remediation approaches to support a client in addressing modifiable impairments (with the client's approval) while being reflectingly cautious that interventions which overmedicalize and focus on normalization are eliminated from the approaches being used. However, OTPs must recognize that many Disabled clients experience problems with engaging in occupations that are unrelated to their impairment or illness, due to issues such as ableist attitudes or access and financial barriers.[48]

However, many OTPs fail to recognize these barriers.[49] Occupational therapy academic programming often fails to even educate OT students about these barriers or methods for practically addressing them.[50] Embracing disability as a form of human variation calls on OTPs to address participation barriers at the individual client level as well as by addressing structural, systematic, process, and attitudinal barriers through advocacy and policy efforts.[51] To be effective, OTPs must also have structural knowledge and structural competency.

Structural Competency of OT When Working with Clients

To truly apply strengths-based approaches and uphold anti-ableist practices as an OTP demands critical analysis of how the profession's models and theories are primarily informed by ableism that promotes and propagates ideals of independence and normativity. Ableism results in experiences of exclusion, marginalization, and segregation at the individual level as we see in research describing the consequences of ableism.[52] However, structural discrimination created by and supported through systems, organizations, and institutions targets the collective of the Disabled community and produces and reproduces occupational injustices such as occupational imbalance, deprivation, and alienation. To realistically achieve comprehensive goals of social inclusion and participation of Disabled clients, an OTP must consider these barriers in goal setting with the client and in intervention design. This requires the OTP to share the knowledge of the social determinants of health and occupation, thoughtfully plan strategies with clients to widen opportunities to achieve participation in meaningful occupations, promote occupational choice, and support occupational engagement.[53] This demands practitioners and the profession work to achieve structural competence and a broader understanding of the social contexts of clients' lives.[54] Failure to do so fails the client and contributes to occupational injustices. If all an OTP focuses on when working with an individual client is achieving independence in dressing, the client will be left only to get dressed but with nowhere to go and no meaningful choices in the occupations to participate in.

Without structural competency, it is far too easy for OTPs to stay focused on individualist approaches. An overemphasis on individual independence, activities of daily living or instrumental activities of daily living, and work / return to work is not only steeped in ableism but overlooks many of the authentic and meaningful ways of occupational engagement and occupational forms that contribute to a high quality of life for many Disabled people.

Endnotes

1 Linton, S. (1998). Disability studies/not disability studies. *Disability & Society, 13*(4), 525–539. https://doi.org/10.1080/09687599826588, p. 525.
2 Sheth, A. J., Kish, J., VanPuymbrouck, L. H., Heffron, J. L., Lee, D., & Mahaffey, L. (2021). "A legitimate place in the profession": Author reflections on the 2005 disability studies special issue. *American Journal of Occupational Therapy, 75*, 7504180005. https://doi.org/10.5014/ajot.2021.045294
3 Patten, K. K. (2022). Finding our strengths: Recognizing professional bias and interrogating systems. *The American Journal of Occupational Therapy, 76*(6). https://doi.org/10.5014/ajot.2022.076603
4 Harrison, E. A., Sheth, A. J., Kish, J., VanPuymbrouck, L. H., Heffron, J. L., Lee, D., Mahaffey, L., & Occupational Therapy and Disability Studies Network. (2021). Disability studies and occupational therapy: Renewing the call for change. *The American Journal of Occupational Therapy, 75*(4). https://doi.org/10.5014/ajot.2021.754002
5 Overton, G. L., Marsa-Sambola, F., Martin, R., & Cavenagh, P. (2024). Understanding the self-identification of autism in adults: A scoping review. *Review Journal of Autism and Developmental Disorders, 11*, 682–702. https://doi.org/10.1007/s40489-023-00361-x
6 Brewer, E. (2018). Coming out mad, coming out disabled. In E. J. Donaldson (Ed.), *Literary disability studies* (pp. 11–30). Springer International Publishing. https://doi.org/10.1007/978-3-319-92666-7_2
7 Sheth, A. J., Kish, J., VanPuymbrouck, L. H., Heffron, J. L., Lee, D., & Mahaffey, L. (2021). "A legitimate place in the profession": Author reflections on the 2005 disability studies special issue. *American Journal of Occupational Therapy, 75*, 7504180005. https://doi.org/10.5014/ajot.2021.045294
8 Bogart, K. R., Lund, E. M., & Rottenstein, A. (2018). Disability pride protects self-esteem through the rejection-identification model. *Rehabilitation Psychology, 63*(1), 155–159. https://doi.org/10.1037/rep0000166
9 Kielhofner, G. (2009). *Conceptual foundations of occupational therapy practice*. F.A. Davis Company.
10 ibid.
11 ibid.
12 Harrison, E. A., Sheth, A. J., Kish, J., VanPuymbrouck, L. H., Heffron, J. L., Lee, D., Mahaffey, L., & Occupational Therapy and Disability Studies Network. (2021). Disability studies and occupational therapy: Renewing the call for change. *The American Journal of Occupational Therapy, 75*(4). https://doi.org/10.5014/ajot.2021.754002
13 Kielhofner, G. (2009). *Conceptual foundations of occupational therapy practice*. F.A. Davis Company.
14 Patten, K. K. (2022). Finding our strengths: Recognizing professional bias and interrogating systems. *The American Journal of Occupational Therapy, 76*(6). https://doi.org/10.5014/ajot.2022.076603
15 Sheth, A. J., Kish, J., VanPuymbrouck, L. H., Heffron, J. L., Lee, D., & Mahaffey, L. (2021). "A legitimate place in the profession": Author reflections on the 2005 disability studies special issue. *American Journal of Occupational Therapy, 75*, 7504180005. https://doi.org/10.5014/ajot.2021.045294
16 Union of the Physically Impaired Against Segregation. (1975). *The Union of the Physically Impaired Against Segregation and The Disability Alliance discuss fundamental principles of disability*. https://disability-studies.leeds.ac.uk/wp-content/uploads/sites/40/library/UPIAS-fundamental-principles.pdf
17 Oliver, M. (1990). *The politics of disablement*. Macmillan.
18 Zaks, Z. (2023). Changing the medical model of disability to the normalization model of disability: Clarifying the past to create a new future direction. *Disability & Society*. https://doi.org/10.1080/09687599.2023.2255926
19 Albrecht, G. L., & Bury, M. (2001). The political economy of the disability marketplace. In G. L. Albrecht, K. Seelman, & M. Bury (Eds.), *Handbook of disability studies* (pp. 585–609). Sage.
20 ibid, p. 588.
21 Snyder, S. L., & Mitchell, D. T. (2006). *Cultural locations of disability*. The University of Chicago Press.
22 ibid.
23 Kafer, A. (2013). *Feminist, queer, crip*. Indiana University Press, p. 6.
24 Overton, G. L., Marsa-Sambola, F., Martin, R., & Cavenagh, P. (2024). Understanding the self-identification of autism in adults: A scoping review. *Review Journal of Autism and Developmental Disorders, 11*, 682–702. https://doi.org/10.1007/s40489-023-00361-x
25 Kapp, S. K., Gillespie-Lynch, K., Sherman, L. E., & Hutman, T. (2013). Deficit, difference, or both? Autism and neurodiversity. *Developmental Psychology, 49*(1), 59–71. https://doi.org/10.1037/a0028353
26 Broderick, A. A., & Roscigno, R. (2022). Autism, Inc.: The autism industrial complex. *Journal of Disability Studies in Education, 2*, 77–101. https://doi.org/10.1163/25888803-bja10008
27 Campbell, F. (2009). *Contours of ableism: The production of disability and abledness*. Springer.
28 ibid.

29 Zaks, Z. (2023). Changing the medical model of disability to the normalization model of disability: Clarifying the past to create a new future direction. *Disability & Society*. https://doi.org/10.1080/09687599.2023.2255926
30 Campbell, F. (2009). *Contours of ableism: The production of disability and abledness*. Springer.
31 ibid.
32 Brown, N., & Leigh, J. (2020). *Ableism in academia: Theorising experiences of disabilities and chronic illnesses in higher education*. UCL Press.
33 Calder-Dawe, O., Witten, K., & Carroll, P. (2020). Being the body in question: Young people's accounts of everyday ableism, visibility and disability. *Disability & Society, 35*(1), 132–155. https://doi.org/10.1080/09687599.2019.1621742
34 ibid.
35 Friedman, C. (2019). Mapping ableism: A two-dimensional model of explicit and implicit disability attitudes. *Canadian Journal of Disability Studies, 8*(3), 95–120. https://doi.org/10.15353/cjds.v8i3.509
36 ibid.
37 Greenwald, A. G., McGhee, D. E., & Schwartz, J. L. (1998). Measuring individual differences in implicit cognition: The implicit association test. *Journal of Personality and Social Psychology, 74*(6), 1464–1480. https://doi.org/10.1037//0022-3514.74.6.1464
38 Friedman, C. (2019). Mapping ableism: A two-dimensional model of explicit and implicit disability attitudes. *Canadian Journal of Disability Studies, 8*(3), 95–120. https://doi.org/10.15353/cjds.v8i3.509
39 ibid.
40 Friedman, C. (2023). Explicit and implicit: Ableism of disability professionals. *Disability and Health Journal, 16*(4), 101482. https://doi.org/10.1016/j.dhjo.2023.101482
41 Friedman, C. (2019). Mapping ableism: A two-dimensional model of explicit and implicit disability attitudes. *Canadian Journal of Disability Studies, 8*(3), 95–120. https://doi.org/10.15353/cjds.v8i3.509
42 ibid.
43 Nario-Redmond, M. R., Kemerling, A. A., & Silverman, A. (2019). Hostile, benevolent, and ambivalent ableism: Contemporary manifestations. *The Journal of Social Issues, 75*(3), 726–756. https://doi.org/10.1111/josi.12337
44 Shakespeare, T., & Watson, N. (2010). Beyond models: Understanding the complexity of disabled people's lives. In G. Scambler & S. Scambler (Eds.), *New directions in the sociology of chronic and disabling conditions: Assaults on the lifeworld* (pp. 57–76). Palgrave Macmillan UK.
45 Friedman, C. (2023). Explicit and implicit: Ableism of disability professionals. *Disability and Health Journal, 16*(4), 101482. https://doi.org/10.1016/j.dhjo.2023.101482
46 Hyslop, B. (2020). "Not safe for discharge"? Words, values, and person-centred care. *Age and Ageing, 49*(3), 334–336. https://doi.org/10.1093/ageing/afz170
47 Paul-Ward, A. (2009). Social and occupational justice barriers in the transition from foster care to independent adulthood. *The American Journal of Occupational Therapy, 63*(1), 81–88. https://doi.org/10.5014/ajot.63.1.81
48 Shakespeare, T. (2007). Debating disability. *Journal of Medical Ethics, 34*(1), 11–14. https://doi.org/10.1136/jme.2006.019992
49 Turcotte, P.-L., Carrier, A., Roy, V., & Levasseur, M. (2018). Occupational therapists' contributions to fostering older adults' social participation: A scoping review. *The British Journal of Occupational Therapy, 81*(8), 427–449. https://doi.org/10.1177/0308022617752067
50 VanPuymbrouck, L., Chun, E. M., Hesse, E. D., Ranneklev, K., & Sanchez, C. (2024). Developing client self-advocacy in occupational therapy: Are we practicing what we preach? *Occupational Therapy International, 2024*(1), 1662671. https://doi.org/10.1155/2024/1662671
51 Barclay, L., McDonald, R., Lentin, P., & Bourke-Taylor, H. (2016). Facilitators and barriers to social and community participation following spinal cord injury. *Australian Occupational Therapy Journal, 63*(1), 19–28. https://doi.org/10.1111/1440-1630.12241
52 Gappmayer, G. (2021). Disentangling disablism and ableism: The social norm of being able and its influence on social interactions with people with intellectual disabilities. *Journal of Occupational Science, 28*(1), 102–113. https://doi.org/10.1080/14427591.2020.1814394
53 Hammell, K. W. (2020). *Engagement in living: Critical perspectives on occupation, rights, and wellbeing*. Canadian Association of Occupational Therapists. https://caot.ca/client/product2/908/item.html
54 Pitonyak, J. S., Mroz, T. M., & Fogelberg, D. (2015). Expanding client-centred thinking to include social determinants: A practical scenario based on the occupation of breastfeeding. *Scandinavian Journal of Occupational Therapy, 22*(4), 277–282. https://doi.org/10.3109/11038128.2015.1020865

CHAPTER 3

Neurodiversity and Occupation

AARON R. DALLMAN AND MELANIE E. WRIGHT

What Is Occupation?

As occupational therapy practitioners (OTPs) and other clinicians work to improve outcomes in various Neurodivergent populations, a central question undoubtedly emerges—what is a meaningful outcome for Neurodivergent populations? Is an ideal outcome alleviating *symptoms* of one's neurodivergence (i.e. autism characteristics), or is the more ideal outcome aligning a client's environment to their occupations? In some cases, the occupation's focus may be the authentic expression of self at work while avoiding actions that make others feel uncomfortable (e.g. a patient may want to avoid stimming at work). However, a more optimal outcome would be aligning a client's work setting to match their authentic expression (e.g. coaching employers to understand the differing emotional regulation tools of Neurodivergent individuals).

We will attempt to answer these questions throughout this chapter, by suggesting that meaningful and successful occupational participation is the optimal endpoint for all individuals. We will argue that successful occupational participation reflects a commitment to supporting an individual's participation in activities that are meaningful to them while living in a complex society. We do not suggest that occupations are solely at the individual level and we recognize that societal limitations can prevent one from accessing meaningful participation. However, we adopt a pragmatic approach and argue that these societal limitations reflect barriers that can be addressed. Although there are many competing definitions of occupation, OTPs typically agree that occupations include the things that people need, want, or have to do throughout their lives and include the doing, being, becoming, and belonging aspects of life.[1] While occupations can be mundane everyday tasks such as sweeping one's cooking area or listening to a favorite song, they can include the complexities of participating in a skydiving experience or defending oneself in court. Because occupations include *doing*, it is hard, if not impossible, to imagine not being engaged in an occupation. The monk who seemingly sits for hours in meditation is still *doing* something; they are engaging in the practice of meditation. An Autistic adolescent who is stimming to regulate their emotions is actively participating in, or doing, an emotional regulation activity. Similarly, individuals with intellectual and developmental disabilities (IDD) who engage in stimming or sensory-fulfilling behaviors often report experiencing benefits from these actions and consider them to be leisure activities. A fundamental element of meaningful occupational participation involves understanding the diverse ways individuals engage in activities that are integral to their lives. Behaviors like stimming, which are frequently misunderstood, should be recognized as a valued and essential occupation for many Neurodivergent individuals. Clearly, a human life is an occupied life, filled with participation that thrusts us through time and leads us to a meaningful life.

Occupations, though, are not all positive and many are not socially sanctioned. A core belief of the occupational therapy profession is that occupations are connected to well-being. Some occupations may serve to promote health (e.g. walking) while others may be detrimental to long-term well-being (e.g. smoking). While adolescent drinking can help establish a young person's identity as a rebel or relieve anxiety, this occupation can also establish a potentially unhealthy coping tool that diminishes their quality of life. Other occupations may not be culturally sanctioned (e.g. sex work in the United States, substance use), but have significant value to the individual themselves and are highly regarded in other cultures or time points. Hallucinogens, for example, were used as a central component in spiritual rituals for over 2000 years,[2] including in the United States. However, since 1970, many hallucinogenic drugs like psilocybin have been banned in the United States and possession of them can lead to federal convictions and incarceration. Even in cases where occupations may not be illegal, social sanctions can prevent one from freely engaging in a respective occupation.

To demonstrate the impact of social stigma on the occupations of Neurodivergent populations, consider the stigma associated with auditory hallucinations or hearing voices among those with schizophrenia. The reader is likely familiar with horror or crime films where the perpetrator of the violence did so at the direction of a voice they heard (think *Psycho*). While there is some evidence that hearing voices can cause negative emotions or lead people to do negative actions, there is also evidence that some people have feelings of positive or neutral emotions when hearing voices.[3] Non-clinically diagnosed patients also report hearing voices and, similar to those with psychiatric diagnoses, report that these voices can be calming and can provide a source of relief.[4] If hearing voices might provide a sense of calm in the same way as meditating or humming a favorite song, why is it that humming a song as I walk around the grocery store is acceptable, but responding to internal voices is not?

The answer lies in the social and federal limitations on occupation, and these restrictions have important implications for Neurodivergent populations. If one's occupations are pathologized, then it is expected that one would avoid publicly participating. Even if one rejects the desire for social acceptance and proceeds with their occupations anyway, federal or local laws might prevent participation. In many countries and states, causing a disturbance (e.g. talking to oneself to respond to an internal monologue) might cause alarm and result in imprisonment. When possible, OTPs should find ways to support their clients in engaging in the occupations that are meaningful to them but recognize that people live within a society that might constrain these occupations. It may be worthwhile to identify ways an Autistic client can stim without disrupting their daily routines and provide ways for an individual who hears voices to participate without causing alarm. Although this task is not easy, it will likely have long-term impacts on the well-being of clients. For instance, offering a Neurodivergent student brief breaks to engage in stimming behaviors before returning to a task can be an effective approach for achieving daily goals and maintaining focus. Clinically, I have observed this approach's effectiveness, as several of my students have learned to request breaks to meet their stimming needs when they experience dysregulation. I offer a designated break period, mutually agreed upon, and then support their return to the task, which helps improve their attention to the task at hand.

In conclusion, occupations are culturally situated, meaningful activities that are performed by individuals, groups, and populations for identity formation, maintenance of self, exploration of self, and connecting to others. Here, we do not use the self in the Western, egocentric viewpoint, but instead propose that the self encompasses a variety of layers of interconnectedness such as families, organizations, and communities. Our definition is in line with the Occupational Therapy Practice Framework (OTPF), which defines OTPs' role in addressing occupation at these levels.

A Phenomenological Understanding of Occupation

This discussion of what occupation is and the various impacts of participation is particularly relevant to the Neurodivergent community, whose occupations have largely been misunderstood, stigmatized, and repressed. As noted throughout this text, Neurodivergent individuals have faced decades of occupational injustices which have, in turn, led to a limited understanding of the needs and preferences of this community. Neurodivergent writers have shared detailed accounts of their own experiences and provided rich descriptions of the meaning of their occupations in books such as *The Reason I Jump*, *How to Keep House While Drowning: A Gentle Approach to Cleaning and Organizing*, *Me, Myself, and Them*, and *The Secret Life of a Black Aspie*. Outsider perspectives (i.e. anyone who is not the individual) fail to understand the lived daily experiences that can only be obtained from the insider perspective. Because a comprehensive understanding of the occupations of Neurodivergent individuals is missing from the scientific and peer-reviewed literature, this discussion will be guided based on the clinical experience of the authors, published research, and blogs of Neurodivergent individuals. By welcoming the range of evidence encompassed within evidence-based practices, we hope to address what occupational scientists have critiqued as the over-dominance of outsider perspectives in autism research that have largely exoticized behaviors and marginalized populations.[5]

Although outsider perspectives are problematic for all populations, they are particularly problematic for Neurodivergent populations where a colonialist rhetoric has led to decades of treatment focused on alleviating and reducing Autistic behaviors. Outsiders are historically inaccurate when judging the emotions and experiences of others. Consistently, Autistic self-advocates and researchers have shared that Autistic behaviors remain constantly dehumanized and stigmatized and lead to feelings of Otherness.[6] Likewise, stimming behaviors among other groups of Neurodivergent individuals also result in these groups feeling Othered. A large social media community of self-identified women with ADHD shared personal accounts of their stimming being perceived in a derogatory manner, bringing about feelings of Otherness. One user recounted their childhood experience of flapping their hands and arms, noting that those around them, including their parents, would mock them, even suggesting that they might "fly away" if they continued the movements.[7] Meanwhile, these stimming behaviors are supportive of the individual's well-being and individuality. Thus, understanding the lived experience of the members themselves must be the gold standard for defining and describing occupations for Neurodivergent individuals.

The Beautiful and Diverse Voices of Neurodivergent Individuals

Neurodivergent heterogeneity refers to the wide range of ways in which individuals experience neurodivergence, with connections between certain phenotypes and genotypes. This suggests that observable traits (phenotypes) and their genetic underpinnings (genotypes) should be sufficiently linked to connect various aspects of neurodivergence. However, Waterhouse[8] argues that the heterogeneity within autism leads to negative effects, such as ineffective drug regimens and behavioral treatments lacking clinical evidence, and that transdiagnostic endophenotypes—traits beyond specific diagnoses linked to underlying biology or genetics—may help prevent these effects when placed under certain constructs (e.g. sensory dysfunction, impaired social motivation, impaired social attention, social withdrawal, lack of social communication, poor interaction quality, indexing of cognitive functioning, measures of ADHD behaviors, measures of anxiety). These endophenotypes could offer a better framework for understanding and grouping Neurodivergent individuals to better support their needs.

Ultimately, this reinforces the idea that neurodivergence should not be seen as a single, uniform concept, but as a spectrum with diverse expressions and experiences. While there are overlaps in genotypes and phenotypes among Neurodivergent individuals, we must consider the high variability within this population. Neurodiversity is inherently multifaceted, and the boundary between neurotypical and Neurodivergent is not always clear-cut. For instance, Neurodivergent individuals often exhibit high cognitive variability, excelling in some areas while struggling in others during psycho-cognitive and executive function assessments. In contrast, neurotypicals tend to show more consistent cognitive performance across different domains.[9] Consequently, the binary classification of Neurodivergent versus neurotypical fails to capture the full complexity and diversity of cognitive experiences within this population. Environmental, emotional, and societal factors can obscure the true abilities of some Neurodivergent individuals, causing neurotypical observers to misinterpret certain behaviors as symptoms of a diagnosis. For instance, Dr. Mary Doherty, an Autistic consultant anesthetist, makes the argument that we cannot claim an Autistic individual appears to have IDD when relying on rigid benchmarks, as a Neurodivergent individual may possess significant intellect that only becomes apparent when provided with an effective communication method.[10] These types of oversimplifications overlook the varied strengths and challenges faced by Neurodivergent individuals, emphasizing the need for a more flexible and individualized approach that goes beyond mere categorization and standardized protocols. Instead, providing appropriate supports and optimizing an individual's environment are favorable strategies for improving outcomes among Neurodivergent populations, rather than reinforcing divisions (i.e. lack of support for those who need it) that derive from heterogeneity. OTPs have the expertise to adapt and modify environments and occupations to support Neurodivergent individuals' differing needs and unique strengths. Therefore, it is essential for OTPs to implement neurodiversity-affirming practices to celebrate the identities of Neurodivergent individuals, while cultivating positive relationships and a sense of belonging as they work toward achieving their goals.

Throughout this chapter, we will prioritize the voices of Neurodivergent individuals to inform the directionality and phenomenology of meaningful occupation. In so doing, we recognize that personal experiences and motivations are inextricable from occupations. While systems and policies may shape one's occupational participation, policies and systems alone do not dictate individual and differential performance in occupation. Thus, we assume that some established occupations meaningful to neurotypical populations may not fully be reflective of

Neurodivergent individuals' unique phenomenological preferences in neurotypical occupations. For example, a goal to encourage Neurodivergent individuals to move in ways similar to the neuro-majority (e.g. without stimming) would neglect the phenomenological reasons why an individual might stim. Rather than harmfully mandating neurotypical behaviors onto Neurodivergent individuals, OTPs have a moral obligation to rethink occupation and allow Neurodivergent individuals to redefine occupation in their own way. OTPs can embody a neurodiversity-affirming practice by intentionally valuing individual differences, supporting self-advocacy, and involving clients in the development and selection of interventions. This approach includes applying a strengths-based perspective, encouraging inclusion, and creating supportive environments. Additionally, OTPs can build positive relationships by providing education to teachers, caregivers, providers, and other community members for and with Neurodivergent individuals.

Occupations Through the Neurodivergent Lens

Occupations often share similar characteristics for individuals regardless of neurotype, but there is limited research about the specific occupations of Neurodivergent individuals. Taylor[11] theorized that occupational science, a field that focuses on describing and understanding occupation, has rendered Autistic behaviors invisible and consequentially maintained the dominance of ableist systems. While all individuals regularly engage in occupations for maintenance of self, such as eating/feeding, bathing, and participating in leisure activities, Neurodivergent populations likely have unique experiences of these occupations. Eating a new food might be a novel and enjoyable experience for some, but for those with sensory sensitivities, the new food may be a source of anxiety. Similarly, all individuals also engage in occupations for the presentation of self which may include occupations such as doing makeup and brushing one's hair, or may include other elements such as responding to blogs online. Although the OTPF classifies occupations as activities of daily living (ADLs), instrumental activities of daily living (IADLs), health management, rest and sleep, education, work, play, leisure, and social participation, this chapter organizes the discussion around the *why* behind the occupation, as opposed to the form. From our lens of critical phenomenology, we recognize that the subjective experiences are essential components of occupation and that these individualized meanings are situated for the individual.

Occupations for the Maintenance and Presentation of the Self

Neurodivergent individuals engage in a variety of occupations that serve to maintain and create a presentation of the self. Some of these occupations serve self-regulatory purposes and can help one to cope with difficult emotions. We have already discussed how auditory hallucinations (e.g. internal voices) can provide positive coping tools for some individuals. Other occupations assist Neurodivergent individuals in their presentations of self. For example, some individuals choose the clothes they wear in order to manage the impressions of others. This careful curation of personal appearance can be a strategic tool for navigating social interactions and performing elements of identity. Other individuals strategically (whether conscious or not) modify their movements, tone, and language to modify the impressions of others. For example, students in one of the author's classroom are markedly different in their tone and language when the class officially begins and when it ends. The immediate cessation of personal identities in favor of embodying the role of a student is apparent. As a clinician, one of the authors worked with one Autistic adult who reported strategically using "extroverted"-like behaviors to get ahead at work. During work meetings or events, this individual would arrive early, plan five meaningful conversations that would make an impact on the listener, and then depart to go home and recharge. Although the person preferred to keep to themselves, they adopted a new way of being to *present* as a good player at work. Furthermore, one individual with IDD, who one of the authors worked with closely, chose to wear a championship wrestling belt during the day while participating in structured program routines. This symbolic act helped boost their confidence and provided a sense of empowerment as they navigated their daily activities under the persona of a "winner." These types of identity switching can serve important functions for Neurodivergent populations, allowing them to navigate social and personal challenges with a sense of agency and self-assurance.

Stimming, also known as repetitive behaviors or stims, includes a wide class of behaviors such as hand flapping, jumping, rocking, twisting, twirling, singing, vocalizations, and skin picking that may be central to an individual's identity and culture.[12] Although stimming is typically discussed in the context of autism,[13,14] one observational and non-epidemiological study found that 20% of non-Autistic individuals stim.[15] Most individuals I know stim in some way to regulate their attention. As you read this chapter, you might find that you are twirling your hair, biting your thumb, or clicking a pen. These repetitive behaviors help you to focus and are important elements of who you are. Scholars have recently asserted that stimming is an improvisatory practice that constitutes an individual's aesthetics and sensory experiences.[16] Improvisation and stimming can be better understood as forms of spontaneous expression[17] that arise from a shared sense of creativity and self-regulation. This beautiful and evocative conceptualization of stimming explains why it helps individuals, both Neurodivergent and neurotypical, manage otherwise adverse sensory or environmental barriers (e.g. loud sounds in public like a baby crying) and create a pleasing situation. Stimming is painting one's aesthetic on a world that resists your ways of being; it is a tool to emplace one's identity and self into structures and environments that have often neglected your reality. Some people stim with the aid of technology or other devices (e.g. a string or preferred object) and others stim just using their body (e.g. rocking). Thus, stimming transforms the world and its objects into part of the Neurodivergent individual's tableau and becomes an element of active resistance. The painting extends beyond individuals and projects into the world. While stimming has frequently been a target of medical intervention, recent studies highlight just how important the self-regulatory components of stimming are, including helping Neurodivergent individuals to regulate their emotions and helping individuals regulate when they experience negative sensory stimuli.[18]

Problematically, many stims only become acceptable when integrated into the neuro-majority's behaviors and improvisatory actions. For example, scientists and public health experts encouraged neurotypical individuals during the COVID-19 pandemic to take advantage of fidget toys or to move their bodies in specific ways (e.g. toe tapping) in order to prevail through working from home and to manage potential bodily (i.e. mental, physical, emotional) discomfort associated with the environmental change.[19] Further, since 2020, smartphone cases that possess built-in fidgets have become increasingly popular and utilized to provide a calming sensory experience for the user. These mainstreamed stimming devices have now gained social acceptance and can be readily used by Neurodivergent individuals in the community. Other stims, though, such as rocking and flapping, have not gained social acceptance and are oppressed. One social media user shared their stimming practices for managing anxiety, describing how they position their body in "contortionist-like" poses, press their fingers into their ribcage, and knead or apply pressure to their shoulders or collarbone as a form of self-soothing. Despite finding comfort in these actions, they expressed unease performing them in public due to fear of societal judgment. To help alleviate this fear, an OTP might suggest more discreet alternatives, such as wall push-ups for providing intense proprioceptive input or using a handheld massage device to address their upper body sensory needs in a way that feels more socially acceptable. However, OTPs should approach these adaptations with care, recognizing that encouraging clients to suppress or hide their natural regulation strategies can be re-traumatizing. The goal is not to promote social conformity, but to create environments that make authentic self-regulation safe, supported, and accepted.

When stimming is suppressed, Neurodivergent individuals experience increased health disparities such as feelings of reduced autonomy, self-esteem, motivation, and increased feelings of learned helplessness and lack of control which result in the masking of Neurodivergent behaviors.[20] With continued suppression and masking behaviors, Neurodivergent individuals tend to experience shutdowns and sensory over-stimulation to behave in ways that are deemed acceptable in neurotypical settings.[21,22] Despite this, some clinicians still espouse clinical approaches that aim to reduce stimming behaviors even if they offer no negative ill effects. For example, approaches that encourage quiet hands, whole-body listening, and listening with your eyes/ears are just a few examples of approaches that might limit the stimming behaviors of individuals. Efforts to suppress stims can also lead to Autistic burnout,[23] which is a type of chronic exhaustion that causes a loss of skills and reduced tolerance to a stimulus. In place of whole-body listening and approaches alike, we suggest that whole-body learning can be used as a practical alternative. Whole-body learning acknowledges that all individuals learn differently, and one framework from Autism Level UP! encourages students to explore how they utilize various body parts—such as their head (mission control), hands and arms (tactile manipulators), legs and feet (mobility units), and internal systems (fuel and rest)—to facilitate their learning process.[24] Embracing whole-body learning and movement-based approaches not only respects the individuality of Neurodivergent individuals, but provides an environment where they can thrive, leading to improved sensory processing, enhanced motor skills, and better overall well-being.

Ultimately, Neurodivergent individuals experience increased health disparities when they are made to feel that their desired occupations are inappropriate forms of behavior. Therefore, it is imperative that OTPs continue to explore the nuance of stimming along with other meaningful occupations that have been self-identified by Neurodivergent populations.

Occupations for Recreation and Leisure

Neurodivergent individuals engage in a range of diverse and unique types of play throughout the lifespan. While play is typically believed to be the primary occupation of childhood, play and leisure activities are often practiced throughout the lifespan. From early classifications of autism[25] to the present day,[26] researchers have observed that Autistic children line up toys during their play experiences. While some clinicians are eager to target lining up toys because it appears on the surface to be irregular, we encourage clinicians to look beyond their interpretation of the aesthetics of the play occupation and to consider the meaning behind the occupation itself. Further, it is vital for all clinicians to recognize that the function of play and leisure is, at least in part, up to the player. Thus, goals targeting "functional play" that are evaluated/measured by outsiders (e.g. the OTP) may miss the very point of play. Many Autistic children get great enjoyment when lining up toys. Instead of trying to change how an individual experiences joy through play, we should support them by teaching those who are most involved in their environment how to engage with the individual's unique play styles (e.g. challenging ableist approaches in school settings, such as imposing behavioral expectations that require them to suppress natural stimming behaviors or other forms of self-regulation). The process of lining up toys provides an opportunity to learn about colors, shapes, sizes, and categories, which may serve as important prerequisite knowledge for learning mathematics.

Games, whether online or physical, are common recreational activities for Neurodivergent individuals. Board games can provide an opportunity for individuals to learn social rules, navigate complex rules, and learn negotiation tools that can be addressed both in the games and in real life. Individuals with ADHD report differing experiences and preferences engaging with board games; for some, they flourish with the structure and complexity of the unfolding game dynamic, whereas others report a misalignment between board games and their processing patterns. For example, some individuals report difficulty following game rules, remembering their turns, or feeling anxious about making mistakes during play. OTPs can collaborate with clients to combat these feelings by implementing accommodations to participate in the game, such as checklists that clearly state each simplified direction or using a special object like a token to pass among players to let the person know it is their turn. These strategies can help reduce anxiety, support attention, and offer a more enjoyable and inclusive gaming experience. Other sources of recreation and leisure may be fitness classes, reading about a focused interest, or playing with language (e.g. scripting). Although these types of play may not be seen as such from an outside point of view, they can provide the structure, relaxation, and opportunities for engagement and growth that are characteristic of recreation.

Many Neurodivergent individuals also play online games, including massively multiplayer online role-playing games (MMORPGs).[27] These immersive environments offer an opportunity to develop friendships and other types of social connection with peers. These virtual environments provide a unique opportunity for players to escape the potential challenges of the real world and creatively explore a new world to find belonging and acceptance. The often direct styles of communication required in MMORPGs may play to the strengths of Neurodivergent individuals. The anonymity and flexibility offered by online gaming can make it more comfortable for them to express themselves and to explore new interests and experiences. For example, the vast virtual environments of the Final Fantasy series can provide Neurodivergent individuals an opportunity to explore different types of personal characteristics through their interactions with other online players. Through shared quests, battles, and in-game events, players can develop strong friendships and bonds that transcend the digital world and thus become an important source of recreation; this opportunity may not always be possible/achievable in real-world social interactions due to the fear or discomfort associated with violating implicit societal norms. In turn, players can utilize a low-pressure setting to experience a sense of belonging within a community of other players through these experiences. Furthermore, the structured nature of many MMORPGs can provide a sense of predictability and routine that can be comforting for some Neurodivergent individuals who may find sudden changes difficult.

Neurodivergent individuals across the lifespan often engage in sensory play—a type of play that offers an opportunity for enjoyment, learning, and development through sensory experiences. While most play includes sensory components, sensory-oriented play specifically focuses on engaging the senses for their unique calming, stimulating, or educational effects. For instance, some children may be fascinated by water, enjoying the opportunity to place their hands under a faucet or watch water dance out of the spout. Others may engage with slime or other sensory-rich materials to enjoy soothing tactile experiences. One Autistic child one of the authors had the pleasure of learning from created their own play by watching the blades of a fan spin rhythmically while also inviting in the cool air on their face. Higashida[28] provides a rich account of childhood experiences with sensory play through the act of spinning objects; Prahlad[29] describes watching particles of dust dance in light. Other Neurodivergent individuals I have worked with clinically and non-clinically view bubble blowing and popping as a rich sensory experience, engaging multiple senses at once. The act of pulling the lips together to push out air onto the wand, the visual dance of the bubbles, the tactile pleasure of feeling them burst on the skin, and the satisfying sound of each pop combine to create a calming and captivating activity that resonates as play. These experiences demonstrate how sensory play provides both calming comfort and active engagement, much like how many Neurodivergent children and adults use sensory toys, such as plushies or a favorite stuffed animal, to regulate sensory needs, enhance arousal, and create joyful connections with their surroundings. In essence, sensory play is a vital tool for Neurodivergent individuals, providing them with the opportunity to feel more connected to both their inner and outer worlds while fostering emotional regulation, learning, and skill development.

Neurodivergent individuals commonly report focused interests. Although a pervasive stereotype of autism might suggest that these are "restricted interests"[30] and are limited to trains, cars, and robots, a wide body of research has shown that Neurodivergent individuals have varied interests. Recently, scholars have posited that a core feature of Neurodivergent conditions is monotropism, that is a person has a high degree of intensity for a few interests. Polytropism, a lesser degree of interest in many areas, is believed to be reflective of the interest distribution among the neuro-majority. Thus, while early reports of autism often reported that these interests are specific and gendered, new evidence about the gender spectrum in autism has suggested that there is no such simplistic view of interests in autism. These focused and highly intense interests have been likened to flow, an experience of immersion, and engagement.[31] Individuals experience intense focus, motivation, and enjoyment, resulting in complete immersion in the present moment. When considered in this way, these strong interests represent a core occupation of Autistic community members and serve as a foundational feature of recreation/leisure in the autism population. As one of the authors sits here, a close relative is learning to play the drum, actively engaged in practicing rhythms and learning notation. As family members call their name, they miss these social calls and instead stay immersed in this recreational activity. Although the family might make jokes, we welcome this newfound interest. However, if that same individual were diagnosed with some form of neurodivergence, they might have this type of intense focus pathologized and problematized. In fact, they might even be encouraged to branch out in their interests or be given medication to change their arousal levels with social stimuli. When this reconceptualization of focused interests is applied to the Neurodivergent population, the focus of intervention becomes celebrating these interests, providing time to explore them, and developing techniques to shift away from these interests to others as appropriate.

Importantly, while we have highlighted some leisure occupations of Neurodivergent populations, it is important to recognize that environments are often not designed with the sensory needs and experiences of Neurodivergent children. Consequentially, many leisure activities enjoyed by the neuro-majority may be more enjoyable (and thus leisurely) for Neurodivergent individuals when their sensory needs are met. Creating inclusive spaces for all individuals may require confronting the often disparate needs of a Neurodivergent population. Such realities are evident when considering individuals who are hyposensitive and hypersensitive to stimuli. Some organizations have laid out plans to design these flexible and adaptive environments (see Cusack[32] for one example). Airports (Newark Airport in NJ for example) are beginning to incorporate sensory-designated rooms for individuals to utilize to manage the sensory-related stressors of air travel (e.g. loud noises from announcements and crowds, long lines, unfamiliar smells, bright lights). Similarly, hospitals are adopting sensory rooms into their practices to better support patients with unique sensory needs. This is demonstrated by Atlantic Health Systems in Morristown, NJ which has created a sensory room for Autistic patients to mitigate discomfort associated with getting their blood drawn. Likewise, to address a mismatch between students' sensory processing and environments, Pennsylvania State University added a sensory room to Beaver Stadium to help fans with unique sensory needs avoid feelings of overwhelm often associated with large sporting events. The design and implementation of environments like sensory rooms that accommodate the diverse sensory needs of Neurodivergent individuals can promote inclusivity and accessibility to further increase occupational engagement.

Occupations for Finding Belonging and Building Community

While all types of occupations are important and offer critical roles in living a good life, the most important occupations are undoubtedly tied to finding and participating in a community where one feels a sense of belonging. Although there is not a clear definition of belonging in the literature, a recent review paper proposed an integrated framework.[33] This novel framework suggests that belonging occurs at the intersection of competencies, opportunities, perceptions, and motivations, all of which occur within a social, cultural, environmental, and temporal context and experience. Although the purpose of this chapter is not to review theories associated with occupation, the reader may wish to review the tenets of this integrated framework with complementary theories of occupation to understand how OTPs can support belonging. In general, OTPs have a role in supporting individuals to develop their individual competencies, while providing opportunities, shaping perceptions, and understanding their motivations. Competencies arise out of the opportunities afforded in an environment. OTPs have a role in developing supportive contexts, which may include helping a parent understand their Neurodivergent child's needs and communication methods, which will foster an environment that supports the child's growth, providing opportunities for communication, promoting intrinsic motivation and sense of belonging. Similarly, an OTP can help a parent understand the monotropic interests of a child with ADHD, thus helping the child to feel included and welcomed at home, promoting their own motivations. By understanding and addressing individual needs and interests, OTPs will support the cultivation of environments that empower individuals and enhance a profound sense of belonging within communities.

Problematically though, very few studies have investigated belonging among individuals with disabilities. Generally, researchers assert that Neurodivergent individuals report less belonging than their neuro-majority peers, including Autistic individuals,[34] individuals with intellectual disabilities,[35] and others. Interestingly, one study found that individuals with physical disabilities demonstrated similar rates of thwarted belonging as individuals without disabilities. However, the state of the science remains too new to understand what may lead to a thwarted sense of belonging among Neurodivergent individuals. As a result, our limited understanding of the unique challenges individuals with disabilities face in forming connections and feeling included has the potential to obstruct the trajectory toward fostering a strong sense of belonging within this population.

OTPs should view belonging as a fragile and situated concept, one that can shift with changes in policies, social attitudes, and resources. OTPs should also encourage their clients to explore their interests, which is an occupation in and of itself that can promote belonging. Engaging in activities we enjoy can significantly improve our overall well-being and provide a sense that we belong in this context. Interests provide a sense of purpose, fulfillment, and connection to the world around us. By exploring one's passions, an individual can enhance their quality of life, reduce stress, build connections to a community, develop metacognitive skills related to their own learning styles, and foster a positive mindset. Additionally, engaging in said passions can help clients develop a deeper understanding of their personal strengths, challenges, and values, which contributes to a greater sense of self-awareness and confidence. OTPs can guide individuals in identifying activities that not only bring joy but also align with their personal goals, empowering them to take an active role in their own therapeutic process. This approach supports the holistic development of the client, promoting not just physical or cognitive improvement, but also emotional and social well-being.

Conclusion

The concept of occupation must prioritize the voices and experiences of Neurodivergent individuals in order to effectively and collaboratively apply their diverse perspectives and preferences. Historically, the concept of occupation tends to be defined and integrated through neurotypical ideals, often failing to encompass the nuanced realities and self-reported values of Neurodivergent communities. By actively seeking feedback and allowing ourselves to learn from and with Neurodivergent individuals, we can enhance our understanding of meaningful occupation in ways that reflect this population's unique needs, aspirations, and occupational identities. Neurodivergent health and well-being priorities are best designated by Neurodivergent communities themselves. This reiterates the importance of fostering a sense of shared agency and support within Neurodivergent communities, enabling individuals to come together to advocate for their needs and desires. Further, this approach strengthens the ability of Neurodivergent individuals and communities to influence systems, policies, and practices that impact their lives, ultimately promoting autonomy and inclusivity. This shift enriches our understanding of health and well-being from the lens of occupation while challenging us to embrace the diversity of the lived human experience as we collectively reconceptualize what it means to prosper through occupational engagement.

Endnotes

1 Wilcock, A., & Hocking, C. (2024). *An occupational perspective on health*. Taylor & Francis.

2 Begola, M. J., & Schillerstrom, J. E. (2019). Hallucinogens and their therapeutic use: A literature review. *Journal of Psychiatric Practice*, *25*(5), 334. https://doi.org/10.1097/PRA.0000000000000409

3 Woods, A., Jones, N., Alderson-Day, B., Callard, F., & Fernyhough, C. (2015). Experiences of hearing voices: Analysis of a novel phenomenological survey. *The Lancet Psychiatry*, *2*(4), 323–331. https://doi.org/10.1016/S2215-0366(15)00006-1

4 Faccio, E., Romaioli, D., Dagani, J., & Cipolletta, S. (2013). Auditory hallucinations as a personal experience: Analysis of non-psychiatric voice hearers' narrations. *Journal of Psychiatric and Mental Health Nursing*, *20*(9), 761–767. https://doi.org/10.1111/jpm.12008

5 Taylor, E. (2022). Beyond "bad" behaviors: A call for occupational scientists to rethink autism. *Journal of Occupational Science*, 1–16. https://doi.org/10.1080/14427591.2022.2136231

6 ibid, p. 577.

7 SituationMiddle. (2025). *Judged / teased for stimming behavior (hand over mouth)*. www.reddit.com/r/adhdwomen/comments/1hth2lo/judged_teased_for_stimming_behavior_hand_over

8 Waterhouse, L. (2022). Heterogeneity thwarts autism explanatory power: A proposal for endophenotypes. *Frontiers in Psychiatry*, *13*, 947653. https://doi.org/10.3389/fpsyt.2022.947653

9 Goldberg, H. (2023). Unraveling neurodiversity: Insights from neuroscientific perspectives. *Encyclopedia*, *3*(3), 972–980. https://doi.org/10.3390/encyclopedia3030070

10 Doherty, M. (2023). Weaponized heterogeneity only harms the most vulnerable Autistic people. *Spectrum*. https://doi.org/10.53053/WDPZ6657

11 Taylor, E. (2022). Beyond "bad" behaviors: A call for occupational scientists to rethink autism. *Journal of Occupational Science*, 1–16. https://doi.org/10.1080/14427591.2022.2136231

12 Felepchuk, E. (2021). Stimming, improvisation, and COVID-19: (Re)negotiating Autistic sensory regulation during a pandemic. *Disability Studies Quarterly*, *41*(3), Article 3. https://doi.org/10.18061/dsq.v41i3.8426

13 Kapp, S. K., Steward, R., Crane, L., Elliott, D., Elphick, C., Pellicano, E., & Russell, G. (2019). "People should be allowed to do what they like": Autistic adults' views and experiences of stimming. *Autism*, *23*(7), 1782–1792. https://doi.org/10.1177/1362361319829628

14 Felepchuk, E. (2021). Stimming, improvisation, and COVID-19: (Re)negotiating Autistic sensory regulation during a pandemic. *Disability Studies Quarterly*, *41*(3), Article 3. https://doi.org/10.18061/dsq.v41i3.8426

15 Nwaordu, G., & Charlton, R. A. (2023). Repetitive behaviours in Autistic and non-Autistic adults: Associations with sensory sensitivity and impact on self-efficacy. *Journal of Autism and Developmental Disorders*. https://doi.org/10.1007/s10803-023-06133-0

16 Felepchuk, E. (2021). Stimming, improvisation, and COVID-19: (Re)negotiating Autistic sensory regulation during a pandemic. *Disability Studies Quarterly*, *41*(3), Article 3. https://doi.org/10.18061/dsq.v41i3.8426

17 Nachmanovitch, S. (1990). *Free play: Improvisation in life and art*. Penguin and Putnam.

18 Kapp, S. K., Steward, R., Crane, L., Elliott, D., Elphick, C., Pellicano, E., & Russell, G. (2019). "People should be allowed to do what they like": Autistic adults' views and experiences of stimming. *Autism*, *23*(7), 1782–1792. https://doi.org/10.1177/1362361319829628

19 Felepchuk, E. (2021). Stimming, improvisation, and COVID-19: (Re)negotiating Autistic sensory regulation during a pandemic. *Disability Studies Quarterly*, *41*(3), Article 3. https://doi.org/10.18061/dsq.v41i3.8426

20 Sandoval-Norton, A. H., Shkedy, G., & Shkedy, D. (2019). How much compliance is too much compliance: Is long-term ABA therapy abuse? *Cogent Psychology*, *6*(1), 1641258. https://doi.org/10.1080/23311908.2019.1641258

21 McGill, O., & Robinson, A. (2020). "Recalling hidden harms": Autistic experiences of childhood applied behavioural analysis (ABA). *Advances in Autism* (ahead-of-print). https://doi.org/10.1108/AIA-04-2020-0025

22 Pearson, A., & Rose, K. (2021). A conceptual analysis of Autistic masking: Understanding the narrative of stigma and the illusion of choice. *Autism in Adulthood*, *3*(1), 52–60. https://doi.org/10.1089/aut.2020.0043

23 Taylor, E. (2022). Beyond "bad" behaviors: A call for occupational scientists to rethink autism. *Journal of Occupational Science*, 1–16. https://doi.org/10.1080/14427591.2022.2136231

24 Fede, J., & Laurent, A. (2022). *Bumper: A whole-body learner*. Autism Level UP! https://cdn.sanity.io/files/p6bm7moz/production/99d189ab413e0ccab0329aaa52658ad68b2f7875.pdf

25 Baron-Cohen, S. (1987). Autism and symbolic play. *British Journal of Developmental Psychology*, *5*(2), 139–148. https://doi.org/10.1111/j.2044-835X.1987.tb01049.x

26 Woods, S. E. O., & Estes, A. (2023). Toward a more comprehensive autism assessment: The survey of Autistic strengths, skills, and interests. *Frontiers in Psychiatry*, *14*. https://doi.org/10.3389/fpsyt.2023.1264516

27 Gallup, J., Serianni, B., Duff, C., & Gallup, A. (2016). An exploration of friendships and socialization for adolescents with autism engaged in massively multiplayer online role-playing games (MMORPG). *Education and Training in Autism and Developmental Disabilities*, *51*(3), 223–237.

28 Higashida, N., Yoshida, K. A., & Mitchell, D. (2016). *The reason I jump: The inner voice of a thirteen-year-old boy with autism*. Random House.

29 Prahlad, A. (2017). *The secret life of a Black Aspie: A memoir*. University of Alaska Press.

30 American Psychiatric Association (Ed.). (2022). *Diagnostic and statistical manual of mental disorders: DSM-5-TR*™ (5th ed.). American Psychiatric Association Publishing.

31 Heasman, B., Williams, G., Charura, D., Hamilton, L. G., Milton, D., & Murray, F. (2024). Towards Autistic flow theory: A non-pathologising conceptual approach. *Journal for the Theory of Social Behaviour*, *54*(4), 469–497. https://doi.org/10.1111/jtsb.12427

32 Cusack, J. (n.d.). *Autistica inclusive spaces plan*. Autistica. www.Autistica.org.uk/downloads/files/Autistica-Inclusive-Spaces-Plan.pdf

33 Allen, K.-A., Kern, M. L., Rozek, C. S., McInerney, D. M., & Slavich, G. M. (2021). Belonging: A review of conceptual issues, an integrative framework, and directions for future research. *Australian Journal of Psychology*, *73*(1), 87–102. https://doi.org/10.1080/00049530.2021.1883409

34 Milton, D., & Sims, T. (2016). How is a sense of well-being and belonging constructed in the accounts of Autistic adults? *Disability & Society*, *31*(4), 520–534. https://doi.org/10.1080/09687599.2016.1186529

35 Van Gaasbeek, E. K., & Tassé, M. J. (2024). Constructing a preliminary model of school belonging for students with intellectual disability. *Journal of Intellectual Disabilities*, *28*(3), 591–614. https://doi.org/10.1177/17446295231164438

SPOTLIGHT

The Occupations of Communication and Playwriting

SOFI GHASSAEI AND BRYDEN CARLSON-GIVING

Sofi Ghassaei is an Autistic Nonspeaker who is a playwright, poet, composer, and so much more. One of Sofi's groundbreaking plays, *Love Letters—A True-ly Short Epistolary Romance,* explores the romance between two Autistic Nonspeakers, Melody and Luke, who fall in love with each other over email. As their connection deepens, they confront the complex realities of having sensory processing differences in a world that was not designed for them. *Love Letters* is the first musical by and about Autistic Nonspeakers. *Love Letters* serves as a testament (and a good reminder for non-Autistic individuals) of the capabilities of individuals with high support needs. Just because someone cannot speak or does not speak in traditional ways does not mean they have nothing worthwhile to say.

Sofi wrote the play using the technique of Spelling to Communicate, a technique that bypasses the oral-motor barriers of conventional speech. By pointing to letters on a board, Nonspeakers can express themselves by creating an intimate bridge between mind and body. This technique promotes synchrony between cognitive and motor systems, allowing individuals like Sofi to share their voices. *Love Letters* required hundreds of hours of spelling, and it took Sofi two years to bring the project to life. The musical features not only Sofi's original songs, but also compositions by other Nonspeakers, reflecting their often unspoken emotional worlds.

There are so many aspects of *Love Letters* that I am incredibly fond of, with one in particular standing out: the play dismantles the dominating myth that Nonspeaking individuals and Disabled individuals with high support needs are not sexual beings. Luke and Melody express the same heart-pounding love, vulnerability, and longing we all experience when falling for someone, a familiar tune of romantic angst.

For example, below is an email shared by the character Melody to her friend Kelsey expressing the heart-pounding nervousness and excitement you feel when being around your crush (shared with permission by Sofi):

> Dear Kelsey,
>
> I am looking forward to meeting you when we come to Canada. Yes, I would really love to come over for a boat ride. I absolutely love water and wind. I am excited to see you and Luke. I hope Luke doesn't think I am loud and talk too much. I speak and type, but much of what I say is garbage I don't mean to say. That's my trouble with speaking. Or I might be too nervous to speak in front of Luke. Sometimes I can't talk when I am anxious, other times I get really nervous or excited then I start obnoxiously verbalizing. I am only making noise, not communicating. I need space and time to settle my nerves. I'm just worried about looking completely ridiculous when I meet him, but I am counting the days!
>
> Melody

Sofi shared the following on why she engages in the occupation of playwriting: "I write so people will know what it's like to be Nonspeaking. It isn't just a lack of words. Mouth words are not actually my calm way to communicate. The best way to explain it is a brain-body translation issue. My brain knows none of the same languages my body does, so it's always flipping through the dictionary wondering what the hell is going on."

The real questions we must ask ourselves are: Why have we made occupational therapy so that *we* never have to step outside our comfort zones to understand others? Why do we let assumptions about communication and what it means to be human go unchallenged? The truth is, the real barrier is not that Nonspeakers have nothing to express—it's that we are the barrier. We have created a world so steeped in assumptions about speech and competence that we've forgotten (or really have never realized) the diverse ways in which communication can occur. In Sofi's world, words are not just mouth sounds; they are movements of the mind, the body, and the soul. The future of occupations related to communication lie not in silencing those who don't speak the way we do, but in embracing the possibility that there are endless ways to be heard.

The power of communication is not in the sound of our voices. It is in the space between us where true understanding lives. Thank you, Sofi, for allowing us to share your story and work!

Practical Implications for Occupational Therapy Practitioners

- From a conversation with Nonspeaking advocate Isaiah Grewal: "Get educated about Nonspeaking apraxia; Nonspeaking doesn't mean 'nonthinking'!"[1]

- Examine your own biases about what Nonspeaking individuals can or cannot do, and engage in practices that center the person's autonomy.

- Think about whether or not you are making space for the person you are supporting to express themselves in a way that feels authentic to them, and not how you think communication should look like.

- How can you challenge your own assumptions about the capabilities of Nonspeaking individuals to ensure you are not limiting their opportunities for full self-expression?

Where to Follow Sofi

youtube.com/@sofighassaei

youtube.com/@theaterofpossibility

instagram.com/sofighassaei

i-asc.org/our-team/sofi-ghassaei

The play, *Love Letters*, was premiered by (or first produced by) Theater of Possibility, directed by Lauren Marshall, in Seattle, WA in June 2023, and it may be viewed on YouTube @TheaterofPossibility

Endnote

1 Grewal, I. T. (2024, March 6). Nonspeaking autism—My point of view. *Bened Life*. https://benedlife.com/blogs/news/nonspeaking-autism-my-point-of-view

CHAPTER 4

Collective Liberation

Honoring Disability Justice and Indigenous Wisdom in Occupational Therapy

BRYDEN CARLSON-GIVING AND LAVONNE FOX

with Maya Brandsen, Sam Brandsen, Diamond Rashad, Razan Hamad, Khalilah R. Johnson, Shayda Kafai, Toni Saia, Georgia Vine, and Daryl Patrick Yao

> "Perhaps the most compelling survival tool that Disabled, Queer, Gender Non-conforming, and Transgender communities of color have is their dreamwork. Dreaming is not passive. In dreaming, our communities materialize a world where, through fury and love, transformation in all its rebelliousness thrives."[1]

The phrase "the future is Disabled" invites reflection and critical engagement, challenging societal norms and envisioning a future where disability is embraced as an essential aspect of human diversity. We kindly ask you to reflect on the following: Do you support a Disabled future? Does occupational therapy as it stands support such a future?

Disabled individuals continue to be taught that we are not welcome and that we shouldn't exist (intense we know, but true). For Disabled individuals to be present in mainstream society, and to do so unapologetically and thrivingly, is a radical act of justice and self-love.[2] Imagine if occupational therapy cultivated this self-love and fostered environments where we authentically belonged. Despite ableism and its attempts to separate and disempower Disabled individuals, we are finding and liberating each other.

The disability justice movement was started by Patty Berne of Sins Invalid, a disability-justice-focused performance project. Sins Invalid is also an advocacy organization led by Disabled people of color, rooted in the belief that disability is a vital aspect of human diversity. Sins Invalid challenges societal norms around beauty, sexuality, and disability. Sins Invalid was created to address the gaps followed by the disability rights movement (which critics[3] have shared centered on white experiences and those with physical disabilities). The organization is known for its powerful performances and transformative advocacy, which blend art and activism to create spaces where Disabled voices are amplified and celebrated.[4] At the center of Sins Invalid and the disability justice movement is the disability justice framework, ten liberating principles created by Sins Invalid (as illustrated in Figure 4.1).

Figure 4.1—Sins Invalid's Disability Justice Principles

Occupational therapy often falls short in providing services that authentically support disability as an identity. Occupational therapy, in its current state of prioritizing non-disabled and Western ways of living, does not support a Disabled future as well as it could. Our profession's framework and knowledge base are informed by the medical model of disability, leading our services to implicitly support ableism in that disability is an imperfection in the human experience and needs to be fixed rather than an identity to be embraced (while also recognizing the challenges that come with being Disabled). We don't think about how we will all be Disabled at some point, and yet we make the very notion of normalizing disability a bad thing.

Many of our practices rest on standardized norms that do not reflect Disabled perspectives. There is also a lack of Disabled representation in the field. As occupational therapy practitioners (OTPs), we are uniquely positioned to advocate for our clients in ways of living, being, and doing that are meaningful to them. We dream of a profession that embraces disability justice as a guide, and OTPs can provide anti-ableist approaches that are essential for fostering equitable and empowering services. This chapter aims to support OTPs and their ability to incorporate Sins Invalid's disability justice principles into their practice. Additionally, this chapter will explore Indigenous perspectives on disability, offer a critique of Eurocentric views of disability, and contribute to a broader and more inclusive understanding of disability. OTPs will be invited to challenge dominating concepts of disability and reflect on Disabled experiences often left out of disability conversations.

Reflections and Applications of the Disability Justice Principles

This section of the chapter will introduce all ten of Sins Invalid's disability justice principles with brief descriptions. Sins Invalid utilizes the power of the art form and stories as primary forms of advocacy, and to honor that, we have invited Disabled activists, scholars, and allies to provide reflections on what a specific principle means to them. These intimate narratives offer a window into the living meaning of these principles, and we invite you to reflect alongside these intimate narratives and how they may resonate with your own experiences. To support your journey in applying these principles, actionable steps are provided on how to implement and uphold each principle within occupational therapy practice.

Intersectionality

Description: Intersectionality recognizes that social identities, such as disability, race, and gender, overlap and affect how people experience discrimination and privilege. This principle highlights that ableism is interconnected with other forms of oppression, like racism and sexism. Understanding intersectionality is essential for appreciating the unique challenges faced by individuals in Marginalized communities and for advocating effectively for disability justice. Oppression compounds itself because of these multiple forms of inequities, and these intricacies cannot be ignored.

Activist Reflection

> "Dear Sins Invalid,
>
> Your principle of *intersectionality* resonates within me like the echo of a song that has always lived in my Jordanian heart. I have lived a life stitched together by threads of many identities—a Middle Eastern woman, an immigrant to America, a mother, an educator, and an advocate for social and educational justice. Each thread holds its unique tension, its own story of struggle and triumph. Yet, it is only through embracing intersectionality that I have come to see the beauty of this tapestry.

Intersectionality, as you have taught us, is not just a lens—it is a lifeline. It acknowledges the fullness of humanity in all its layered, complex forms. For me, it has meant carrying the weight of cultural expectations while daring to step outside them, striving to uplift my children and students while navigating systems not built for those who look or think like me. It is the fierce recognition that justice for one cannot exist without justice for all. This principle calls me to honor every voice, every story, and every fight that shapes the whole. And it reminds me that my struggles and privileges intersect with those of others, creating both opportunities for solidarity and responsibilities to act. It also reminds me that our emotional scars are milestones for journeys taken and battles fought well. I wear mine proudly.

In occupational therapy, your principle of intersectionality has the potential to transform practice. When practitioners recognize the intersecting identities of their clients—disability, race, gender, culture, socioeconomic status—they move beyond seeing a diagnosis and begin to see the person. This principle asks OTPs to design care that honors the whole person, understanding that access and healing look different for everyone. It calls for humility, curiosity, and a commitment to dismantling systemic barriers, one client and one system at a time.

Sins Invalid, you remind us that the path to justice is collective, and every intersection is a meeting place where humanity blooms. For this, and so much more, I thank you. You are the light in the shadowed places, showing us how to build a world where everyone belongs."—RAZAN HAMAD

Application of Intersectionality Within Occupational Therapy Practice

- Assess contextual and environmental factors, such as centering assessment tools that assess environmental support and barriers (see assessment figures in Chapter 9).

- Ask clients open-ended questions on their less seen/more invisible aspects of functioning related to their intersectionality, such as "What aspects of your well-being do you feel are often overlooked in discussions about your experiences or identities?"

- Ensure you are co-creating goals with clients by incorporating their experiences and priorities related to their identities (e.g. a Queer and Disabled person may like support locating and navigating social spaces so they feel accepted).

- Consider having therapy services include supporting clients in desired social justice initiatives, such as promoting their performance in the occupation of protesting including storytelling, mutual aid, and participating in solidarity groups). When working within systems that rely on insurance reimbursement, OTPs can still support these goals by documenting them in terms of functional performance or contextualized participation. Maybe instead of "client participated in meaningful advocacy activity," frame it like "client will engage in community-based social participation activities requiring navigation of complex environments and supporting self-regulation."

- For researchers, ensure you are obtaining first-hand lived experiences from intersectional Disabled individuals to add contextual value to your quantitative data; when possible, prioritize including qualitative research methods (e.g. narrative approaches, focus groups).

Leadership of the Most Impacted

Description: This principle highlights that those who experience the most oppression—such as Disabled individuals from Marginalized backgrounds—are best positioned to lead the movement for change. Their lived experiences offer valuable insights and solutions that can effectively address systemic issues like ableism and racism. By listening to and uplifting these voices, we create a stronger, more inclusive disability justice movement. The movement prioritizes the voices and experiences of individuals who are most affected by systemic issues such as ableism, racism, sexism, transmisogyny, and police violence.

Activist Reflection

> "As the second principle of disability justice, leadership of the most impacted has a rebel, killjoy heart. It signals our attention and demands action. To advocate for the leadership of the most impacted is to remember that those of us who wrestle with systemic oppressions are the ones who best know how to dismantle it. This principle invites a powerful reframing of who we turn to for answers. We, dear ones, are the experts we have been waiting for. We know most about the violences of the systemic oppressions impacting our communities because *we* experience them. We are the ones with creative and intergenerational resistance strategies, the hacks and interventions moving us closer and closer toward liberation: community fridges,[5] crip mutual aid networks,[6] KN95 mask drives, fragrance-free femme of color resource shares,[7] depression cookbooks,[8] and Queer and Trans-affirming warm lines.* We do not need to wait or look beyond our communities for restorative and transformative practices; our bodyminds wield solutions. Coalition building, healing, and activism, after all, have always originated from our unmet needs.
>
> I arrived to myself because of intersectional community, because of the archives

* Unlike traditional mental health hotlines like the 988 Suicide and Crisis Lifeline, warm lines are anti-carceral and do not involve police.

of knowledge and healing I found there. I write this reflection as a Disabled, Mad Queer femme of color who for so long felt small, pliable, and silent until community helped me unlearn the deeply rooted effects of ableism, sanism, and heterosexism with direction and tenderness. Leadership of the most impacted for me means wisdom creation by crip of color doulas,[9] Black feminists, and Queer and Trans of color femme elders. This principle is also a call, a love letter. Dear ones: I need you to know that it is an act of love to find ourselves again, to ground ourselves in the activist stories of our communities. I need you to know that you matter, that revolution circulates throughout your bodyminds. You possess ancestral legacies of dissent, of resistance building, and together, we are seed banks. We are wild gardens of change-making."—SHAYDA KAFAI

Application of Leadership of the Most Impacted Within Occupational Therapy Practice

- Organize training sessions at your workplace or occupational therapy program that are led by Disabled individuals, such as hosting a panel discussion of Disabled OTPs to discuss the lived experiences of being Disabled and navigating ableism within the profession and society.

- Amplify diverse narratives by prioritizing stories and education with intersecting identities, such as inviting (and paying) a BIPOC Disabled individual to speak out on their experiences, and translating these insights into practice.

- Instead of relying primarily on peer-reviewed literature about disability, often created by non-disabled researchers, seek out gray literature and resources actually created by Disabled individuals (e.g. blogs, social media, podcasts, community resources, and toolkits). Of course, definitely consider peer-reviewed research if it includes the lived experiences of Disabled individuals!

Anti-Capitalism

Description: This principle recognizes how our economic system prioritizes profit and productivity over well-being, and our society often judges the worth of its members by how much they produce. This also extends to how humans exploit the land and natural resources for profit. Disabled individuals are automatically devalued by society because they are seen as not able to contribute to the economy. Capitalism relies on wealth accumulation for some (the white ruling class) at the expense of others. Our worth as human beings is not dependent on what and how much we can produce. Productivity is measured by ableist standards and marginalizes those who are unable to meet these "normative" standards of output. We must create an economic system that prioritizes the well-being not only of people, but also of the Earth.

Activist Reflection

"Anti-capitalism and Marxism critique capitalism's ableist social norms and standards that are sustained from independence and productivity.[10] These social norms that are unrepresentative of the Disabled population are imbedded within healthcare resulting in occupational therapists knowingly or unknowingly perpetuating ableism.

Occupational therapy training and practice reinforce this neoliberal view within the occupational therapy process as often goals are about social conformity and less about quality of life.[11] For example, as a child with cerebral palsy, I was made to work on occupations like cutting my food to meet societal norms when the reality of cutting up food causes me too much pain and I'd much rather work on other occupations. As a child I enjoyed playing the piano and this had a lot of meaning for myself and my family, therefore I valued playing the piano more and wanted to work on these skills rather than cutting up my food. Another example, and the most obvious example when we think about capitalism, is work. Disabled people may be unable to work as often or not work as often, yet this neoliberalist factor should not be a measure of our social value.[12] I work full-time and I am fortunate as someone with chronic health that I can, but just because I do doesn't mean I should be valued more than Disabled people who don't work full-time or cannot work, which happens due to multiple ableist reasons.

One reason is due to inspirational porn: I often get told I'm inspiring for being a Disabled occupational therapist who works full-time, yet I find this quite patronizing. I was the average age when I went to university, then I left university and got a job. Yes, there were more challenges, but I did what a lot of people my age do. It wasn't out of the ordinary and it wasn't inspiring. This is also very damaging to the person who uses the same amount of energy I use to do a full day's worth of work to get out of bed. The amount of time I spend working doesn't value my worth as I work full-time due to the cost of living. Yes, I'm lucky I can do this, but what people don't see is the weekends when I struggle to get out of bed. Therefore, my work has nothing to do with my worth in society; of course being in the career that I'm in feeds into my self-worth, but that's more because of my passion for what I do, not because I'm meeting 'societal norms.'

I don't assign value to my life based on how much money I earn, and how much economic influence I have on society. I value my role in terms of how much of a difference I have made with the people I work with. Yes, I'm very fortunate to be in the role that I'm in within academia so early on in my career, but I'm in that position because I'm passionate about what I do, and I want to make a difference. Outside of work, as cliché as it is, I find a lot of meaning in spending time with family and friends, and that's what I value. Being Disabled is expensive due to the extra cost of living, but I'm surrounded by family and friends that help me manage my disability and that's what matters to me."—GEORGIA VINE

Application of Anti-Capitalism Within Occupational Therapy Practice

- Center human needs over productivity, emphasize the value of rest, leisure, and creativity overachieving milestones or productivity goals with clients as a focus of their service plans; center approaches that emphasize mental, emotional, and social well-being.
  - You can do this by using assessment tools that focus on the client's personal interests, hopes, dreams, and overall well-being rather than tools that measure discrete performance patterns or body structures (see the Vault for a 20+ page resource for recommended assessment tools).

- Redefine success with your clients in terms of empowerment, self-expression, personal fulfillment, and self-efficacy rather than employability.
  - Collaborate with clients to ensure they have a goal that resonates with how they define success for themselves, whether it's enjoyment in a particular activity or personal growth rather than outcomes focused on work or academics.

- If you own a practice, consider implementing a sliding-scale payment system that enhances accessibility to services for Marginalized individuals or those who have limited access to resources, or collaborate with local organizations to provide free or low-cost outreach programs that service the most marginalized.

Cross-Movement Organizing

Description: This principle emphasizes how we can't fully embrace disability justice without engaging with other social justice movements, such as racial justice, Queer and Trans movements, anti-police terror, the genocide against Palestinians,[13,14] prison abolition, environmental justice, and so many more. Cross-movement organizing highlights how these movements are interconnected and why these movements must collaborate with each other if we really want to empower all human beings. It also encourages other movements to confront any ableist attitudes within their own ideals and specific movements, which is so powerful!

Activist Reflection

"Audre Lorde famously said, 'we do not live single-issue lives.' This truth is a call to action. A demand that we reject siloed struggles and embrace the power of intersectional, cross-movement organizing. Justice for Disabled people cannot be won in fragments; liberation requires us to recognize the interconnectedness of our fights. To build a truly accessible and just world, we must unite across ongoing oppression, communities, cultures, and identities, understanding that our collective strength lies in solidarity. This collective strength allows us to reimagine occupational therapy as more than just a practice but rather a partnership that actively fights the struggles while celebrating the wins with clients. More importantly, this partnership demands that occupational therapists recognize a fundamental truth: clients do not exist solely within the four walls of the occupational therapy room. Disabled people are shaped by systemic forces, community struggles, and intersecting identities that extend far beyond a single session.

Occupational therapists have the power and the responsibility to dismantle barriers that limit Disabled people's access, autonomy, and justice. To do this effectively, OTPs must go beyond traditional practice of 'servicing an individual'; they must actively collaborate, immerse themselves in social justice movements, and commit to addressing the rampant ableism that exists within the profession and larger society. As a Disabled woman who has been on the receiving end of many services (including occupational therapy), **do not be a gatekeeper, be a 'life hacker'** as we navigate systems that were not built for us."—TONI SAIA

Application of Cross-Movement Organizing Within Occupational Therapy Practice

- Help build alliances across movements, such as partnering with organizations focused on Queer rights, racial justice, disability rights, and other social issues to really foster a collective approach to advocacy (e.g. an OTP collaborates with the Black Youth Project (BYP) and the Trevor Project to host an event where resources are shared pertaining to screenings, healthcare resources, and combatting houselessness).

- Promote shared advocacy work by getting involved in community programming that addresses various social justice issues (e.g. an OTP engages in developing an accessible garden in a mixed-income neighborhood, holding meetings with Disabled community members, and environmental activities to provide the space for these groups to come together and create a shared plan).

- *Example*—An OTP in a public education setting develops a mentorship program where peers from similar backgrounds and experiences support each other (e.g. Disabled 11th and 12th graders mentoring Disabled 9th and 10th graders), and together they partner with other student-led organization groups to host a "Diversity and Disability Justice Week" at school.

Recognizing Wholeness

Description: This principle emphasizes that Disabled people should not be reduced to their disability or impairments but celebrated for their full humanity. Embracing wholeness promotes acceptance, self-love, and a deeper appreciation for the contributions of all individuals. "Each person is full of history and life experience. Each person has an internal experience composed of our own thoughts, sensations, emotions, sexual fantasies, perceptions, and quirks" (p. 19).[15] Disabled individuals are multifaceted human beings, just like non-disabled individuals, and Disabled people have diverse skills, passions, and experiences that enrich our community and society.

Activist Reflection

> "Recognizing wholeness means understanding that we are not defined by our flaws or incomplete moments, but by all parts of ourselves. It's easy to fall into the trap of thinking we need to fix our disabilities in order to feel whole, but true wholeness comes from acceptance. Every experience, whether positive or negative, contributes to our overall sense of self. By embracing both our strengths and our vulnerabilities, we can begin to see that we were never broken to begin with. Wholeness is about acknowledging that we are complete, not because we lack challenges or imperfections, but because we are continuously evolving and learning to accept all that we are meant to be."—MAYA BRANDSEN

Application of Recognizing Wholeness Within Occupational Therapy Practice

- Remember, clients are being vulnerable in sharing their experiences with you. Believe their experiences and shift the focus from "fixing" to supporting (your goal is not to "fix" clients but instead to promote empowerment and achieve their definition of success on their terms).

- Interrogate your initial feeling that you need to focus on gathering information about the client's deficits, and instead center the evaluation on the client's passions and life story (e.g. "What life experiences have shaped who you are today?") and how you, as the OTP, can dismantle barriers and adapt their activities to promote their engagement in their prioritized occupations.

Sustainability

Description: This principle emphasizes that we must create and maintain environments where Disabled individuals thrive not just in the short-term but long-term. Advocates must listen to what our bodies need to avoid advocacy burnout.

By listening to our bodies, we are moving away from the white supremacy component of urgency culture, and instead fostering a slow but deep transformative wave of justice and liberation.

Application of Sustainability Within Occupational Therapy Practice

- Recognize that the current discourse on self-care is rooted in colonized standards of hygiene, sanitation, nutrition, and other means of caring for oneself that are achieved through capitalistic means. Commit to this unlearning and historize that the concept of self-care is connected to the Black feminist movement empowered by activist Audre Lorde, and is described by Lorde as not self-indulgence but self-preservation. When Marginalized individuals prioritize their well-being in a society that oppresses them, engaging in self-care becomes a means of resistance and a refusal to accept an unjust society. Lorde also shares how self-care extends beyond taking care of oneself but acknowledges the importance of collective healing.[16]
  - When working with clients, incorporate discussions on how engaging in self-care connects with broader activism, and help clients to consider how managing their well-being is integral to their capacity to be involved in advocacy work (e.g. whether it is systems-level such as legislative or policy reform, or even micro-level, such as advocating to a student's IEP team for the inclusion of neurodiversity-affirming goals and accommodations).

- Reduce the chance of activist burnout by collaborating with clients to complete the ABCD of self-care for activists[17] and a wellness plan[18] to promote the occupation of rest.

- To amplify a client's (and your) sustainability, OTPs play a significant role in helping clients recognize and nurture the various aspects of their identities beyond their role as activists. Facilitate conversations with clients that explore their various roles (e.g. partners, parents, friends, or hobbyists). Use assessments/conversations to support clients in articulating their interests, values, and the importance of these roles in their lives.

Cross-Disability Solidarity

Description: Commitment to cross-disability solidarity honors the lived experiences and voices of all Disabled individuals. Though Disabled individuals experience varying levels of oppression depending on their identities, we can be a collective and unite against systemic discrimination. All Disabled people benefit from disability justice. Whether you are Mad, Deaf, Neurodivergent, or have a physical or intellectual disability (non-exhaustive list), your voice matters. No Disabled community is left behind!

Activist Reflection (a Merging of Sustainability and Cross-Disability Solidarity)

> "As I reflect on sustainability and cross-disability solidarity as principles of disability justice, I am reminded of my experiences as a 23-year-old newly minted occupational therapist (OT) practicing in metropolitan Atlanta and rural northern Georgia, and its profound impact on my learning and unlearning about disability. I had a good understanding of disability rights but had not yet learned about disability justice and my role as an OT in materializing its promise. One of the observations I made quickly was although I worked in a large diverse city, the vast majority of service recipients were white, Disabled, middle- to late-aged adults, who lived in mixed-income communities. I did not understand why I was not seeing Black and Brown patients, but what I did understand was that there were a lot of racially Marginalized people in these communities and that those who needed OT services were not accessing them for whatever reason. I was committed to doing the work to not only understand why this was happening but to do something about it. Little did I know, these early experiences would change how I saw myself as an OT.
>
> What I learned from clients and disability advocates in my community was that OT was more than ensuring quality therapeutic services; it was challenging employers to update facilities to accommodate clients' needs, identifying and developing policies that would hold colleagues accountable when clients were harmed, collaborating with community partners to ensure our practice was community-centered, encouraging my state organization to participate in public health efforts—it was ongoing advocacy that had become an embodied part of my practice. But these efforts did not cease at the end of each business day, they became integral to everything I was doing day in and day out. As you may imagine, the load I was carrying was not sustainable as I had not yet learned to build capacity through my practice or how to align the work with others with similar values and goals. I began to sit (longer) with elder advocates and activists, mostly Disabled Black women outside of OT (e.g. educators, epidemiologists, clergy, domestic workers), to learn more about strategic and sustainable advocacy and what it really meant to engage a justice praxis to change the culture of where I worked but also OT.
>
> What did that look like? It was learning when to engage and when to rest, to only commit to sustainable activities that were established by and in collaboration with Disabled activists and their families in and around the community, working with providers who valued disability justice and fostered inclusive practice environments, partnering with churches and other faith-based groups that were committed to teaching community members that loving everyone included the

liberation of Disabled people to be able to thrive at the intersections of all aspects of their identities. It was calling in OT practitioners in my community to practice from a justice lens, to disrupt discourses, and dismantle the false narrative that one's race or ability status are predictors of their outcomes and successes and frame those consequences as being mediated by systems of oppression and ideologies about disability."—KHALILAH R. JOHNSON

Application of Cross-Disability Solidarity Within Occupational Therapy Practice

- Like racism (and other prejudices), we are all socialized to harbor harmful attitudes and assumptions about disability. Being Disabled does not exempt anyone from having an ableist attitude toward other disability communities (e.g. an Autistic ADHDer labeling someone with bipolar disorder as "dangerous" or "emotionally unstable"). Reflect on your personal biases, acknowledge your assumptions, and learn about the cultural norms and goals of other disability communities to foster mutual empowerment.

- Support and engage in advocacy efforts across disabilities. This may include but is not limited to joining local disability advocacy organizations and assisting in establishing and enacting advocacy priorities; supporting the legislative priorities or nationally representative disability organizations (e.g. New Disabled South, Disability Rights Advocates, Ramp Your Voice); and participating in conferences or workshops that represent many disability communities (e.g. Disability: IN Annual Conference, National Disability Rights Network Annual Conference, the Annual African American Conference on Disabilities).

- Consider sharing personal insights and your own disability experiences (if applicable) and how they relate to your clients' experiences; being open about your disability journey may help to humanize conversations around disability.

Interdependence

Description: Eurocentric colonialism disrupted the interdependent nature of Indigenous communities, prioritizing individualism over community-based living, which has contributed to our societal pressure on individualism today. There is a beauty in that we are all connected, and this connection is woven into the fabric of who we are as human beings. Think about it! We depend on fishers and farmers for food, healthcare workers for lifesaving care, and delivery drivers for items we are so excited to receive. From the coffee mug that holds our morning brew to the engineers who ensure our homes stay warm, there is nothing we do in our daily lives that doesn't involve relying on the contributions of others. Interdependence fosters a sense of belonging where all individuals can contribute to each other's lives, and that is okay!

Activist Reflection

"We work to meet each other's needs as we build toward liberation."[19]

"The principle of interdependence invites us to reflect on how our lives are woven together, reminding us that our strength lies in supporting one another. Moreover, it feels like a nod to my roots. I grew up in the Philippines, where the idea of supporting one another is engraved in our values and culture. We even have a word for it: *Bayanihan*. This concept goes beyond mere communal assistance; it embodies a rich tradition of collective responsibility and shared joy. It is often depicted through images of neighbors coming together to lift a nipa hut. However, as colonialism imposed Western ways of being, thinking, and doing, the emphasis shifted toward individualism. *Bayanihan* is reduced to a buzzword used mainly in times of crisis. Many people began to prioritize personal upliftment over uplifting the community. As a result, people are left behind—people who are Marginalized and Disabled by the actions, attitudes, and apathy of others. Colonialism undermined our rich traditions and diminished the strength of our social fabric. The call to embrace interdependence is, therefore, a call to decolonize knowledge and society, urging us to go back to the wisdom of our ancestors. We have much to learn from the values our forefathers passed down—particularly the importance of mutual support and interdependence. In fact, the world could benefit significantly from listening to cultures that have long been silenced and deemed inferior.

This challenge to embrace interdependence extends to occupational therapy practices in the Philippines and globally. The field has traditionally been informed by a Western focus on independence, often shaping interventions and goals around the ability to perform tasks alone. Yet, we must recognize the profound truth in the saying, 'no man is an island.' Our survival as a species has always depended on our ability to form interconnected communities. Thus, therapy services should not solely aim for independence but should instead foster meaningful participation in occupations. For instance, a client may wish to play with their grandchild, regardless of whether they can dress independently. They have family, friends, and personal assistants to support them. Embracing the principle of interdependence can radically transform how occupational therapy sets goals and designs programs, positioning it as a better ally to the disability community.

To strive toward disability justice and liberation, embracing interdependence is crucial. By meeting each other's needs, we ensure that no one is left behind. Our every action affects the lives of others. By acknowledging and embracing interdependence, we can reinvigorate our commitment to one another, nurturing a sense of community. In our journey, let us remember that progress lies not in individual endeavors but in the care and support of the community. By reclaiming and practicing interdependence, we can build a more just and inclusive world for all."—DARYL PATRICK YAO

Application of Interdependence Within Occupational Therapy Practice

- Recognize and affirm interdependence as a beautiful aspect of being human rather than making independence the benchmark for success. From childhood to benefiting from assistance as we age, embrace the reality that everyone relies on each other at various points of life. Make sure you are not forcing clients to conform to ableist standards of self-sufficiency! For instance ask yourself this: "How can I use their social environment to facilitate meaningful participation of my client?"

- Celebrate interdependence in daily life, such as framing the use of assistive devices, personal assistance, familial members, community members, and other forms of support as empowered choices. Don't hesitate to engage in an open conversation with your clients and their social circle (e.g. family and friends) about independence and interdependence. Explore together what true success looks like for the individual and how it can be defined on their own terms. It's important to help clients and their loved ones reframe what it means to live a meaningful and fulfilling life.

- As OTs, we should recognize that greater joy and meaning can be found in participating in meaningful activities with support rather than adhering to an ideal of independence. It's essential to honor each person's preference regarding their participation in daily life. For some individuals, relying on others for assistance—rather than striving for independence—may be a more practical, fulfilling, and authentic way to engage in the world.

- Serve as a bridge that connects your clients to one another. By fostering peer connections, you can create opportunities for mutual support, shared learning, and collective empowerment. When clients are connected to others, they can build a sense of community that can facilitate their acceptance of their Disabled identity and amplify their shared advocacy.

Collective Access

Description: Collective access advocates that all members of a community need to work together to ensure that spaces, resources, and opportunities are accessible to everyone, especially Disabled individuals and those experiencing the most oppression. Access isn't just changing the physical environment. It's creating an inclusive culture that values diverse needs and experiences. It is not solely the responsibility of Disabled individuals to advocate for our needs; we need support from non-disabled allies. It's a shared responsibility!

Activist Reflection

> "The good thing is that if we understand that our built environment and social environment are created by people, then we know that these are things that people can change."[20]

> "I see collective access as a commitment to develop spaces where everyone's needs are considered and are part of the shared responsibility of communities. In occupational therapy, I see this as an opportunity to create for each person: within the profession, with clients we collaborate with, and with transformed systems.
>
> I have the pleasure of visiting the first accessible bookstore in my area pretty frequently (The Stacks Bookstore in Savannah, Georgia). The store owner has created space for everyone to thrive with physical (ramp, automatic push to open plates, rolling shelves) and sensory (natural lighting, no perfumes or loud music, accessible colors and contrast on signage) adaptations. In addition to these universal changes, the booksellers regularly emphasize in personal conversations, during event promotions, and marketing that further individual accommodations can be made. From their intentional efforts, visitors and regulars know that access needs can be articulated privately, in a collective, or within the community. It embodies 'for us, by us' with creative solutions as the community grows. Further, because intersectionality matters, the bookstore hosts a variety of books and book clubs that highlight and support LGBTQIA+ authors, Black and Brown authors, Disabled authors, as well as authors that may fall into several identities.
>
> This is what I hope to see in the occupational therapy profession: prioritizing the voices of Disabled individuals, honoring differences, supporting autonomy, and considering intersectionality. In every community that we collaborate in; we hold a responsibility to do so."—DIAMOND RASHAD

Application of Collective Access Within Occupational Therapy Practice

- Advocate to your workplace to require professionals to complete a disability-justice- or neurodiversity-focused continuing education every few years to ensure practices are in line with the disability community's priorities and to decrease your chance of implementing ableist practices (e.g. education examples could be Learn Play Thrive's continuing education trainings, STAR

Institute's Neurodiversity Virtual Summit, Autism Level UP!'s online workshops, or having *Disability Justice in Healthcare: Promoting Anti-Ableism in Medical Settings*[21] a required onboarding lesson for employees/colleagues).

- Think about how your treatment plans can be comprehensive advocacy plans for your clients! By creating client-led goals that infuse their hopes and dreams, promoting your client's self-advocacy skills within meaningful environments, and equipping clients with information about their rights as a Disabled individual (yes, this includes educating Neurodivergent children that they do not need to conform to neurotypical learning styles), you are fostering disability justice. Knowledge is truly power. Consider including goals that involve clients taking concrete steps to advocate for their needs (e.g. teaching a student or client how to advocate for their accommodations, and you can practice role-playing scenarios).

- There is an inherent distrust of the medical system from Black, Indigenous, communities of color, and Disabled communities because of historical injustices and ongoing discrimination. That is a reality that OTPs must acknowledge if they wish to build rapport and provide effective (and equitable) support. Make sure you are validating your clients' stories about their barriers to seeking medical help. If a client says your practices are in some way negatively impacting their well-being or do not resonate with their identity, be open-minded and open-hearted to this feedback (it can be hard in the moment, and that is okay). Express gratitude for their vulnerability and make the necessary changes to your services instead of feeling defensive; think about this as valuable insight into the client's experiences and an opportunity for you to grow as an ally.

Collective Liberation

Description: Collective liberation refers to the idea that the freedom and well-being of one Marginalized community are connected to the freedom and well-being of all Marginalized communities. The liberation of Disabled individuals is linked to a global fight against various forms of oppression and injustice (e.g. racism, sexism, homophobia, transphobia, classism). By all of us moving and marching forward together, true justice can be achieved for everyone rather than focusing on the liberation of one community.

Activist Reflection

"I believe this principle follows automatically from the belief that all humans have inherent value. If we truly believe in the value of each and every person, then naturally, we would not want anyone to be left behind or to go without basic human rights. However, even beyond this, two additional thoughts come to mind regarding collective liberation.

The first is that we truly need all perspectives. So often, inclusivity initiatives are framed as a sort of (well-intentioned) charity with the goal of helping Marginalized individuals face fewer barriers. For example, many institutions will justify initiatives to support Neurodivergent students by noting that Neurodivergent students are struggling in various ways, and it's worth developing accommodations if it helps these students. While this is certainly true, what is often left out is the fact that the inclusion of Neurodivergent individuals helps *everyone*. When Neurodivergent students are excluded, the rest of the student body is also worse off for their absence, and I believe that overlooking that also overlooks the depth of what Neurodivergent individuals (and Marginalized individuals) have to offer. The rest of the student body is missing out on valuable friendships that could have been, perspectives they could have learned from, information about accessibility they could have learned, and potentially a chance to develop a more neurodiversity-affirming approach. It is my belief that ableism ultimately hurts everyone, as it will always demand more productivity, more ability, and more success. We must create an environment where Disabled and Neurodivergent individuals can thrive, which will help everyone.

The second is that the inclusion of the most Marginalized individuals will likely automatically result in universal inclusion. Thus, for both practical and moral reasons, I imagine that true inclusion must necessarily start with those who are most marginalized—and may also require an expanded definition of marginalization, encompassing both Marginalized identities (related to racial or ethnic identity, age, gender identity, orientation, disability, socioeconomic status, etc.) as well as other factors or experiences which may often be overlooked even within social justice spaces (e.g. whether one has had access to advanced education, whether one has experienced / is experiencing food insecurity or housing insecurity, access to healthcare, job stability, one's current immigration status). To give a specific example, conditions such as schizophrenia or psychosis are often stigmatized, even within mental health circles. However, places that are inclusive of individuals with schizophrenia and/or psychosis tend to also be very accepting of individuals with other mental health conditions, such as anxiety and depression. Likewise, many types of ableism are deeply rooted in cognitive ableism (or prejudice toward people with cognitive disabilities). For example, if an Autistic person without an intellectual disability is told 'you don't have to label yourself as Autistic, you're too smart to be Autistic,' that can be very dismissive or invalidating of their Autistic identity and of course overlooks the diversity of support needs/abilities within the autism spectrum. However, it is also often rooted in the deeper belief that there is something wrong with having an intellectual disability and the presumption that one would naturally want to distance oneself from a label that sometimes co-occurs with intellectual disability. Finally, if we can build environments that are accessible for multiply Marginalized individuals, the environments will likely remain accessible for individuals who share one of the Marginalized identities and will also fill a crucial need for those who are multiply Marginalized and may have experienced very few truly inclusive spaces in their lives."—SAM BRANDSEN

Application of Collective Liberation Within Occupational Therapy Practice

- Consider including an anonymous feedback form to empower clients to provide feedback on your implementation of neurodiversity-affirming practices, which helps to ensure all voices can feel heard and valued without fear of repercussion, especially those who are multiply Neurodivergent (e.g. intersectional increase of ableism experienced every day).

- Organize community workshops that bring together Disabled individuals and those from other Marginalized communities to discuss shared experiences, intersectional identities, and occupational therapy (e.g. an OTP hosts a community forum focused on how disability intersects with other identities, allowing invited guests or speakers to share how these factors impact their access to health services and changes needed within the occupational therapy profession).

- Advocate for therapy spaces and natural environments of the client to embody universal design principles (e.g. physical accessibility [making sure furniture arrangements have ample access for wheelchairs], sensory inclusivity [quiet spaces, accessible sensory tools], visual aids and supports) to ensure these spaces are accessible for individuals of all bodies and minds. Consider implementing regular staff training on universal design and how you can implement them effectively!

Impact of Colonization on Disability Perception

For the remainder of the chapter, we will explore Indigenous perspectives on disability and provide ideas on how the profession can embody Indigenous ways of knowing into their practice to support disability justice. Before we dive into Indigenous perspectives, we must begin with a conversation on the impact of colonization and disability. Colonization profoundly influenced perceptions of ability and disability, imposing European ideals that marginalized Indigenous understandings.[22] In her writings, Ineese-Nash identifies one of the core axioms as "that disability exists in the contexts of colonialism through explicit structures of oppression."[23] These

Western notions of health and ability often conflicted with Indigenous views, which recognized diverse abilities as a natural part of human diversity.[24]

Disability Within Colonized Contexts

In colonized regions, Western medical models pathologized disabilities, marginalizing individuals further through productivity-focused structures that embedded systemic barriers and limited opportunities for those labeled as Disabled.[25] This marginalization was deepened by the ideology of eugenics, which, emerging in the late 19th and early 20th centuries, promoted the removal of "undesirable" traits to ostensibly improve human populations.[26] This reinforced the colonial perspective that viewed disabilities as deviations from the ideal human form, intensifying the focus on "normalcy" and categorizing disabilities as defects to be eliminated.

Such beliefs profoundly influenced medical and institutional practices, leading to segregation, sterilization, and restrictive immigration policies under the guise of societal improvement. These harmful ideologies were embedded into government policies, resulting in restrictive laws and oppressive measures against those deemed "unfit." Clear examples of these, for Indigenous peoples, are placement on reservations and the boarding school era. Understanding the role eugenics played in reinforcing colonial attitudes toward disability provides insights into the historical and systemic roots of discrimination. This connection highlights the urgent need for contemporary efforts to dismantle these oppressive legacies that have formed the basis of institutionalized racism and discrimination.

Colonization profoundly reshaped the understanding and treatment of disability in Indigenous communities. Western medical models pathologized disabilities, dismissing Indigenous spiritual perspectives and casting them as conditions needing correction.[27] Economic systems focused on productivity marginalized those deemed less productive, while restrictive educational and legal policies embedded systemic inequalities. Cultural erasure further suppressed Indigenous practices, imposing foreign norms that undermined traditional teachings. Colonial infrastructures neglected accessibility, creating enduring physical and social barriers. Despite these challenges, Indigenous communities displayed resilience, adapting their practices to support individuals with disabilities within oppressive colonial frameworks. This legacy highlights the ongoing need to dismantle these historical influences, promoting inclusive practices that respect both diversity and cultural heritage.

Indigenous Perspectives on Disability and Neurodiversity

In response, movements have emerged to reclaim Indigenous perspectives, emphasizing community-centered approaches that celebrate the strengths of individuals with disabilities. Many Indigenous cultures view individuals born with a disability as having a spiritual gift due to their ability to experience the world in novel and unique ways. A beautiful example is the Cree word, *kakanaticichek*,* which means "the gifted and special people."[28] Like many Indigenous communities, the Diné don't even have a universal word for disability. For many Indigenous communities, mainstream discussions about disability (such as the medical model of disability and the social model of disability) often do not resonate because they are described in Western definitions of health. Within numerous Indigenous cultures, all individuals are viewed as having a purpose and can contribute to the community. No matter how small the contribution may seem to Westerners, all contributions are valued. The very idea of there being an "ideal" bodymind or a "diverging" body/mind is a concept that isn't often a part of Indigenous conversations. Lovern flips the Westernized concept of disability on its head with the following:

> "As there is no 'ideal' person or way of existing, no human body or mind is necessarily preferential. Instead, differences in body and mind allow for differing relationships at all levels and allow for differing knowledge. For this reason, Indigenous peoples often talk of each person needing to teach or to learn, often both throughout one's life, and sometimes beyond body death. Differences in bodies or in minds allow for the expansion of knowledge beyond a single set of shared constructs or shared theories... The emphasis is not on whether a person has physical or mental limitations, as it is understood that every being has limitations of some type. The emphasis for Indigenous peoples is how one upholds the responsibilities experienced in these *(communal)* relationships."[29]

This conversation about disability extends to the topic of neurodiversity.

Indigenous scholars have shared how the term "neurodiversity" often doesn't fit within the Global South's** conceptualizations of bodymind. Historically, explorations of the bodymind experience existed long before the Global North introduced the "neurodiversity" definition, which tends to highlight these differences as a Neurodivergent/neurotypical binary. With Indigenous communities, variations of the bodymind experience are seen as opportunities to gain unique insights, which helps to foster a holistic understanding of interpersonal relationships and the world. This perspective emphasizes what unique skills they bring to their communities versus their bodily differences. The mainstream definition of "neurodiversity" is a Global North idea, and we as OTPs must think about neurodiversity as being *one* of the theories exploring the bodymind universe versus *the* theory.[30] A fantastic starting point is to understand how a culture views bodymind diversity and its different manifestations. Though there are no universal Indigenous frameworks or approaches to disability, common constructs

* The Cree, or nehinaw, are a North American Indigenous people who live primarily in Canada and northern Montana.

** See Chapter 6 for an in-depth explanation of the Global North and Global South.

of difference focus on relationships, interdependence, and wellness (whereas in Western cultures, differences are defined by physical and mental impairments).[31]

> It has been found that Indigenous individuals often rely on their cultural values to protect themselves against the Western idea of "disability" and even have described this concept as oppressive. There is a dire need to decolonize our conceptualizations of disability and ensure the voices most impacted by colonization are leading these conversations.[32]

The Seven Grandfather Teachings

Rooted in many Indigenous cultures, the Seven Grandfather Teachings provide a moral framework to guide how to live well while also providing knowledge on the meaning of life. While each Indigenous culture adapts the teaching to reflect its own values and traditions, they all often contain the seven guiding principles: truth, respect, love, courage, honesty, wisdom, and humility. Table 4.1 describes practical ways for OTPs to apply the Grandfather Teachings illustrated in Figure 4.2. We invite you to embrace the Grandfather Teachings as a foundation for integrating Indigenous ways of knowing and supporting neurodiversity and disability justice in your work. By incorporating these teachings, you can enhance the therapeutic process and promote holistic well-being within the communities you serve.[33]

Table 4.1—Applying the Seven Grandfather Teachings to Occupational Therapy Practice

1. Truth (East): Strive to engage in open dialogue with your clients and communities to truly understand their needs. Align your interventions with the realities and aspirations of those you serve, prioritizing clear and honest communication.
2. Respect (South): Create a welcoming environment that celebrates diversity and honors individual strengths. By acknowledging different backgrounds and experiences, you foster a therapeutic space where everyone feels valued and respected.
3. Love (South): Develop empathetic relationships by actively listening and being present. By fostering a deep emotional connection, you promote healing. When you create a genuinely supportive atmosphere, clients feel safer to express themselves and clients are more engaged in the therapeutic process.
4. Courage (South): Advocate for your clients, helping them address mental health challenges with compassion and courage. Stand up for their rights and needs within healthcare systems, all the while increasing their ability to advocate within their own lives and reducing stigma.
5. Honesty (West): Build trust through transparency in the therapeutic process. Set realistic goals and communicate openly about treatment options, progress, and challenges, fostering a safe and trusting environment.

cont.

6. Wisdom (North): Utilize community-defined evidence practices and draw on community insights to continuously refine your approaches. Embrace feedback for ongoing learning and service improvement, ensuring interventions are both effective and relevant to their culture.
7. Humility (North): Cultivate a collaborative culture by listening and learning from clients and community members. Recognize and appreciate their strengths and knowledge, and work together to achieve common goals.

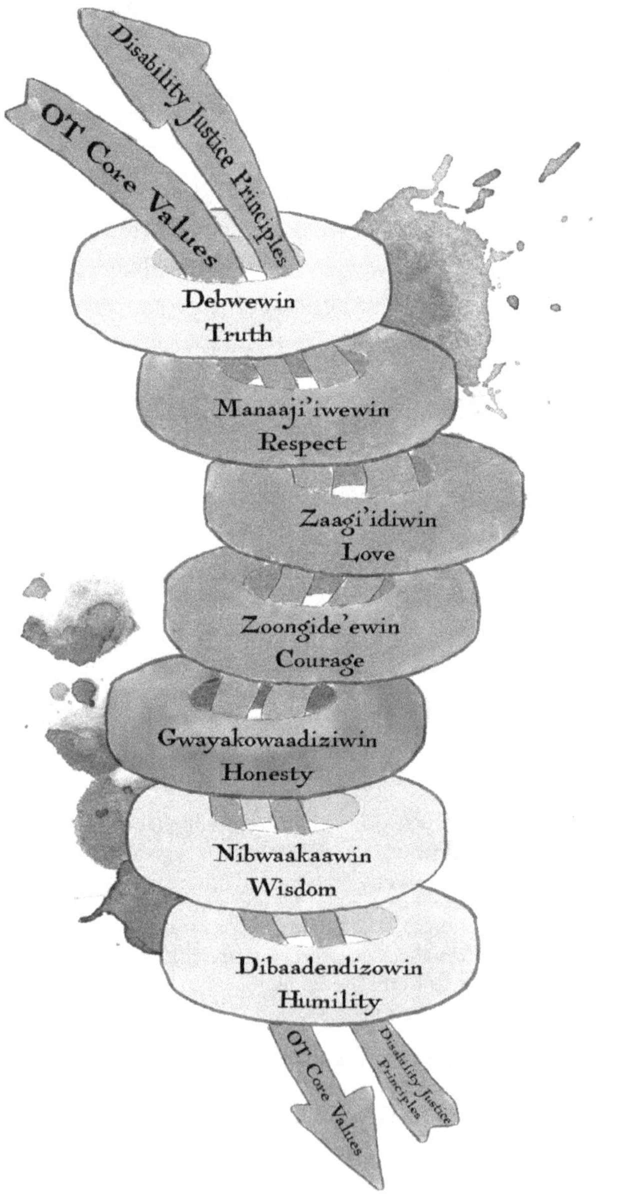

Figure 4.2—The Seven Grandfather Teachings

Note. Design concept created by Frankie Morin. A Vault item exists, that describes how to apply each of these teachings into OT practice.

By integrating these teachings into your daily practice, you can create more meaningful and effective interactions, ultimately enhancing your impact on mental health and community well-being.

Conclusion

This chapter offered an exploration of how Sins Invalid's disability justice principles and Indigenous perspectives of disability can reshape occupational therapy practice toward a more equitable future. By incorporating these tenets within our work, our practices can challenge ableist narratives of occupational participation and affirm the inherent dignity and worth of everyone. As you have completed this chapter, we hope you are reminded of how powerful community can be. Embracing these concepts requires a commitment to self-reflection and continuous learning while also recognizing that our journey as advocates and allies must be steeped in resilience, collective action, and love. Give yourself patience and grace, and never stop dreaming!

Endnotes

1 Kafai, S. (2023). *Crip kinship: The disability justice and art activism of Sins Invalid.* Arsenal Pulp Press, p. 16.
2 Piepzna-Samarasinha, L. L. (2022). *The future is disabled: Prophecies, love notes, and mourning songs.* Arsenal Pulp Press.
3 Ellis, K. (2023). The forgotten activists: Black people in the disability rights movement. *University of Miami Race & Social Justice Law Review, 14*(1), 54. https://repository.law.miami.edu/umrsjlr/vol14/iss1/5
4 Sins Invalid. (2019). *Skin, tooth, and bone: The basis of movement is our people* (2nd ed.). Sins Invalid.
5 Oung, K. (2021). Community fridges are lifelines for the neighborhoods they serve. *Vox.* www.vox.com/the-goods/22285863/community-fridges-neighborhoods-free-food
6 Piepzna-Samarasinha, L. L. (2021). *How disabled mutual aid is different than abled mutual aid.* Disability Visibility Project. https://disabilityvisibilityproject.com/2021/10/03/how-disabled-mutual-aid-is-different-than-abled-mutual-aid
7 Piepzna-Samarasinha, L. L. (2024). *Fragrance free femme of colour genius.* Brown Star Girl. https://brownstargirl.org/fragrance-free-femme-of-colour-genius
8 Smith, S. E. (2023). "Depression cooking zine" is a reminder that sometimes eating is an accomplishment. *Eater.* www.eater.com/23834841/depression-cooking-sonali-menezes-zine-creator-profile
9 Wong, A. (Host), Piepzna-Samarasinha, L. L. (Guest), & Milbern, S. (Guest). (2017, October 22). Labor, care work, and disabled queer femmes (No. 6) [Audio podcast episode]. In *Disability Visibility Podcast.* https://disabilityvisibilityproject.com/2017/10/22/ep-6-labor-care-work-and-disabled-queer-femmes
10 Hammell, K. W. (2023). A call to resist occupational therapy's promotion of ableism. *Scandinavian Journal of Occupational Therapy, 30*(6), 745–757. https://doi.org/10.1080/11038128.2022.2130821
11 ibid.
12 ibid.
13 United States Holocaust Memorial Museum (2024). *What is genocide?* United States Holocaust Memorial Museum. https://encyclopedia.ushmm.org/content/en/article/what-is-genocide
14 United Nations. (2025). *Genocide, displacement and starvation in Gaza: The urgent need for a permanent ceasefire and protection of civilians—letter from the state of Palestine.* United Nations—The Question of Palestine. www.un.org/unispal/document/letter-from-the-state-of-palestine-23apr25
15 Sins Invalid. (2019). *Skin, tooth, and bone: The basis of movement is our people* (2nd ed.). Sins Invalid, p. 19.
16 SAIC Office of Diversity, Equity, and Inclusion. (2024). *Research guides: Learn & unlearn: Anti-racism resource guide: Radical self-care.* Research Guides at School of the Art Institute

of Chicago. https://libraryguides.saic.edu/learn_unlearn/wellness5

17 Frontline AIDS. (2018). *Self-care and prevention of burnout among activists—tools for everyday life*. Frontline AIDS. https://frontlineaids.org/resources/self-care-and-prevention-of-burnout-among-activists-tools-for-everyday-life

18 The Audre Lorde Project. (n.d.). *Breaking isolation: Self-care and community care tools for our people*. The Audre Lorde Project. https://alp.org/breaking-isolation-self-care-and-community-care-tools-our-people

19 Sins Invalid. (2019). *Skin, tooth, and bone: The basis of movement is our people* (2nd ed.). Sins Invalid.

20 Ly, V. (2019, May 13). *When creating inclusive spaces, talk to disabled people* [Video]. YouTube. www.youtube.com/watch?v=lpf_gS8mozY

21 Andrews, E. E. (2024). *Disability justice in healthcare: Promoting anti-ableism in medical settings*. San Francisco State University. https://ibhequity.sfsu.edu/sites/default/files/documents/Webinar%20%236%20Accessible%20PowerPoint%20Slides.pdf

22 Norris, H. (2014). Colonialism and the rupturing of Indigenous worldviews of impairment and relational interdependence: A beginning dialogue towards reclamation and social transformation. *Critical Disability Discourses, 6*. https://cdd.journals.yorku.ca/index.php/cdd/article/view/39665

23 Ineese-Nash, N. (2020). Disability as a colonial construct: The missing discourse of culture in conceptualizations of disabled Indigenous children. *Canadian Journal of Disability Studies, 9*(3), 28–51. https://doi.org/10.15353/cjds.v9i3.645

24 Piepzna-Samarasinha, L. L. (2022). *The future is disabled: Prophecies, love notes, and mourning songs*. Arsenal Pulp Press.

25 Powell, R. M. (2021). Confronting eugenics means finally confronting its ableist roots. *William & Mary Journal of Women and the Law, 27*(3), 607. https://scholarship.law.wm.edu/wmjowl/vol27/iss3/2

26 ibid.

27 Yellowhorse, S. (2023). *Indigeneity and disability: The teachings of our ancestors and being in relation towards harmonious outcomes*. Disability Visibility Project. https://disabilityvisibilityproject.com/2023/06/18/indigeneity-and-disability-the-teachings-of-our-ancestors-and-being-in-relation-towards-harmonious-outcomes

28 Morgan, K. P. (2025). To see or not to see. Am I blind or is that just another colonial label? In J. T. Ward (Ed.), *Indigenous disability studies* (pp. 71–81). Routledge.

29 Lovern, L. (2021). Indigenous concepts of difference: An alternative to Western disability labeling. *Disability Studies Quarterly, 41*(1). https://dsq-sds.org/index.php/dsq/article/view/8468/6302

30 Nair, V. K. K., Farah, W., & Boveda, M. (2024). Is neurodiversity a Global Northern white paradigm? *Autism: The International Journal of Research and Practice*. https://doi.org/10.1177/13623613241280835

31 Lovern, L. (2021). Indigenous concepts of difference: An alternative to Western disability labeling. *Disability Studies Quarterly, 41*(1). https://dsq-sds.org/index.php/dsq/article/view/8468/6302

32 Daniels-Mayes, S. (2023). Researching Indigenous people living with a disability: The urgent need for an intersectional and decolonising approach (BlakAbility). *First Nations and Health and Wellbeing—The Lowitja Journal, 1*, 1–5. www.lowitjajournal.org.au/article/S2949-8406(23)00004-9/fulltext

33 Nahwegiizhic, L. G. (2025). Neurodiversity from an Indigenous perspective. In J. T. Ward (Ed.), *Indigenous disability studies* (pp. 94–103). Routledge.

CHAPTER 5

Trauma, Interoception, and Occupational Therapy

KATIE O'DAY AND KELLY MAHLER

Introduction

Trauma-informed approaches (TIAs) and interoception are pivotal concepts in occupational therapy, offering a comprehensive framework for understanding and addressing the complex needs of Neurodivergent individuals. TIA is a transformative approach that acknowledges the pervasive impact of trauma on individuals, shifting the focus from "What's wrong with you?" to "What happened to you?" This perspective is crucial for understanding the experiences of clients, particularly those who are Neurodivergent, as it allows therapists to tailor interventions that are sensitive to their unique challenges and histories.[1]

Interoception, often referred to as the "eighth sense," plays a critical role in this framework by helping individuals recognize and respond to their internal bodily signals. For Neurodivergent individuals, who may experience differences in sensory processing and emotional regulation, interoception is essential for fostering self-awareness and emotional regulation. Key studies in neuroscience have also shown that one's interoceptive awareness can be impacted by trauma. Neurodivergent individuals may already have some inherent differences in their interoceptive awareness as part of their neurology.[2]

Together, TIA and interoception create a holistic approach that aligns with the core values of occupational therapy, emphasizing client-centered practice, empowerment, and holistic care. This integrated approach not only enhances therapeutic outcomes but also contributes to the overall well-being of clients, fostering resilience and self-advocacy. By creating inclusive environments that prioritize safety, trust, and empowerment, occupational therapists can support Neurodivergent individuals in reclaiming their autonomy and agency, ultimately leading to improved health and well-being outcomes across communities. Utilizing a trauma-informed approach in daily practice not only improves therapeutic outcomes but also contributes to the overall well-being of clients, fostering resilience and self-advocacy. Trauma-informed care on a systems level is essential for overall health and well-being throughout communities.

Understanding Trauma

Trauma is a complex and multifaceted experience that can have profound effects on an individual's physical, mental, and social well-being. It is generally categorized into three types: acute, chronic, and complex trauma. Acute trauma refers to the emotional and psychological response to a single, distressing event perceived as harmful or life-threatening, such as an accident or natural disaster. Chronic trauma involves prolonged exposure to distressing events, often occurring in contexts where the individual feels trapped, such as ongoing bullying or systemic discrimination. Complex trauma refers to exposure to multiple traumatic events, often of an invasive and interpersonal nature, typically occurring during critical developmental periods. Table 5.1 elaborates on the types of trauma and considerations for OTPs.

Table 5.1—Types of Trauma

Type of Trauma	Definition or Description	Examples	Implications for Neurodivergent Individuals	Considerations for Occupational Therapy Professionals
Acute Trauma	Emotional and psychological response to a single, distressing event perceived as harmful or life-threatening.	Accidents, natural disasters, violent incidents.	May manifest as heightened anxiety, fear, or avoidance behaviors, impacting daily activities.	• Consider incorporating the Classroom Sensory Screening Tool (which can be adapted to fit other contexts) as a 'sensory audit' for your therapy space to identify potential triggers and create a calming environment. Additionally, provide immediate coping strategies such as deep breathing exercises or grounding techniques to help clients manage acute anxiety. Always work to utilize trauma-informed approaches.

				• Incorporate the Trauma Expression and Connection Assessment (TECA) to help clients articulate their trauma responses and coping strategies, enhancing their self-awareness and emotional regulation.
Chronic Trauma	Prolonged exposure to distressing events, often in a context where the individual feels trapped.	Ongoing bullying, persistent sensory overload, systemic discrimination.	Can lead to difficulties in emotional regulation, social interactions, and academic performance.	• Regularly offer breaks and continue to assess clients' own self-determined client-centered goals. Consider their emotional state through both verbal and non-verbal indicators. Use visual schedules and clear communication to create predictability in sessions, which can help reduce anxiety. Offer the individual frequent opportunities to make choices on how therapy occurs. Always work to utilize trauma-informed approaches. • Utilize the Interoception Curriculum to help clients develop interoceptive awareness and coping strategies, which is crucial for emotional regulation.
Complex Trauma	Exposure to multiple traumatic events, often of an invasive and interpersonal nature, typically during critical developmental periods.	Early childhood neglect, forced conformity to neurotypical standards, systemic discrimination.	May result in disconnection from body signals and emotional needs, complicating engagement in therapeutic activities.	• Incorporate interoceptive awareness practices, such as mindfulness exercises or body scans, to help clients reconnect with their internal experiences. Create a safe space for clients to express their feelings without judgment, fostering trust and openness. Always work to utilize trauma-informed approaches. • Implement mindfulness techniques to support emotional regulation and resilience, helping clients manage anxiety and stress.

cont.

Role of Occupational Therapy Professionals:

OTPs play a vital role in supporting Neurodivergent individuals through TIA. By creating environments that prioritize safety, validation, and empowerment, therapists can help clients navigate their emotional landscapes and develop healthier coping mechanisms. This approach contrasts with compliance-driven and even potentially traumatic therapies like applied behavioral analysis (ABA), which often prioritize behavioral conformity over individual needs, potentially leading to interoceptive disconnection and long-term harm. We as OTPs need to be aware of how interventions focused on promoting neurotypicality such as reinforcement, token systems, and tolerance of sensory input can be traumatizing as well. Listening to the voices of individuals with lived experiences of neurodiversity and trauma are key considerations for OTPs.

Call for Trauma-Informed Support:

Research and lived experiences indicate that Neurodivergent individuals are increasingly advocating for trauma-informed approaches. They seek professionals who understand the unique interplay between neurodivergence and trauma, and who can provide support that honors their experiences and fosters genuine growth and healing. By embracing TIA, OTPs can lead the shift toward more compassionate and effective therapeutic practices.

Principles of Trauma-Informed Approach

TIA is built upon six foundational principles[3] (SAMSHA) (Figure 5.1) that guide practitioners and organizations in creating environments conducive to healing and empowerment. These principles are particularly crucial in occupational therapy, where understanding and addressing the unique needs of Neurodivergent individuals can significantly enhance therapeutic outcomes. The principles of TIA are:

- **Safety**: Ensure both physical and emotional safety. Create environments that are predictable and non-threatening, helping individuals feel secure and supported.

- **Trustworthiness and Transparency**: Build trust through openness and honesty. Clearly communicate actions and intentions, ensuring that processes are transparent and understandable.

- **Peer Support**: Leverage the power of shared experiences. Encourage connections among peers to foster mutual understanding, support, and healing.

- **Collaboration and Mutuality**: Promote collaborative relationships. Engage individuals as equal partners in the healing process, valuing their input and fostering shared decision-making.

- **Empowerment, Voice, and Choice**: Highlight individual strengths and encourage self-determination. Create an environment where individuals can express their preferences and have control over their decisions and actions.

- **Cultural, Historical, and Gender Issues**: Recognize the impact of cultural, historical, and identity factors. Adapt approaches to be sensitive and responsive to the diverse backgrounds and experiences of individuals.

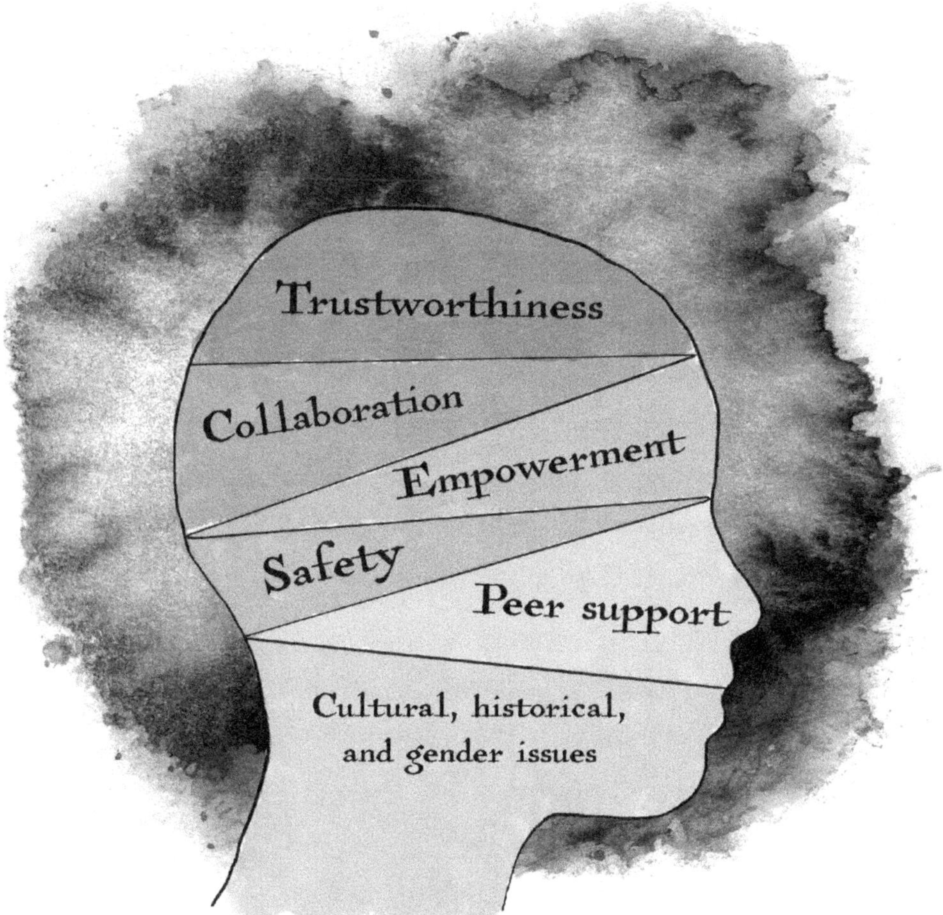

Figure 5.1—Principles of Trauma-Informed Approach

Table 5.2—Applying Trauma-Informed Principles in OT Practice

Principle	Description	Practical Application in Occupational Therapy	Role of OTPs in System-Wide Implementation	Strategies for Supporting Neurodivergent Individuals	Advocacy and Education Initiatives	Additional Considerations for OTPs
Safety	Clients feel physically and psychologically safe.	Create a welcoming space, maintain clear boundaries, and ensure privacy during sessions. Adapt environments to minimize sensory overload (e.g. noise-canceling headphones, minimizing fluorescent light, remind clients they can stim however they like).	Advocate for sensory-friendly environments in schools, workplaces, and community settings.	Use sensory-friendly tools and techniques to create a calming environment. Provide clear communication and predictable routines.	Educate community members on the importance of safety in therapeutic and community settings.	• Most Neurodivergent individuals, including those who have experienced/are experiencing trauma, have sensory processing differences. Be mindful of individual sensory profiles and adjust the environment accordingly. • Deficit-based approaches can be particularly harmful to historically marginalized populations, as they often reinforce feelings of inadequacy and disempowerment. Such approaches may fail to create a sense of safety and belonging, which is crucial for effective therapeutic engagement (e.g. talking about sensory processing differences as deficits that need fixing with clients).
Trustworthiness and Transparency	Building trust through transparency and consistency in care practices and communication.	Clearly explain treatment options, involve clients in decision-making, and follow through on commitments.	Promote transparent communication practices across healthcare systems.	Use clear, consistent communication and follow through on promises. Validate experiences and acknowledge past invalidations.	Develop training programs on trust-building for healthcare professionals.	• Be aware of past experiences of betrayal or invalidation that may affect trust (remember in Chapter 4 and the discussion of Marginalized individuals often having an inherent distrust of the medical system). • Clearly outline treatment goals and processes, ensuring clients understand their role in decision-making (e.g. before using a new intervention strategy, the OTP explains the *why* it's being used and how it connects to the client's goals).

Peer Support	Peer support and mutual self-help are key as vehicles for establishing safety and hope, building trust, enhancing collaboration, and utilizing their lived experience to promote recovery and healing.	Utilize peer support workers in therapy sessions to enhance trust and engagement. Facilitate group sessions or community activities that encourage peer interaction and support.	Facilitate the creation of peer support networks within communities.	Organize group activities that allow Neurodivergent individuals to connect with peers.	Advocate for peer support programs in educational and healthcare settings.	• Encourage clients to share their stories and support one another in a safe environment (e.g. an OTP collaborates with social work to facilitate a group where challenges are normalized, clients learn how to celebrate small wins, and form friendships to reduce feelings of isolation).
Collaboration and Mutuality	Importance is placed on partnering and leveling power differences between provider and service participants.	Involve clients and their families in goal-setting and treatment planning discussions.	Foster interdisciplinary collaboration to ensure comprehensive care.	Empower clients to take an active role in their care, respecting their preferences and needs.	Promote collaborative practices in policy development and service delivery.	• Involve clients and their families in goal-setting and treatment planning discussions, ensuring their input is valued and respected. • Foster interdisciplinary collaboration to ensure comprehensive care (e.g. the OTP models co-regulation techniques alongside the client's behavior technician to demonstrate relationship-based and trauma-informed approaches. This collaboration aims to help the technician reframe the client's behaviors and reduce harm).

cont.

Principle	Description	Practical Application in Occupational Therapy	Role of OTPs in System-Wide Implementation	Strategies for Supporting Neurodivergent Individuals	Advocacy and Education Initiatives	Additional Considerations for OTPs
Empowerment, Voice, and Choice	Supporting clients in recognizing their strengths and making informed choices about their care. Consider implementing a strengths checklist	Encourage clients to set their own goals and provide options for treatment that align with their preferences. The Visual Activity Sort[4] is a strengths-based trauma-informed self-determination tool.	Advocate for client-centered care models that prioritize empowerment.	Focus on skill-building activities that enhance self-advocacy and confidence. Celebrate progress and nurture growth potential.	Lead workshops on empowerment strategies for healthcare providers.	• Use self-determination theory to empower clients to take an active role in their care, respecting their preferences and needs (e.g. Self-Determined Kids provides various resources grounded in self-determination theory, such as the Self-Determination Toolkit, the Captain Me program, and professional learning opportunities). • Consider maximizing empowerment and the client's voice by using the occupational profile curated by the Chapter 9 co-authors found in the Vault.
Cultural, Historical, and Gender Issues	Recognizing and addressing the impact of cultural, historical, and gender-related factors on trauma experiences. Consider exploring the Cultural Identity Assessment in the Vault, with more information in Chapter 9.	Tailor interventions to be culturally sensitive and inclusive, considering the unique backgrounds of each client.	Promote cultural competence and inclusivity in all aspects of care. For example, utilize interpretation services when the individuals' primary language is not the one utilized in therapy, demonstrate allyship and advocacy with using an individual's pronouns.	Honor clients' cultural identities and experiences. Adapt therapy practices to be culturally relevant and inclusive.	Develop cultural competence training for healthcare and educational professionals.	• Utilize a non-Westernized theory like the Kawa Model to assess how environmental factors impact the individual's flow of life and well-being, allowing for a more personalized approach to cultural sensitivity when considering one's occupational engagement (e.g. the OTP facilitates a life-story group where clients use art, journaling, or photography to reflect on personal strengths, coping skills, and hopes for recovery).

Table 5.2 comprehensively outlines the principles of TIA and provides specific strategies and examples for OTPs to implement these principles with individuals and within systems and communities. It highlights the distinct role of OTPs in fostering a trauma-informed approach that supports Neurodivergent individuals and promotes healing and empowerment.

Implementing Trauma-Informed Approaches in Occupational Therapy

Implementing TIA in occupational therapy involves creating environments that prioritize safety, support, and empowerment for all clients, particularly those who are Neurodivergent. This approach requires a shift in perspective and practice, focusing on understanding and addressing the impact of trauma on individuals' lives.

Importance of Assuming Trauma Exposure in Neurodivergent Individuals

In the context of TIA, it is essential for OTPs to assume that all clients may have experienced trauma, especially for Neurodivergent individuals. Research indicates that Neurodivergent individuals often face unique challenges that can lead to trauma, including social stigma, bullying, and non-affirming treatment approaches. These experiences can result in significant emotional and psychological distress, which may manifest in various ways, such as anxiety, depression, or behavioral challenges. Trauma directly impacts an individual's interoceptive awareness, and utilizing TIA can reduce the potential for further harm.

By utilizing TIA, OTPs can create a more inclusive and supportive environment that acknowledges the potential for trauma in every client. This approach shifts the focus from "What is wrong with you?" to "What has happened to you?" This reframing is crucial for building trust and rapport, allowing clients to feel safe and validated in their experiences. Recognizing the prevalence of trauma among Neurodivergent individuals not only enhances therapeutic relationships but also informs the development of more effective, individualized treatment plans.

The Importance of Active Listening and Validating Client Experiences

Active listening helps build trust and rapport between therapists and clients. By being present, attentive, and responsive to clients' verbal and non-verbal cues, therapists can validate clients' feelings and experiences. This validation is essential for clients who may have previously felt misunderstood or dismissed. By fostering open communication, therapists can create a therapeutic alliance that encourages clients to share their stories and engage more fully in the therapeutic process.

The NEAR Framework

The NEAR Framework—comprising Neurobiology, Epigenetics, ACE studies, and Resilience—provides a comprehensive understanding of how trauma impacts individuals. This framework emphasizes the interconnectedness of these four components, illustrating how trauma can shape not only brain function but also emotional and social development (see Table 5.3).

Neurobiology: How Trauma Affects Brain Function and Development

Within the NEAR Framework, neurobiology plays a critical role in understanding how trauma and interoception affect brain function. Neurobiology is the study of the nervous system, including the brain, spinal cord, and nerves, and how these structures and their functions are influenced by genetic, environmental, and experiential factors. Trauma can alter key brain regions such as the amygdala, hippocampus, and prefrontal cortex, while interoception influences how individuals process internal sensory experiences. OTPs can leverage this understanding to develop interventions that promote emotional regulation and self-awareness.

Trauma has a profound impact on brain function, particularly in areas responsible for emotional regulation, memory, and stress response. Key brain regions affected include the insula, amygdala, hippocampus, and prefrontal cortex. The insula is crucial for processing internal sensory experiences, known as interoception, which can be disrupted by trauma, leading to difficulties in recognizing and responding to bodily signals. The amygdala, responsible for processing emotions and fear, can become hyperactive in response to traumatic experiences, resulting in heightened anxiety and emotional dysregulation. Conversely, the hippocampus, essential for memory formation and emotional regulation, may shrink in size due to chronic stress, impairing an individual's ability to process and recall memories accurately. The prefrontal cortex, vital for executive functions such as decision-making and impulse control, may also exhibit reduced activity, leading to difficulties with self-regulation and behavioral control.

For Neurodivergent individuals, these neurological changes can exacerbate existing challenges. For example, a person with depression may already experience differences in sensory processing and emotional regulation, and trauma can further complicate these issues. Understanding the neurobiological impact of trauma allows OTPs to be more empathetic and understanding of the client as well as tailoring interventions that address these specific challenges, promoting emotional regulation and self-awareness.

Table 5.3—The NEAR Framework

NEAR Component	Description	Implications for Neurodivergent Individuals	Recommended Strategies for Occupational Therapy Professionals	Potential Challenges or Considerations
Neurobiology	Examines how trauma affects brain function, particularly in areas responsible for emotional regulation, memory, and stress response.	Neurodivergent individuals may experience heightened anxiety and emotional dysregulation due to differences in brain structure and function.	Implement TIA that prioritizes safety and sensory-friendly environments. Use mindfulness and trauma-informed sensory techniques to support emotional regulation. Consider partnering and exploring the client's sensory processing differences, such as the sensory processing wheel in the *Neurodivergent Friendly Workbook of DBT Skills*.[5]	Neurodivergent individuals may have unique sensory processing needs that require personalized interventions and adaptations to their environmental contexts. Research shows that an individual's sensory processing and in particular interoceptive awareness are impacted by trauma; consider incorporating the Comprehensive Assessment of Interoceptive Awareness to assess potential interoception differences.
Epigenetics	Studies how environmental factors influence gene expression without altering DNA sequences. Trauma can lead to epigenetic changes affecting stress response and health.	Neurodivergent individuals may have altered stress responses, increasing the risk of mental health disorders.	Create supportive environments that mitigate negative effects of trauma on gene expression. Focus on validation and empowerment to foster resilience. Ways to promote empowerment are involving the individual in collaborative goal setting as well as offering transparency, clear expectations, and flexibility throughout the therapy experience.	Understanding individual genetic predispositions may be complex and require collaboration with other healthcare professionals. Be aware that generational trauma can come into play alongside an individual's lived experiences.

cont.

NEAR Component	Description	Implications for Neurodivergent Individuals	Recommended Strategies for Occupational Therapy Professionals	Potential Challenges or Considerations
Adverse Childhood Experiences studies	Focuses on the impact of ACEs on emotional and social development. ACEs can lead to long-term health and social issues.	Neurodivergent individuals may have experienced multiple ACEs, leading to difficulties in emotional regulation, trust, and social interactions.	Assume individuals may have experienced ACEs and always use TIA. Create a safe and supportive environment without necessarily bringing up specific traumatic experiences. Use trauma-informed practices such as providing choices, maintaining clear boundaries, and fostering a sense of safety and trust.	Identifying and addressing ACEs can be challenging and may require specialized training and resources. Avoid re-traumatizing conversations by focusing on creating a safe and supportive environment. Demonstrate care and reliability through small actions, such as remembering details they have shared from previous sessions and following through on any promises you made (e.g. sending clients that handout you mentioned).
Resilience	Emphasizes the importance of building resilience to help clients cope with and overcome trauma. Resilience involves the ability to bounce back from adversity, adapt to challenges, and maintain a sense of well-being.	Neurodivergent individuals may face challenges in developing resilience, making it critical for healing. They may experience difficulties in emotional regulation, social interactions, and maintaining a positive outlook due to past trauma.	Strengths-based approach: Focus on identifying and building on the client's strengths and resources. Collaborate with clients to set realistic and achievable goals. Teach and practice mindfulness, deep breathing, and other relaxation techniques. Be aware that deficit-based approaches may be harmful, causing the individual to feel further marginalized, judged, and ashamed.	Individual variability: Resilience can vary widely among individuals, and what works for one person may not work for another. Building resilience is a long-term process that requires patience and consistent support. Make sure to include the individual's important family members, peers, or community supports to strengthen relational connections and foster resilience.

Epigenetics: The Impact of Trauma on Gene Expression

Epigenetics refers to the study of how environmental factors can influence gene expression without altering the underlying DNA sequence. Trauma can lead to epigenetic changes that affect an individual's stress response and overall health. For instance, exposure to ACEs can result in modifications to genes associated with stress regulation, potentially increasing the risk of mental health challenges and chronic health conditions later in life.

In occupational therapy, recognizing the epigenetic implications of trauma can inform treatment approaches. By creating supportive and affirming environments, therapists can help mitigate the negative effects of trauma on gene expression. This may involve implementing trauma-informed practices that prioritize safety, validation, and empowerment, ultimately fostering resilience and promoting healthier outcomes for Neurodivergent individuals. OTPs play a key role in educating and training others about the role of trauma and epigenetic changes that can persist across generations.

Adverse Childhood Experience Studies

The ACE Study,[6] conducted by Kaiser Permanente and the CDC, has been instrumental in highlighting the long-term impact of trauma. The study revealed that more than half of the general population has experienced at least one ACE, with significant disparities based on socioeconomic status and race. For instance, children living below the Federal Poverty Line are five times more likely to experience four or more ACEs. The study established a clear link between the number of ACEs experienced and a range of negative health outcomes in adulthood, including chronic health conditions, mental health issues, and social challenges.

The long-term impact of ACEs extends beyond physical and mental health, affecting educational attainment and employment. Individuals with high ACE scores are at increased risk of high school non-completion, unemployment, and living below the poverty line. These socioeconomic factors further compound the effects of childhood trauma, creating a cycle of disadvantage that can persist across generations. Moreover, ACEs can impact interpersonal relationships, leading to difficulties in trust, emotional regulation, and forming healthy connections. Recognizing the prevalence of trauma and its long-term effects is essential for developing effective interventions that address the needs of individuals with ACE histories, emphasizing the importance of TIA in healthcare, education, and social services. A table of the implications for each key finding from the ACE study is available for download within the Vault.

Resilience

Emphasizing resilience enables OTPs to support clients in building and maintaining meaningful connections and coping strategies. Resilience involves the ability to bounce back from adversity and adapt to challenges. By fostering resilience, OTPs can help clients develop the skills and strengths needed to navigate and overcome the effects of trauma. OTPs play a key role in helping support resilience for Neurodivergent populations utilizing strengths-based approaches with collaborative goal setting. OTPs can promote resilience by incorporating mindfulness and social support networks, utilizing trauma-informed practices, and demonstrating cultural competence.

Trauma Responses

Trauma significantly impacts behavior and emotional regulation, especially in Neurodivergent individuals. Understanding these effects is crucial for OTPs and other practitioners to provide effective and compassionate care. Trauma responses such as fight, flight, freeze, fawn, hyperarousal, and hypoarousal are automatic reactions of the autonomic nervous system to perceived threats:

- *Fight:* The nervous system prepares to confront and combat the threat, characterized by increased aggression and a heightened sense of urgency.

- *Flight:* The nervous system primes the individual to escape the threat, involving a strong urge to flee and increased physical activity.

- *Freeze:* The nervous system causes immobility or unresponsiveness when neither fight nor flight is viable, conserving energy and reducing detection.

- *Fawn:* The nervous system prompts appeasement or pleasing of the threat to avoid conflict, involving submissive behaviors and a focus on others' needs.

- *Hyperarousal:* The nervous system is overactivated, leading to heightened anxiety, panic, and constant alertness, often exhibiting fight or flight responses.

- *Hypoarousal:* The nervous system is underactivated, leading to numbness, dissociation, and shutdown of emotional and physical responses, often exhibiting freeze or fawn responses.

These responses are deeply rooted in neurobiology and essential for survival. The "window of tolerance," developed by Dr. Dan Siegel, explains how individuals respond to stress and trauma. It is the optimal zone where a person can manage and process stress and emotions effectively. An expanded table describing how OTPs can address each trauma emotional expression is available for download within the Vault.

How Trauma Affects Behavior and Emotional Regulation

Trauma disrupts brain function, particularly in areas responsible for emotional regulation and stress response. The amygdala may become hyperactive, leading to heightened anxiety and emotional dysregulation. The hippocampus may shrink due to chronic stress, impairing memory and emotional regulation. The prefrontal cortex may exhibit reduced activity, resulting in difficulties with self-regulation and behavioral control.

For Neurodivergent individuals, who may already experience differences in sensory processing and emotional regulation, trauma can exacerbate these challenges. This can lead to increased anxiety, hypervigilance, withdrawal, aggression, and difficulties with social interactions. For example, a Neurodivergent individual might experience meltdowns or shutdowns in response to overwhelming stimuli, often misinterpreted as "challenging behavior" rather than valid reactions to an unsupportive environment.

Other behavioral responses may include avoidance of certain situations, impulsivity, and difficulties articulating feelings or needs. These behaviors are often coping mechanisms developed in response to trauma and can be exacerbated by the individual's Neurodivergent traits. For instance, an individual with ADHD may have heightened auditory perception, making them more susceptible to sensory overload in loud environments.

Interoception, Our Eighth Sense: A Crucial Concept for Trauma-Informed Approaches

Interoception, often referred to as the "eighth sense," is a sensory system that allows us to notice, interpret, and respond to internal body signals such as a racing heart, growling stomach, tight chest, sore muscles, sweaty skin, heavy eyes, a full bladder, and so forth. These body signals provide us with vital clues to our **homeostatic emotional** experiences (e.g. knowing when we are hungry, thirsty, in pain or sick, hot or cold, need to pee or poop, sexually aroused, etc.) as well as our **affective emotional** experiences (e.g. knowing when we are scared, anxious, excited, content, etc.). Interoception not only helps us understand how we feel but also plays a crucial role in recognizing what our body needs for health and regulation in each moment.

The process of noticing, interpreting, and responding to interoceptive sensations can be referred to as interoceptive awareness (IA), and each aspect of this process is important:

1. BODY: Notice body signals
2. EMOTION: Connect body signals to the meaning or emotion
3. ACTION: Regulate body signals with an action

For example, someone might notice a tight sensation spanning across the chest and a churning feeling brain (BODY); they have learned over time that this is a clue that they are anxious (EMOTION); and through experimenting they learned that going for a walk is an action that helps regulate their body during this internal experience (ACTION). These Body, Emotion, Action connections are unique to each person. With the right support, individuals can develop body knowledge and gain a deeper understanding of their interoceptive identity.

Interoceptive Awareness: The Bridge Between Co-Regulation and Self-Regulation

Not enough is known about the development of the interoceptive system, but from a practical standpoint, most infants are naturally wired to notice interoceptive comfort and discomfort and express those internal experiences to caregivers. On day one of life, an infant likely does not have a high-level understanding of their interoceptive world (e.g. they probably do not recognize *This feeling means I am hungry; I need food* or *This feeling means I am cold; I need a blanket*). However, their interoceptive system is already attuned to detecting basic comfort and discomfort sensations, signaling when something feels off in their body.

It then falls to an attuned caregiver to respond with curiosity—making thoughtful guesses about the source of the infant's discomfort and offering co-regulation strategies, such as feeding or providing warmth. When the infant's interoceptive needs are met, they experience feel-good sensations from the caregiver, reinforcing a sense of safety and strengthening their secure bond and attachment (see Figure 5.2). This reinforces attachment theory's central idea that early co-regulation and emotional attunement lay the groundwork for later emotional and social development.

Through consistent co-regulation, infants not only have their interoceptive needs met but also receive ongoing messages that their internal experiences are valid and worth expressing. If this co-regulation cycle happens consistently, many growing children begin to refine knowledge about their body (e.g. "this feeling in my body means I'm hungry, and when I eat this feeling in my body gets better"), thus building the interoceptive awareness—the body, emotion, action connections—which is the foundation of self-regulation.

Figure 5.2—Building the IA Bridge from Co-Regulation to Self-Regulation

Therefore, IA, which largely develops through co-regulation and attuned, affirming, and curious relationships, provides the bridge from co-regulation to self-regulation. Caregivers and supporters must remember that due to ableism shadowing the world, even in loving relationships, IA breakdowns can still occur. However, as OTPs, we play a crucial role in combating ableism, and by doing so we can reduce harm and minimize opportunities for IA breakdowns.

Neurodivergent Trauma and Interoception Differences

Interoception differences are common across all neurotypes, including in individuals who have experienced early life trauma, most likely due to the disruption in the co-regulation process leading to:

- inadequate internal curiosity and validation from support partners
- the need to suppress, mask, or dissociate from the pain/discomfort resulting from unmet interoception needs
- countless missed opportunities for interoception learning.

Even in the most attuned and affirming early relationships, Neurodivergent individuals often face other traumas due to a mismatch between their neurology and the world around them. Rather than solely early life events, this trauma is often lifelong, persistent, and rooted in systemic invalidation, ableism, and non-affirming approaches.

Given this, it is unsurprising that many Neurodivergent individuals experience interoception differences. For example, Fiene, Ireland, and Brownlow[7] found that 74% of Autistic adults reported interoception differences and Bruton et al.[8] found that, across 17 studies, ADHDers consistently reported statistically significant interoception differences. While research has mixed findings as to the interoception experiences of Neurodivergent people (primarily due to lack of comprehensive standardized interoception assessments as well as inclusion of input from Neurodivergents themselves within the research), lived experiences shared by the community emphasize that many environments are not naturally accommodating for individuals with interoceptive differences. As a result, these individuals often lack the opportunities to authentically and safely explore and understand their unique internal experiences.

Interoceptive differences are a valid and inherent aspect of the human experience, with variations in how individuals perceive their internal bodily sensations. While these differences are natural, trauma can sometimes intensify them, leading to more amplified breakdowns in IA.

When There Is a Breakdown in Interoceptive Awareness

Interoception differences can involve a breakdown in one, two, or all three aspects of IA, making self-regulation difficult. Some may struggle to notice body signals due to muted (too quiet) or intense (too overwhelming) sensations. Others may notice their signals but struggle to interpret or figure out the meaning behind them. Some may recognize both the signals and their meaning but are uncertain about how to change the way their body feels.

Toileting Regulation Breakdown

- **Breakdown in Noticing** → An individual doesn't feel their bladder filling, leading to accidents.
- **Breakdown in Connecting** → They notice the sensation of their bladder filling, but are unsure what it means, leading to accidents.
- **Breakdown in Regulating** → They know they need to go but don't know how to help their body feel safe in an overwhelming bathroom, leading to accidents.

Sensory Overwhelm Breakdown

- **Breakdown in Noticing** → An individual doesn't register rising discomfort from loud noises until they are in complete shutdown.
- **Breakdown in Connecting** → They notice bodily discomfort but don't realize it's a sign of sensory overload from environmental noise, leading to a shutdown.
- **Breakdown in Regulating** → They recognize the discomfort is sensory overwhelm from the noise but don't know how to seek relief, leading to a shutdown.

People can experience this breakdown in IA for one or many homeostatic or affective emotions, affecting their ability to self-regulate the emotion impacted. When this breakdown occurs, they will most likely rely on co-regulation to support unmet interoceptive needs.

Reclaiming Our Role: OTPs Leading the Shift Toward Interoception-Affirming Practices

Culturally, once children reach a certain age, they are often expected to manage their homeostatic and affective emotions independently, with little to no co-regulation.

> When Neurodivergent individuals struggle to meet this expectation due to IA breakdowns, they are often mislabeled with ableist terms such as "challenging," "oppositional," or "attention-seeking," when the issue actually lies in the unrealistic demands.

These labels often push Neurodivergent individuals into non-affirming approaches that mirror early life trauma, lacking curiosity, validation, and co-regulation of their internal experiences. Rather than fostering body knowledge, these approaches often prioritize compliance, leading individuals to suppress or mask discomfort instead of learning from it—deepening IA breakdowns, compounding dysregulation, and ironically often worsening the "behavior concerns."

As OTPs, we can lead the charge in transforming how Neurodivergent individuals are supported. Recognizing the interoception impact of common intervention approaches—such as compliance, gaslighting, desensitization, and normalization—is the first step. By addressing these gaps, we can shift toward neuro-affirming practices that prioritize exploration, validation, and self-understanding. Through modeling co-regulation, inner curiosity, and inner validation we can create safe spaces for individuals to reconnect with their body signals in ways that are empowering. Beyond our direct work, we can advocate for systemic change, inspiring others to move away from compliance-based approaches and toward affirming interoception-informed supports. Without this shift, many supports will continue to reinforce trauma and IA breakdowns.

Recognizing the Trauma and Interoception Impact of Common Approaches

The Cost of Compliance-Based or Behavior Modification Approaches

Compliance is embedded in nearly every system—educational, medical, judicial, and families. Widespread compliance-based interventions—including, but not limited to, ABA, a profession rooted in compliance—often condition individuals to override their interoceptive signals in order to please others and earn external reinforcement. These approaches prioritize obedience over unmet needs, teaching individuals to mask or suppress interoceptive discomfort rather than notice, understand, and regulate to their body signals. Over time, this interoceptive disconnect can lead to chronic, lifelong dysregulation created by a diminished IA.

Why Compliance Appears to Work (and Why It's Harmful)

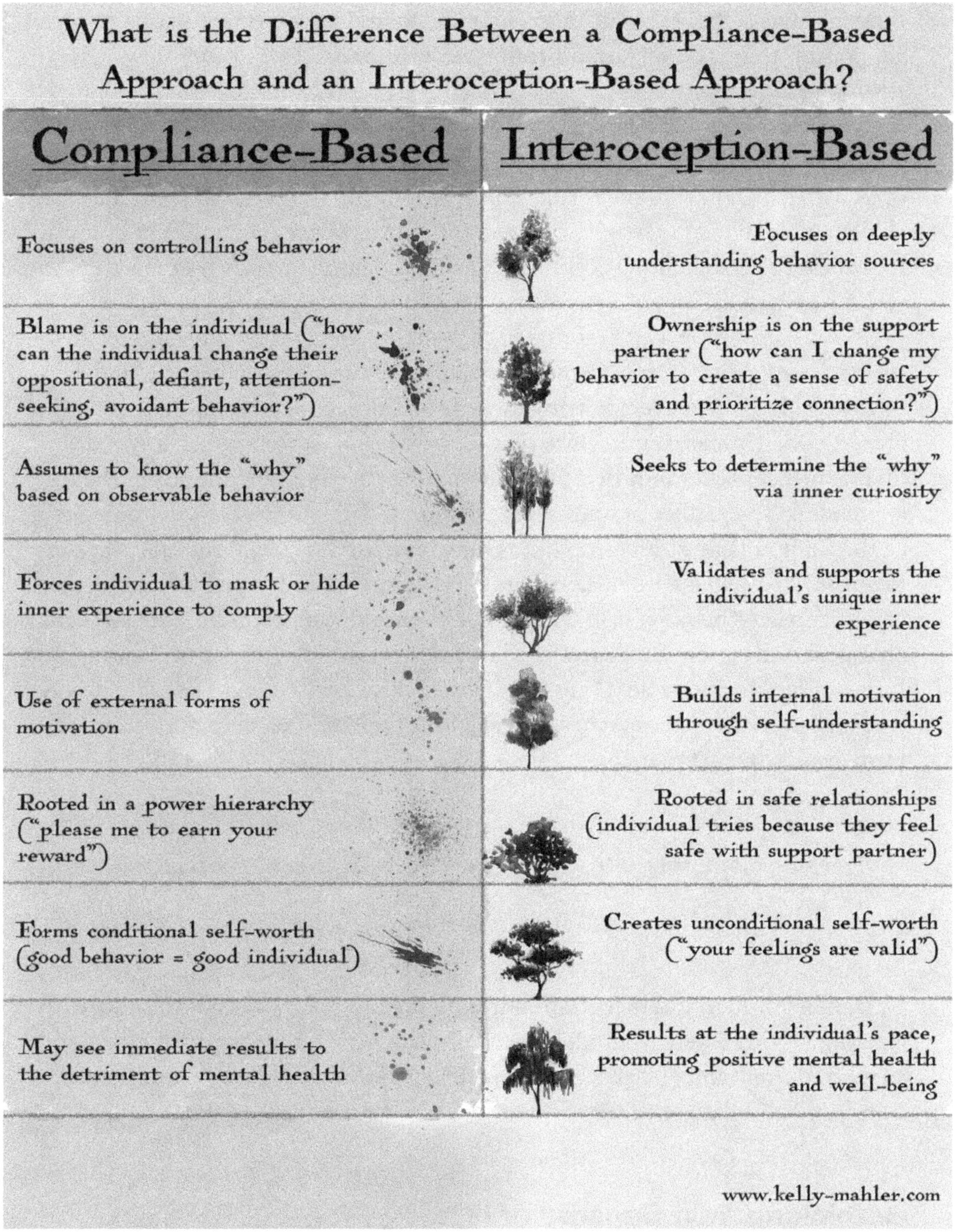

What is the Difference Between a Compliance-Based Approach and an Interoception-Based Approach?

Compliance-Based	Interoception-Based
Focuses on controlling behavior	Focuses on deeply understanding behavior sources
Blame is on the individual ("how can the individual change their oppositional, defiant, attention-seeking, avoidant behavior?")	Ownership is on the support partner ("how can I change my behavior to create a sense of safety and prioritize connection?")
Assumes to know the "why" based on observable behavior	Seeks to determine the "why" via inner curiosity
Forces individual to mask or hide inner experience to comply	Validates and supports the individual's unique inner experience
Use of external forms of motivation	Builds internal motivation through self-understanding
Rooted in a power hierarchy ("please me to earn your reward")	Rooted in safe relationships (individual tries because they feel safe with support partner)
Forms conditional self-worth (good behavior = good individual)	Creates unconditional self-worth ("your feelings are valid")
May see immediate results to the detriment of mental health	Results at the individual's pace, promoting positive mental health and well-being

www.kelly-mahler.com

Figure 5.3—Compliance-Based Versus Interoception-Based Approaches

Many compliance-based approaches are deemed successful because they produce outward behavioral conformity. However, what is actually happening is a trauma response—where an individual is forced to suppress or mask their authentic responses in order to avoid punishment or gain approval. Masking, once thought of as a choice to "fit in," is now understood as an unconscious trauma adaptation to unsafe or non-affirming environments. Over time, this survival strategy erodes body trust and interoceptive connection, leaving individuals disconnected from their internal needs in order to stay safe. While these strategies may appear effective in the short term, they come at a steep cost—derailment of IA with a high likelihood of Neurodivergent burnout, increased mental health challenges, and even a heightened risk of suicide. The expectation to comply, regardless of personal interoceptive experiences, erodes a healthy connection to self and perpetuates long-term harm.

As OTPs, we have a critical role in challenging these ableist norms and advocating for approaches that foster interoceptive awareness, body trust, and self-understanding. However, shifting away from compliance-based models is not always easy. Unmasking itself is often a privileged experience; many Neurodivergent people remain in environments that are not yet safe for authentic expression. This makes our advocacy even more vital. OTPs can use tools such as the Camouflaging Autistic Traits Questionnaire (CAT-Q)[9] and the Masking Regulator[10] to help identify when masking is occurring and to guide supports that prioritize safety, belonging, and agency. We must also push for broader systemic change, ensuring environments and policies evolve to reduce oppression and make unmasking possible. OTPs may face pushback from teams that are deeply entrenched in these approaches, particularly when they seem to produce short-term results. But at what cost?

> True support must prioritize long-term well-being over momentary behavioral control.

By standing firm in interoception-affirming practices, OTPs can lead the way in creating a future where Neurodivergent individuals are understood, validated, and supported—not simply managed or controlled. Please see Figure 5.3 for interoception-based alternatives to common compliance-based approaches.

Rethinking "Is It Sensory or Is It Behavior?" – a False Dichotomy

The long-standing debate in occupational therapy—*"is it sensory or is it behavior?"*—demands serious reflection. When this question first emerged, there was far less understanding of neuro-affirming supports, and while some practitioners may have unintentionally operated within an ableist framework, we now know better.

The reality is that everything is both sensory and behavior, but also a lot more! Every action, reaction, or response is shaped by a complex interplay of many factors including, but not limited to, sensory processing, interoceptive awareness, nervous system regulation, communication, language, executive functioning, and so on. The question itself has developed into a false dichotomy—one that is sometimes used to oversimplify complex human experiences and, in many cases, justifies compliance-based approaches. If the concern does not neatly fit into what is determined to be a "sensory" cause, then what happens within this dichotomy? Individuals are often labeled as "challenging" and subjected to interventions that focus on control rather than support.

As Meg Ferrell highlights, this binary thinking forces professionals into narrow intervention pathways.[11] If we assume something is sensory, we may focus only on sensory accommodations and miss other contributing factors like executive function, communication, or predictability needs. If we assume something is behavioral, we risk falling into harmful compliance-based interventions that assume intentionality, demand control, and fail to address the root cause of distress. Either way, we are missing the bigger picture—one that requires curiosity, not control.

If we continue to participate in the "sensory versus behavior" debate, we are not just oversimplifying human experiences; we are actively upholding the ableism behind behaviorism. As OTPs, our training equips us to look beyond observable behavior, to ask better questions, and to make meaningful adjustments to environments and tasks. Our clients deserve support that is affirming and responsive—not interventions that force them into compliance. It's time to leave this outdated debate behind and focus on what truly matters: exploring, understanding, and validating.

Gaslighting and Dismissal of Internal Experiences

Neurodivergent individuals frequently experience gaslighting, where their sensory, emotional, and medical experiences are dismissed or invalidated. This can condition them to distrust their interoceptive signals, leading to long-term IA breakdowns, self-doubt, and increased dysregulation. Common statements that contribute to this harmful dynamic include:

- "It's not that loud in here."
- "You're being too sensitive."
- "Stop overreacting."
- "What's the size of the problem?"

- "We see nothing medically wrong in the tests, so your symptoms are nothing to worry about."

These messages—whether explicit or implicit—reinforce the idea that an individual's internal experience is untrustworthy or wrong, deepening the interoceptive disconnect.

OTPs play a crucial role in countering gaslighting and helping individuals rebuild trust in their interoceptive signals. By approaching each person's internal experience with deep curiosity and validation, we can support them in noticing, understanding, and regulating their bodily needs using statements such as:

- "I see you covering your ears. What's going on? Is there something I can do to help?"
- "I see you crying. I'm here with you" (offer a co-regulation strategy based on your hypothesis of their unmet interoceptive need until you find something that meets that need).
- "Ugh. I'm having a hard time right now. Are you too?"
- "I notice you are reaching for more squeezes. Let's do it! Show me where they feel best."
- "I see your body wiggling like this (playfully imitate their movements). I wonder how your body feels right now?"
- "We didn't find anything on the medical tests, but I know you are still having symptoms. Let's talk about some next steps that we can try to see if we can help your body feel better."

Until the world becomes more neuro-affirming, part of our work must involve pushing back against systemic invalidation while amplifying Neurodivergent voices. By standing as allies, we can ensure that Neurodivergent individuals are not only heard but empowered to shape their own interoceptive identities with confidence.

Emotion "Teaching" and Emotion Labeling

Neurodivergent individuals often experience emotion labeling and teaching, both of which—though well-intended—can contribute to interoceptive doubt. When others label an individual's emotions ("it looks like you are frustrated"), they are making a guess based on external observation, often misinterpreting the actual experience. Repeated mislabeling can cause Neurodivergent individuals to doubt their own interoceptive signals, leading them to question whether their internal experience is "wrong."

Similarly, traditional emotion teaching presents emotions as having universal bodily signals ("Anger is a high-arousal red-zone emotion" or "You know you're hungry when your stomach growls"). In reality, emotions manifest differently in every body—hunger might feel like zaps all over the skin instead of a growling stomach, and anxiety might present as muscle shutdown rather than a racing heart. Teaching a singular emotional footprint can cause Neurodivergent individuals to mistrust their own interoceptive experiences, leading them to memorize emotion words for compliance rather than authentic self-expression.

The *Double Empathy Problem*[12] highlights that misunderstanding goes both ways—just as Neurodivergent individuals may struggle to read neurotypical emotions, neurotypicals often misinterpret Neurodivergent emotional expressions. However, because neurotypical interpretations are treated as the default, Neurodivergent individuals are expected to conform, reinforcing emotional mislabeling and self-doubt.

OTPs can help by shifting away from external labeling and predefined emotion definitions, instead guiding Neurodivergent individuals in exploring their own body signals and using them as unique emotional clues. For example, *The Interoception Curriculum*[13] is a framework that is used to sequentially develop IA within a neuro-affirming lens, starting by using hands-on, concrete learning activities to practice noticing body signals (*how does my body uniquely feel?*); and then moving to activities that guide connection of the body signals noticed to emotions (*what do these body signals uniquely mean for me?*); and then finally exploring a wide variety of actions that promote "feel-good" or comfortable body signals (*what does my body uniquely need for comfort?*).[14] By fostering curiosity rather than correction, we can help rebuild interoceptive trust, ensuring Neurodivergent individuals feel validated in their bodily and emotional experiences and empowered in their self-understanding.

Desensitization Approaches

Many desensitization-based therapies—such as exposure-based sensory or feeding interventions aimed at normalization—are rooted in outdated thinking. These methods operate on the assumption that discomfort should be ignored or overridden rather than understood. Forcing someone to "get used to" a sensation or specific food conditions them to suppress their interoceptive signals, reinforcing the harmful idea that their natural bodily responses are wrong. Over time, this can lead to chronic IA breakdowns, increased dysregulation, and a diminished ability to trust one's own needs.

> Beardon's *Golden Equation*—Autism + Environment = Outcome—reminds us that the person remains constant; it's the environment that determines whether the outcome is positive or negative.[15]

Desensitization-based approaches attempt to change the person by forcing them to override or mask their discomfort, rather than recognizing that it is the environment that needs to shift. If a Neurodivergent individual is struggling, the focus should not be on forcing them to adapt but on adjusting the environment to meet their needs. This often, but not always, involves shifting the attitudes and behaviors of the people within that environment. While Beardon's work is specific to autism, this equation applies broadly across neurodivergence. Whether an individual has trauma, sensory processing differences, or is otherwise Neurodivergent, their nervous system and interoceptive needs remain constant—it is the external conditions that dictate whether they will experience regulation or distress.

When we apply this thinking to real-world scenarios, we see that success comes not from forcing desensitization but from creating conditions where a person feels safe and supported. For example, in feeding therapy, rather than pressuring a person to endure distressing food exposure, we can create an environment that fosters interoceptive safety around food. This includes adjusting sensory factors like lighting, noise, and smells; finding eating positions and tools that feel best; keeping to safe foods and only expanding when the person expresses interest; and finding alternative forms of nutrition if there is a medical concern. When the environment prioritizes safety and autonomy, the person can engage with food in a way that honors their interoceptive signals—without fear or force. See Chapter 10 for more neurodiversity-affirming approaches to support feeding.

The same principle applies in the classroom, where sensory overwhelm is often met with behavior management strategies rather than environmental adjustments. Instead of using a token economy to push a student through a sensory-hostile environment, we can adapt the space to support their regulation. This might mean adjusting the sensory environment, allowing for movement breaks, providing noise-canceling headphones, modifying tasks to align with the student's needs, and training staff to see sensory distress as a need rather than a behavior to fix. When the environment is designed to work for the student, coercive systems become unnecessary, and authentic engagement becomes possible. Recognizing that the outcome depends on the environment, OTPs have the power to drive systemic change, shaping truly inclusive, neuro-affirming spaces. This is the heart of occupational therapy: we don't force individuals to endure harm—we transform environments so they foster success. With our expertise, we can lead the shift toward interoception-centered, neuro-affirming approaches that empower every person to thrive.

Normalization and the Denial of Neurodivergent Experiences

Normalization efforts aim to make Neurodivergent individuals conform to neurotypical standards, often at the cost of their well-being. Whether it's discouraging stimming, forcing eye contact, extinguishing self-soothing behaviors, or requiring the memorization of the social rules of a different neurotype, these approaches send a harmful message: *Your natural way of being is wrong.* Over time, this repeated invalidation erodes self-trust and creates breakdowns in IA, as individuals learn to suppress or ignore the signals their body is giving them in order to meet external expectations.

Interoception is deeply tied to social safety. When a person is in an environment where their natural social way of being is controlled or corrected, they may experience interoceptive distress, but in favor of "getting it right," they may need to disconnect from their interoceptive cues entirely. This can make it harder to recognize when a social environment is unsafe or exhausting, leaving Neurodivergent individuals vulnerable to social forms of abuse and Neurodivergent burnout.

OTPs can lead the shift away from harmful normalization practices toward approaches that foster genuine connection. Rather than teaching scripted social skills that prioritize neurotypical norms, OTPs can use the power of meaningful occupation to facilitate social experiences centered on shared interests—like gaming groups, writing clubs, or movement-based activities—where connection happens naturally and authentically. Additionally, OTPs can integrate interoception work, helping clients (re)explore what they need to feel safe in social situations while reducing social vulnerability and increasing self-advocacy. Instead of compliance-driven social training, we can support individuals in understanding their own boundaries, empowering them to engage in relationships on their own terms.

Leading the Shift: How Trauma-Informed, Interoception-Based OTPs Can Foster Lasting Change

By creating safe, supportive, and engaging environments, OTPs can facilitate positive neuroplastic changes that promote healing. As OTPs, we are uniquely positioned to be powerful allies to the Neurodivergent community. Our expertise allows us to assess environments, foster interoceptive exploration, and support individuals in reconnecting with their internal experiences—many of whom have experienced trauma due to non-affirming approaches. Luke Beardon's *Golden Equation* reminds us that autism (and neurodivergence) itself does not determine an outcome—rather, the environment does. If we seek positive outcomes, we must focus on shifting the environment, which often means rethinking the systems, approaches, and people within it.

Interoception is at the heart of this shift. By centering curiosity, validation, and co-regulation, we can move beyond outdated compliance-based models and into affirming, trauma-informed practices that empower rather than suppress. This work is not always easy, but it is necessary. OTPs have the power to reshape the narrative—creating spaces where Neurodivergent individuals are not forced to conform but instead are supported in understanding, trusting, and advocating for their own interoceptive experiences. The path forward is clear: let's rise to the occasion and lead the change.

Endnotes

1 Perry, B. D., & Winfrey, O. (2021). *What happened to you? Conversations on trauma, resilience, and healing*. Flatiron Books.

2 Shah, P., Hall, R., Catmur, C., & Bird, G. (2016). Alexithymia, not autism, is associated with impaired interoception. *Cortex; a Journal Devoted to the Study of the Nervous System and Behavior, 81*, 215–220. https://doi.org/10.1016/j.cortex.2016.03.021

3 Substance Abuse and Mental Health Services Administration's Trauma Justice Strategic Initiative. (2014). *SAMHSA's concept of trauma and guidance for a trauma-informed approach*. Substance Abuse and Mental Health Services Administration. https://library.samhsa.gov/product/samhsas-concept-trauma-and-guidance-trauma-informed-approach/sma14-4884

4 O'Day, K. (2023). *Visual activity sort (VAS)*. www.visualactivitysort.com

5 Wise, S. (2019). *The Neurodivergent friendly workbook of DBT skills*. Lived Experience Educator. www.livedexperienceeducator.com/store/p/Neurodivergent-friendly-workbook-of-dbt-skills

6 Felitti, V. J., Anda, R. F., Nordenberg, D., Williamson, D. F., Spitz, A. M., Edwards, V., Koss, M. P., & Marks, J. S. (1998). Relationship of childhood abuse and household dysfunction to many of the leading causes of death in adults. The Adverse Childhood Experiences (ACE) Study. *American Journal of Preventive Medicine, 14*(4), 245–258. https://doi.org/10.1016/s0749-3797(98)00017-8

7 Fiene, L., Ireland, M. J., & Brownlow, C. (2018). The Interoception Sensory Questionnaire (ISQ): A scale to measure interoceptive challenges in adults. *Journal of Autism and Developmental Disorders, 48*(10), 3354–3366. https://doi.org/10.1007/s10803-018-3600-3

8 Bruton, A., Levy, L., Rai, N. K., Colgan, D. D., & Johnstone, J. (2025). Diminished interoceptive accuracy in attention-deficit/hyperactivity disorder: A systematic review. *Psychophysiology, 62*(2), e14750. https://doi.org/10.1111/psyp.14750

9 Hull, L., Mandy, W., Lai, M.-C., Baron-Cohen, S., Allison, C., Smith, P., & Petrides, K. V. (2019). *The Camouflaging Autistic Traits Questionnaire (CAT-Q)*. NovoPsych. https://novopsych.com.au/assessments/formulation/camouflaging-Autistic-traits-questionnaire-cat-q

10 Fede, J., & Laurent, A. (2023). *The masking regulator*. Autism Level UP! https://cdn.sanity.io/files/p6bm7moz/production/4de925ca8a61578a68a0a9bc506484fbdf1f9e27.pdf

11 Ferrell, M. (2020). *Is it sensory or is it behavior... or are we asking the wrong question?* Learn Play Thrive. https://learnplaythrive.com/is-it-sensory-or-is-it-behavioror-are-we-asking-the-wrong-question

12 Milton, D. E. M. (2012). On the ontological status of autism: The "double empathy problem." *Disability & Society, 27*(6), 883–887. https://doi.org/10.1080/09687599.2012.710008

13 Mahler, K. (2019). *The interoception curriculum: A step-by-step guide to developing mindful self-regulation*. Kelly Mahler. www.kelly-mahler.com/product/the-interoception-curriculum-a-step-bystep-guide-to-developing-mindful-self-regulation

14 ibid.

15 Beardon, L. (2019). *Autism and Asperger syndrome in childhood: For parents and carers of the newly diagnosed*. Sheldon Press.

SPOTLIGHT

Trauma-Informed Approaches for Supporting Individuals with IDD

SAM BRANDSEN

Trigger warning: abuse, partner violence

A trauma-informed approach is especially critical when working with the IDD (intellectual and developmental disability) community, given that people with IDD are disproportionately likely to have experienced abuse, intimate partner violence, bullying, and trauma.[1,2]

One key component of a trauma-informed approach is understanding the various types of trauma, as well as indicators that someone might be experiencing abuse. While there are many outstanding general resources on abuse, such as the Power and Control Wheel, people with IDD may additionally experience relatively IDD-specific forms of abuse. In the context of intimate partner violence, an abuser* might use their partner's sensory sensitivities against them by purposefully playing distressing noises or otherwise causing sensory overwhelm as part of the abuse. Likewise, an abuser may use their partner's memory-related disabilities or differences in social communication to claim that their partner's recollection of events is inaccurate. One specific real-life example is an individual with a pattern of abusive behavior who threatened her partner and later tried to claim that the threats were sarcasm and that her partner was simply "too Autistic" to realize it was actually sarcasm. There can also be relatively IDD-specific signs of control, such as controlling how someone discloses their disabilities or controlling their

* I generally avoid using the term "abuser" because I don't believe that people should be fully defined by their harmful actions; and I also realize that people can often have multiple relationships to abuse throughout the course of their life (in some cases, people are victimized in certain relationships and abusive in others). However, I am using the term here as I think it makes the writing clearer (compared to longer phrases like "person who is treating their partner abusively").

access to medications, therapies, or accommodations. It is worth noting that, unfortunately, abuse exists within any community and people of all identities and abilities can be capable of abuse—while ableism often leads to the victimization of people with IDD being overlooked, in some instances it can lead to an infantilization that causes the abusive behaviors of people with IDD to be overlooked.

When working with people with IDD who have a history of trauma, it can be particularly important to use a collaborative approach which emphasizes autonomy and consent. The rest of this section will discuss specific topics related to a trauma-informed approach and include actionable suggestions where possible.

Proactive accessibility and feedback. Trauma often involves uncertainty, and the anxiety that often accompanies uncertainty can be even greater when someone is in a vulnerable situation (such as seeking care/therapy). Letting patients*/clients know in advance that you welcome feedback and also providing information about what they can expect can be helpful. For example, one might provide potential patients with pictures of the therapeutic space and nearby parking area/entrance or with a list of potential accommodations offered and an offer to discuss any other accommodation needs that come up. In addition to welcoming feedback more generally, it may be beneficial to outline to patients how you usually approach feedback, as this information can ease anxiety about how you might react to constructive criticism or more "difficult" feedback. For some patients, it can also be beneficial to periodically check-in with them explicitly to ask whether there are any changes they would like to see in the therapy relationship.

Humility and acknowledging limitations. Part of a commitment to inclusivity and accessibility is recognizing when one isn't the best therapeutic fit and helping connect the patient to someone who is. Personally, I had an extremely stressful therapy experience with a therapist who I genuinely believe is a wonderful, inclusive person overall. However, when we began meeting, there were several stressful misunderstandings and (likely unintentional) dismissive reactions regarding autism that seemed to be in part due to her not having a deep knowledge of autism at the time. In hindsight, being referred to someone with more knowledge on the topic probably would have saved a great deal of shame or self-doubt. In some cases, it might be worth seeing if a patient would prefer to be connected to a clinician with a shared identity (I know that I personally really benefited from later working with an Autistic clinician). Likewise, if a therapist has an intense workload or

* I know many clinicians who prefer the word "client," as it is generally less associated with the medical model and an idea of "fixing" people and some also find that the word "client" is more associated with concepts like autonomy and agency. Personally, I feel that "patient" does a better job of conveying the vulnerability and expectation of care in the relationship (a more eloquent version of this comment can be found on Dr. Natalie Russ' website). I also believe that, in an ideal world, a collaborative and non-pathologizing approach would be a part of all clinical interactions, whether between a medical doctor and patient or between a therapist and patient/client; and so am hesitant to assume that the word "patient" inherently involves a negative or harmful approach.

external stressors, does not have the capacity to meet frequently, or otherwise has an extremely unpredictable schedule and/or prolonged breaks, attempting therapy with a patient who needs more consistent care and engagement can be harmful. The patient might begin to feel like a burden and the therapist might feel even further over-extended or overwhelmed.

Understanding different ways that trauma can appear. One simple but important note is that individuals with IDD may not express distress or trauma in the way that is typically expected. For example, an Autistic individual might say "I feel overwhelmed" in a neutral, quiet tone of voice while indeed feeling incredibly overwhelmed internally. Unfortunately, expectations about what distress looks like and the non-verbal signs that people expect to accompany it such as crying, distressed facial expressions, a change in tone of voice, etc. are so deeply entrenched that clinicians may inadvertently **overlook or underestimate distress** in Autistic individuals.

Avoiding re-traumatization: developing flexible yet robust boundaries. Some flexibility in clinical boundaries can help patients/clients feel safer or more trusting of the clinician they are working with. For example, a "blank slate" approach where a therapist discloses almost nothing about themselves or their beliefs can lead to increased uncertainty in some patients. Suppose that a patient self-identifies as Autistic but has no idea what the clinician thinks about self-identification. They may then hesitate to bring up any considerations or experiences related to their autism due to this uncertainty. In some cases, therapists disclosing their own neurodivergence and/or general approach to care can be extremely helpful for building a sense of what to expect. Likewise, given that people with IDD often go through life being treated as "socially broken" or being overly therapized or scrutinized at times, a more "human" approach to therapy—such as genuinely engaging with the patient/client in discussing their special interests, using a slightly more human or conversational approach, or even suggesting external community resources as appropriate—may be beneficial for the patient/client.

However, while I personally believe that therapy in general could benefit from skewing toward a more flexible and collaborative approach, there can also be a risk of significant (potentially delayed) confusion and harm when boundaries become overly blurry. Critically, the underlying power dynamic in therapy exists even when clinicians may wish to use a more collaborative or non-hierarchical approach, and interactions which may be perfectly healthy in another setting can be deeply (even if unintentionally) exploitative or harmful when in the context of a clinical relationship. Below are some examples of potential questions/considerations related to flexible boundaries:

- *Is it sustainable?* For example, being frequently available for out-of-session contact may not be sustainable and could potentially lead to either clinician burnout/resentment or confusion from the patient/client if the clinician suddenly withdraws an established pattern of communication.

- *Would I be sad, upset, hurt, etc. if the client/patient wanted to go back to "stricter" boundaries?* One therapist wrote anonymously about a patient who had asked for small talk / light conversation at the beginning of sessions. After some time, the patient's needs changed, and the patient wanted to switch to more of a blank slate approach. The therapist adapted her approach, but realized she missed the friendly conversation and had a hard time not feeling hurt by the change. If you realize that you might be unable to easily accept or integrate feedback from the patient, that could be a "red flag" or at least a "yellow flag."

- *Would I be hesitant for my supervisor or peers that I otherwise trust to learn about the way that I am interacting with this client/patient?* If you find yourself frequently making exceptions for a patient/client in a way that you wouldn't want others to know about, that is certainly a red flag. Likewise, if you feel you would need to provide extensive context or explanations to justify your interactions with a patient/client, that may be a sign that the relationship is becoming overly complex.

- *What is the worst semi-realistic scenario?* For example, are you disclosing something about yourself that is so personal or vulnerable that you would be upset or unable to maintain objectivity if a patient responded to your self-disclosure in an unexpected or dismissive way? If you do have a couple of roles in the patient's life (e.g. social or professional overlap), is there a potential for conflict or disagreement with the patient? If so, what impact might it have on the patient if someone who they are trusting to provide support and healing is suddenly expressing criticism or frustration? Personally, I don't think that flexible boundaries need to be completely avoided just because of a potential risk. But if the degree of potential risk is substantial, that could be a reason to use a more cautious approach and/or seek additional consultation.

- *Is the patient/client showing signs (including potentially subtle signs) of strain, stress, or confusion?* In some cases, a patient/client will directly communicate that they are struggling or will appear more withdrawn or disengaged. However, in still other cases a patient/client might develop a very strong attachment to their therapist/clinician—while this can be a sign that therapy is a safe environment for the person, in some cases it can also be a sign that boundaries in therapy are unclear. Many patients who have experienced

> therapy harm at one point idealized their therapist and thought they were happily consenting to changes in the therapy relationship; only to later feel hurt or exploited that a relationship which was meant to help them heal ended up re-traumatizing them. I still don't know exactly when a collaborative approach crosses into an issue of consent. I do believe that patients should be able to request adaptations in therapy (e.g. from a blank slate to a slightly more conversational approach), but I also believe that there is a degree and type of self-disclosure or general flexibility which patients simply can't fully consent to, and which may end up being harmful in the long run.

If interested, Sam also created a Vault item that dives more into trauma-informed approaches specific to supporting caregivers who are significantly involved in the care of their loved one(s). The following are general steps that are often part of an accessible or trauma-informed approach:

- Begin with rapport-building by participating in activities of interest prior to formally starting the evaluation.
- Consider having a visual schedule of the layout of the evaluation activities available (e.g, first is engaging in an activity of interest, then assessment tool time, etc.).
- Be mindful of triggers related to past restraint use (those with IDD are much more likely to have been physically restrained), medical procedures, or sensory overwhelm.
- Make sure you are incorporating the individual's AAC or familiar communication partners to reduce anxiety and ensure understanding.
- Prioritize observation of natural participation in meaningful contexts and activities over standardized testing when possible.
- Contextualize behavior—interpret "challenging behaviors" as adaptive responses to stress, fear, or lack of control.
- Offer clients the option to wait in their car and receive a text when it's time to come in, rather than waiting in a busy waiting room.
- Provide photographs or even a short introductory video of the clinician and/or the space to reduce unpredictability of the first appointment.

Endnotes

1 Chirwa, E., Jewkes, R., Van Der Heijden, I., & Dunkle, K. (2020). Intimate partner violence among women with and without disabilities: A pooled analysis of baseline data from seven violence-prevention programmes. *BMJ Global Health*, *5*(11), e002156. https://doi.org/10.1136/bmjgh-2019-002156

2 Fanslow, J. L., Malihi, Z. A., Hashemi, L., Gulliver, P. J., & McIntosh, T. K. D. (2021). Lifetime prevalence of intimate partner violence and disability: Results from a population-based study in New Zealand. *American Journal of Preventive Medicine*, *61*(3), 320–328. https://doi.org/10.1016/j.amepre.2021.02.022

CHAPTER 6

Antiracism Occupational Therapy Practice

Why, What, How?

MUSHARRAT J. AHMED-LANDERYOU

This chapter provides a critical discussion regarding the need for occupational therapists to be antiracist and do antiracism in practice, and contribute toward ending racism. The chapter invites the occupational therapy community to be critically reflexive and activists for antiracism change for the delivery of fair, just, and equitable occupational therapy. The term antiracism is used purposefully here (instead of "anti-racism") to denote that the change required is structural from the profession and professional bodies. A hyphen will not be used when referring to antiracism or antiracist to signify that the change needed is not an add-on set of instructions or action/s, but a necessary approach for fair, equitable, and just occupational therapy to exist and be delivered. The chapter will explore and critically evaluate why and how racism exists in the profession, and provide suggestions on how to change to deliver antiracism practice.

Background: What Is Racism and How and Why Does It Exist?

Racism is based on the social construct categorizing people into two types of humans: white humans from the West as superior, and the rest of humanity as less-valued humans.[1] Racism was designed to justify the colonial project. It was created for capitalist patriarchal gain, reproduced for centuries, and maintained through politics, economics, and culture to justify the maltreatment of individuals, communities, and nations.[2] Additionally, this hierarchy is meant to justify actions such as slavery or medical experimentation on Black intellectually/

developmentally Disabled persons.[3] The colonial project refers to the ongoing exploitation of Indigenous peoples, lands, and waters by colonial states. Whether we want to admit it or not, the occupational therapy profession continues to benefit from racism and the colonial project.

The profession cannot run away from its racist roots and how the profession enacts racism. Racism is the problem, not race. Racism has provided validation for the organizing principle of the hierarchization of people, knowledge, and constructions of power structures.[4,5] Colonization is about power and oppression. Colonization prioritizes Western domination and the spreading of Western ideas as the "supreme" and "right" source of knowledge. This results in every person being evaluated against a "colonial yardstick" to determine who is a valuable human being. This hierarchy of power favors traits such as white, male, Christian, Eurocentric, heterosexual, non-disabled, educated, affluent, and English-speaking. Everybody else is categorized as lesser.

We see the concept of the "colonial yardstick" in occupational therapy practice, with occupational therapy practitioners (OTPs) prioritizing Western norms and values, assessment tools not being standardized with those who are Black, Indigenous, and people of color (BIPOC), and the strong focus on individualism. Many Marginalized OTPs have shared how racism has been the bedrock of the occupational therapy profession, often implicitly. The profession emerged in the 20th century as a response to the needs of individuals impacted by war and mental health challenges, and occupational therapy was not immune to the racial inequities impacting access to occupational therapy services and what supports were provided. The very roots of the profession were influenced by prevailing societal norms that marginalized BIPOC communities. Have you ever thought about your goals emphasizing independence and self-sufficiency, and how this may overlook the importance of community and connecting in cultures that value the enhancing quality of interdependence? We even see this in our early years, where developmental milestones themselves are Eurocentric cultural conventions that do not resonate with Indigenous cultures. And yet, we have designated these milestones as the foundation for practice within pediatric practice at large.[6]

Antiracism is trying to disrupt the five monocultures of colonial representation of knowledge,[7] as shown in Figure 6.1. The monocultures are a concept that highlights how one side of the world determines what knowledge is considered valuable and who gets to participate in knowledge creation and sharing. This references Santos'[8] concept of the "five modes of production of non-existence." In terms of knowledge production, the Global South is viewed as a reservoir of resources and information that is siphoned by the Global North, which is seen as the authoritative expert in analyzing and controlling these resources (see Figure 6.2).[9]

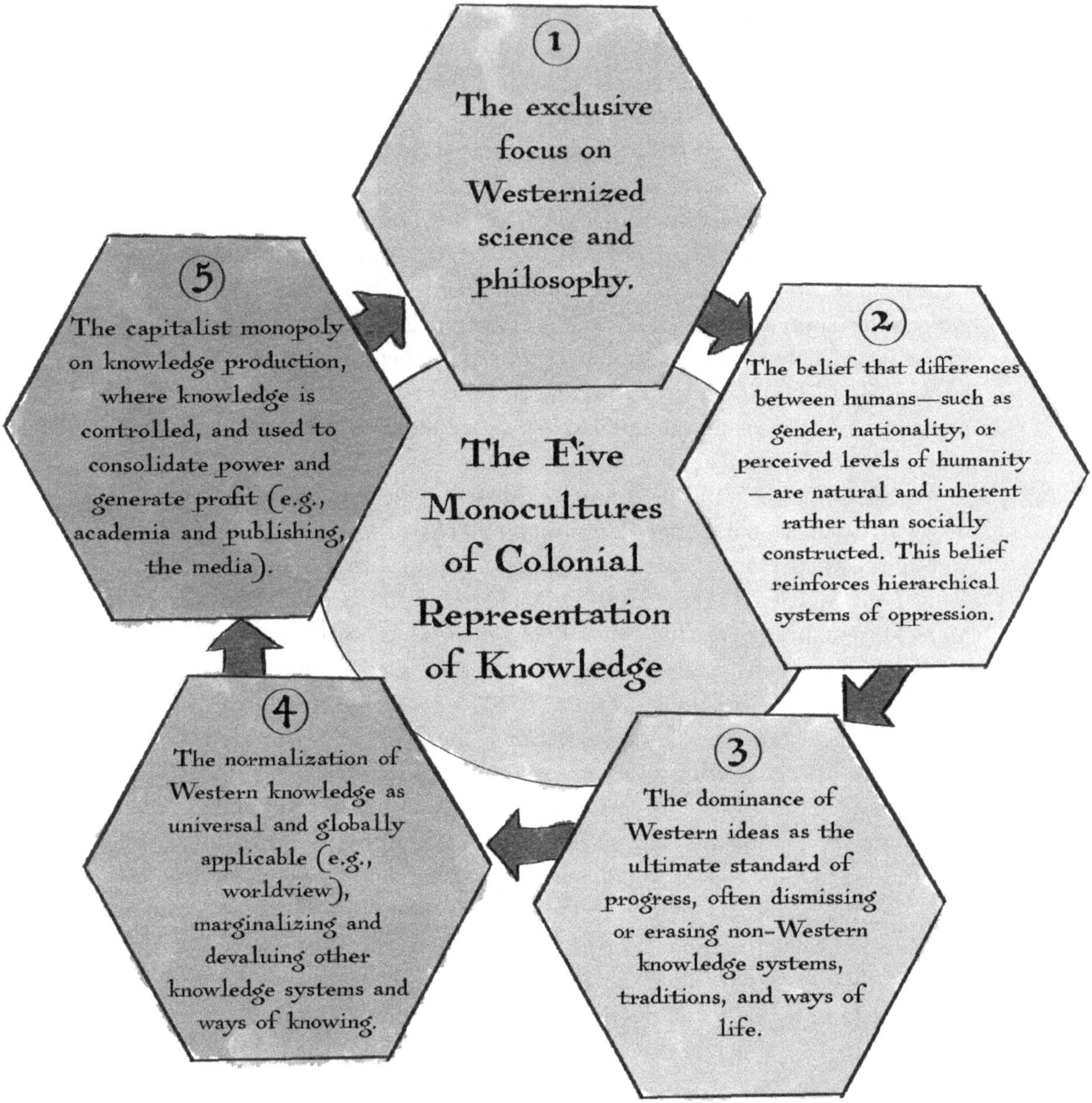

Figure 6.1—The Five Monocultures of Colonial Representation of Knowledge
Note. Adapted from Santos.[10]

The Global North includes the United Kingdom, the United States, Australia, the European Union, Canada, Israel, Japan, South Korea, and New Zealand. The Global South includes countries within South America, those in Africa, Latin America, and the Caribbean, and countries not within the Global North in the Middle East, Asia, and Oceania. This relationship reflects a power dynamic rooted in historical colonization, where not only are the cultures and peoples of the Global

South oppressed, but their insights and traditional knowledge systems are controlled and undervalued by the dominant narratives of the Global North.[11] This is exemplified in Tuhiwai Smith's[12] observation that "The colonizer did not simply design an education system. They designed an education especially to destroy Indigenous cultures, value systems, and appearance." Antiracism doesn't benefit just BIPOC communities but addresses wider discriminations because it deals with the "knottiest" intersecting problems for BIPOC, and in the end benefits the wider populations, including white people. White supremacy harms white people and has led to a harmful culture of perfectionism, quantity over quality, power hoarding, individualism, and an intense sense of urgency.

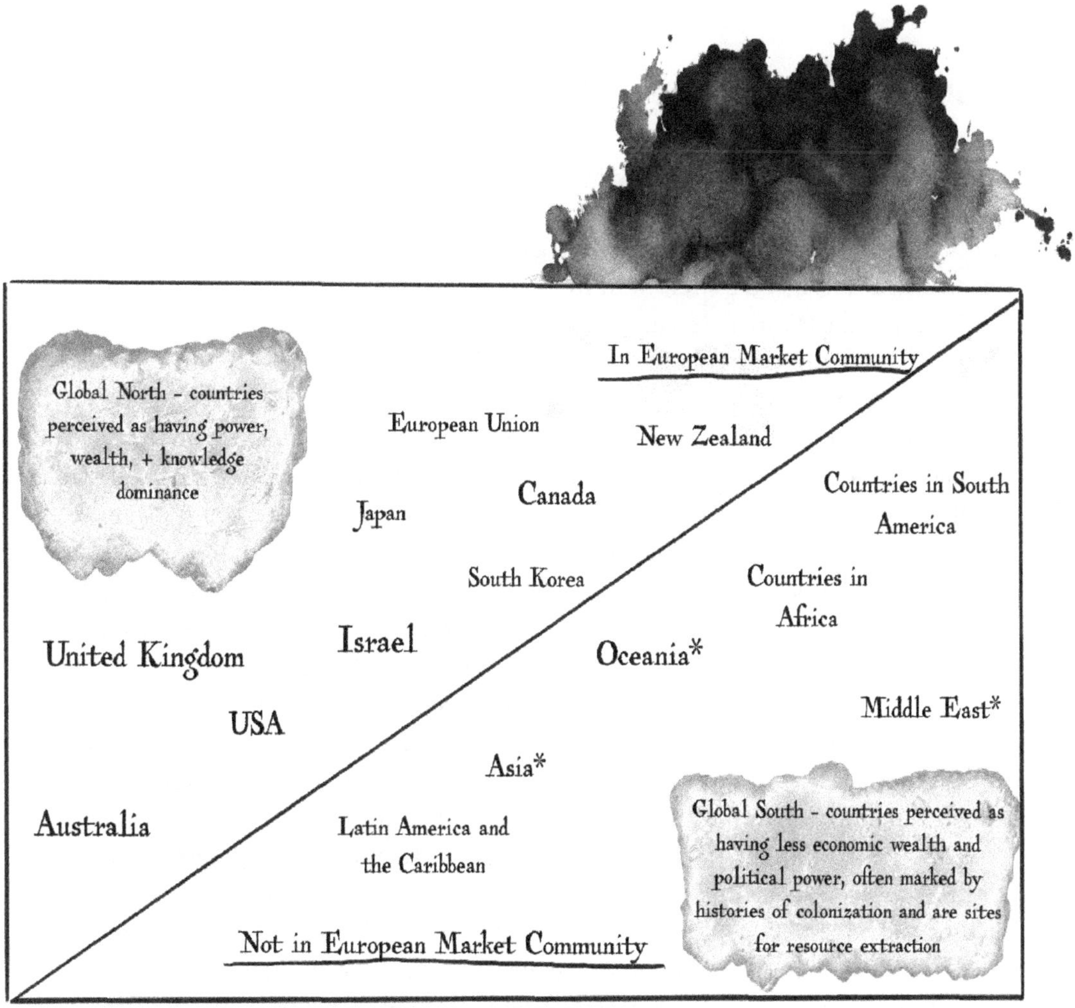

*All countries besides those within the Global North

Figure 6.2—The Global North and the Global South

But white people or those that align with whiteness must always be vigilant that they center actions to deal with racism experienced by BIPOC and not just center themselves as "do-gooders" or victims of antiracism change.[13] Additionally, all health and social care services should challenge whataboutery. Whataboutery is a maneuver to delegitimize and undermine any callouts of racism in the system or service; if not challenged, it enables the continuation of harming people from Black and Marginalized backgrounds and/or with protected characteristics.[14] Unfortunately, the focus on racism and broader health factors tends to fluctuate. Though these issues spark an interest in antiracism and instill hope for meaningful change, the interest in antiracism is often temporary and results in short-lived efforts.

Political Perspectives of Occupational Therapy Practice

Human rights are political because the pursuit of existence involves navigating complex power structures meant to inhibit access for diverse populations. Similarly, healthcare is political because the very lives of various communities are influenced by social determinants and governmental policies. Human rights and healthcare cannot be understood in isolation. Currently, political and societal attitudes in the West are leaning more and more toward the alt-right, often leading to demonizing Marginalized and society's most vulnerable people, including people who are not white, Western, non-disabled, or heterosexual.[15]

Alt-right politics are not just an abstract concept; they are already negatively impacting occupational therapy practice through upholding colonialism. Alt-right policies often prioritize budget cuts to social services and decreased funding for healthcare, directly impacting the availability of occupational therapy services. Additionally, these policies promote a singular cultural narrative undermining the necessity for occupational therapy to be culturally responsive, and resist policy changes aimed at equity and inclusion because these changes are a threat to the status quo. In the United States, there have been various hard-right legislators attempting to appeal the Affordable Care Act (ACA), one of the primary ways many clients access occupational therapy services due to the ACA's expansion of Medicaid, allowing millions of low-income individuals to access rehabilitation services.[16] Additionally, this leadership is leading to cuts in many states, directly influencing access to mental health and disability services. In the UK, the new Labour government is taking harsher sanctions on elderly and Disabled persons by reducing benefits (e.g. support in paying winter bills for the elderly) or reducing maintenance support to "encourage" Disabled persons to look for work.[17]

The existing power structures are not acting responsibly, failing to hold those in positions of power and privilege accountable. There is a lack of antiracism commitment to our healthcare systems operating with a commitment to "do no harm," and in turn, there is a call for antiracism changes in these systems including occupational therapy. Remember, advocates have shared that embedding antiracism into practice improves equitable outcomes not only for clients but also for the practitioners themselves. However, resistance to antiracism change arises from individuals who fear that it could threaten their power and privilege, leading them to perceive antiracism as a personal risk rather than recognizing its potential benefits for everyone. This mindset halts progress toward a more equitable healthcare system and a more just occupational therapy profession.

Critically Exploring Why Occupational Therapy Must Embrace Antiracism

The occupational therapy community must reflect on how colonialism manifests within our profession, and how these corrupted foundations must be examined before pursuing antiracism practices. Simply adding positive initiatives to a broken system will not create meaningful change; we must question our occupational therapy history, our roots, and how racism has influenced occupational therapy from the very beginning.

Kronenberg[18] states it has taken occupational therapy 105 years to acknowledge racism and systemic racism. This interruption/disruption occurred because after father, partner, son, brother, and peer George Floyd was publicly murdered, it became clear to some in the occupational therapy community that the silence from the professional bodies and the majority of the community was showing complicity in the wrongdoing.[19] The silence highlights a privilege that allows the profession to disregard the pain and struggles of Black individuals, betraying that the profession's principles of inclusion, belonging, and justice-infused occupational therapy may be applied to only a select group of people. In partaking in this silence, institutional racism in occupational therapy was exposed, many thanks to BAMEOTUK,[20] DisruptOT, and Justice Based Occupational Therapy.[21] As a result, occupational therapy remains complicit in institutional racism. Performative efforts to address racism in occupational therapy practice have been evident with occupational therapy professional bodies, such as superficial diversity initiatives and a failure to address systemic barriers that BIPOC OTPs experience in education and employment.

The knowledge and episteme of allied health, including occupational therapy, are mostly based on Western and Eurocentric ideas and often overlook cultural differences.[22] Those who were/are denied humanity automatically were/are denied any advantages. Ahmed-Landeryou's paper[23] identified there continues to be a dominance of white leaders, lead authors, and researchers in occupational therapy and science, perpetuating ethnocentrism in the discipline and theory. We need to question why in the US the first and only Black occupational therapist to be awarded the Eleanor Slagle Lecture was in 1969, to Dr. Lela Llorens, PhD,[24] and in the UK the first and only Black occupational therapist to deliver the prestigious Elizabeth Casson Lecture was in 1996, delivered by Elizabeth Yates on equalizing opportunities in occupational therapy.[25] We do not question in the UK why it took until 2022 for Odeth Richardson to be the first Black chair of council to be elected to the Royal College of Occupational Therapists since it became a professional body in 1932. The exploration and explanation of these occurrences lie within the topics of racism, institutional racism, and white supremacy. Ignoring or remaining silent makes the profession further complicit in perpetuating the status quo rather than engaging in antiracism to improve itself, policies, practice, culture, and leadership. Practical implications for supporting antiracism are summarized in Figure 6.3.

OTPs must recognize that engaging in antiracism work is inherently political, philosophical, and requires cultural humility. By doing so, practitioners enable individuals seeking their services to flourish rather than merely exist. As practitioners, we must connect and enhance occupational therapy service delivery and interventions to address and reduce racial and other disparities. To deliver antiracism occupational therapy, we must understand the colonial and Western-focused foundations of contemporary occupational therapy practice and how to make contextual change actions to disrupt its perpetuation.

Colonial Power Influences Within Occupational Therapy

The colonial matrix of power indicates that many contemporary institutional, social, and cultural power relations can be traced back to the structures and cultures established during the colonial period.[26] If the colonial matrix of power is driving the presentation of current knowledge systems, then these systems are also inputting the design and behavior of other systems including occupational therapy services. Quijano[27] frames the actions and impacts of racism through his colonial matrix of power that includes the three key players of colonialism, patriarchy, and racism, and how these key players impact the four intersecting domains to control, oppress, and dominate people (see Figure 6.4).

As a counter to Domain Four, some may say there is the Kawa model of occupational therapy practice as a means to move away from Western-centrism, acknowledging that the Kawa model is notable for integrating Eastern philosophies and ways of knowing into a predominantly Western-centric occupational therapy. However, Wada's[28] criticism of the model is that it perpetuates individualism not collectivism and does not integrate the power of the Japanese concept of belonging in collective communities, *seken*, which refers to the community a person shares their life with. This concept would strengthen the model's claim of including Eastern philosophy, particularly in terms of well-being.

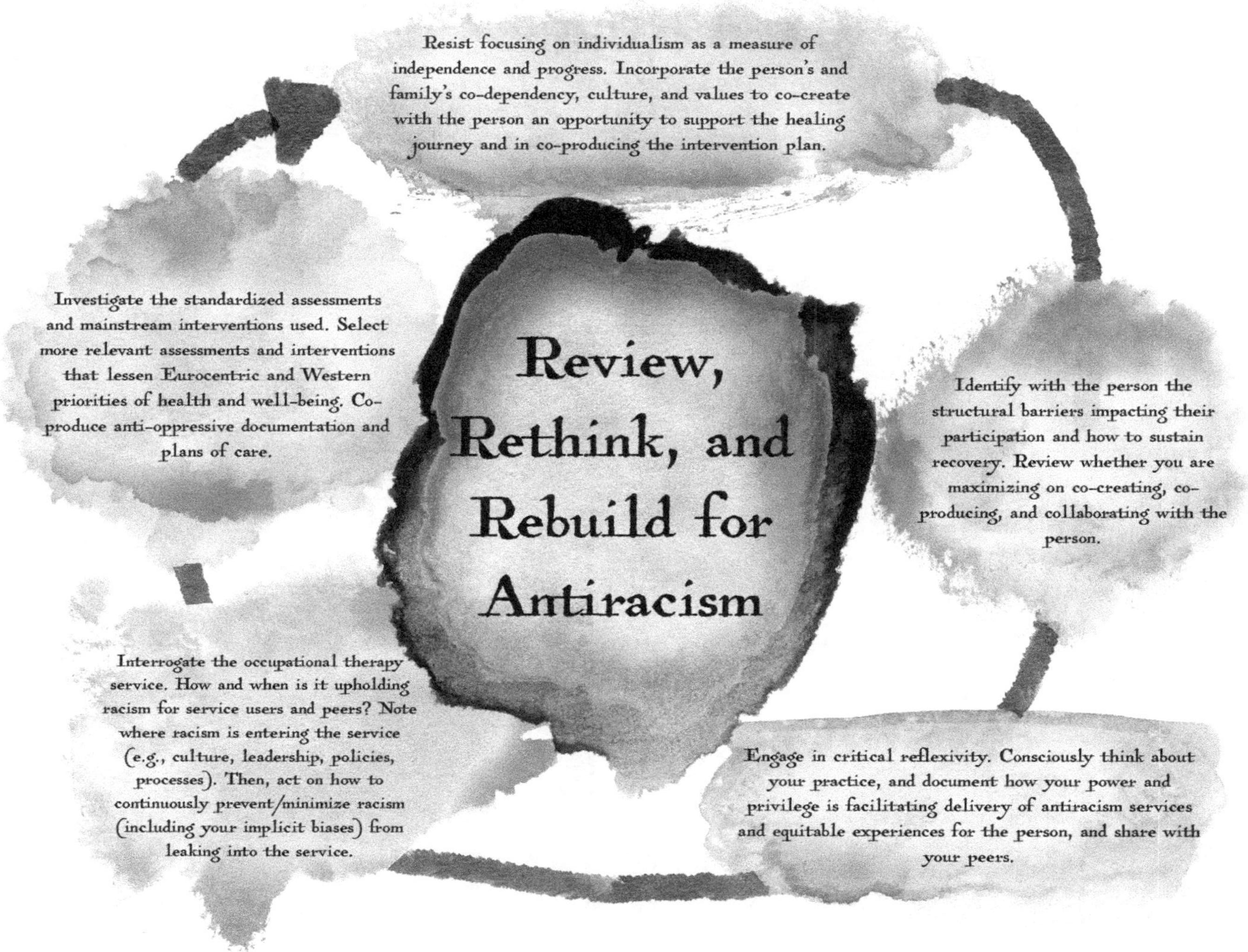

Figure 6.3—Review, Rethink, and Rebuild for Antiracism

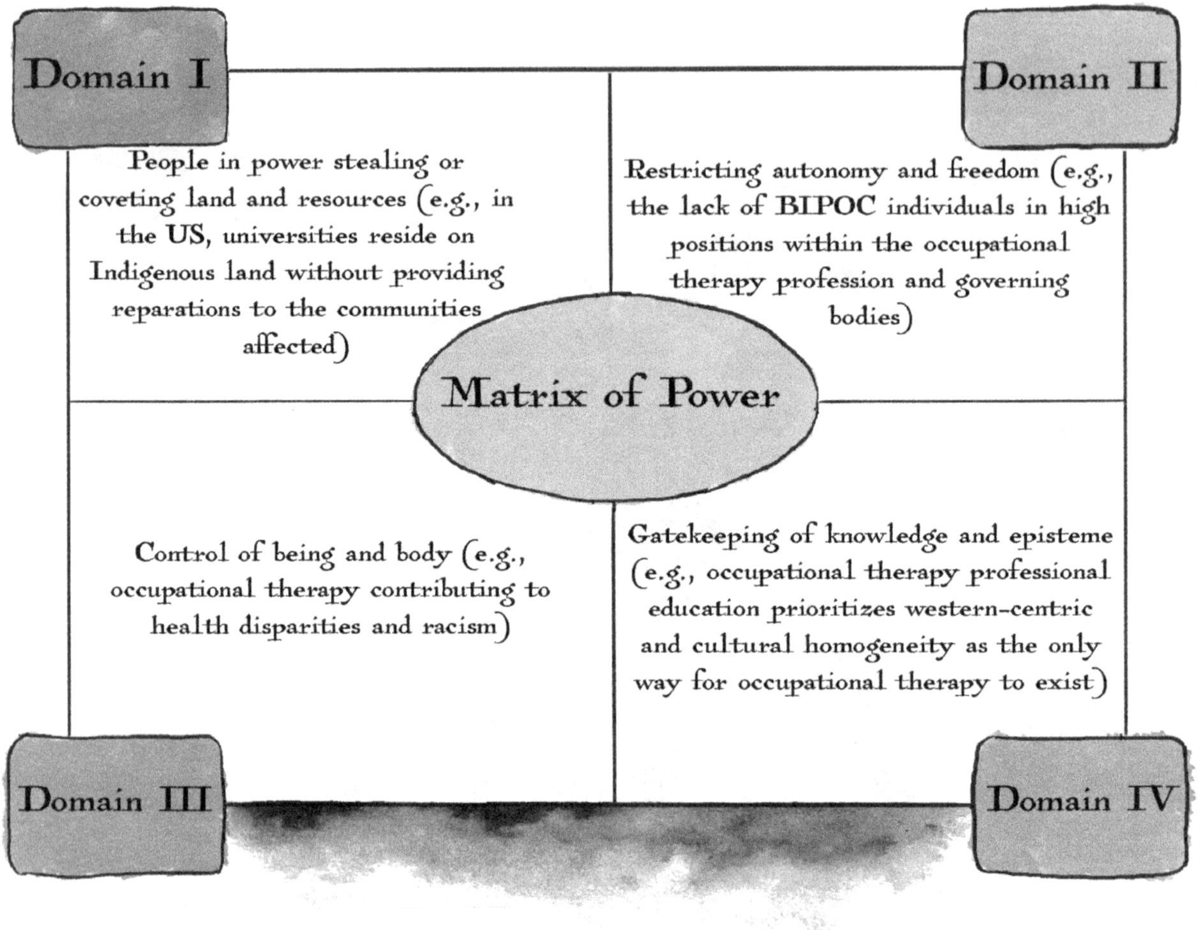

Figure 6.4—Colonial Matrix of Power for Occupational Therapy
Note. Adapted from Quijano.[29]

Occupational therapy promotes itself on the principles of person-centeredness, belonging, and human rights. But how can these principles and values align with the reality of occupational therapy, given that its knowledge and frameworks are predominantly Western-focused and homogeneous? Additionally, the profession lacks staff diversity, e.g. in the UK, USA, and Canada, and there is unchecked and unaccountable racism in practice education toward Black and Marginalized students.[30] The World Federation of Occupational Therapists (WFOT)[31] has a public statement on systemic racism, but it lacks any strategic actions associated with itself or follow-through. This kind of statement indicates that the organization does not see racism as a structural problem within the profession. Remember, the WFOT sanctions occupational therapy courses across the globe, and in doing so supports the recycling of coloniality within courses.

An example of the lack of diversity of occupational therapy registrants can be seen in the data from the Health and Care Professions Council (HCPC), which is the registering body for occupational therapists in the UK. On looking at the data from HCPC,[32] which hasn't changed much over the years, the diversity data shows that 84% of occupational therapists identify as white and 89% as female. We know from the literature that lack of diversity in staff leads to poorer public health outcomes for Black and Marginalized individuals accessing healthcare.[33] Additionally, research shows that when organizations, including those in occupational therapy, effectively and sustainably maintain staff diversity,[34] they benefit from increased creativity and innovation. This, in turn, leads to higher satisfaction among staff and service groups.[35]

The discussion thus far indicates that occupational therapy is perpetuating coloniality and contributing to institutional racism through its Western-centric and ethnocentric knowledge, frameworks, and practices, as well as its lack of diversity within the profession. This exclusivity reflects a supremacist nature in its daily operations. Furthermore, this highlights the need for occupational therapy practice to adopt an antiracism approach. To help readers better identify racism within their practice, Table 6.1 provides examples of racism in occupational therapy practice.

Table 6.1—Specific Examples of Racism Within Occupational Therapy Practice

Aspect of Practice	Example
Evaluation	**Assessment bias**—Assessment tools are evaluated and interpreted from a narrow Western perspective. This excludes service users from non-Western cultures (e.g. those who do not aspire to be independent). Some cultures view maintaining interdependency as a sign of progress, while Western narratives often consider it as an inferior approach. In communities where symbols are more the norm than text, a child may be deemed developmentally delayed by an OTP due to this cultural difference when in reality their communication is effective within their community and culture.
Evaluation	**Eurocentric milestones**—Most standardized assessment tools used by OTPs are normed predominantly on white populations and typically do not have cross-cultural referencing or norming. Underwood et al.[36] further elaborate that when it comes to Indigenous communities, standardized measures and screening tools often pathologize Indigenous ways of living and may wrongly suggest that the children are underdeveloped or the caregivers are struggling with parenting. Such outcomes reinforce harmful stereotypes, and OTPs should identify tools that are culturally responsive or are designed for that individual's community. Examples include the Ethno Cultural Assessment[37] or the Multicultural Mental Health Outcomes and Assessment Tools.[38]

cont.

Aspect of Practice	Example
Intervention	**Resistance to cultural transformation of practice**—When OTPs resist adapting approaches to accommodate the culture of their clients, OTPs reinforce racism in the system, uphold white ignorance,[39] and prioritize whiteness.[40] This is a power play that not only creates barriers for service users to fairly access the service but also sends a message that not all are welcome to receive occupational therapy services. For example, this can lead to taking a person-centered individualistic approach, instead of a family-centered approach to recovery, potentially underserving the person's environmental needs and contributing to occupational injustice.
Intervention	**Ignoring traditional practices**—OTPs may overlook cultural practices central to the client's identity. For example, an OTP with an Indigenous client might dismiss enhancing the treatment journey by incorporating the client's traditional healing practices into intervention planning in favor of Western medical practices. Another example is an OTP who might envision a family structure that is specific to the immediate family, whereas, for example, in many Black, Asian, or Indigenous cultures, family extends to the broader community, and not honoring these communal relationships may undermine the crucial support system to the client's recovery.
Education	**Occupational therapy education is built on Eurocentric theories, principles, and pedagogy**—Adopting an antiracism approach means embracing an intersectional perspective that enhances education rather than diminishes it. For example, for the endpoint assessment methods why not have a variety; if coursework is usually written add an audio recording, or for the PhD oral exam send questions to the student before the oral exam so they are prepared to answer. Thomas and Quinlan[41] identify areas for curriculum improvement, ethnic diversity of students and staff, positive portrayals of ethnic communities, challenging power, and inclusive classroom interactions. Or bringing in theories such as social occupational therapy from Brazil,[42] or Indigenous authors' writings on occupational therapy, into the learning materials.

Antiracism and Neurodiversity

OTPs must address the intersection of race and neurodivergence; you cannot be neurodiversity-affirming without being antiracist, and you cannot fully embrace neurodiversity without addressing the challenges experienced by Neurodivergent individuals of color. The experiences of Neurodivergent individuals are not just impacted by challenges related to systemic barriers pertaining to disability, but also racism. Racism impacts access to resources, treatment, and social inclusion. For example, BIPOC individuals are more likely to experience delayed diagnosis or misdiagnosis because racial biases cause healthcare providers to categorize behaviors as problems if they deviate from white, middle-class cultural norms (e.g. a BIPOC child with characteristics of ADHD may be labeled as simply being behaviorally challenged and judgment is placed on their family). BIPOC individuals are more likely to be met with suspicion and skepticism by healthcare providers, and BIPOC individuals are less likely to be believed regarding their symptoms or when reporting pain to their healthcare providers.[43] This suspicion then extends to healthcare providers labeling BIPOC individuals with the harmful description of being "uncooperative" or "aggressive." The intersection of race and neurodivergence influences a person's lived experience and identity. This complex intersection means that BIPOC Neurodivergent individuals are more likely to face greater stigma and discrimination, which can increase their vulnerability to mental health challenges such as depression, anxiety, and trauma.[44] We also need to recognize the neurodiversity movement itself has much work to do, with neurodiversity still entrenched in whiteness in how it is described and perceived.[45] In a panel discussion that was focused on amplifying Neurodivergent individuals of color, a white Neurodivergent woman expressed discomfort with the panelists "bringing race" into conversations around neurodivergence. Within the article analyzing this interaction, Giwa Onaiwu[46] further elaborates on the "invisibilizing" of BIPOC Neurodivergent individuals:

> "like in nearly everything else, white is the 'default' and everything else is merely Other. White is the foundation upon which neurodiversity rests; white is the standard Neurodivergent individuals are measured against; white is the *de facto* status quo... Whiteness demands that it must be the sole focus at all times, then naturally white people must also be the sole focus at all times, and anything that does not perpetually center this toxic whiteness is perceived as a threat... In reality, however, experiences like those *(white Neurodivergent individuals expressing outrage to intersectional conversations on disability)* are the norm, and are unfortunately representative of the erasure, disregard, and dismissal people of color encounter from members of our neurodiversity community on a daily basis. They are, at least in part, the reason why so few of us remain visible and active in the public discourse surrounding neurodiversity."

OTPs must recognize the complexity of their clients' identities and experiences, and OTPs cannot fully embrace neurodiversity without addressing the challenges experienced by Neurodivergent individuals of color and interconnections to racism. Failing to acknowledge the ways racism, ableism, and neurodivergence intersect and the discriminations and disparities that can occur only perpetuates and reinforces systemic injustices.

Suggestions on How to Deliver Antiracism Occupational Therapy Practice

To disrupt the status quo of institutional racism and ethnocentrism to transform into an antiracism occupational therapy practice, OTPs need a systems approach.

This includes micro- (individual), meso- (e.g. education, practice, research, professional body), and macro- (e.g. regulator, government) levels. The focus of this section will be on two of the three levels, the micro- and meso-levels.

Micro-Level

To be able to see the change needed in occupational therapy, individuals have to commit to unlearning and learning themselves and changing their practice:

1. A present and active critical thinker. Start by acknowledging institutional racism exists and learn and unlearn the part you have played in its continuation. The critical thinker is combining different questions to create multiple actions; see Table 6.2 for different areas to ask questions. This type of thinker knows that reflection into action is connected to knowledge and understanding of the problems of theory and their practice in the pursuit of social justice. Chapter 8 dives further into how to be a critically reflexive OTP.

2. Being a change agent. Make antiracism change matter to you on a personal level and do some work on yourself because it is the right thing to do. A change agent is an activist, not an advocate. An activist is a person who is there "engaging in action or involvement as a means of achieving political, social, economic, cultural, or environmental goals with the desire to make changes in society toward a perceived greater good,"[47] whereas an advocate negotiates for, recommends for, and supports a person, cause, or policy.[48] As an occupational therapy staff or student, it is important that you are not silent or hiding in the shadows for others to act justly for antiracism in occupational therapy. For three accessible action steps you can do to start your antiracism journey, see Table 6.2. Your silence and inaction do not make you neutral but demonstrate complicity in keeping with the status quo of institutional racism and ethnocentrism in the profession and knowledge.

3. You don't have to do activism alone; it involves building relationships, collaborating for social change, shifting power, and holding occupational therapy accountable for being antiracist. Find those support networks that will enable you to become an activist, where you feel safe to be vulnerable, share knowledge, and be able to apply your established professional skills to contribute to social change.[49]

4. Inform your professional body and regulators that institutional racism, ethnocentrism, and white supremacy must not be allowed to persist in the profession, practice, education, and research of occupational therapy.

Hold them accountable and ensure they take responsibility for promoting antiracism in the profession as part of a unified collaboration. Collaborate with Marginalized-led OTP groups to co-create and co-produce position statements with your professional bodies for them to operationalize.

Meso-Level

The meso-level focuses on the communities, services, and organizations, and their interactions and connectivity within occupational therapy. In this section, we will apply the antiracism principles, guidance, and toolkit provided by the Wellcome Trust, summarized on page four of their guide.[50] These principles can also be contextually relevant to all organizations and services.

The document identifies five "to do" areas: i) prioritize, ii) investigate, iii) involve Black and Marginalized people, iv) counteract racism, and v) make measurable progress. The Wellcome Trust emphasizes that organizations must dedicate time and effort to achieve structural change and allow workers the time away from their regular duties to engage in antiracism efforts.[51] This applies equally to occupational therapists and their services. Nearly all health and social care places have a zero-tolerance statement, or something similar, regarding racism and discrimination as part of their diversity, equity, and inclusion strategy. However, these strategies have not stopped racism, racial harassment, racial discrimination, and more within the workplace regarding staff[52,53] and service users.[54] For antiracism to be genuinely embedded within occupational therapy services, organizational boards and leaders must develop strategies that outline a comprehensive antiracism action plan. This includes allocating funds, resources, and appointing a manager along with a task team dedicated to implementing the strategy as an ongoing effort, rather than a one-time initiative, and ensuring it is integrated into the annual budget and planning.[55] There is no one-size-fits-all strategy for implementing antiracism within the workplace. Strategies need to be contextualized to people and place. The occupational therapy service antiracism strategy must align with the corporate strategy.

An Example of a Potential Occupational Therapy Service Antiracism Strategy

- An overarching vision—"Our vision is to cultivate an equitable and inclusive occupational therapy service that actively embodies antiracism."
- The mission statement could be "By aligning our occupational therapy service strategy with our corporate strategy, we will foster a culture of collaboration and accountability, ensuring that every aspect of our practice contributes to dismantling systemic racism and promoting social justice in healthcare."

- The core values could be being responsive, compassionate, and engaging in active listening and antiracism actions.
- The strategic actions (typically outlined within a time frame of five years) could include embedding antiracism in service delivery, clinical practices, organizational culture, and quality care, among other areas.

Without those in positions of power prioritizing antiracism efforts, it becomes challenging to start, let alone gain momentum, for authentic change. OTPs must identify a person in power to support their antiracism work for impact and sustainability, as Dobbin et al.'s[56] research identified for corporate America.

Example of Methods to Employ for a Potential Occupational Therapy Service Antiracism Strategy

Identify what policies, practices, and processes are enabling racism in the system. An example of an institutionally racist policy comes from a non-profit group called Ladders for Action, which noted that UKRI research grants for COVID-19 were not awarded to any projects led by Black individuals.[57] Ladders for Action found that grant applications were associated with well-known white researchers, whether this was intentional or not. To address inequities due to institutional racism, we must collect and analyze data to understand the disparities in health outcomes and staff career progression within your service, while also considering the diversity of your team. This analysis involves disaggregated data, which helps to reveal differences among various groups. By gathering this information, we can begin to examine the underlying culture, practices, and processes at play within the workplace. Examples of data collection methods include:

- distributing surveys and questionnaires to clients and staff to gather information about their experiences and perceptions related to care and workplace culture
- completing regular audits and reviews of service delivery to assess the diversity of staff and identify areas of improvement
- creating key performance indicators related to diversity, equity, and inclusion, and regularly measuring progress against these metrics.

Regarding data, be explicit about what data is being collected to be transparent as to why this data is collected, and be sensitive to the histories of colonial harm in relation to the data.[58] The data collected must be mixed (i.e. quantitative and qualitative) to gain a deeper understanding of the specific context, which helps to identify patterns and trends within the service. This process isn't always about generating new data; it can involve analyzing existing data to uncover what is excluded, what remains invisible, and who benefits or suffers from these dynamics.

To explicitly see the reality from the data it must be disaggregated and you need the data to analyze the reality. For example, to understand in your service where the disparities are in health outcomes and staff career progression, analyze the diversity of the team. By collecting this data, you start to investigate the culture, practice, and processes. You might notice that a specific assessment or intervention strategy has poorer outcomes for Black and Marginalized groups. This discovery could then prompt you to explore why this may be happening and be diligent about assessment tools and intervention strategies that honor BIPOC lives and culture. An example from my workplace is we provide the questions to job interviewees before the interview, and we added an equity question because our staff diversity was not improving. We were seeing diverse sets of applicants but following the interview white peers were being appointed to the positions. Today, our staff diversity has changed from 12% to 39%.

Service design, policies, practices, and work culture are created by humans and can be dismantled and restructured by teams. By doing these checks and balances and exposing racism, it builds up a realistic picture of what is hindering and enabling the antiracism approach within the service. This understanding allows for the development of a targeted plan for change that is tailored to the specific context of the service.

Ways to Bring People with You for Successful Antiracism Strategy

This is fundamental: any antiracism work includes collaboration with those directly affected by the current policies and practices of the service and ensuring their participation throughout the entire process. When collaborating with Black and Marginalized individuals, groups, or communities, be cognizant of historical wrongs and of being extractive of free labor, and be humble. Do not pressure them; instead, work around their commitments and needs, provide choices that enable their participation, go to them rather than expecting them to come to you, and don't expect them to conform to the organization's agenda. Above all, be respectful.

Start by bringing the racial literacy of the staff to a standard base level of acceptability, provide annual antiracism training, and measure their progress through their professional development objectives. Make sure to evaluate your service through a culturally aware framework (e.g. such as the Global Critical Race and Racism Framework),[59] then act and identify and apply racial equity measures for service evaluation and accountability. The reference list at the end of this chapter can be viewed as a list of resources, and the author of this chapter delivers a bespoke antiracism workplace transformation workshop.*

Resist, interrupt, and disrupt racial inequity through positive action. Positive action means taking steps to equalize the accessibility to opportunities within environments that are discriminating and disadvantaging people with protected

* https://shortcourses.lsbu.ac.uk/consultancy/organisational-development

characteristics. In the UK, protected characteristics include "age, disability, gender reassignment, marriage and civil partnership, pregnancy and maternity, race (including ethnic or national origins, color, and nationality), religion or belief (including lack of belief), sex, and sexual orientation."[60] Examples of positive actions are: mentoring with racialized matching, additional training, reconstructing the application form content (so that only skills, qualifications, and references are required and no CV is needed), reframing the interview process so questions are given to the applicant prior to the interview, and making sure that there is artificial intelligence (AI) available to help communicate with people who are not English speaking. Positive action is not positive discrimination, as the latter is choosing someone based solely on their protected characteristics, which is illegal. See a summary of the micro-, meso-levels of antiracism change for occupational therapy in Table 6.2.

Table 6.2—Applying Micro-Level and Meso-Level Antiracism Practices Within Occupational Therapy

Micro-Level	
Critical thinker:	*Questions to answer to help develop practice action/s:*
i) Reasoning applying the skills of analysis, evaluation, and logical arguments learned in education and applied in relation to antiracism practice	How am I delivering equitable delivery of practice? If I am delivering equitable service delivery, am I able to document the actions I am taking?
ii) Engaging in reflexivity	How does who I am create a power difference between me and my peers and service users and how could that create or not create a safe space?
iii) Interrogating self-beliefs	Why do I think there is equality between a white person with neurodiversity and a Black/Brown/Indigenous person with neurodiversity in opportunities?
iv) Own values	My values are about respecting all people and enabling their dignity, but why do I not engage in speaking out when I see this not happening at work?
v) Existing knowledge	Assessments are based on specific white majority populations; what am I doing to make sure I am using the relevant assessment to match the person in front of me?
vi) Worldviews	Occupational therapy is based on the colonial yardstick, so what can I do in my work to interrupt this?
vii) Doing action for the continuous development of an antiracist environment	How are you showing citizenship, challenging assumptions and falsehoods, and contributing to transforming inequity due to power structures and practices?

Being a change agent—questions for change to develop accessible actions:
i) Why haven't I engaged in this change? I need to list actions I want/need to take toward antiracism change. Then I must co-create action in changing with stakeholders and peers with reference to the list, and document what I do and the outcomes.
ii) How am I committing myself to reading a book or article a year specifically to unlearn and learn? Think about how to apply this in my work and try what I read in my practice, document what happened, and keep the cycle going, reading, planning, testing, evaluating, changing, and doing again. For example, I could suggest a monthly antiracism workshop.
iii) Who in power can I access to support and resource my antiracism change work? I identify the people at work who can support me in the change-making and hold people accountable if they are not being responsible in evolving their antiracism practice.

Meso-Level

Wellcome Trust Antiracist Guidance and Toolkit[61]

Do:	*Action for occupational therapy:*
i) Prioritize—Insist that the organization must make the time and effort for structural change and enable the workers to have time away from their chores to do the antiracism approach.	The occupational therapy services build in space within work time for antiracism task and finish projects, to be co-developed, delivered, monitored, evaluated, and further developed.
ii) Investigate—Insist that for staff who are involved in the antiracism work for change, time is allocated and protected away from their daily chores, and a timeline is composed and shared for implementation.	It is important to interrogate the service to fully understand what aspects of the occupational therapy service are delivering the antiracism approach and what is hindering delivering the approach. This is from identifying where and what are the racial inequity pattern/s being seen in the data. You need to map the policies and processes of the service end to end, who and what, especially from the viewpoints of all stakeholders, deliverers, and receivers of the service.
iii) Involve people of color (I appreciate this term is not acceptable to all, but it is used in the document)—This is fundamental. No antiracism redesign should be devoid of collaborating with the very people harmed by the current services' policies, practices, and processes, from the beginning with everyone involved.	Those who come to the table and are service users or unwaged volunteers should be paid, so as not to replay the colonial master–slave relationships, keeping the power dynamic unequally within the organization.[62] Center the individuals, groups, and communities' voices; don't make them the problem solvers. Those harmed by the system shouldn't bear the burden of fixing it. Change should be a collaborative effort, with the primary responsibility for action resting on the organization.

cont.

Do:	*Action for occupational therapy:*
iv) Counteract racism—Visibly "counteract racism by taking positive action or other targeted approaches to redress racial inequity" (p. 14).	Again, map and record when, where, and what actions have been taken to counteract racism. Enacting the antiracism approach will lead to identifying patterns and trends to keep on developing and evolving to disrupt institutional racism and coloniality in the occupational therapy service.
v) Make measurable progress—People in power should make transparent what measures have collaboratively been decided upon to demonstrate antiracism impact.	Staff should push the service and organization with stretch goals of progress annually to rapidly counter racism. Leaders hold the power to be responsible in delivering antiracism occupational therapy, such that measuring progress holds the service and organization accountable toward racial equity.

The macro level is not included within the book itself as this is more about leadership, boards, and management, and this chapter focuses on practice. However, there is a supplemental download in the Vault that provides this information.

In essence, taking an intersectionality approach can help counteract racism. This concept, pushed forward by Professor Crenshaw in her doctoral research and work on critical legal studies, examines how a person's intersecting identities, such as race and sex, can lead to discrimination and disadvantage in relation to the law, policies, practices, and cultural norms.[63] By taking this approach to expose and address structural disadvantages and institutional racism, we can begin to foster an antiracism culture shift in occupational therapy.

Intersectionality has been referenced as an important component of neurodiversity (historically, intersectionality is one of the paradigm's building blocks), though the intersectionality of race and neurodivergence has been rarely explored. This has contributed to the overrepresentation of whiteness in the neurodiversity movement, which is designated "white neurodiversity." What can we do? Well, explore literature explaining how mainstream definitions of neurodiversity are a Global North ideal, and discover and understand other global ideas of the bodymind experience (or alternatives to neurodiversity to supplement what you thought you knew about neurodiversity). Ensure your resources about neurodiversity and the movement include diverse voices, such as highlighting Indigenous and Global South perspectives.[64]

Conclusion

This chapter is calling on the occupational therapy community to act now for antiracism change and for occupational therapy governance to align with antiracism praxis. It is not enough for the occupational therapy community to publish statements of solidarity regarding the injustices experienced by Black and Marginalized individuals and communities and then hope that this will be enough as an act of allyship. We in occupational therapy, our leaders, and our institutions are people in positions of power. We are people with privilege who continue working in systems designed to be institutionally racist and colonial, resulting in racial and health disparities also marginalize Neurodivergent individuals and uphold norms of ableism. If we in the occupational therapy community do not take action to disrupt the system for change, we become complicit in its continuance and the status quo. Make change meaningful to leaders, boards, and the occupational therapy community at large by linking the change needed to aspects such as reputation, salary, and opportunity. When change is valued, it translates into action that can be monitored, evaluated, and measured over time. Black and Marginalized people experiencing injustice in health and social care seek change actions from the occupational therapy profession, not just empty words or platitudes. Actions clearly communicate that we, as a community, are ready to commit to consciously and conscientiously initiating antiracism and neurodiversity-affirming change to disrupt the continuance of ongoing practices that perpetuate harmful ethnic neutrality.

Endnotes

1 Grosfoguel, R. (2016). What is racism? *Journal of World-Systems Research*, *22*(1), 9–15. http://dx.doi.org/10.5195/jwsr.2016.609

2 ibid.

3 Sowemimo, A. (2023). *Divided, racism, medicine and why we need to decolonise healthcare*. Wellcome Collection.

4 Grosfoguel, R. (2016). What is racism? *Journal of World-Systems Research*, *22*(1), 9–15. http://dx.doi.org/10.5195/jwsr.2016.609

5 Christian, M. (2019). A global critical race and racism framework: Racial entanglements and deep and malleable whiteness. *Sociology of Race and Ethnicity*, *5*(2), 169–185. https://doi.org/10.1177/2332649218783220

6 Underwood, K., Ineese-Nash, N., & Haché, A. (2019). Colonialism in early education, care, and intervention: A knowledge synthesis. *Journal of Childhood Studies*, *44*(4), 21–35. https://doi.org/10.18357/jcs444201919209

7 Ahmed-Landeryou, M. J. (2023). A critical reflection from inside, looking back and forward: Theorising perspectives on decolonising occupational science theory and practice. *Journal of Occupational Science*, *31*(1), 32–46. https://doi.org/10.1080/14427591.2023.2246986

8 ibid, pp. 172–175.

9 ibid.

10 Santos, B. (2016). *Epistemologies of the south, justice against epistemicide*. Routledge.

11 Tuhiwai Smith, L. (2012). *Decolonizing methodologies: Research and Indigenous peoples* (2nd ed.). Zed Books.

12 ibid, p. 22.

13 Gillborn, D. (2024). *White lies: Racism, education and critical race theory*. Routledge.

14 Ganguly, M. (2017). Engaging in "whataboutery" instead of protecting rights. *Brown Journal of World Affairs*, *XXIV*(1), 39–52. www.hrw.org/news/2018/03/01/engaging-whataboutery-instead-protecting-rights

15 Norris, P. (2022, November 1). A powerful theory of why the far right is thriving across the globe. *New York Times*. www.nytimes.com/2022/11/01/opinion/ezra-klein-podcast-pippa-norris.html

16 Pritchard, K. T., Fisher, G., McGee Rudnitsky, K., & Ramirez, R. D. (2019). Policy and payment

changes create new opportunities for occupational therapy in acute care. *The American Journal of Occupational Therapy: Official Publication of the American Occupational Therapy Association, 73*(2), 7302109010p1–7302109010p8. https://doi.org/10.5014/ajot.2018.732002

17 Sharland, H. (2024). Reeves just confirmed Labour is carrying on dangerous DWP WCA reforms. *The Canary*. www.thecanary.co/uk/news/2024/10/30/dwp-wca-changes-autumn-budget

18 Kronenberg, F. (2020, November 26). *Systemic racism in occupational therapy: Dealing with the skeleton in our closets* [Video]. YouTube. www.youtube.com/watch?v=NwlcdG65e5k

19 BAMEOTUK. (2021, March 26). *Let's talk white supremacy and occupational therapy—Episode 9* [Video]. YouTube. www.youtube.com/watch?v=5kZ77S-inyl&t=4107s

20 ibid.

21 Justice Based Occupational Therapy [@JusticeOT1]. (2020, June 17). The murder of a Black man, George Floyd, by a White police officer was not the first, but one of many [Tweet]. Twitter. https://x.com/JusticeOT1/status/1273312742942875654

22 Nancarrow, S., & Borthwick, A. (2021). *The allied health professions: A sociological perspective*. Policy Press.

23 Ahmed-Landeryou, M. J. (2023). A critical reflection from inside, looking back and forward: Theorising perspectives on decolonising occupational science theory and practice. *Journal of Occupational Science, 31*(1), 32–46. https://doi.org/10.1080/14427591.2023.2246986

24 American Occupational Therapy Association (AOTA). (2024). *AOTA spotlights history of Black occupational therapy practitioners during Black History Month*. www.aota.org/about/for-the-media/aota-news/aota-spotlights-history-of-black-otps-during-black-history-month

25 Yates, J. E. (1996). The Casson memorial lecture 1996: Equalising opportunities. *British Journal of Occupational Therapy, 59*(8), 352–356. https://doi.org/10.1177/030802269605900802

26 Quijano, A. (2000). Coloniality of power, eurocentrism and Latin America. *Nepantla: Views from the South, 1*(3), 533–580. https://edisciplinas.usp.br/pluginfile.php/347342/mod_resource/content/1/Quijano%20(2000)%20Colinality%20of%20power.pdf

27 ibid.

28 Wada, M. (2011). Strengthening the Kawa model: Japanese perspectives on person, occupation, and environment. *Canadian Journal of Occupational Therapy, 78*(4), 230–236. https://doi.org/10.2182/cjot.2011.78.4.4

29 ibid.

30 Tayson, S., Miller, O., & Mutsvairo, V. T. (2024). Experiences of racism in occupational therapy clinical placement settings. In M. J. Ahmed-Landeryou (Ed.), *Antiracist occupational therapy: Unsettling the status quo* (pp. 84–100). Jessica Kingsley Publishers.

31 World Federation of Occupational Therapists (WFOT). (2021). *WFOT statement on systemic racism*. https://wfot.org/wfot-statement-on-systemic-racism

32 Health Professions and Care Council (HCPC). (2024). *Diversity data occupational therapists January 2024*. www.hcpc-uk.org/resources/data/2024/diversity-data-occupational-therapists-2024

33 Bradley, E. H. (2020). Diversity, inclusive leadership, and health outcomes. *International Journal of Health Policy and Management, 9*(7), 266–268. https://doi.org/10.15171/ijhpm.2020.12

34 Dobbin, F., Kalev, A., & Kelly, E. (2007). Diversity management in corporate America. *Contexts, 6*(4), 21–27. https://doi.org/10.1525/ctx.2007.6.4.21

35 McKinsey & Company. (2023). *Diversity matters even more: The case for holistic impact*. McKinsey & Company. www.mckinsey.com/featured-insights/diversity-and-inclusion/diversity-matters-even-more-the-case-for-holistic-impact

36 Underwood, K., Ineese-Nash, N., & Haché, A. (2019). Colonialism in early education, care, and intervention: A knowledge synthesis. *Journal of Childhood Studies, 44*(4), 21–35. https://doi.org/10.18357/jcs444201919209

37 Finley, L. Y. (1990). *Ethno cultural assessment*. PRIME Institute. www.psychrehabassociation.org/sites/default/files/series-documents/ho_3_multicultural_assessment_guide.pdf

38 Transcultural Mental Health Centre. (n.d.). *Multicultural mental health outcomes and assessment tools*. www.dhi.health.nsw.gov.au/transcultural-mental-health-centre-tmhc/resources/multicultural-mental-health-outcomes-and-assessment-tools

39 Mills, C. W. (2007). White ignorance. In S. Sullivan & N. Tuana (Eds.), *Race and epistemologies of ignorance* (pp. 11–38). State University of New York Press.

40 Gillborn, D. (2024). *White lies: Racism, education and critical race theory*. Routledge.

41 Thomas, D. S. P., & Quinlan, K. M. (2022). Reimagining curricula: Effects of cultural (in) sensitivity of curricula on racially minoritised students' engagement. *Studies in Higher Education, 48*(2), 283–298. https://doi.org/10.1080/03075079.2022.2134332

42 Lopes, R. S., & Malfitano, A. P. S. (2020). *Social occupational therapy: Theoretical and practical designs*. Elsevier.

43 Hamed, S., Bradby, H., Ahlberg, B. M., & Thapar-Björkert, S. (2022). Racism in healthcare:

A scoping review. *BMC Public Health, 22*(1). https://doi.org/10.1186/s12889-022-13122-y

44 Horner-Johnson, W., Akobirshoev, I., Amutah-Onukagha, N. N., Slaughter-Acey, J. C., & Mitra, M. (2021). Preconception health risks among US women: Disparities at the intersection of disability and race or ethnicity. *Women's Health Issues: Official Publication of the Jacobs Institute of Women's Health, 31*(1), 65–74. https://doi.org/10.1016/j.whi.2020.10.001

45 Giwa Onaiwu, M. (2020). I, too, sing neurodiversity. *The Journal of Autistic Culture, 2*(1), 58–67. https://doi.org/10.9707/2833-1508.1048

46 ibid, pp. 62–65.

47 Fila, M. (2021). How I became an activist lesson plan. *Global Feminism Project, University of Michigan*. https://sites.lsa.umich.edu/globalfeminisms/how-i-became-an-activist-lesson-plan-2

48 ibid.

49 Brian, H., Cook, S., Taylor, D., Freeman, L., Mundy, T., & Killaspy, H. (2015). Occupational therapists as change agents in multidisciplinary teams. *British Journal of Occupational Therapy, 78*(90), 547–555. https://doi.org/10.1177/0308022615586785

50 Puvanendran, K., Agbalaya, T., & Christies, S. (2021). *Anti-racist principles, guidance and toolkit*. Wellcome Trust. https://cms.wellcome.org/sites/default/files/2021-06/Wellcomes-Anti-racist-principles-and-toolkit-2021.pdf

51 ibid.

52 NHS England. (2024). *Workforce race equality standard 2023*. www.england.nhs.uk/publication/nhs-workforce-race-equality-standard-2023-data-analysis-report-for-nhs-trusts

53 Beagan, B. L., Sibbald, K. R., Bizzeth, S. R., & Pride, T. M. (2022). Systemic racism in Canadian occupational therapy: A qualitative study with therapists. *Canadian Journal of Occupational Therapy, 8*(1), 51–61. https://doi.org/10.1177/00084174211066676

54 NPEU. (2023). *MBRRACE-UK perinatal confidential enquiry: A comparison of the care of Asian, Black and White women who have experienced a stillbirth or neonatal death*. www.npeu.ox.ac.uk/mbrrace-uk/reports

55 Dobbin, F., Kalev, A., & Kelly, E. (2007). Diversity management in corporate America. *Contexts, 6*(4), 21–27. https://doi.org/10.1525/ctx.2007.6.4.21

56 ibid.

57 Adelaine, A. (2020). *Knowledge is power—an open letter to UKRI*. www.researchprofessionalnews.com/rr-news-uk-views-of-the-uk-2020-8-knowledge-is-power-an-open-letter-to-ukri

58 Sowemimo, A. (2023). *Divided, racism, medicine and why we need to decolonise healthcare*. Wellcome Collection.

59 Christian, M. (2019). A global critical race and racism framework: Racial entanglements and deep and malleable whiteness. *Sociology of Race and Ethnicity, 5*(2), 169–185. https://doi.org/10.1177/2332649218783220

60 Skills Development Scotland. (2020). *A guide to positive action 2020/2021*. Skills Development Scotland. www.skillsdevelopmentscotland.co.uk/media/q2ge1wem/a-guide-to-positive-action.pdf, p. 4.

61 Puvanendran, K., Agbalaya, T., & Christies, S. (2021). *Anti-racist principles, guidance and toolkit*. Wellcome Trust. https://cms.wellcome.org/sites/default/files/2021-06/Wellcomes-Anti-racist-principles-and-toolkit-2021.pdf

62 Ahmed-Landeryou, M. (2023). Developing an evidence-informed decolonising curriculum wheel—A reflective piece. *Equity in Education & Society, 2*(2), 157–180. https://doi.org/10.1177/27526461231154014

63 Crenshaw, K. (2016, December 7). *The urgency of intersectionality* [Video]. YouTube. www.youtube.com/watch?v=akOe5-UsQ2o

64 Nair, V. K. K., Farah, W., & Boveda, M. (2024). Is neurodiversity a Global Northern white paradigm? *Autism: The International Journal of Research and Practice*. https://doi.org/10.1177/13623613241280835

CHAPTER 7

Strengths-Based Approaches

Foundations for Practice and Anti-Ableist Occupational Therapy Education

KAVITHA MURTHI AND KRISTIE K. PATTEN

Background

Ableism is a form of pervasive structural discrimination and prejudice that is intended to classify and segregate Disabled communities in favor of normative standards of structure and functioning.[1,2] By exercising control through division, ableism has ideologically contributed to creating a world that perpetuates harm and exploitation of Disabled communities so certain groups can hold onto privileges associated with position in society, wealth, and power through its manifestation as professional biases.[3,4]

Raymaker[5] asserted that the Neurodivergent and intellectual disability communities are "The last to benefit from civil rights gains." Milton et al.[6] emphasized that the unique abilities and perspectives of Autistic and other Neurodivergent individuals continue to be framed as deficits. Healthcare professionals, including occupational therapy practitioners (OTPs), often design "interventions" to alter these differences, driven by a goal to normalize Neurodivergent individuals rather than embrace their neurodivergence.[7] As described in Chapter 2, this discrimination and subjugation is perpetuated by bias, which is either covert and explicitly perpetuated or implicit and internalized as demonstrated through unconscious bias.[8] Practices for Neurodivergent communities rooted in ableism often shape research development, subsequently influencing educational approaches and policies.[9] Hence, the community has consistently called on researchers and practitioners to acknowledge their unique differences and actively involve them in addressing challenges collaboratively through the incorporation of their strengths or capabilities.[10,11]

To foster practices that recognize and celebrate the strengths of Neurodivergent communities, Murthi et al.[12] emphasize three key factors that were developed from critically examining Neurodivergent individuals' priorities about strengths-based practices: presuming competence, building authentic partnerships, and fostering collaboration across research, education, and practice. These principles can be applied to a variety of these communities. Additionally, strengths-based practices advocate for creating safe and supportive environments that enable Neurodivergent individuals to explore, practice, and apply their unique strengths.[13] Figure 7.1 illustrates the strengths-based principles and Table 7.1 offers practical examples of their application in occupational therapy. In this chapter, we will incorporate the principles of strengths-based practice using a relational lens, holistic perspective, and constructive cooperation.

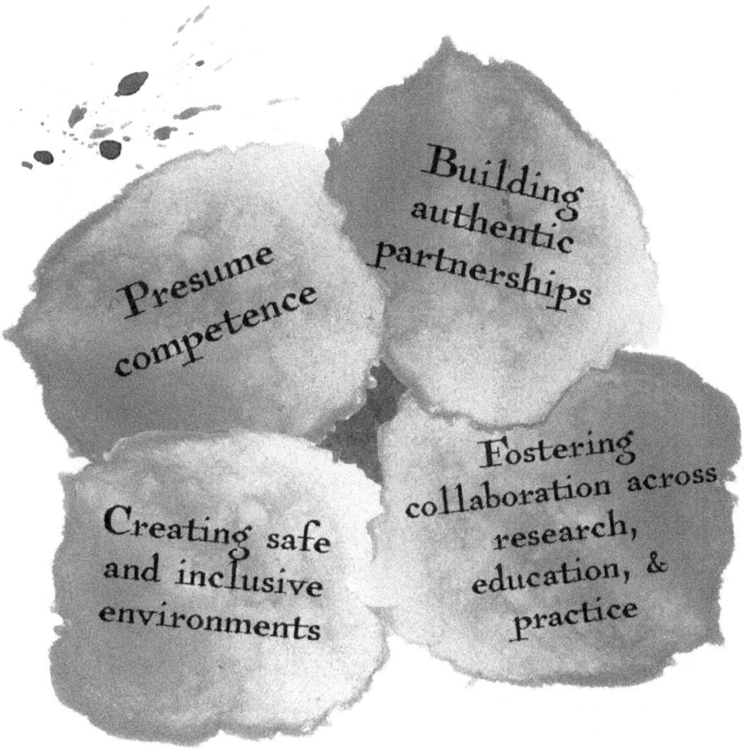

Figure 7.1—Principles of Strengths-Based Approaches

What Encompasses Strengths-Based Practice?

We should emphasize the significance of creating a paradigm shift when considering incorporating elements of strengths-based practice. Transitioning from viewing deficits as central to Disabled communities and fully acknowledging their abilities and challenges could be the first step toward developing practices focusing on strengths. Once we shift away from centering our practices around deficits, we can view ourselves as supporters rather than facilitators or correctors who seek to eliminate disabilities from Disabled communities. Then the next question is: *Can every OTP value the strengths of their clients? If so, how can we do that?*

To answer these questions, we want to start by recognizing Patten's[14] call to action in her Eleanor Clarke Slagle Lecture to "Be willing to be wrong, be curious, be better," so we can interrogate our occupational therapy practice and research standards for biases as a professional community. Only through critical interrogation and questioning personal choices and clinical judgments can every OTP move beyond the limitations of the medical model of disability.

We must heed Patten's call and start by *unlearning* what we have been socialized to learn as practitioners. We need to give up our position as experts on disability and accept that we need to learn from the lived experiences of our clients and service users.

Strengths-based practices are defined in many ways by a variety of health professions. In the broadest perspective, they align with value-based practices, including practices that combine elements from the person's lived experiences, capabilities, and contemporary evidence.[15] When we explored strengths-based practice specifically for the Autistic community using a content analysis approach from a roundtable discussion with Autistic community members, we noted that the community highlighted presumption of competence, authentic and organic collaboration in education, research, and practice, and creation of supportive environments as pillars of strengths-based practice.[16,17] Building on this understanding, it is important to recognize that strengths-based theory and practice do not dismiss challenges or deficits. Instead, they encourage OTPs and researchers to adopt a nuanced perspective that acknowledges challenges while emphasizing the capacities and resources of individuals, groups, and organizations.[18]

Table 7.1—Components of Strengths-Based Practice

Strengths-Based Practice Component	Characteristics of the Strengths-Based Approaches	Practical Applications to OT
Building Authentic Partnerships and Fostering Collaboration Across Research, Education, and Practice	1. **Reflective practice:** Practitioners can continually learn from their experiences and develop reflexive skills to understand how they impact communities. 2. **Valuing multiple knowledges:** Practitioners recognize and integrate evidence, professional expertise, with the lived experiences of their clients and their families. 3. **Intentional prioritization:** OTPs need to critically consider why certain forms of knowledge or evidence (e.g. research evidence) are emphasized in their practice over others (e.g. clients' lived experiences). 4. **Collaborative decision-making:** Practitioners need to include clients' feedback and insights in shared, informed decision-making. 5. **Co-production of knowledge:** OTPs need to actively partner with clients and colleagues to generate shared understanding and solutions. 6. **Professional growth:** OTPs need to identify skill or mindset gaps and engage in continuous learning to strengthen strengths-based competence. 7. **Supportive mentorship:** OTPs need to promote strengths-based values in supervision and the professional development of new graduates.	• Challenge deficit-based or purely medicalized viewpoints of neurodivergence by introducing neurodiversity-affirming research or client testimonials on the impact of your neurodiversity-affirming care. • Consider adopting a strengths-based lens for yourself, as you would for your clients. For example, emphasize competence and adaptability, not perfectionism. – *"I'm learning to adjust my approach quickly when clients need something different,"* rather than *"I need to stop being so inconsistent."* • List the sources of your intervention approaches: textbooks, clinical guidelines, client feedback, personal experience, or community-led resources. • Reflect on whose voices are missing (e.g. have you read writing by Disabled scholars or advocates?) • Intentionally integrate non-published research knowledge sources (blogs, podcasts, community trainings) into continuing education plans. • Instead of matching skills to problems (e.g. "I help clients reduce meltdowns"), match them to how you support their well-being ("I help clients identify regulation tools that work for their sensory processing patterns").

cont.

Strengths-Based Practice Component	Characteristics of the Strengths-Based Approaches	Practical Applications to OT
Presume Competence	1. **Empathy and respect:** Practitioners need to demonstrate empathy and genuine respect for clients' perspectives and their experiences. 2. **Commitment to neurodiversity:** Practitioners must understand neurodivergence and apply neurodiversity-affirming, strengths-based approaches in collaboration with their clients. 3. **Self-awareness and core beliefs**: Practitioners need to recognize, understand, explore, and include strengths, including their own. by bringing personal values, ideologies, and motivations to guide their practice and research decisions. 4. **Human rights and inclusion perspective:** Practitioners need to frame their interventions and supports within a human rights and social justice context, advocating for equitable participation for their clients by bringing their voices to the forefront across environments. There is a focus on developing aspirational goals that value the inherent worth of Neurodivergent interests and abilities. 5. **Ethical and reflective decision-making**: Practitioners need to make ethical decisions through informed choices that value their beliefs, ideologies, and commitment to person-first, strength-oriented care provision. 6. **Commitment to lifelong learning:** Strengths-based practitioners continuously need to expand their knowledge of neurodivergence, co-production, and neurodiversity-affirming practices by understanding the intrinsic power of "yet."	• An OTP is working with a Nonspeaking client and speaks directly to the client rather than only to the adults/caregivers. • Incorporate assessment tools that utilize visuals to support access for those with communication differences (see the recommended assessment tool resource in the Vault). • Moving away from solely using deficit-based or standardized assessments that ignore meaningful occupations or clients' aspirations. • All intervention supports are co-created and selected by the person receiving support. • The individual's strengths, interests, aspirations, and preferences are deeply explored, recognized, respected, and included. • Setting goals that reflect self-determined aspirations (e.g. "developing an online art portfolio") rather than only daily living tasks. • Co-writing goals with clients using language that feels empowering and authentic to them. • Supporting advocacy or leadership goals, such as presenting about neurodivergence acceptance or mentoring others. • Recognizing and documenting Neurodivergent expertise (e.g. a client's deep knowledge of a topic) as a strength and source of occupational meaning.
Creating Safe and Inclusive Environments	1. The OTP invests in developing neurodiversity-affirming and sensory-friendly environments. 2. The OTP respects and utilizes maximum access and self-regulation communication strategies. 3. The OTP prioritizes the safety of the Neurodivergent individual, regardless of their sexual orientation, gender identity, culture, or ethnicity.	• Make sure you are using inclusive and affirming language (ask clients how they would like to describe their disability and/or neurodivergence). • Don't hesitate to adjust interventions based on the client's feedback and lived experiences; celebrate these moments as growth in your neurodiversity-affirming journey! • Normalize different ways to self-regulate, such as stimming or using accommodations (e.g. wearing noise-cancelling headphones yourself, dimming the lighting, using flexible seating).

Presumption of Competence

The presumption of competence is rooted in child development. Parents presume the competence of their non-Neurodivergent infants during early interactions, such as gesturing, babbling, and making eye contact.[19] This presumption of competence is also embedded in early literacy education when teachers and educators assume non-Neurodivergent students' capacity to learn as they introduce novel educational concepts. Biklen and Burke argue that the educational system fails Neurodivergent individuals by perceiving them as incompetent and concentrating on their deficiencies rather than their strengths. Once Neurodivergent students are labeled in school, their cognitive abilities are questioned. Biklen and Burke add that the responsibility is placed on these students to prove their capabilities in environments that are not developed to be inclusive so they can receive the services they rightfully deserve.[20] This also consists of the Non-speaking Neurodivergent community, who are often compelled to adopt communication methods that do not align with their preferences. This may involve using approaches that aim to remediate or normalize their communication styles rather than honoring their natural ways of expressing themselves. As a result, they risk being perceived as less cognitively competent, further marginalizing their voices and autonomy. OTPs are well-positioned to presume the competence of our Neurodivergent clients as we propagate our alignment with ideologies of empathy and client-centeredness.[21]

Using the Growth Mindset to Presume Competence

Mindsets are interconnected belief systems regarding whether personal qualities, such as intelligence or extraversion, are fixed or adaptable. Some individuals perceive these traits as inherent and unchangeable, while others view them as dynamic attributes that can be developed through effort, learning, and experience. Although fixed and growth mindsets generally represent enduring cognitive orientations,[22] research suggests situational factors can also influence them, shaping how individuals respond to challenges and opportunities for growth.[23] Occupational therapists can incorporate elements of these mindset theories to inform their practice specifically for the Neurodivergent community. The growth mindset can shape how therapists approach the presumption of competence of their Neurodivergent clients by instilling the power of "yet."[24] In this way, practitioners can shape environments to support skill development and Neurodivergent people's natural ways of being. The word "*yet*" holds immense potential to shift the paradigm, encouraging a transformative mindset among practitioners, family members, teachers, and the broader community. It reframes skill development as a dynamic, ongoing process rather than a fixed endpoint, recognizing that abilities can evolve and vary across different environments. By embracing the power of *yet*, we foster a culture of growth, patience, and possibility, empowering Neurodivergent individuals to be themselves and encouraging Neurodivergent growth authentically. Doing so can shift the focus from viewing the individual as high- or low-functioning to understanding that the context is high- or low-functioning.[25] The growth mindset also encourages mistakes, productive failure, and practice as indispensable concepts of any learning process.[26] A Vault item is available that provides a list of initial thoughts and questions that can support practitioners to start incorporating the power of "yet" in their practice.

Shifting the Labels of High- and Low-Functioning

Terms like "high-functioning" and "low-functioning" individuals fail to capture the diverse experiences within the Neurodivergent community. They are detrimental characterizations and categorizations that often lead to a) an underestimation of abilities (e.g. assuming a Nonspeaking individual cannot advocate their hopes, dreams, and healthcare needs) or b) an overestimation of abilities (e.g. assuming an individual is "neurotypical enough" and they don't need supports). There is no reason to describe any individual as high- or low-functioning. Describing the environment's support for individual needs is more constructive.[27,28,29] There is a power in turning the high- versus low-functioning individualistic descriptions into descriptions of environments, which allows the occupation therapy practitioner to not only advocate for these high-functioning environments but to use their reasoning skills and understanding of the importance of the environment to provide a very different lens through which to view the flourishing of an individual, *within* a high- versus low-functioning environment.

OTPs must be willing to examine the environments that they work in, advocate for, and create for those they serve. Table 7.2 outlines characteristics of low- and high-functioning environments, and what they look like in occupational therapy practice.

Any one of these characteristics can impact Neurodivergent individuals in negative ways, no matter what individual characteristics they embody. Conversely, high-functioning environments can allow any Neurodivergent individual a place to thrive with the individual characteristics they bring to that environment.

Table 7.2—Qualities of Low- and High-Functioning Environments

<table>
<tr><th colspan="2">Aspects of Low-Functioning Environments</th></tr>
<tr><th>Characteristic</th><th>What It Looks Like in Practice</th></tr>
<tr><td>A bias toward remediation of deficits that have been categorized and pathologized by primarily the medical model, and language that typifies this bias.</td><td>• OTP prioritizes societal expectations of occupation, such as developmental milestones and prescribed behaviors, over the client's interests or goals.
• Interventions focus on correcting and modifying the Neurodivergent individual to fit in the environment.
• Interventions focus on deficits rather than on building existing skills in preferred and non-preferred activities and occupations.</td></tr>
<tr><td>A lack of consideration of the sensory environment and its potential impact.</td><td>• A client reports that their workplace is ableist and wants support in learning how to advocate or educate their employer. But the OTP determines this is not within the scope of occupational therapy goals.
• An individual shares that a particular meaningful space is overwhelming or overstimulating, and the OTP expects the individual to "simply get used to it."</td></tr>
<tr><td>An underutilization of multiple means of communication.</td><td>• Limited options for communication beyond spoken language.
• An OTP assumes that a Nonspeaking individual is unable to communicate their sensory preferences.</td></tr>
<tr><td>Failure to design the environment for maximum access (i.e. visual supports, interest-based activity centers, etc.).</td><td>• An OTP in the schools has services focused on pull-out sessions indefinitely, versus pushing into the classroom and supporting the student's engagement in naturally occurring settings.</td></tr>
<tr><th colspan="2">Aspects of High-Functioning Environments</th></tr>
<tr><td>Utilization of a strengths-based lens that is asset-driven, while understanding challenges.</td><td>• Starting evaluations with interest and strength inventories, cultural and individual preferences, rather than deficit checklists (see Chapter 9).
• Designing interventions that expand on existing skills (e.g. using a client's love of gaming to build fine motor or executive functioning strategies).</td></tr>
</table>

cont.

Fundamental commitment to valuing Neurodivergent interests, ways of thinking, behaving, socializing, communicating, and more as a difference versus a deficit.	• Educating colleagues and families about Neurodivergent communication norms (e.g. directness, echolalia, scripting, info-dumping, or avoidance of eye contact). • Supporting authentic social participation by helping create environments where different interaction styles are accepted rather than trained out. • Modeling acceptance of stimming and sensory regulation behaviors in shared spaces.
Creation of "just right" sensory comfort spaces with unfettered access to these spaces.	• Designing calming spaces that are always available. • Educating general education staff in a school on sensory inclusivity and providing ways to make classrooms sensory inclusive for all (a Vault download exists with a sample presentation). • Supporting clients in identifying and articulating sensory needs and documenting these as essential supports (not privileges).
Utilization of multiple means of communication with a presumption of competence and receptive understanding as a "do no harm" proposition, and to look at all behavior through a deep understanding of this competence.	• Assuming receptive understanding even when expressive communication differences exist. • Offering and modeling AAC options, visuals, typing, drawing, gestures, or sign language alongside verbal communication.

Note. Adapted by Onwumere et al.[30]

The key to a high-functioning environment and the impact of a low-functioning environment fundamentally lies in the attitudes and biases of OTPs, which are often rooted in our professional training. Negative implicit bias grew or stayed the same during occupational therapy education, as witnessed in the study by Friedman and VanPuymbrouck.[31]

As Patten[32] asked: Does occupational therapy (OT) education reinforce ableist attitudes? What happens when new practitioners enter the profession with the preconceived notion that disability is negative, harmful, or something to be fixed with their expertise? What practices must the OT educational system change?

Ableist Practices in Occupational Therapy Education

OTPs as a professional community have historically made limited efforts to engage with, acknowledge, or integrate the substantial and influential body of scholarship developed by Disabled scholars and disability theorists over the past several decades.[33] Addressing this oversight is essential for advancing a more inclusive, socially responsive, and critically informed approach to occupational therapy that fully embraces the voices and expertise of those with lived experiences of disability.

Occupational therapy has upheld the idea that integrating thoughtfully selected occupations that are important to service users promotes the attainment of personally significant goals, reinforcing this philosophy in education practice. However, numerous occupational therapy educational programs still focus heavily on gatekeeping ableism, thus acting as controllers of disability identity.[34,35] Therefore, educators, practitioners, and researchers must critically examine existing educational standards and question *how* and *what* content we expose to our newly graduated practitioners and scholars.

Strengths-Based Strategies to Promote Anti-Ableist Practices in Education

Aligning occupational therapy educational practices to the Universal Design of Learning (UDL) principles can improve access and engagement with the learning process.[36] UDL focuses on learner autonomy and empowerment, reducing the skewed power dynamics between educators and students. This framework decreases the control educators have over students, enabling students to take charge of their learning by independently engaging with the materials. Furthermore, UDL places the burden of learning not on students but on the learning environment, which can be modified, hyperindividualized, and tailored by educators to meet the learning needs of every student.[37]

UDL targets ableist practices using intentional knowledge and skill development while creating spaces to promote community building and critical reflection within the learning environment.[38] For example, to reduce ableist practices in occupational therapy education, programs could start by acknowledging the mistakes or wrongdoings of our profession as the first step.

Let us consider the example of an educator intending to teach the technologically driven, diverse communication patterns used by the Autistic community. At this stage, to recognize the harm caused by ableist perspectives, diverse perspectives from the Nonspeaking Autistic community must be included through evidence or lived experiences. Students can then reflect on and brainstorm ways to support Nonspeaking Autistic communication.

Then, the educator and students can reflexively act on the knowledge by using their biases as a starting point and infusing a curiosity-driven approach through constant questioning, looking at the community for answers, and understanding stereotypes.[39] Through this process, the educator ensures that the environment is safe for students and that the social and educational demands are achievable. The educator can provide real-life problems that the students could solve by confronting their biases around communication styles, patterns, and modes. Then, the educator provides authentic learning experiences built on personalization, cultural relevance, and those that further confront implicit ableist ideologies. By doing so, the learners develop a sense of belonging to their learning community and can work interdependently to solve real-world problems using novel ideas.[40]

Areas of Opportunities in Occupational Therapy Education to Develop an Anti-Ableist Curriculum

Occupational therapy education requires scrutiny to develop future generations of anti-ableist practitioners. Harrison et al.'s paper[41] is a call to action for practitioners, educators, and researchers to recognize the value that disability studies bring to occupational education. As explored in Chapter 2, disability studies research recognizes the disability community, rather than practitioners or researchers, as the primary experts on disability. Harrison and their team urged the professional community to create pathways for assimilating disability studies into occupational therapy educational curricula.

ACOTE Standards

The Accreditation Council for Occupational Therapy Education (ACOTE) accredits entry-level occupational therapy and occupational therapy assistant (OTA) programs in the U.S., ensuring they meet the standards necessary to prepare graduates for national certification. As ACOTE establishes, approves, and manages educational standards to evaluate programs for training occupational therapists and occupational therapy assistants, it is essential to use these standards as a foundation for initiating our inquiry and exploration.[42] The foundational content requirements aim to prepare students to grasp the concepts of disability and the biological, social, and psychological dimensions of occupational performance. Although this chapter does not encompass a comprehensive discussion of all the standards, we will concentrate on standard B and explore how we can view it from a strengths-based perspective as a model.

While studying the structure of the human body, lifespan development, and human behavioral development are essential content areas, we must establish a pathway to normalizing the "non-standard" as endorsed by Hammell.[43] In this context, normalizing the non-standard includes opening up lessons and inquiries to incorporate diverse perspectives of community members and moving away from deficit-centered concepts infused from the medical model of disability.

The curriculum must start assimilating concepts that promote biological and neurological diversity. By including differences from the outset, the focus will move away from comparing these differences from a deficit perspective and to the acceptance that biodiversity and neurodiversity are established norms of evolution.[44] Some areas of deficit-based learning approaches in healthcare education include disability simulations and ingraining of the "expert" positionality.[45,46] Many disability theorists consider these practices as entrenched ableism, stemming from the simulation of helplessness that arises when emulating a Disabled individual by recreating a day in their lives. Using language highlighting productiveness and functions, we shape a narrative of preferring non-disabled productivity standards, functions, and occupations. Disability simulations reinforce disability stereotypes by emphasizing associated challenges without examining or showcasing the abilities or strengths a Disabled individual possesses or exploring how the environment can affect participation.[47]

Hammell[48] also criticized the perceived division between non-disabled OTPs and the Disabled community, where the former provides the expertise and prioritizes the latter to live a productive and meaningful life. Promoting this rhetoric has created a dilemma for Disabled occupational therapists and students to choose one of their identities over their other equally indispensable identities as they provide services or participate in occupational therapy schools.[49] Table 7.3 provides some recommendations on adapting our ACOTE educational standards to adopt an anti-ableist, strengths-based curriculum.

Including Neurodivergent voices can help students understand how societal barriers shape their experiences and highlight the intersection of factors like age, gender, and economic status in health outcomes. This perspective fosters awareness of social determinants of health, cultural influences, and systemic inequities, promoting person-centered, equitable occupational therapy practice to students during their training. Thus, it impacts their clinical reasoning right at the onset of their journeys as practitioners.

Since practitioners rely on research to provide evidence-based services, the Neurodivergent community urgently calls for participatory research approaches that amplify their voices in the research process. Excluding their voices reinforces skewed power dynamics, ableist perspectives, and colonial biases, particularly in Indigenous and Global South communities.[50,51] Ethical tensions around inclusion highlight the need to support diverse communication preferences and ensure transparency when direct participation is impossible.[52]

As mentioned in Chapter 2, ableism is rooted in hegemony, which seeks to perpetuate the standardization of non-disabled perspectives, abilities, skills, and talents over the community's knowledge. Political, fiscal, and economic impacts on occupational choices afforded to the Neurodivergent community and the effect on mental health must be incorporated into the occupational therapy curricula.[53] In the post-modern age, occupations are valued and measured based on productivity and profit metrics. This concept is called neoliberalism, and it supports a global capitalist system focused on promoting consumerism and maximizing private profits.[54]

Incorporating Neurodivergent-led theories, such as Autistic flow states theory, in occupational therapy education can help students recognize Neurodivergent differences early, thus fostering the development of holistic, anti-ableist professionals.[55] Community input also shapes the language used to describe neurodivergence, but merely updating terminology is not enough; occupational therapists must engage in critical reflexivity, challenge biases, and adopt a curiosity-driven approach.[56,57]

The Anti-Ableist Student Becomes an Anti-Ableist Practitioner: Strengths in Action

Students empowered by anti-ableist educational programs have the potential to share the most authentic versions of themselves to employ practices and strategies using a holistic approach rooted in strengths. When our students commit to learning from Neurodivergent community partners by confronting and informing their biased perspectives, their expertise can scaffold our knowledge structures and help us support these communities holistically.[58] Leveraging our professional strengths and establishing anti-ableist educational standards can develop future anti-ableist occupational therapy leaders and advocates.

As proponents of anti-ableist practices, new graduates can be primed to incorporate a strengths-based lens to deliver their practices right from the start of their careers. By adopting a respectful and authentic partnership with their service users, anti-ableist professionals can exercise cultural sensitivity to enquire about their past trauma and lived experiences to gain a comprehensive understanding.[59] This approach can propel early-career anti-ableist practitioners to employ critical reflexivity and creativity to improve their skills through perseverance, effort, and learning.

Table 7.3—ACOTE Standards: Recommendations to Add Anti-Ableist Language

Current ACOTE Standards	Anti-Ableist Recommendations to Standards
Demonstrate knowledge of: • The structure and function of the human body that must include the biological and physical sciences, neurosciences, kinesiology, and biomechanics. • Human development throughout the lifespan (infants, children, adolescents, adults, and older adults). Course content must include, but is not limited to, developmental psychology. • Concepts of human behavior that must include the behavioral sciences, social sciences, and science of occupation.	Demonstrate knowledge of: • The structure and function of the human body **including differences in neurology and biology of Neurodivergent communities** that must include the biological and physical sciences, neurosciences, kinesiology, and biomechanics. • Human development throughout the lifespan (infants, children, adolescents, adults, and older adults). **Focus must be placed on recognizing differences in the Disabled communities.** Course content must include, but is not limited to, developmental psychology. • Concepts of human behavior **and the differences in behavior in Neurodivergent communities** must include the behavioral sciences, social sciences, **critical disability studies**, and science of occupation.
Apply and analyze the role of sociocultural, socioeconomic, and diversity equity and inclusion factors, as well as lifestyles in contemporary society to meet the needs of persons, groups, and populations. Course content must include, but is not limited to, introductory psychology, abnormal psychology, and introductory sociology or introductory anthropology.	Apply and analyze the role of sociocultural, socioeconomic, and diversity equity and inclusion factors, as well as lifestyles in contemporary society to meet the needs of persons, groups, and populations. **The impact of ableism, racism, and other intersectional factors, along with their detrimental effects on the limited opportunities available to Neurodivergent communities, will be explored and highlighted.** Course content must include, but is not limited to, introductory psychology, abnormal psychology, **critical disability studies**, **disability studies**, and introductory sociology or introductory anthropology.
Demonstrate knowledge of the social determinants of health for persons, groups, and populations with or at risk for disabilities and chronic health conditions and distinguish the epidemiological factors that impact the public health and welfare of populations.	Demonstrate knowledge of the social determinants of health for persons, groups, and populations with or at risk for disabilities and chronic health conditions and distinguish the epidemiological factors that impact the public health and welfare of populations. **Lived experiences from specific Neurodivergent communities will be used to understand the impact of social determinants.**

cont.

Current ACOTE Standards	Anti-Ableist Recommendations to Standards
Demonstrate the ability to use quantitative statistics and qualitative analysis to interpret tests and measurements for the purpose of establishing and delivering evidence-based practice.	Demonstrate the ability to use quantitative statistics and qualitative analysis to interpret tests and measurements for the purpose of establishing and delivering evidence-based practice. **Students will also demonstrate the ability to use participatory research approaches by learning the different types of participatory research methodologies and collaborating with Neurodivergent community partners.**
Apply, analyze, and evaluate scientific evidence, theories, models of practice, and frames of reference that underlie the practice of occupational therapy to guide and inform interventions for persons, groups, and populations in a variety of practice contexts and environments.	Apply, analyze, and evaluate scientific evidence, theories, models of practice, and frames of reference that underlie the practice of occupational therapy to guide and inform interventions for persons, groups, and populations in a variety of practice contexts and environments. **Theories will also be included from disability studies, to understand the impact of these theories on occupations and opportunities afforded to Neurodivergent communities.**
Analyze and evaluate occupational therapy history, philosophical base, theory, and socio-political climate and their importance in meeting society's current and future occupational needs as well as how these factors influence and are influenced by practice.	Analyze and evaluate **history from the lens of occupational therapy and the impact of colonialism, ableism, racism, and other social determinants of health**, philosophical base, theory, and socio-political climate and their importance in meeting society's current and future occupational needs as well as how these factors influence and are influenced by practice.
Apply, analyze, and evaluate the interaction of occupation and activity, including areas of occupation, performance skills, performance patterns, context, and client factors.	Apply, analyze, and evaluate the interaction of occupation and activity, including areas of occupation, performance skills, performance patterns, context, and client factors. **The impact of ableism on these factors will be explored to critically analyze their impact on volition, choices, and availability of occupations for Neurodivergent communities.**
Explain to the community of interest (e.g. consumers, potential employers, colleagues, third-party payers, regulatory boards, policymakers, and the public) the distinct nature of occupation and the evidence that occupation supports performance, participation, health, wellness, and well-being.	Explain to the community of interest (e.g. consumers, potential employers, colleagues, third-party payers, regulatory boards, policymakers, and the public) the distinct nature of occupation and the evidence that occupation supports performance, participation, health, wellness, and well-being. **Emphasis will also be placed on how ableism and other aspects of intersectionality impact occupations, performance, health, wellness, and well-being. Focus will be placed on physical and social environments and their limitations.**

<table>
<tr><td>Apply and analyze scientific evidence to explain the importance of:
• Balancing areas of occupation.
• The role of occupation in the promotion of health and wellness.
• The prevention of disease, illness, and dysfunction for persons, groups, and populations.</td><td>Apply and analyze scientific evidence to explain the importance of:
• Balancing areas of occupation.
• The role of occupation in the promotion of health and wellness. The influence of environments in supporting participation or limiting access to various occupations.
• The prevention of disease, illness, and dysfunction for persons, groups, and populations using participatory research approaches to include the needs of the Neurodivergent communities.</td></tr>
<tr><td>Demonstrate activity analysis in areas of occupation, performance skills, performance patterns, context, and client factors to formulate the intervention plan.</td><td>Demonstrate activity analysis in areas of occupation, performance skills, performance patterns, context, and client factors to formulate the intervention plan. Focusing specifically on occupations and activities that are coerced on Neurodivergent communities and that have the potential to cause harm.</td></tr>
<tr><td>Demonstrate therapeutic use of self, including one's personality, insights, perceptions, and judgments, as part of the therapeutic process in both individual and group interaction.</td><td>Demonstrate therapeutic use of self, including one's personality, insights, perceptions, and judgments, as part of the therapeutic process in both individual and group interaction. Demonstrating critical reflection and reflexivity by understanding individual positionality and biases in a situation and acting as a change agent.</td></tr>
<tr><td>Demonstrate professional reasoning to evaluate, analyze, diagnose, and provide occupation-based interventions that:
• Address client factors, performance patterns, and performance skills.
• Focus on creation, promotion, establishment, restoration, maintenance, modification, and prevention.</td><td>Demonstrate professional reasoning to evaluate, analyze, diagnose, and provide occupation-based interventions that:
• Address client factors, performance patterns, and performance skills.
• Focus on creation, promotion, establishment, restoration, maintenance, modification, and prevention.
• Critically focusing on the environmental barriers that restrict access to occupational participation.
• Questioning ableist practices in the environment to increase access and inclusion.</td></tr>
</table>

cont.

Current ACOTE Standards	Anti-Ableist Recommendations to Standards
Interpret evaluation findings, including: • Occupational performance and participation deficits. • Results based on psychometric properties of tests considering factors that might bias assessment results (e.g. culture and disability status related to the person and context). • Criterion-referenced and norm-referenced standardized test scores on an understanding of sampling, normative data, standard and criterion scores, reliability, and validity.	Interpret evaluation findings, including: • **Strengths, abilities, interests, passions, and communication patterns of Neurodivergent communities.** • Occupational performance and participation deficits. • Results based on psychometric properties of tests considering factors that might bias assessment results (e.g. culture and disability status related to the person and context). • Criterion-referenced and norm-referenced standardized test scores on an understanding of sampling, normative data, standard and criterion scores, reliability, and validity.
Recommend and provide direct interventions and procedures to persons, groups, or populations to enhance safety, health and wellness, chronic condition management, and performance in occupations. This must include the ability to collaborate with the occupational therapy assistant related to interventions and selecting and delivering occupations and activities: • Occupations as a therapeutic intervention • Interventions to support occupations including therapeutic exercise • Interventions to support well-being (e.g. complementary health and integrative health) • Interventions to support self-advocacy related to persons, groups, or populations • Virtual interventions.	Recommend and provide direct interventions and procedures to persons, groups, or populations to enhance safety, health and wellness, chronic condition management, and performance in occupations. This must include the ability to collaborate with the occupational therapy assistant related to interventions and selecting and delivering occupations and activities: • Occupations as a therapeutic intervention • Interventions to support occupations including therapeutic exercise • Interventions to support well-being (e.g. complementary health and integrative health) • Interventions to support self-advocacy related to persons, groups, or populations • Virtual interventions. **Interventions must not be provided to Neurodivergent communities solely with normalization as a goal; instead, they must aim to incorporate strengths to build on areas of challenges. Moving away from interventions to provision of support in preferred activities or occupations must be the goal.**
Select, design, and implement occupation-based interventions using the strategies of establish, restore, and modify approaches to address deficits in performance skills.	Select, design, and implement occupation-based interventions using the strategies of establish, restore, and modify approaches to address deficits in performance skills **using strengths of Neurodivergent people and interest-driven occupations**.

Apply the principles of assessment to identify appropriate features of assistive technologies and durable medical equipment to support the client's participation. Demonstrate the ability to design, fabricate, apply, fit, and train in assistive technologies and devices (e.g. aids for communication, mobility, sensory loss, computer access, seating, and positioning systems) used to enhance occupational performance. Document a justification to secure funding.	Apply the principles of assessment to identify appropriate features of assistive technologies and durable medical equipment to support the client's participation. Demonstrate the ability to design, fabricate, apply, fit, and train in assistive technologies and devices (e.g. aids for communication, mobility, sensory loss, computer access, seating, and positioning systems) used to enhance occupational performance. **Assistive technology must also accommodate preferred communication modes using various technologies chosen by Neurodivergent communities.** Document a justification to secure funding.
Demonstrate and evaluate the principles of the teaching-learning process using educational methods and health literacy education approaches: • To design activities and clinical training for persons, groups, and populations. • To instruct and train the client, caregiver, family, significant others, and communities at the level of the audience.	Demonstrate and evaluate the principles of the teaching-learning process using educational methods and health literacy education approaches: • To design activities and clinical training for persons, groups, and populations. • To instruct and train the client, caregiver, family, significant others, and communities at the level of the audience. **Training caregivers and family members to recognize, build, and advocate for strengths-based practices and opportunities for Neurodivergent communities.**
Identify and analyze evolving service delivery models; changing federal, state, and local laws and regulations; and payment reform to advocate for occupational therapy. Articulate the distinct knowledge and skills of OTPs to the community of interest.	Identify and analyze evolving service delivery models; changing federal, state, and local laws and regulations; and payment reform to advocate for occupational therapy. Articulate the distinct knowledge and skills of OTPs to the community of interest. **Include and leverage collaboration with Neurodivergent communities to advance their goals and healthcare service priorities and needs.**
Select, apply, and interpret quantitative and qualitative methods for analyzing evidence to inform occupational therapy practice, including: • Basic descriptive, correlational, and inferential quantitative statistics. • Analysis and synthesis of qualitative data.	Select, apply, and interpret quantitative and qualitative methods for analyzing evidence to inform occupational therapy practice including: • Basic descriptive, correlational, and inferential quantitative statistics. • Analysis and synthesis of qualitative data. • **Include participatory research approaches, including community-based participatory research.**

Note. The suggested changes are in bold.

Endnotes

1 Hammell, K. W. (2023). A call to resist occupational therapy's promotion of ableism. *Scandinavian Journal of Occupational Therapy, 30*(6), 745-757. https://doi.org/10.1080/11038128.2022.2130821

2 Patten, K. (2024). Ableism's pervasive impact in healthcare: A time for action. *Developmental Medicine and Child Neurology, 66*(9), 1120–1121. https://doi.org/10.1111/dmcn.15889

3 Patten, K. (2022). Finding our strengths: Recognizing professional bias and interrogating systems. *The American Journal of Occupational Therapy, 76*(6), 7606150010. https://doi.org/10.5014/ajot.2022.076603

4 Raymaker, D. M. (2024). Disrupting oppression: Critical systems thinking and ethics in autism research. In A. Bianchi & J. A. Vogt (Eds.), *Intellectual disabilities and autism: Ethics and practice*. Springer. https://doi.org/10.1007/978-3-031-61565-8_11

5 ibid, p. 139.

6 Milton, D. E., Waldock, K. E., & Keates, N. (2023). Autism and the "double empathy problem." In F. Mezzenzana & D. Peluso (Eds.), *Conversations on empathy: Interdisciplinary perspectives on empathy, imagination and othering* (pp. 78–97). Routledge.

7 Patten, K. (2024). Ableism's pervasive impact in healthcare: A time for action. *Developmental Medicine and Child Neurology, 66*(9), 1120–1121. https://doi.org/10.1111/dmcn.15889

8 Friedman, C., & VanPuymbrouck, L. (2021). Impact of occupational therapy education on students' disability attitudes: A longitudinal study. *The American Journal of Occupational Therapy, 75*(4). https://doi.org/10.5014/ajot.2021.047423

9 Grenier, M. L. (2021). Patient case formulations and oppressive disability discourses in occupational therapy education. *Canadian Journal of Occupational Therapy, 88*(3), 266–272. https://doi.org/10.1177/00084174211005882

10 Raymaker, D. M. (2024). Disrupting oppression: Critical systems thinking and ethics in autism research. In A. Bianchi & J. A. Vogt (Eds.), *Intellectual disabilities and autism: Ethics and practice*. Springer. https://doi.org/10.1007/978-3-031-61565-8_11

11 Murthi, K., Chen, Y.-L., Shore, S., & Patten, K. (2023). Strengths-based practice to enhance mental health for Autistic people: A scoping review. *The American Journal of Occupational Therapy, 77*(2). https://doi.org/10.5014/ajot.2023.050074

12 ibid.

13 Urbanowicz, A., Nicolaidis, C., Houting, J. D., Shore, S. M., Gaudion, K., Girdler, S., & Savarese, R. J. (2019). An expert discussion on strengths-based approaches in autism. *Autism in Adulthood, 1*(2), 82–89. https://doi.org/10.1089/aut.2019.29002.aju

14 Patten, K. (2022). Finding our strengths: Recognizing professional bias and interrogating systems. *The American Journal of Occupational Therapy, 76*(6), 7606150010. https://doi.org/10.5014/ajot.2022.076603, pp. 6–7

15 Department for Health and Social Care & Social Care Institute for Excellence. (2019). *Strengths-based approach: Practice framework and practice handbook*. Social Care Institute for Excellence. www.scie.org.uk/strengths-based- approaches/practice-framework-handbook

16 Murthi, K., Chen, Y.-L., Shore, S., & Patten, K. (2023). Strengths-based practice to enhance mental health for Autistic people: A scoping review. *The American Journal of Occupational Therapy, 77*(2). https://doi.org/10.5014/ajot.2023.050074

17 Urbanowicz, A., Nicolaidis, C., Houting, J. D., Shore, S. M., Gaudion, K., Girdler, S., & Savarese, R. J. (2019). An expert discussion on strengths-based approaches in autism. *Autism in Adulthood, 1*(2), 82–89. https://doi.org/10.1089/aut.2019.29002.aju

18 Coghlan, D. & Brydon-Miller, M. (2014). Strengths-based approach. In D. Coghlan & M. Brydon-Miller (Eds.) *The SAGE encyclopedia of action research, 2* (pp. 733–735). SAGE Publications Ltd. https://doi.org/10.4135/9781446294406.n322

19 Biklen, D., & Burke, J. (2006). Presuming competence. *Equity & Excellence in Education, 39*(2), 166–175. https://doi-org.proxy.library.nyu.edu/10.1080/10665680500540376

20 Bottema-Beutel, K., Sasson, N. J., McKinnon, R., Braun, C., Guo, R., Hand, B. N., Kapp, S. K., Espinas, D. R., Bailin, A., Lester, J. N., & Yu, B. (2024). Recognizing and resisting ableist language in schools: Suggestions for school-based speech-language pathologists and related professionals. *Language, Speech, and Hearing Services in Schools, 55*(4), 1025–1038. https://doi.org/10.1044/2024_LSHSS-24-00036

21 Hammell, K. W. (2023). A call to resist occupational therapy's promotion of ableism. *Scandinavian Journal of Occupational Therapy, 30*(6), 745–757. https://doi.org/10.1080/11038128.2022.2130821

22 Robins, L. R. W., & Pals, J. (2002). Implicit self-theories in the academic domain: Implications for goal orientation, attributions, affect, and self-esteem change. *Self and Identity, 1*, 313–336. http://dx.doi.org/10.1080/15298860290106805

23 Mrazek, A. J., Ihm, E. D., Molden, D. C., Mrazek, M. D., Zedelius, C. M., & Schooler, J. W. (2018). Expanding minds: Growth mindsets of self-regulation and the influences on

effort and perseverance. *Journal of Experimental Social Psychology*, *79*, 164–180. https://doi.org/10.1016/j.jesp.2018.07.003

24 Dweck, C. S. (2006). *Mindset: The new psychology of success*. Random House.

25 Patten, K. (2022). Finding our strengths: Recognizing professional bias and interrogating systems. *The American Journal of Occupational Therapy, 76*(6), 7606150010. https://doi.org/10.5014/ajot.2022.076603

26 Dweck, C. S. (2006). *Mindset: The new psychology of success*. Random House.

27 Patten, K. (2022). Finding our strengths: Recognizing professional bias and interrogating systems. *The American Journal of Occupational Therapy, 76*(6), 7606150010. https://doi.org/10.5014/ajot.2022.076603

28 Bottema-Beutel, K., Sasson, N. J., McKinnon, R., Braun, C., Guo, R., Hand, B. N., Kapp, S. K., Espinas, D. R., Bailin, A., Lester, J. N., & Yu, B. (2024). Recognizing and resisting ableist language in schools: Suggestions for school-based speech-language pathologists and related professionals. *Language, Speech, and Hearing Services in Schools*, *55*(4), 1025–1038. https://doi.org/10.1044/2024_LSHSS-24-00036

29 Onwumere, D., Akrofi, N. S., Murthi, K., Ellzey, L. M., & Patten, K. (in press). Strength-based frame of reference for Autistic individuals. In P. Kramer (Ed.), *Frames of reference for pediatric occupational therapy* (5th ed.). Lippincott Williams & Wilkins.

30 Onwumere, D., Akrofi, N. S., Murthi, K., Ellzey, L. M., & Patten, K. (in press). Strength-based frame of reference for Autistic individuals. In P. Kramer (Ed.), *Frames of reference for pediatric occupational therapy* (5th ed.). Lippincott Williams & Wilkins.

31 Friedman, C., & VanPuymbrouck, L. (2021). Impact of occupational therapy education on students' disability attitudes: A longitudinal study. *The American Journal of Occupational Therapy*, *75*(4). https://doi.org/10.5014/ajot.2021.047423

32 Patten, K. (2022). Finding our strengths: Recognizing professional bias and interrogating systems. *The American Journal of Occupational Therapy, 76*(6), 7606150010. https://doi.org/10.5014/ajot.2022.076603

33 Hammell, K. W. (2023). A call to resist occupational therapy's promotion of ableism. *Scandinavian Journal of Occupational Therapy*, *30*(6), 745–757. https://doi.org/10.1080/11038128.2022.2130821

34 ibid.

35 Patten, K. (2022). Finding our strengths: Recognizing professional bias and interrogating systems. *The American Journal of Occupational Therapy, 76*(6), 7606150010. https://doi.org/10.5014/ajot.2022.076603

36 CAST. (2025). *Universal Design for Learning Guidelines version 3.0*. https://udlguidelines.cast.org

37 ibid.

38 Bouldin, A. S. (2017). Reflection is not reflexive. *American Journal of Pharmaceutical Education*, *81*(9), 6832. https://doi.org/10.5688/ajpe6832

39 Way, N. (2011). *Deep secrets: Boys' friendships and the crisis of connection*. Harvard University Press.

40 CAST. (2025). *Universal Design for Learning Guidelines version 3.0*. https://udlguidelines.cast.org

41 Harrison, E. A., Sheth, A. J., Kish, J., VanPuymbrouck, L. H., Heffron, J. L., Lee, D., Mahaffey, L., & Occupational Therapy and Disability Studies Network. (2021). Disability studies and occupational therapy: Renewing the call for change. *The American Journal of Occupational Therapy*, *75*(4). https://doi.org/10.5014/ajot.2021.754002

42 Accreditation Council for Occupational Therapy Education. (2023). *2023 Accreditation Council for Occupational Therapy Education (ACOTE®) standards and interpretive guide*. ACOTE Online. https://acoteonline.org/accreditation-explained/standards

43 Hammell, K. W. (2023). A call to resist occupational therapy's promotion of ableism. *Scandinavian Journal of Occupational Therapy*, *30*(6), 745–757. https://doi.org/10.1080/11038128.2022.2130821

44 ibid.

45 Patten, K. (2022). Finding our strengths: Recognizing professional bias and interrogating systems. *The American Journal of Occupational Therapy, 76*(6), 7606150010. https://doi.org/10.5014/ajot.2022.076603

46 Bottema-Beutel, K., Sasson, N. J., McKinnon, R., Braun, C., Guo, R., Hand, B. N., Kapp, S. K., Espinas, D. R., Bailin, A., Lester, J. N., & Yu, B. (2024). Recognizing and resisting ableist language in schools: Suggestions for school-based speech-language pathologists and related professionals. *Language, Speech, and Hearing Services in Schools*, *55*(4), 1025–1038. https://doi.org/10.1044/2024_LSHSS-24-00036

47 Murthi, K., Chen, Y.-L., Shore, S., & Patten, K. (2023). Strengths-based practice to enhance mental health for Autistic people: A scoping review. *The American Journal of Occupational Therapy*, *77*(2). https://doi.org/10.5014/ajot.2023.050074

48 Hammell, K. W. (2023). A call to resist occupational therapy's promotion of ableism. *Scandinavian Journal of Occupational Therapy*, *30*(6), 745–757. https://doi.org/10.1080/11038128.2022.2130821

49 Pooley, E. A., & Beagan, B. L. (2021). The concept of oppression and occupational therapy:

A critical interpretive synthesis. *Canadian Journal of Occupational Therapy, 88*(4), 407–417. https://doi.org/10.1177/00084174211051168

50 Patten, K. (2024). Ableism's pervasive impact in healthcare: A time for action. *Developmental Medicine and Child Neurology, 66*(9), 1120–1121. https://doi.org/10.1111/dmcn.15889

51 Pihama, L. (2019). Colonization and the importation of ideologies of race, gender, and class in Aotearoa. In E. A. McKinley & L. T. Smith (Eds.), *Handbook of Indigenous education* (pp. 1–20). Springer Nature.

52 Raymaker, D. M. (2024). Disrupting oppression: Critical systems thinking and ethics in autism research. In A. Bianchi & J. A. Vogt (Eds.), *Intellectual disabilities and autism: Ethics and practice*. Springer. https://doi.org/10.1007/978-3-031-61565-8_11

53 Botha, M. (2021). Academic, activist, or advocate? Angry, entangled, and emerging: A critical reflection on autism knowledge production. *Frontiers in Psychology, 12*, 727542. https://doi.org/10.3389/fpsyg.2021.727542

54 Gruber, B., & Scherling, J. (2020). The relevance of unmasking neoliberal narratives for a decolonized human rights and peace education. *International Journal of Human Rights Education, 4*(1), 3. https://repository.usfca.edu/ijhre/vol4/iss1/3

55 Heasman, B., Williams, G., Charura, D., Hamilton, L. G., Milton, D., & Murray, F. (2024). Towards Autistic flow theory: A non-pathologising conceptual approach. *Journal for the Theory of Social Behaviour, 54*(4), 469–497. https://doi.org/10.1111/jtsb.12427

56 Murthi, K., Chen, Y.-L., Shore, S., & Patten, K. (2023). Strengths-based practice to enhance mental health for Autistic people: A scoping review. *The American Journal of Occupational Therapy, 77*(2). https://doi.org/10.5014/ajot.2023.050074

57 Bottema-Beutel, K., Sasson, N. J., McKinnon, R., Braun, C., Guo, R., Hand, B. N., Kapp, S. K., Espinas, D. R., Bailin, A., Lester, J. N., & Yu, B. (2024). Recognizing and resisting ableist language in schools: Suggestions for school-based speech-language pathologists and related professionals. *Language, Speech, and Hearing Services in Schools, 55*(4), 1025–1038. https://doi.org/10.1044/2024_LSHSS-24-00036

58 Patten, K. (2022). Finding our strengths: Recognizing professional bias and interrogating systems. *The American Journal of Occupational Therapy, 76*(6), 7606150010. https://doi.org/10.5014/ajot.2022.076603

59 Botha, M. (2021). Academic, activist, or advocate? Angry, entangled, and emerging: A critical reflection on autism knowledge production. *Frontiers in Psychology, 12*, 727542. https://doi.org/10.3389/fpsyg.2021.727542

SPOTLIGHT

Supporting Individuals with High Support Needs Through a Strengths-Based Approach

LUCIO SERIO, KELSIE REED, BREEA M. ROSAS, AND HALEY BIDDANDA

Supporting individuals with high support needs requires a shift from traditional deficit-rooted models to a strengths-based, neurodiversity-affirming approach. A traditional approach typically relies on the medical model of disability, falling short in meaningfully recognizing the full spectrum of abilities one can possess. This leads to a hyperfocus on deficits, overlooking the diverse strengths and potential that could inform more tailored support strategies.[1] These traditional methods offer an especially limited perspective for individuals with high support needs, as this approach emphasizes services designed to remediate perceived weaknesses, rather than cultivate strengths and autonomy. This can lead to reduced opportunities, lower expectations, and supports that are disconnected from the individual's interests and goals.

Occupational therapy practitioners (OTPs) are uniquely positioned to redefine how students with high support needs are perceived and supported. Our evaluations and supports shape not only outcomes but also life trajectories. By presuming competence, centering individual interests, and providing purposeful, affirming supports, OTPs can support individuals in developing essential skills while still fostering self-determination and supporting quality of life. See below for a vignette that compares a deficit-based approach with a strengths-based approach.

Vignette: Supporting Gabby in Achieving Her Goals

Gabby is a 17-year-old high school student who enjoys shopping with her sister, baking with her mom, and musical theater. She is a strong reader, has an impressive memory for phone numbers, and recently joined the gospel choir at her church. Gabby was diagnosed with Down syndrome at birth and experiences hypotonia, which affects her muscle endurance and, at times, her speech clarity. She has an Individualized Education Program (IEP) due to her identification as an individual with an Intellectual Disability (ID). She navigates her school campus independently with occasional monitoring from her aide and uses checklists to support organization. Gabby has repeatedly expressed a desire to work at a local eatery or coffee shop, hoping her IEP team will help her prepare for employment.

Deficit-Based Approach: Under a traditional model, Gabby's support plan involves school staff and family members making most decisions about her day. Her IEP goals are framed around general life skills such as stocking shelves, sweeping, and cleaning, based on the assumption that she has reached her academic potential. Occupational therapy services focus on isolated fine motor tasks that work on general grasp strength and finger dexterity. When discussing her transition plan, the team steers conversations toward sheltered employment programs without fully exploring Gabby's own aspirations. The language in her record emphasizes deficits, using terms like "executive functioning deficiencies" and "motor planning delays" without acknowledging her problem-solving skills or strong memory. While these services are well-intentioned, they reinforce the belief that Gabby's growth has plateaued, leading to stagnant supports that do not help her reach her full potential.

Strengths-Based Approach: In contrast, a strengths-based approach prioritizes Gabby's voice, ensuring that Gabby makes choices throughout her day, from selecting which staff member to work with to deciding the order of task completion. Her transition goals reflect her desire to work in a bakery, incorporating opportunities to follow recipes using visual step-by-step guides and video modeling. Occupational therapy sessions incorporate fine motor skill development tied to her real-world needs as defined by Gabby, such as measuring ingredients, using adaptive cooking tools, and handling utensils needed for baking. In addition, Gabby's IEP team works with her to help her secure an internship at a local bakery where she can apply her skills in a meaningful way. The language in her records focuses on her capabilities and the supports that help her succeed, using terms such as "works best with visual supports and structured routines" and "demonstrates strong memory skills." This approach empowers both Gabby and her team to continue building autonomy and self-efficacy. Table S1 outlines the key shifts made in practice that moved Gabby's supports from a traditional, deficit-based approach to one that is empowering.

Table S1—Deficit-Based Versus Strengths-Based Approach

Approach	Deficit-Based Lens	Strengths-Based Lens
Choice and Autonomy	Daily schedules and routines are dictated by staff or family members, with minimal input from the individual. Activities and supports are determined *for* them rather than *with* them.	Individuals are provided with maximum choice and autonomy in their daily routines, including seating options and selecting preferred support staff. Empowering individuals in this way fosters a sense of agency and ownership over their lives.
Presumption of Competence	Assumptions are made about the individual's capabilities based on diagnoses or perceived limitations. Unnecessary and harmful prompting, such as hand-over-hand assistance, is frequently used.	Competence is presumed unless the individual explicitly requests help. Supports are provided as needed, reinforcing dignity and encouraging self-determination.
Role in Decision-Making	Decisions about goals, accommodations, and supports are made primarily by caregivers and professionals, with little direct input from the individual. Conversations about the individual often happen *in front of* them rather than *with* them.	Individuals are active participants in decisions that impact their lives. Their preferences and perspectives are prioritized in discussions about services, supports, and future planning.
Language	Documentation focuses on deficits, using terms such as "delays," "limitations," or "deficits." Goals are framed around what the individual cannot do. *Example:* "Requires visual supports due to significant deficits in executive functioning."	Documentation highlights strengths and support needs using affirming and individualized language. *Example:* "Works best with visual supports and structured routines to enhance organization and task completion."
Focus of Services	Services focus on the remediation of weaknesses, often prioritizing isolated skill-building over meaningful application. *Example:* Fine motor skill development through tasks determined to be meaningful by the team (without Gabby), such as stacking blocks rather than real-world activities.	Services leverage strengths and interests to support skill development. *Example:* Fine motor skills are developed through meaningful tasks identified by Gabby, like measuring ingredients, using adaptive cooking tools, and handling baking utensils, aligning with the individual's interests.
Long-Term Planning	Professionals set goals based on their own perceptions of what is "realistic," often shaped by ableist assumptions about a client's abilities, rather than centering the client's hopes and dreams. Options may be limited to sheltered employment opportunities.	Future plans align with the individual's goals and interests. *Example:* Gabby is interested in working at a bakery and is supported in developing relevant job skills, using adaptive tools that enhance success, and accessing employment opportunities.

The Strengths-Based Collective (https://www.strengthbasedcollective.com), led by Kelsie Reed, is a magnificent resource of tools and strategies to support strengths-based practice. A few recommended items include:

- Strength-Based and Neurodiversity-Affirming IDEA Definitions (provides a powerful reframing of the disability categories as defined by the Individuals with Disabilities Education Act) [FREE]: https://www.strengthbasedcollective.com/product-page/strength-based-and-neurodiversity-affirming-idea-definitions
- My Self-Advocacy Map (strengths-based student interview tool to help maximize student voice in IEPs): https://www.strengthbasedcollective.com/product-page/my-self-advocacy-map-bundle-pack
- Character Trait Strength Cards (use these visual cards to help individuals identify their strengths): https://www.strengthbasedcollective.com/product-page/strength-trait-cards-complete-k-12-bundle
- Strength-Based Checklist for Neurodivergent Learners (a checklist designed to identify strengths often found in Neurodivergent individuals) [FREE]: https://www.strengthbasedcollective.com/product-page/strength-based-checklist-for-neurodivergent-learners

Social Media Handles/Websites

- Lucio Serio: @bookworm_edpsych (Instagram), www.bookwormedpsych.com
- Kelsie Reed: @dr.kelsiereed, @bestrengthbased (Instagram and Bluesky), www.strengthbasedcollective.com
- Breea M. Rosas: @ndaffirming_sp (Instagram), www.ndaffirmingsp.com
- Haley Biddanda: @haleybiddanda (Instagram and Bluesky)

Endnote

1 Reed, K., Serio, L., Rosas, B., & Biddanda, H. (2025). *Igniting potential: Redefining assessments for students with high support needs* [PowerPoint slides]. National Association of School Psychologists Annual Convention, Seattle, WA.

PART II

Application

CHAPTER 8

Critical Reflexivity

JULIA STERMAN AND JANET NJELESANI

Critical reflexivity is essential for occupational therapy practitioners (OTPs), as it supports the development of critical thinking and clinical reasoning required for professional competency. Critical reflexivity can enhance service delivery and promote more equitable care by influencing clinical decision-making. Critical reflexivity also bridges the gap between theory and practice, improving professional development by encouraging practitioners to adapt their practice based on experience. Additionally, being critically reflexive can open new discussions around understanding neurodiversity and challenge existing practices within occupational therapy. By using critical reflexivity, OTPs can address the social and systemic structures that perpetuate ableist practices in therapy and promote a more inclusive, person-centered approach that values the autonomy, preferences, and well-being of Neurodivergent individuals. This shift not only enhances the therapeutic experience for Neurodivergent individuals and their families but also challenges and disrupts systemic barriers that perpetuate marginalization in occupational therapy (OT) practices.

What Is Critical Reflexivity?

In this chapter, the term critical reflexivity is used to highlight reflection and action aimed at transforming OT practice; it is defined as the processes of examining the assumptions underlying clinical practice, including beliefs, values, and social and systemic structures, and how such dimensions influence our daily professional practice.[1] To question something, one must be aware of these beliefs, values, and structures. Critical reflexivity therefore not only prompts OTPs to question existing ideologies but also motivates them to initiate change by applying their newfound understanding to guide their actions. Critical reflexivity can serve as a tool for practitioners to examine the unchallenged and prevailing beliefs that shape their personal lives and professional practices.[2]

Critical reflexivity involves an examination of the socially ingrained assumptions, beliefs, and values that underpin established clinical practices and ways of thinking. Assumptions are ideas that we assume to be right or common sense and that are taken for granted.[3]

Critical reflexivity is NOT about criticism, being cynical, or only pointing out what is wrong. Instead, it involves recognizing our assumptions and taken-for-granted ideas as well as understanding our position in the world. This approach helps reveal the boundaries of our knowledge and fosters a deeper appreciation for the perspectives and realities of others.

Critical reflexivity goes beyond critical reflection, which focuses on self-critique, examining how one's assumptions, behavior, biases, and power relations shape OT practice.[4] Similarly, while positionality focuses on an individual explicitly acknowledging their assumptions tied to their social context and practice setting, critical reflexivity challenges those assumptions and seeks ways to address them.[5] Finally, professional identity refers to how individuals view themselves within their professional environment and how they convey themselves in their work.[6] Critical reflexivity involves addressing issues of identity and positionality by prompting individuals to critically examine how professional discourses and the knowledge that informs practice are formed and shaped.[7]

In OT practice with Neurodivergent individuals, critical reflexivity encourages practitioners to examine how their personal and professional assumptions and beliefs about neurodiversity shape their clinical approaches. Assumptions are not fixed and can be changed over time, so there is an opportunity for practitioners to change if they learn that some ways of thinking are contributing to problems. For example, a practitioner might reflect on how traditional OT models often prioritize neurotypical behaviors and question whether these frameworks truly meet the needs of Neurodivergent clients. Critical reflexivity can lead practitioners to adopt more inclusive practices that embrace Neurodivergent strengths and preferences rather than focusing on modifying behaviors to align with societal norms. Additionally, practitioners may reconsider the systemic structures in healthcare and education systems that marginalize Neurodivergent individuals and advocate for changes that promote greater autonomy and client-centered care. By continuously reflecting on and challenging these assumptions, OTPs can create a more equitable and inclusive therapeutic environment that respects the unique experiences of Neurodivergent people.

What Are the Benefits of Being Critically Reflexive?

Culturally Responsive Care

Critical reflexivity enhances culturally responsive care by encouraging practitioners to deeply examine their own biases, assumptions, and values about different cultural, social, and identity groups, as well as the structural systems and cultural norms that influence their practice. By engaging in this process, practitioners are better able to provide care that is attuned to the diverse cultural, social, and personal contexts of individuals, particularly those whose identities intersect in ways that may compound marginalization and inequity.

As mentioned in previous chapters, intersecting identities refer to the multiple, overlapping social identities an individual holds, such as race, ethnicity, gender, age, socioeconomic status, sexual orientation, religion, disability, and more. These identities do not exist in isolation but interact with one another in complex ways, often influencing how an individual experiences privilege, oppression, and access to services. For instance, a practitioner working with a Black Disabled woman might unconsciously prioritize one aspect of the individual's identity—such as their disability—while overlooking or minimizing the impacts of race or gender on their experience. By being reflexive, the practitioner can confront these biases, acknowledging how intersecting identities impact the individual's lived experiences and access to care, resulting in the OTP adjusting their practice. This creates a more inclusive, respectful, and person-centered approach to care, such as promoting the following:

- **Enhanced Professional Growth**: Critical reflexivity encourages continuous self-evaluation, helping practitioners refine their skills, improve decision-making, and stay open to learning from their experiences.
- **Bridging Theory and Practice**: Critical reflexivity helps practitioners apply theoretical knowledge more effectively in real-world situations, closing the gap between what is taught and what is practiced.
- **Greater Ethical Awareness**: By being critically reflexive of their actions and decisions, practitioners can better navigate ethical dilemmas, leading to more responsible and transparent practices.
- **Innovation in Practice**: Critical reflexivity prompts practitioners to question traditional methods and explore alternative approaches, fostering innovation and improvements in practice, such as integrating new perspectives on neurodiversity.
- **Improved Client–Professional Relationships**: Reflexive practitioners are more aware of power dynamics in their interactions, which can lead to more empathetic and equitable relationships with individuals, families, and communities.

Ethical and Professional Standards

Occupational therapy practitioners have an ethical and professional obligation to engage in critical reflexivity. These obligations are reflected in the professional standards of the regulatory bodies within the countries where OTPs work. Table 8.1 includes examples of how these requirements are reflected in selected English-speaking countries.

Table 8.1—International Ethical and Professional Standards Regarding Critical Reflexivity

Country	Examples of Related Standards
Australia	Australian Occupational Therapy Competency Standards, 2019[8] 2.8 reflects on practice to inform current and future reasoning and decision-making and the integration of theory and evidence into practice. 3.7 reflects on practice to inform and communicate professional reasoning and decision-making.
South Africa	Occupational Therapy Association of South Africa (OTASA) Guidelines, 2024[9] Occupational therapy services shall not allow prejudice, discrimination, or stigmatization toward a patient/client based on race, culture, language, gender, age, sexual orientation, health condition, disability, or socio-economic status, to result in an infringement of their privileges or rights.
United Kingdom	Health and Care Professions Council Standards for Occupational Therapy, 2023[10] 5.3 recognize the potential impact of their own values, beliefs, and personal biases (which may be unconscious) on practice and take personal action to ensure all service users and carers are treated appropriately with respect and dignity. 7.3 understand the characteristics and consequences of verbal and non-verbal communication and recognize how these can be affected by differences of any kind, including, but not limited to, protected characteristics, intersectional experiences, and cultural differences. 15.2 understand how social, economic, and environmental factors (wider determinants of health) can influence a person's health and well-being.
United States	American Occupational Therapy Association Occupational Therapy Code of Ethics, 2020[11] 1f. How to seek new and relevant knowledge to meet diverse client needs, the demands of a dynamic profession, and an ever-changing healthcare environment. 3b. Embrace cultural humility through reflective practice and self-assessment of one's biases to effectively interact and create a therapeutic relationship with persons who have backgrounds different from their own. 3f. Demonstrate professional civility to professionally engage with all clients, families, significant others, and professionals in constructive engagement that is inclusive, collaborative, and respectful in thought. 4d. Promote "occupational justice and... [empower] clients to seek and obtain resources to support health, well-being, and occupational participation." 4e. "Create an inclusive, supportive environment to enable clients to feel safe in expressing themselves authentically."

Neurodiversity Shifts and Reflexivity

What kinds of things can OTPs think about when beginning to challenge assumptions with neurodiversity? While sometimes engaging in reflexivity can lead to more questions than answers, it helps to think about specific situations in which to be critical. One idea is to think of what has been taken for granted. For example, as the concept of neurodiversity has gained popularity in the dominant discourse, "Neurodivergent" is often used as a euphemism for "Autistic" or sometimes "ADHD." This alters the term's intent and restricts the multiverse of neurodiversity and Neurodivergent experiences that also include people with intellectual disability, dyspraxia, fetal alcohol spectrum disorder, etc. As an OTP, in what ways can you challenge this shift in language? How would your critique look differently when (a) engaging with individuals and families versus (b) talking to colleagues, or (c) sharing information on social media on behalf of your workplace? When challenging popular discourse, it is important to consider power dynamics and lived experience with the people that you are communicating with. You might support an Autistic parent of a child with dyspraxia and intellectual disability who is involved in disability activism to lead the conversation, while you may need to support a communications director to understand changes to the dialogue regarding neurodiversity.

Occupational therapy practitioners can also think about the dominant values and beliefs about autism, and how they have shifted to better support affirming practice for all Neurodivergent communities. Some aspects of OT have shifted from a medical model of practice to a rights-based approach to working with Autistic children. The focus of advocacy related to autism has started to shift from awareness to acceptance, from groups led by parents of Autistic children to Autistic-led groups, from puzzle pieces and light it up blue to the infinity symbol and light it up red instead, and from person-first language to identity-first language. The dominant narrative has started to shift toward using neurodiversity terms and symbols; however, the prevalence of the terms and symbols does not necessarily mean that the user has engaged in reflection and reflexivity prior to shifting their use. For example, an outpatient clinic may change the paperwork for their social skills groups to talk about "Autistic children" rather than "children with autism." This reflects the change of language without engaging in questioning how their OT practice aligns with the neurodiversity movement or thinking about the systemic changes required to be able to reflect upon and review their biases and prejudices with Autistic and Neurodivergent individuals.

These shifts in the discourse and approach to practice mirror broader shifts in professional support in educational, medical, and community settings. They reflect the priorities of societies and the way that societal beliefs change. For example, many people with disabilities were confined to institutions for their lifetime until Disabled people's advocacy challenged this norm. Following de-institutionalization, services often still segregated Disabled people from non-disabled people. The current shift is toward services embedded in the community that support community inclusion for people with disabilities. For example, the National Disability Insurance Scheme (NDIS) in Australia is focused on increasing choice and control for people with disabilities through services that support community inclusion.[12] Critical reflexivity supports contemporary OTPs to question current norms, as their predecessors did, and envision ways of working and being that should change. The next sections support you, the reader, in considering aspects of your OT practice and wider ways of working that should be challenged, and considering alternatives.

How Can I Be Critically Reflexive?

> Critical reflexivity is not a one-time task but an ongoing commitment to growth.

Applying critical reflexivity involves a continuous process of self-examination and critical thinking about one's own beliefs, assumptions, and practices. See Figure 8.1 and Table 8.2 for one approach to applying critical reflexivity in neurodiversity-affirming practice.

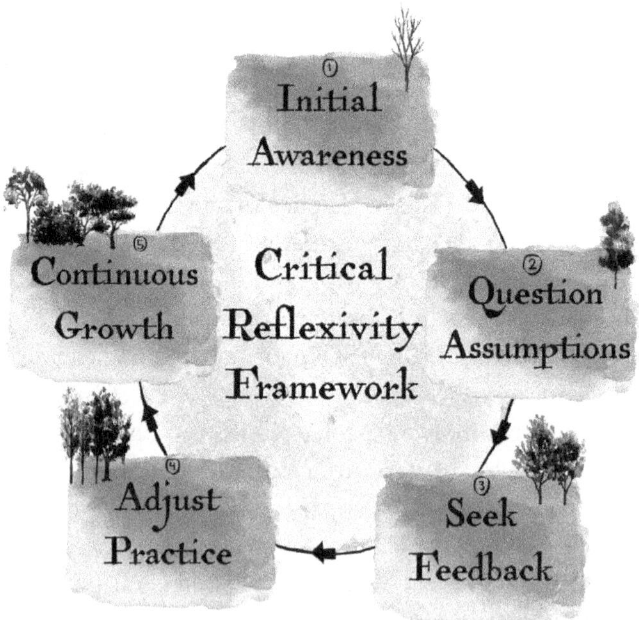

Figure 8.1—The Critical Reflexivity Framework

Table 8.2—Implementing the Critical Reflexivity Framework

Step	Components	General Critical Reflexivity Questions	Critical Reflexivity Questions for Neurodiversity-Affirming Practice
1. Initial Awareness	Begin by acknowledging your values, cultural background, and biases and how they shape your worldview. Reflect on how your personal history, education, social and cultural context, and practice setting influence your decisions and interactions with others.	What assumptions am I making about this situation? How might my background and past experiences influence my views? What are the social and political forces that shape my practice? Who is being neglected or ignored in my area of practice? How is independence socially valued? Where did my beliefs about what constitutes "good" occupations arise? How are these values and beliefs taken up by the people I work with? How can I learn more about critical reflexivity? What continuing professional education should I engage in to learn more?	Am I focusing on weaknesses in the absence of strengths? Am I offering activities and choices that are related to interests? Am I viewing Neurodivergent interests as strengths versus motivators, or worse yet, suppressing them as maladaptive behaviors? Am I combining a strengths perspective with the challenges that are being addressed? What privileges do I hold that may shape my perspective on neurodiversity, and how can I become more aware of how these affect my interactions with clients (e.g. if neurotypical, recognizing privilege by how society was created for my sensory, executive functioning, and mental patterns of processing). How might my perspective on neurodivergence be shaped by the medical model, and how can I shift toward a more inclusive understanding of disability? In my practice setting, how are tasks such as living alone, managing finances, or obtaining employment seen as markers of success for Neurodivergent individuals? How do these expectations align with or differ from my client's own goals and definitions of independence? Am I seeking out resources and training developed or facilitated by Neurodivergent individuals?

cont.

Step	Components	General Critical Reflexivity Questions	Critical Reflexivity Questions for Neurodiversity-Affirming Practice
2. Question Assumptions	Question your internalized shared social values, beliefs, and norms and the assumptions underlying occupational therapy practices that have become second nature / are not questioned in our field. Consider how your assumptions align with or challenge established norms, particularly those related to power, privilege, and social structures. Consider how these dynamics influence your practice or professional behavior. *Tip: journaling or discussing cases with peers can support this process.*	How do my beliefs about behaviors or societal expectations affect my treatment approaches or decision-making? Why do I think this way? Are my beliefs based on evidence or cultural norms? How do these assumptions affect my practice? What are the shared social values, beliefs, and norms where I work? What assumptions are built into the assessments I use? What are the potential unintended harms of these ways of thinking (e.g. Who is being excluded? Who is being seen as a "problem to be fixed"?)?	To what extent do I involve Neurodivergent individuals in the planning and evaluation of their therapeutic interventions? What are the shared cultural values of the disability culture my client resides in (e.g. culture of people with Down syndrome)? How do standardized assessments compare Disabled individuals to non-disabled individuals, and how can that be harmful? How does my perception of the behaviors of Neurodivergent individuals reflect neurotypical ideals (e.g. perception of when someone is being "aggressive")?
3. Seek Feedback	Engage in dialogue with peers, clients, or colleagues to gain perspectives on your actions and assumptions, especially with people with different perspectives. Fostering a sense of collective accountability to create change is important.	How does my social reality differ from the clients that I work with? What areas of practice do others see as needing to change? Whose comfort am I prioritizing when considering interventions? Whose perspectives am I privileging when seeking feedback?	When choosing interventions, do I prioritize practices that align with a classroom or workplace environment's expectations, even if they don't align with the client's preferences or sensory needs? Am I focusing more on making neurotypical individuals comfortable with a Neurodivergent individual's behavior rather than addressing the comfort and needs of the individual themselves?

4. Adjust Practice	Reflexivity often uncovers areas where growth or change is needed. Be prepared to adjust your professional practices or perspectives based on what you learn. Make use of your feelings of discomfort as a greater stimulus for changing and advancing practice.[13] Use your learning to guide meaningful changes in your practice. This could mean modifying how you interact with clients, rethinking therapeutic approaches, or advocating for broader systemic changes. As explored in Chapter 6, think of how to direct change at meso- and macro-levels, as when OTPs direct their strategies toward changing physical, social, and institutional factors, they still tend to focus on the individual level.[14]	What systems and practices uphold an ableist approach in my workplace? What could I do differently? What are the barriers to change within my workplace? Are there ways that I should conceptualize and explain disability differently to others?	What language am I using to describe Neurodivergent individuals, and does it reflect a respectful and empowering view? How do I ensure that I am not unconsciously imposing a "fix-it" mentality on Neurodivergent clients and instead embracing their strengths and perspectives? What are the potential unintended harms of adhering to conventional OT practices, and how can I address them? What aspects of the OT process need to shift to better align with a neurodiversity paradigm (e.g. assessment, goal setting, intervention, monitoring)? In what ways do I ensure that my interventions promote autonomy and self-determination for Neurodivergent individuals within the environment? How might my treatment plans be influenced by a desire to fit clients into socially acceptable norms rather than supporting their unique ways of being? What structural barriers exist in my practice that might limit access to or effectiveness of services for Neurodivergent clients? What are other ways schools could think about classroom expectations? Are the tools and assessments I use designed with Neurodivergent individuals in mind, or do they inherently prioritize neurotypical standards?
5. Continuous Growth	Critical reflexivity is not a one-time event but an ongoing practice. Continuously revisit and reassess your beliefs, values, and approaches to stay responsive to new learning and evolving contexts.	What further societal assumptions should I be considering? How do the clients I work with perceive my adjusted practice?	How can I advocate for systemic changes within my practice or organization that support Neurodivergent individuals more effectively while making my advocacy sustainable for myself?

Examples Applying the Critical Reflexivity Framework in OT Practice

Guided by the above approach, the following are examples of how OTPs could use critical reflexivity to enhance care with Neurodivergent individuals. By using critical reflexivity, practitioners can provide care that is more respectful of the person's neurotype. This approach builds trust with the person and their family. It leads to more meaningful and individualized therapeutic outcomes, as the practitioner's interventions are based on the person's strengths and comfort and create a more effective and inclusive therapeutic approach.

Snapshot: Shawna

Shawna has been practicing for 20 years as an OTP working in school settings in Washington State, United States. Her caseload is children from 3 years to 12 years and predominantly from Marginalized ethnic groups, including Latinx, Somali, and Indian.

Initial Awareness

She feels confident working with her diverse caseload; however, she has started learning about a neurodiversity positive approach, and she thinks that maybe she should learn more about it to see if she needs to change her approach to practice. When she went to university 20 years ago, reflexivity was not something that they talked about. The first thing she does is start to read about reflexivity to learn more[15] as well as the current priorities of Autistic people for OT services.[16]

Adjust Practice

Shawna has identified that her assessments are predominantly developmental, such as the Bruininks-Oseretsky Test of Motor Proficiency-2 (BOT-2) or the Beery-Buktenica Test of Visual Motor Integration (Beery-VMI), rather than focused on well-being. These are likely due to Western societal values of independence and skill development rather than inclusion and belonging. She has consulted with her professional team, families she has worked with, and disability advocates to learn about alternatives to her current assessments that would work in her setting. She has decided to include the Pediatric Volitional Questionnaire (preschool age), Child Occupational Self-Assessment (school-aged), and the Children's Assessment of Participation and Enjoyment (CAPE) in her assessments. To address areas of intersecting marginalization of Autistic children and their families from Marginalized cultural and ethnic backgrounds, such as racism and ableism by OTPs,[17] Shawna seeks to begin to practice with greater cultural humility and awareness of the challenges the children she works with and their families experience. The focus of her goals has shifted from focusing on neurotypical motor development to self-advocacy, positive mental health, and social participation. Approaches to addressing the goals that Shawna uses include teaching children to advocate for the use of their sensory and emotional regulatory tools when needed and providing knowledge and resources to educators addressing differing styles of social communication and participation. She also now collaborates with all teachers to support the development of flexible spaces within classrooms to support sensory needs.[18,19] To support mental well-being and authentic social participation, she has asked her students about their interests and has developed interest-based social groups that students can choose to participate in, including Legos, cooking, and robotics.[20,21,22]

Full Process: Niamh

Niamh has been an OTP for six years in the United Kingdom. She works in a service supporting adults with intellectual disability/learning disabilities (ID/LD) often in addition to other co-occurring neurotypes (e.g. autism, cerebral palsy, Down syndrome, fetal alcohol spectrum disorder) in the National Health Service (NHS). She works in an area of Scotland that has families living in generational poverty. Many of her service users are individuals with high support needs for regulation.

1. Initial Awareness

Niamh's service has started to think about shifting toward a neurodiversity-affirming approach as they have identified that their traditional assessment tools are not fully capturing the service user's strengths and instead are pointing to individual problems to be addressed. She is aware that behavioral approaches are not neurodiversity affirming; however, Positive Behavior Support is considered a gold standard approach within the NHS for people with ID/LD.[23] Niamh and her colleagues have started to question whether their goals are shaped by societal expectations of behavior rather than the unique needs and preferences of the individual.

When making decisions about what opportunities would be best, she considers who are the voices that will be leading the conversation and prioritizes continuing education that comes from the voices of people with ID/LD, especially those from Marginalized backgrounds. She knows that "neurodiversity" is a trendy phrase and thus seeks to be critical of the approach and content of opportunities, even if they call themselves neurodiversity-affirming.

2. Questioning Assumptions

Niamh identifies the following taken-for-granted assumptions held by many practitioners:

- The belief that therapeutic success is achieved by making individuals with ID/LD conform to neurotypical ideals (e.g. prioritizing spoken language instead of validating the unique ways of communicating, such as a combination of augmentative and alternative communication devices, non-verbal communication, and differences in speech patterns).

- The focus of progressing the service user's skills developmentally, which is a Western and colonized ideal (e.g. emphasizing independence in activities of daily living [ADLs] rather than their participation in activities they find meaningful, which may not be ADLs).
- The societal infantilization of adults with ID/LD (e.g. speaking in a condescending manner).

Niamh reflects on her own biases about people with ID/LD, questioning whether her perception of the service user's behavior (e.g. hitting when upset) is shaped by societal norms that prioritize neurotypical communication styles. She considers how if the adults with ID/LD had alternative methods of communicating frustration, they may have fewer behaviors that challenge others. Her service has focused on whether adults with ID/LD are ready for augmentative and alternative communication devices (AAC). This is due to a focus on spoken language rather than introducing AAC early.[24] Niamh begins to question her role in perpetuating these norms and how her beliefs, influenced by societal expectations, may impact the therapy they provide. She realizes that expecting adults with ID/LD to conform to these norms may hinder rather than help their progress and ultimately cause harm. Niamh also considers how adults with ID/LD may be impacted by systemic barriers, such as long waiting lists for services, inappropriate housing provision, or insufficient support from learning disability nurses, forcing adults with ID/LD and their carers to navigate a complex system that does not fully value neurodiversity.

Niamh next considers how the focus on individuals developing skills in a progressive manner is not consistent with Neurodivergent people's "spiky profiles" in development and hinders her ability to practice in a strengths-focused manner. Spiky profiles refer to the uneven set of abilities and capacities, for example strong reading skills while also having impaired verbal expressive language skills.[25] Evaluating her service users' skills in comparison to neurotypical standards focuses on their deficits and is not occupation-focused. Additionally, it does not provide scope for leveraging the strengths of the service user to enable engaging in valued occupations. She considers how the ways that the medical model in which her service sits makes it more challenging to practice in an occupation-focused manner. While Niamh thinks of herself as someone who values all the clients that she works with, she is starting to see how societal assumptions have shaped the way that she thinks about how capable adults with ID/LD are. She considers the way that media portrayals of people with ID/LD and the medical model of care have negatively impacted her perception of what people with ID/LD can do.

3. Seeking Feedback

Niamh and her team start by seeking feedback from the adults with ID/LD and their caregivers who use her service, advocacy organizations such as the Scottish Commission on Learning Disabilities, and other community members such as educators and LD nurses on priorities of support for adults with ID/LD who have co-occurring conditions. They ask about the ways that the service is supporting adults with ID/LD and ways that it is falling short. They ensure that the ways that they seek feedback are inclusive, inviting feedback through verbal, non-verbal, and AAC communication approaches. They ask questions about the goals that should be prioritized, how they should evaluate success, and the approaches to intervention that are valued. They specifically seek to understand, from the perspective of adults with ID/LD, the reasons why they engage in behaviors that challenge others to address the underlying causes (e.g. frustration with communication, sensory overwhelm, challenges with the ability to engage in valued activities, or physical discomfort).

4. Adjusting Practice

Niamh decides to adapt her approach in collaboration with colleagues. To address their ableism that they have uncovered, Niamh and her colleagues explore ways that can challenge their assumptions of what people with ID/LD can do and be. They create a list of media clips,[26] books, podcasts, and films that demonstrate what people with ID/LD are capable of doing and being, and develop a learning circle to discuss their thoughts about these resources in a safe space. They decide to create a series of strengths-based, interest-focused groups for adults with ID/LD[27] that align with the valued occupations identified in Step 3 and support community participation and inclusion. They do not shy away from topics such as sexuality and drinking alcohol that are often not discussed with adults with ID/LD due to their societal infantilization. The focus of strengths-based clubs in the literature has been on Autistic children and adolescents without ID/LD. The team decides to challenge the exclusion of people with ID/LD in this research and pilot these clubs within their service.

Instead of using behavioral evaluations, they shift to using assessments that explore the service user's interests, values, and goals. For example, the Model of Human Occupation Screening Tool (MOHOST), Occupational Identity Questionnaire (OIQ-II), Canadian Occupational Performance Measure (COPM), Visual Activity Sort, and the Adolescent/Adult Goal Setting Tool. They adapt their assessments to include easy-to-read components to increase access. Niamh advocates for the elimination of behavioral approaches within the service but receives considerable pushback from colleagues. She advocates that a way to naturally reduce or eliminate dysregulation responses is to focus on developing skills (e.g. to reduce frustration when engaging in valued occupations), adapting environments (e.g. to reduce sensory overwhelm), and holistically considering other reasons for behaviors (e.g. exploring food intolerances, pain, sleep challenges, or sensory discomfort) and referring to other services as needed. Niamh and her team implemented the use of Sensory Ladders[28] in their therapy sessions to support adults with ID/LD to increase their self-awareness in emotional and sensory regulation to enable better overall regulation. Niamh and her team work with the psychologists and speech and language therapists to shift toward honoring all forms of communication and increasing access to AAC. This focus on communication can reduce behaviors that challenge others by supporting adults with ID/LD to feel heard and valued.

When they sought feedback, Niamh and her team learned that many adults with ID/LD and their families did not know what services and support they were entitled to. Their service now runs a series of workshops co-led with an OTP and an adult with ID/LD to support other adults with ID/LD and their caregivers to develop advocacy skills. These workshops teach participants about systemic structures that may impact their experiences, such as hospital care that does not honor their communication methods. They explain ways adults with ID/LD and caregivers can advocate within these systems, such as helping them secure appropriate accommodations (e.g. access to easy-read documents and AAC) and challenging systemic structures by advocating for more inclusive, strengths-based models of therapy that respect Neurodivergent differences rather than seeking to change them. They also share information about organizations that can support advocacy work, such as the Scottish Commission on Learning Disabilities.[29]

5. Continuous Growth

Niamh and her team regularly review their assumptions and the effectiveness of their practice. They evaluate their groups and advocacy workshops to explore how they have met the needs of participants and ways they need to shift their focus. They stay open to new information, attending workshops on neurodiversity to further challenge traditional models of therapy and integrate more inclusive practices into their work.

What Resources Exist to Support My Critical Reflexivity Journey?

A variety of resources are available to support practitioners on their critical reflexivity journey, offering tools to deepen self-awareness and reflection within clinical practices. Among these is the seven-step framework by Nixon et al.,[30] an iterative process guiding practitioners through a structured reflection on specific aspects of practice. This framework encourages users to scrutinize their assumptions, identify beneficiaries and disadvantaged groups, connect individual practices to broader societal patterns, and envision alternatives to mitigate harm. Initially designed for physical therapists, the model can easily extend to occupational therapy and other fields. Another resource, Cards for Humanity,[31] is a free, accessible online tool designed to enhance the human dimension in clinical care. Cards can be used to prompt critical reflexivity in practice or during discussion at team meetings. Originally for neuromuscular outpatient settings with children, it has proven valuable across various contexts by sparking reflective discussions among teams. The Harvard Implicit Association Test[32] offers a practical way for individuals to uncover implicit biases, which may affect interactions with diverse groups. Additional tools like the Bridges Learning System's Assessment of Individual Ableism,[33] the Neurodiversity Attitudes Questionnaire,[34] the Cross-Cultural Adaptability Inventory,[35] and the Neurodiversity Employers Index (NDEI)[36] provide focused avenues for assessing specific biases and adaptability in clinical and workplace environments. Collectively, these resources guide practitioners toward a more inclusive, reflexive approach, promoting personal and professional growth.

Endnotes

1 Setchell, J., & Dalziel, B. (2019). Using critical reflexivity to enhance clinical care: A clinician perspective. *Journal of Humanities in Rehabilitation*, 1–12. www.jhrehab.org/2019/04/15/using-critical-reflexivity-to-enhance-clinical-care-a-clinician-perspective

2 Rudman, D. L. (2021). Mobilizing occupation for social transformation: Radical resistance, disruption, and re-configuration: Mobiliser l'occupation pour une transformation sociale: résistance radicale, perturbation et reconfiguration. *Canadian Journal of Occupational Therapy*, *88*(2), 96–107. https://ir.lib.uwo.ca/otpub/72

3 Whalley Hammell, K. R. (2015). Client-centred occupational therapy: The importance of critical perspectives. *Scandinavian Journal of Occupational Therapy*, *22*(4), 237–243. https://doi.org/10.3109/11038128.2015.1004103

4 Ng, S. L., Wright, S. R., & Kuper, A. (2019). The divergence and convergence of critical reflection and critical reflexivity: Implications for health professions education. *Academic Medicine*, *94*(8), 1122–1128. https://doi.org/10.1097/ACM.0000000000002724

5 Wilson, C., Janes, G., & Williams, J. (2022). Identity, positionality and reflexivity: Relevance and application to research paramedics. *British Paramedic Journal*, *7*(2), 43–49. https://doi.org/10.29045/14784726.2022.09.7.2.43

6 Neary, S. (2014). Professional identity: What I call myself defines who I am. *Career Matters*, *2*(3). https://repository.derby.ac.uk/item/93z02/professional-identity-what-i-call-myself-defines-who-i-am

7 Farias, L., Laliberte Rudman, D., Pollard, N., Schiller, S., Serrata Malfitano, A. P., Thomas, K., & van Bruggen, H. (2019). Critical dialogical approach: A methodological direction for occupation-based social transformative work. *Scandinavian Journal of Occupational Therapy*, *26*(4), 235–245. https://doi.org/10.1080/11038128.2018.1469666

8 Occupational Therapy Board of Australia. (2019). *Australian occupational therapy competency standards*. www.occupationaltherapyboard.gov.au/Codes-Guidelines/Competencies.aspx

9 Occupational Therapy Association of South Africa. (2024). *OTASA guidelines and principles for ethical and professional conduct*. www.otasa.org.za

10 Health and Care Professions Council. (2023). *The standards of proficiency for occupational therapists*. www.hcpc-uk.org/standards/standards-of-proficiency/occupational-therapists

11 American Occupational Therapy Association. (2020). AOTA 2020 occupational therapy code of ethics. *American Journal of Occupational Therapy, 74*(Suppl. 3), 7413410005. https://doi.org/10.5014/ajot.2020.74S3006

12 National Disability Insurance Scheme (NDIS). (2024, April). *How the NDIS works*. www.ndis.gov.au/understanding/how-ndis-works

13 Yeung, E., Gibson, B. E., Kuper, A., Shaw, J., & Nixon, S. (2021). "Making strange": Exploring the development of students' capacity in epistemic reflexivity. *Journal of Humanities in Rehabilitation*. www.jhrehab.org/2019/11/14/

making-strange-exploring-the-development-of-students-capacity-in-epistemic-reflexivity

14 Phelan, S. K. (2011). Constructions of disability: A call for critical reflexivity in occupational therapy. *Canadian Journal of Occupational Therapy, 78*(3), 164–172. https://doi.org/10.2182/cjot.2011.78.3.4

15 Rogers, M., & Allen, D. (2024). Embedding reflexivity in social work research through the critical reflexive framework. *British Journal of Social Work, 54*(4), 1753–1772. https://doi.org/10.1093/bjsw/bcad245

16 Sterman, J., Gustafson, E., Eisenmenger, L., Hamm, L., & Edwards, J. (2023). Autistic adult perspectives on occupational therapy for Autistic children and youth. *OTJR: Occupation, Participation and Health, 43*(2), 237–244. https://doi.org/10.1177/15394492221103850

17 Sterman, J., Wagland, Z., Scott-Cole, L., Spassiani, N., & Njelesani, J. (under review). Addressing intersectional needs of Autistic children and their families from Black, Asian, and Minority Ethnicity (BAME) backgrounds: A scoping review.

18 Crompton, C., Hallett, S., Axbey, H., McAuliffe, C., & Cebula, K. (2023). "Someone like-minded in a big place": Autistic young adults' attitudes towards Autistic peer support in mainstream education. *Autism, 27*(1), 76–91. https://doi.org/10.1177/13623613221081189

19 Donaldson, A. L., Krejcha, K., & McMillin, A. (2017). A strengths-based approach to autism: Neurodiversity and partnering with the autism community. *Perspectives of the ASHA Special Interest Groups, 2*(1), 56–68. https://doi.org/10.1044/persp2.sig1.56

20 Chen, Y. L., Murthi, K., Martin, W., Vidiksis, R., Riccio, A., & Patten, K. (2022). Experiences of students, teachers, and parents participating in an inclusive, school-based informal engineering education program. *Journal of Autism and Developmental Disorders, 52*(8), 3574–3585. https://doi.org/10.1007/s10803-021-05230-2

21 Lee, E. A. L., Black, M. H., Falkmer, M., Tan, T., Sheehy, L., Bölte, S., & Girdler, S. (2020). "We can see a bright future": Parents' perceptions of the outcomes of participating in a strengths-based program for adolescents with autism spectrum disorder. *Journal of Autism and Developmental Disorders, 50*(9), 3179–3194. https://doi.org/10.1007/s10803-020-04411-9

22 Patten, K. K. (2022). Finding our strengths: Recognizing professional bias and interrogating systems. *American Journal of Occupational Therapy, 76*(6), 7606150010. https://doi.org/10.5014/ajot.2022.076603

23 Care Quality Commission. (2018). *Brief guide: Positive behavior support for people with behaviors that challenge.* Care Quality Commission. www.cqc.org.uk/sites/default/files/20180705_900824_briefguide-positive_behaviour_support_for_people_with_behaviours_that_challenge_v4.pdf

24 Crowe, B., Machalicek, W., Wei, Q., Drew, C., & Ganz, J. (2022). Augmentative and alternative communication for children with intellectual and developmental disability: A mega-review of the literature. *Journal of Developmental and Physical Disabilities, 34*(1), 1–42. https://doi.org/10.1007/s10882-021-09790-0

25 Milton, D. (2012). *So what exactly is autism?* Autism Education Trust. https://capacity-resource.middletownautism.com/wp-content/uploads/sites/6/2017/03/damian-milton.pdf

26 CoorDown. (2024, March 21). *Assume that I can.* www.instagram.com/reel/C4fzdNYOzt4/?-utm_source=ig_embed&ig_rid=b65e728a26b5-47bc-9d89-181709912183

27 Wagland, Z., Sterman J, Njelesani, J., Scott-Cole, L., & Spassiani, N. (in press). Promotion of authentic Autistic identities: A scoping review. *Neurodiversity.*

28 Smith, K. (2024). *Sensory ladders—home.* Sensory Ladders. https://sensoryladders.org

29 Scottish Commission for People with Learning Disabilities (SCLD). (2025). *Scottish Commission for People with Learning Disabilities—home.* Scottish Commission for Learning Disability. www.scld.org.uk/home

30 Nixon, S. A., Yeung, E., Shaw, J. A., Kuper, A., & Gibson, B. E. (2017). Seven-step framework for critical analysis and its application in the field of physical therapy. *Physical Therapy, 97*(2), 249–257. https://doi.org/10.2522/ptj.20160149

31 Holland Bloorview Kids Rehabilitation Hospital. (2019). *Cards for humanity—human dimensions of illness experience.* Physiopedia. www.physio-pedia.com/Human_Dimensions_of_Illness_Experience

32 Project Implicit. (2011). *Implicit association test (IAT).* Project Implicit. https://implicit.harvard.edu/implicit/takeatest.html

33 Bridges Learning System. (2021). *Assessment of individual ableism.* Bridges Learning System. https://bridgeslearningsystem.com/wp-content/uploads/2021/12/SEA-Bridge_Assessment-of-Individual-Ableism.pdf

34 Schuck, R. K., Choi, S., Baiden, K. M., Dwyer, P., & Uljarević, M. (2024). The Neurodiversity Attitudes Questionnaire: Development and initial validation. *Autism: The International Journal of Research and Practice, 28*(11), 2821–2833. https://doi.org/10.1177/13623613241245756

35 Meyers, J., & Kelley, C. (2015). *The cross-cultural adaptability inventory (CCAI).* HRDQ.

36 Autistica. (2025). *The NDEI: Lead the way for neuroinclusion in the workplace.* Autistica. www.Autistica.org.uk/get-involved/employers/ndei

CHAPTER 9

Inclusive Evaluations

LISA MARNELL, KATHRYN L. HANSEN, RACHEL
ROBERTSON, AND BRYDEN CARLSON-GIVING

Introduction

Occupational therapy (OT) evaluations are vital to the therapeutic process. They allow practitioners to identify not only *what* to focus on, but also *how* to evaluate those areas. Choosing the appropriate tools inevitably also means selecting the right philosophical perspectives that underlie their creation and purpose. Furthermore, it is not only the assessment tools used that reflect practitioner values—conducting a truly neurodiversity-affirming evaluation begins before the client or practitioner ever steps through the door. This chapter will provide occupational therapy practitioners (OTPs) with a justification of why shifting to neurodiversity-affirming evaluations is essential and will propose a framework for completing evaluations that support Neurodivergent participation and combat ableism.

Getting into the Right Mindset

In her Eleanor Clarke Slagle lecture at the American Occupational Therapy Association Inspire Conference in 2022, Dr. Kristie Patten explained that our professional bias impacts "not only how our practice may be getting it wrong today but is also perpetuating the systems that prevent us from getting it right tomorrow."[1] As OTPs complete evaluations, it is important to ask—what are we getting wrong, exactly? And how can we revise our approaches to "get things right"? Since neurodiversity-affirming practice means we honor a client's traits as differences and not deficits, we need to ensure that our professional evaluations align with this philosophy. We must not approach evaluations and subsequent intervention with a "we are going to fix them," ableist mindset. In fact, quite the opposite approach is imperative. We must be aware of Neurodivergent characteristics and understand, accept, and support the ways that these drive a client's actions, their activity in the world, and their identification of meaningful goals.

In addition, neurodiversity-affirming evaluations require shifting our perspective away from the confines of the medical model of disability, which pathologizes different ways of being. Current ableist evaluations identify and highlight the individual's deficits, or compare the Neurodivergent individual's participation to a neurotypical's performance in the same occupation. To see common components of ableist and deficit-based OT evaluations, see the list below. Feel free to critically reflect on your own practice. Are there any similarities between the contents of the list and your current approach?

- OTP has the attitude that they are the expert and doesn't facilitate the evaluation as an authentic collaboration between themselves and their client.

- The evaluation focuses on assessing performance components (not prioritized by the client) and body functions to compare to neurotypical norms, such as strength, sensory patterns, reflexes, and cognition.

- Emphasizing the evaluation of activities of daily living (ADLs) as though a hierarchy of occupations exists (e.g. thinking that ADLs are more important than leisure and play).

- No consideration of how the client's environments pose barriers to occupational participation (e.g. attitudes of caregivers and families, accessibility of accommodations at school).

- Assessment tools emphasizing neurotypical norms are the primary focus of the evaluation, such as the BOT-3 (Bruininks-Oseretsky Test of Motor Proficiency—3rd Edition), PDMS-2 (Peabody Developmental Motor Scales—2nd Edition), SPM-2 (Sensory Processing Measure—2nd Edition), FIM (Functional Independence Measure), and the KELS-4 (Kohlman Evaluation of Living Skills—4th Edition), and/or are used as outcome measures.

- Lack of cultural sensitivity or safety (including validating disability as having its own culture[s]).

- Interests are used as a motivator, reinforcement, or reward.

- Deficit-based and harmful language (e.g. not using the language preferences of the community, reporting Neurodivergent actions or traits in ways that judge them negatively).

- Presuming that independence is the ultimate goal for the client, rather than celebrating the beauty and necessity of interdependence.

- Goals are focused on how services will make it easier for the teacher/parent/caregiver instead of focusing on skills that support the individual to lead a self-determined life.

- Service provision focuses on "fixing" traits that deviate from neurotypical expectations, such as expanding so-called "restricted" play interests, encouraging sensory tolerance or conformity to neurotypical sensory patterns, and measuring success by how little the individual relies on accommodations.

- Outcome measures emphasize improving characteristics perceived as "deficits" within the evaluation and how the individual needs to change/improve to better fit the environment.

For example, many of our pediatric assessment tools examining shoe-tying would state that an eight-year-old not being able to tie their shoes is "behind" on that skill. Because we have this underlying assumption that six to seven years old is the ideal functioning threshold for shoe-tying, any differences contrary to this Eurocentric milestone are labeled as "decreased self-care skills," "challenges in shoe-tying," and "developmentally lagging behind their peers." From a neurodiversity-affirming perspective, we would first ask the client whether learning to tie their shoes is important to them, whether they would prefer accommodations or adaptations, or if the skill holds any personal significance at all. Shoe-tying is one skill we assume is important for our clients; imagine all of the other assumptions we make about our clients without even realizing it!

Instead of approaching evaluations with assumed notions of which occupations are meaningful and how they should be performed, neurodiversity-affirming evaluations prioritize the client's perspective, supporting occupations they personally find important for their health and well-being and respecting their preferred ways of engaging in them.[2] Our goal with the remainder of this chapter is to outline guiding principles that can be used to shift toward neurodiversity-affirming practice and can be tailored for Neurodivergent individuals across the lifespan in any context. We will then elaborate on these with descriptive examples of how to be neurodiversity-affirming through each specific component of the evaluation process.

Guiding Principles for Neurodiversity-Affirming Evaluations

To help navigate the evaluation process, it is essential to keep the following guiding principles in mind. Taken together, these will help prioritize affirming shifts and encourage thoughtful, reflexive decision-making. The guiding principles of neurodiversity-affirming evaluations are (see also Figure 9.1):

1. Honor Neurodivergent authenticity.
2. Embrace intersectionality.
3. Advocate for anti-ableism.
4. Center lived experience and collaboration.
5. Highlight strengths and positive identity.
6. Empower autonomy and self-advocacy.
7. Build community and connection.
8. Ensure accessibility and inclusion.

Figure 9.1—Guiding Principles of Neurodiversity-Affirming Evaluations

As we introduce the neurodiversity-affirming evaluation process, we will provide practical examples of how the principles can be implemented in OT practice. When you are working with clients in real-time, have in the back of your mind which of these principles you are embodying, and to what degree. Are your efforts deeply rooted in honoring the individual's identity, or are they surface-level changes, such as simply switching language? Attempting to conceptualize these principles all at the same time is likely overwhelming, and that is okay! Start by choosing one or two and plan how you can incorporate those principles into your evaluations with your next clients.

The Neurodiversity-Affirming Evaluation Process

Stage One: Preparing for the Evaluation

Component #1 – Review Referral for Bias/Ableism

The occupational therapy evaluation process is often initiated via referral from caregivers, teachers, or other professionals in a Neurodivergent person's life. Yet those who refer an individual to OT may have biases and ableist expectations for how things can and should be done. Neurodivergent actions are often described using deficit-based terminology.[3] In fact, attitudes of school staff toward Autistic children were found to be more negative and less supportive than toward non-Autistic children.[4] For examples of how ableist referral concerns can be reframed through an anti-ableist and advocacy-oriented lens, see Table 9.1.

Table 9.1—Ableist Reasons for OT Referral

Ableist Reason for Referral	Flipping the Narrative: Anti-Ableist Considerations and Reflexive Questions
Eight-year-old Jonah is labeled "aggressive at soccer practice" for frequently pushing kids while waiting on the sidelines.	• Affirm Jonah's energy needs and explore alternative ways Jonah can engage in proprioceptive input throughout his day. • Examine Jonah's perception of his friendships and peers during soccer practice and other natural environments. How does Jonah feel about his friendships and relationships? Does Jonah feel understood by his team? • Consider facilitating peer education, such as educating Jonah's coach and his team about sensory processing to support empathy and understanding of Jonah's (and likely their own) sensory processing differences.
45-year-old Tanya wants to learn how to socialize like her neurotypical peers and come across as "less Autistic."	• Does Tanya already have fulfilling, meaningful, and authentic relationships? What are her expectations around relationships? • Is Tanya familiar with her neurotype and communication preferences? Encourage discussions around her Autistic identity and help facilitate Tanya's exploration of her neurotype. • Does Tanya understand masking and the potential costs on mental health? Can we explore internalized ableism and self-image? • Does Tanya have awareness of and access to affirming communities?

Note. An expanded version of the table with more examples is available in the Vault.

As reasons for referral are gathered at the start of the evaluation process, the evaluator must identify whether OT support is truly justified. For example, an adult with anxiety in a community setting may be referred for "social skills intervention" because of their reluctance to take part in social gatherings. Alternatively, an Autistic toddler in early intervention may be referred to OT for their repetitive play schema of lining up toys. These are examples in which Neurodivergent traits are being seen as problems that need to be remediated. The occupational therapist should clarify the intention behind the referral. If the intention is to perform more like a neurotypical or is not in line with the Neurodivergent individual's priorities, the evaluation may not be warranted. Instead, the therapist may provide education to the referring individual. If the intention behind the seemingly ableist referral is increased safety or improved participation in daily life that is meaningful for the individual, one should continue the evaluation to address this occupational performance concern in an affirming way.

Component #2 – Scheduling the Evaluation

Establishing rapport and honoring Neurodivergent differences is essential when planning and carrying out a neurodiversity-affirming evaluation. Offering flexibility and clarity within the scheduling process can help foster comfort and agency of the client. Ways of offering flexibility may include inquiry of preferred time of day for evaluation based on energy levels, tolerance for session length, and asking about sensory and communication preferences. Providing a clear and concise summary or checklist of what to expect for the evaluation can also help Neurodivergent clients mentally prepare.

Component #3 – Incorporating Perspectives for Tailored Evaluations

For OTPs to best meet Neurodivergent needs from the initial encounter, practitioners should consider collecting input from the client and their support system before the evaluation. This can help the practitioner individualize their setup and approach to support a sense of safety for the Neurodivergent client. Regardless of age, Neurodivergent individuals often benefit from interdependence for engagement in at least one major life area. Seeking input from the client's primary social supports in addition to the client can provide rich context and prepare the OTP for being able to anticipate and plan for the client's needs. This can be done by sending out brief surveys or open-ended questionnaires to the client and/or their support system to complete before the evaluation.

> Consider OTs for Neurodiversity's *Neurodivergent Identity Workbook*.[5] The workbook begins with a "My Identity" section where the individual can share words (the workbook also makes it clear clients can use images throughout it) that describe them, how they refer to their disability, strengths, values, and things they don't like. The workbook then provides opportunity for the individual to share their special interests, favorite sensory tools and experiences, their community, and how they define a good life. And finally, the workbook ends with "Self-Actualization," where the client can share how they want to grow, what they are proud of, and how they can nurture their identity to continue growing.

Stage Two: Conducting the Evaluation

Component #4 – Establish a Supportive Environment

Meeting for the Evaluation

Time should be dedicated to clarifying expectations at the start of the evaluation. The practitioner should clarify the neurodiversity-affirming approach and differentiate what *it isn't* (i.e. "fixing," "normalizing," "making less Neurodivergent"). The practitioner should also explicitly share and model an environment for self-advocacy, stim-safety, and responding to body cues as needed. This can be done by having regulation tools and fidgets easily accessible, regularly checking in on the client's well-being and any unmet needs, using observational and curious language versus commands, offering opportunities for breaks as needed throughout, following the lead of the client for preferred positioning and eye contact, and being mindful of the pace.

Embrace a Neurodiversity-Affirming Tone

During evaluations, OTPs are afforded the initial opportunity to set the tone for the therapeutic relationship. From the moment the evaluation begins, it is important to observe and consider signs of your client's arousal level and sense of safety. In turn, your role as a practitioner is to honor their arousal state by prioritizing their autonomy and adjusting the pace, expectations, setup, and matching their energy level to provide the greatest possibility of comfort and safety for the client. In addition, as the initial touchpoint between the client and practitioner, the tone presented in this encounter will inform future ones and signal the safety and relevance of your role in the client's life moving forward. While there is no one "right" way to set a neurodiversity-affirming tone, consideration of the following examples may help inform your approach:

- **Language-use**: Consideration of pronouns, how they refer to their disability (identity-first, person-first), low-demand, neutral or positive description of differences, honoring non-linear conversation, non-rushed.
  - "How do you prefer to identify with your disability? How would you like us to discuss your differences in a way that feels accurate and comfortable for you?"

- **Create a welcoming environment**: Ensure the evaluation space is comfortable and sensory-inclusive, consider factors like lighting, noise levels, seating options, competing stimuli, and access to regulating tools, exit, etc.
  - "Let's take a moment to set up the evaluation space. What sensory elements do you find most comfortable or uncomfortable (e.g. lighting, noise, seating)? Where would you like to sit to feel most at ease during

our session? Are there any tools or items that help you feel calm or focused that I can provide during our evaluation?"

- **Be mindful of body language**: Eye contact, posture, proximity—following the lead of the client.
  - "What non-verbal cues should I be aware of to better understand how you're feeling during our session?"

- **Clarify expectations**: Communicate freedom to stim and regulate as needed, honoring body cues and need for breaks, and remind them of their agency and role as a collaborator for the entire therapy process. *They* are in the driver's seat!
  - "You are welcome to stim or take breaks whenever you need during our session. I want to remind you that you are in control here; your comfort is my priority throughout this process."

- **Respect their communication style**: Avoid pressuring clients to engage in verbal communication if it's not their preferred method. Allow extra time for responses to help reduce anxiety—"Please take all the time you need to think and respond."

- **Offer predictability, flexibility, and structure**: Ensure you are explaining the evaluation process, offer scaffolding around evaluation expectations, such as the use of a visual schedule, and allow flexibility in deviating from the planned structure.
  - "We have some structure today, but if we need to adjust our plan, just let me know."

- **Create a non-judgmental and safe space**: Avoid pathologizing language such as "deficits" or "problems" and reflect their perspectives back to them to show you understand and value their input.
  - "I value your experiences and want to reflect them back to you accurately. Your input matters here."

- **Focus on framing**: When discussing challenges, frame them in a way that acknowledges environmental barriers rather than having it all rest on the individual.
  - "When discussing any challenges you face, I'll frame them as environmental factors rather than personal deficits. Let's talk about any barriers you experience, and I'll focus on how we can address them together."

Component #5 – Creating the Neurodivergent Occupational Profile

Creating the Occupational Profile

While the evaluation process presents differently across settings, it is universally acknowledged as best practice for all evaluations to incorporate an occupational profile (OP). This document is created by the evaluating OTP and includes contexts and environments in which clients function, an analysis of occupational performance, as well as their personal interests and values.[6] Through the development of an OP, Neurodivergent clients can share details about their performance patterns (habits, routines, roles, and rituals), as well as their priorities and goals.[7] When creating an OP within the purview of neurodiversity-affirming practice, the clinician must pay close attention to not adopt a deficit-based view of body functions and structures, and not make assumptions that differences in motor or sensory presentation, for example, are viewed as problems that need "fixing." A clear definition of an OP is lacking within our profession and common tools to ensure therapists gather vital information are neither well-defined nor used by OTPs.[8] The *Neurodivergent Identity Workbook*[9] is suggested as an example questionnaire to be used to gather pertinent client information. Additionally, consider downloading our version of the occupational profile from the Vault to support your evaluations with Neurodivergent individuals.

Promoting Positive Identity

Neurodiversity-affirming evaluations must include a focus on self-empowerment and promoting a positive Neurodivergent identity. Research that includes the voices of Neurodivergent communities increasingly speaks to the importance of cultivating a positive sense of identity and the opportunity to embrace neurodivergence as integral to a person's sense of selfhood that presents both weaknesses and strengths as they navigate their lives.[10] This aspect is vital to supporting positive mental health in our clients, and in valuing our clients to be authentic to themselves.

Component #6 – Center Lived Experiences

Your primary source of information should always be the Neurodivergent clients themselves, even when working with children. For example, research has shown that there are often significant differences in goals and priorities related to health and well-being between Autistic individuals and their parents or caregivers.[11] Keep in mind that relying more on parent/caregiver reports may make your services not align with the hopes and dreams of the Neurodivergent client. Likely, this variation exists more broadly across the Neurodivergent community. To be genuinely neurodiversity-affirming, evaluations must be centered on the Neurodivergent individual's lived experiences, with their narratives and insights being the core focus of the assessment. If you are unable to interview the Neurodivergent individual or they are unable to make their goals and experiences clear, care plans should emphasize promoting the individual's self-efficacy, fostering a positive disability identity, and maximizing the individual's ability to lead a self-determined life.[12] You can also refer to the Vault for a supplemental download that outlines shared health and well-being priorities among Neurodivergent individuals.

Component #7 – Complete Naturalistic Observations

In addition, try to focus on observing the person completing activities in their natural environments, such as in home, school, or community settings. This approach allows you to better assess the real-life barriers that impact occupational participation and ensure that interventions are tailored to the individual's everyday experiences. Naturalistic observations offer valuable insights into sensory processing patterns, communication styles, and the types of supports that may be needed to promote autonomy and well-being. By focusing on what works best for the individual in contexts that matter to them, OTPs can create supports that are both meaningful and sustainable. For OTPs working in outpatient settings or who do not have access to evaluating the client in their natural settings, consider having the client and their family provide videos of the client engaging in everyday tasks, simulating the client's most important tasks in the clinic, and/or utilizing telehealth to observe the client in their natural environment. Maintaining trust, being responsive to the client's cues, and ensuring a collaborative process can make a significant difference in the effectiveness of the evaluation and subsequent intervention.

Component #8 – Consider the "Fit"

During the evaluation, we learn about the client's occupational participation. At times, an occupation holds importance to the client, yet they may be unable to participate without frustration or perceived failure. The evaluating OT can identify the "lack of fit" by examining the interaction of "what is expected" of a Neurodivergent person and "what is possible" given the person's neurology, the environment in which they are functioning, and the occupation or task and the way it is being presented. We can look at each of these factors separately:

1. The person's neurology incorporates interwoven factors which vary day to day. These include emotional regulation, mental health status, sensory processing, social traits and/or social comfort, communication, motor skills and motor planning, and level of fatigue.
2. The environment in which a client functions comprises sensory factors, social expectations, available communication systems, opportunities for movement, as well as cognitive stimulation.
3. The occupation/task considers the actual task, its meaning to a client, and the way it is presented. Specifically, it may require communication, social, or motor demands that do not align with the Neurodivergent person's strengths.

When a client is referred for an occupational therapy evaluation, the OT must consider whether there is a "lack of fit" between what is expected of them and what is possible for them. For example, when a Neurodivergent adult can feed themselves at home but cannot sit with peers at lunch in a group day setting, the OT can use this framework to determine which person factors, environmental factors, and occupation/task factors may be affecting the client's performance. Do keep in mind that the separation of the person from the environment is a Eurocentric idea that may not resonate with other cultures and communities. To learn more about alternative theoretical foundations for addressing evaluation and intervention in OT, particularly from Indigenous cultures, see Chapter 4 and explore Chapter 4's Vault items. If you are interested in reviewing critiques of occupation-based assessments and frameworks from an Indigenous perspective, consider reviewing Price and Pride[13] on the Canadian Occupational Performance Measure (COPM), and Hunter and Pride[14] on the Canadian Model of Client-Centered Enablement (CMCE).

Performance Components in Context

A neurodiversity-affirming OT evaluation should include an assessment of performance components that enable participation in meaningful occupations. These are "person factors" which are important for the evaluating therapist to identify and understand. Neurodiversity-affirming evaluations do not embrace traditional standardized testing. Yet, both structured and unstructured clinical observations, as well as appropriate client/caregiver questionnaires and interviews, enable the OTP to identify clients' challenges in underlying performance capacities. Recognizing the underlying challenges that a Neurodivergent individual faces will enable the development of strengths-based, appropriate goals and supportive accommodations. It is important to integrate the client's input regarding addressing performance components. Do keep in mind that attempting to address performance components without working on the actual occupation (a client wants to get better at gardening but the plan of care focuses on improving strength through exercises) can lead to a disconnect between the client's real-life priorities and therapy goals. Improving performance components without working on the actual activity does not guarantee an "upstream" gain in function or engagement in occupations.[15]

Component #9 – Utilize Inclusive Assessment Tools

One of the most common ways to collect evaluation data is through assessments, necessitating a conversation on standardized assessments. Standardized assessments often compare Disabled individuals to non-disabled individuals, often making neurotypicality or being non-disabled an implicit goal of therapy, and to prove a deviation from the norm; labeling that deviation as a deficit is the opposite of neurodiversity-affirming care.[16] OTPs should carefully evaluate whether these standardized tools truly reflect the functional needs and strengths of Neurodivergent clients. Many common assessment tools, such as the Beery-Buktenica Developmental Test of Visual-Motor Integration—6th Edition (Beery-VMI), Peabody Developmental Motor Scales—2nd Edition (PDMS-2), Bruininks-Oseretsky Test of Motor Proficiency—2nd Edition (BOT-2), and Sensory Processing Measure—2nd Edition (SPM-2), are designed around Eurocentric, neurotypical norms. For example, when using the Functional Independence Measure (FIM) or the Kohlman Evaluation of Living Skills (KELS), clients may prefer to have physical assistance or devices for daily activities (e.g. the client prefers to cook and prepare meals with their family as a form of social engagement rather than doing it alone) or may have different priorities and modalities for instrumental daily activities, rendering much of the KELS irrelevant. This can inadvertently emphasize neurotypical motor skills and sensory processing patterns, which may not be relevant or meaningful for Neurodivergent individuals. Moreover, many of these standardized and criterion-based assessments emphasize structural aspects of the body, aligning with the medical model of disability. This focus can undermine the therapeutic relationship by reinforcing a deficit-based perspective, jeopardizing the potential rapport between the OTP and client, and negatively impacting the client's self-esteem.

> By centering our evaluation systems on neurotypical benchmarks, we risk undermining the client's safety and mental health. Neurodivergent individuals will never be neurotypical, and expecting Neurodivergent individuals to conform is unrealistic, unfair, and harmful.

For OTPs navigating the pressures of reimbursement agencies that require standardized scores—don't worry, we've got you covered! A supplemental download in the Vault explores strategies for handling this complex challenge in ways that align with neurodiversity-affirming practice.

Assessment Tools Emphasizing Lived Experiences and Environmental Considerations

When completing your evaluation, consider incorporating more affirming assessment tools, such as ones that focus on lived experiences, examine environmental supports and barriers, highlight the saliency of identities given the context of care, and/or have been created with or by Neurodivergent individuals. Figures 9.2 and 9.3 feature neurodiversity-affirming assessments for pediatric and adult populations. One such tool is the Cultural Identity Assessment (CIA), which can be especially valuable during the initial clinical encounter to facilitate conversations around sociocultural identities that may influence a patient's experiences, care needs, and treatment outcomes. The CIA includes a cultural identity wheel visual aid, is quick to administer (about 5 minutes), and can be revisited later throughout the occupational therapy process to deepen identity-centered discussions. You can access the CIA and its provider guide for free in the Vault, along with a 20+ page resource that outlines the tools featured in the figures—including descriptions, linked websites (many free), and other helpful details. The downloadable resource also includes additional tools found after the figures were completed.

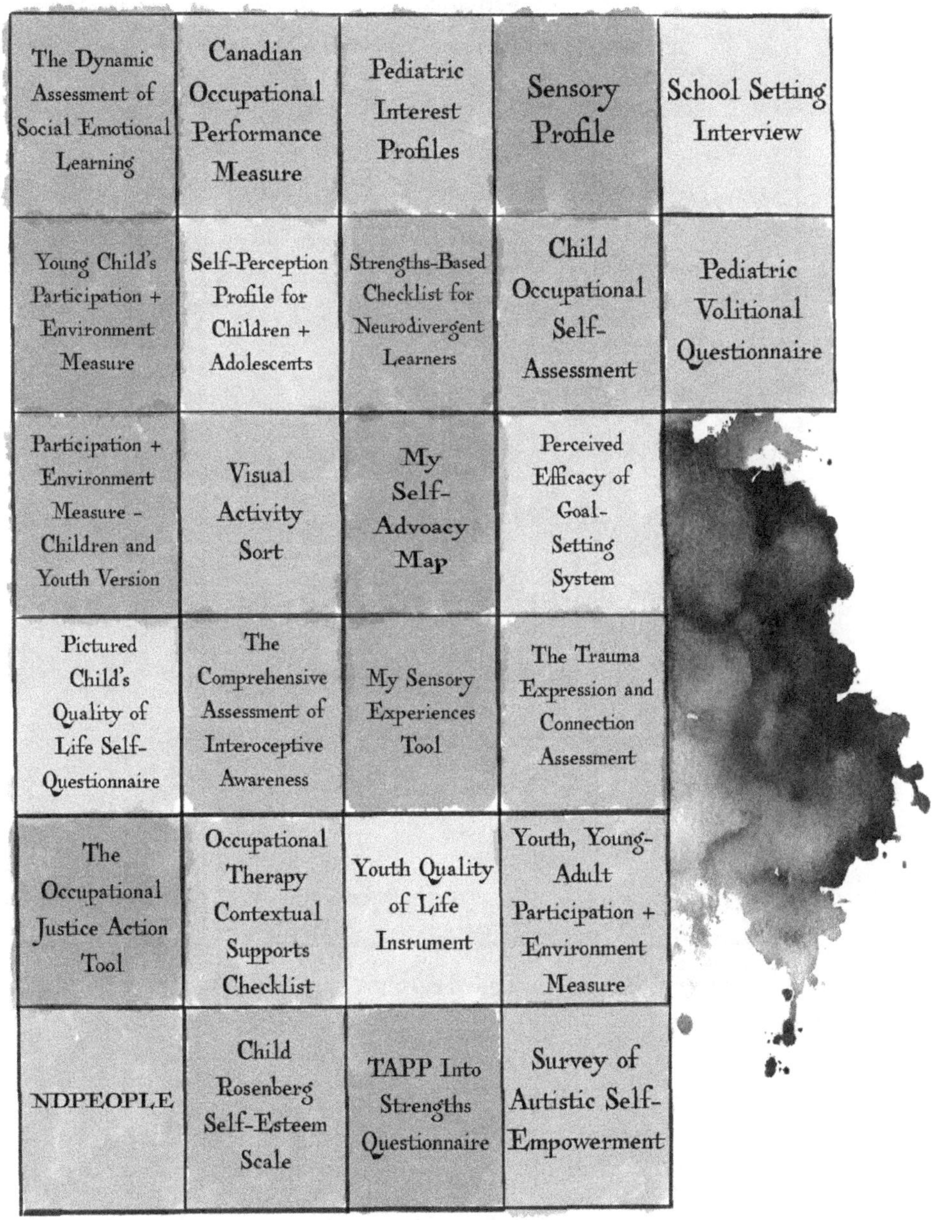

Figure 9.2—Recommended Pediatric Assessment Tools

The Dynamic Assessment of Social Emotional Learning	Canadian Occupational Performance Measure	NDPEOPLE	Sensory Profile
Visual Activity Sort	The Comprehensive Assessment of Interoceptive Awareness	Multidimensional Assessment of Interoceptive Awareness	Youth, Young-Adult Participation + Environment Measure
My Sensory Experiences Tool	Transition-Q	Adolescent/ Adult Goal Setting Tool	Occupational Self-Assessment
Camouflaging Autistic Traits Questionnaire	Online Alexithymia Questionnaire	WHO's Quality of Life Questionnaire	Rosenberg Self-Esteem Scale
Work Environment Impact Scale	Gender Minority Stress Resilience Measure	Model of Human Occupation Screening Tool	Occupational Identity Questionnaire

Figure 9.3—Recommended Adult Assessment Tools

Stage Three: Strengths-Based Reporting and Writing Empowering Goals

Component #10 – Strengths-Based Documentation

> Research shows that the language practitioners use in reports not only shapes the client–caregiver relationship but also influences how caregivers perceive and understand the client. The words we choose matter—they can either empower or diminish the client's sense of identity.

Before you begin, commit to making your reporting process strengths-based. To do so, give the client the space to exercise self-determination, choose how they want to engage with the world, and make decisions for themselves. Remember that clients, parents, and caregivers read these reports, and if the reports are laden with deficit-based language, clients and families internalize these deficits and may even begin to view either themselves or their child as these deficits.[17,18]

Some additional considerations to help in writing strengths-based reports include:[19,20]

1. **Be Descriptive Without Judgment**: Use descriptive language to portray the client's skills and actions without assigning judgment or labels. For instance, instead of saying "Gabriela has difficulty participating in community volunteer activities, demonstrating deficits in social participation," you might describe her actions as "Gabriela joined community volunteer projects and contributed by organizing supplies and supporting event setup. Gabriela did share that she preferred roles that allowed for more behind-the-scenes work rather than direct interaction with large groups." This approach highlights Gabriela's contributions and preferences without framing her involvement negatively.

2. **Highlight Client Self-Determination**: Emphasize the client's autonomy and self-advocacy in their actions. For example, instead of describing a child's behavior as "disruptive" or "difficult," you might say, "During the group activity, Jamie expressed frustration and self-advocated for a quiet space to work, which allowed them to focus better. Jamie's request for a quieter environment was a clear way of communicating their needs and preferences for optimal participation."

3. **Remain Neutral**: Quantitative data can be useful in evaluations, but they do not need to be used to highlight deficits. For instance, instead of stating

"Alex showed difficulty with time management skills, falling short of the expected standards for his age group 50% of the time," you could say, "Alex effectively managed his schedule for several tasks throughout the week 50% of the time, and occasionally needed reminders for deadlines and benefited from the accommodation of a time management app." Neutral phrasing highlights the performance without casting it in a negative light.

4. **Use Preferred Language**: Depending on the client's preference, use language that reflects their identity or personhood. For example, if a client prefers identity-first language, say "Autistic client" or "Schizophrenic" instead of "client with autism" or "client with schizophrenia," or vice versa. This approach affirms the client's identity and respects their preferences. When in doubt, always ask the client their preference.

5. **Skip the "But"**: Reframe your wording to emphasize what the client has achieved without countering it with what they haven't, often seen as the statement being included with a "but." Instead of writing "Mohammed wrote his name but needed help with writing letters," write "Mohammed successfully wrote his name independently, and when provided with additional support, he practiced forming other letters with guidance." This highlights the progress and potential for further growth.

6. **Consider Your Statement Ratio**: If you are unsure how much of your documentation is strengths-based, consider comparing the number of positive statements, negative statements, and neutral ones. How much are you writing about deficits compared to the strengths and emerging skills you are observing? Examining this ratio can increase your awareness of how you compose your documentation! We recognize this is extremely hard, especially given we have been taught to be deficit-based within our practices. You got this!

7. **Putting Norm-Referenced Scores Last**: Instead of centering the evaluation report on the client's scores, center the report on their occupational performance during evaluation, their hopes and dreams, and what they achieved. Place the scores at the end of the report so the strengths-based data you shared isn't overshadowed.

8. **Focus on Abilities Over Comparisons**: Rather than comparing a client's skills to developmental norms or neurotypical standards, focus on what the client *can* do. For example, instead of writing "he is below the developmental standard for fine motor skills," reframe the observation: "Johnny

demonstrated fine motor skills by completing tasks such as using a pencil to draw simple shapes, showing emerging control."

Being strengths-based also includes reporting directly on the client's strengths in an evaluation report. The *TAPP into Strengths Questionnaire* considers a person's strengths to include their personality traits, unique abilities, enjoyable pastimes, and monotropic passions.[21] Strengths may also include concepts such as mental fortitude, power, passion, intensity, skill, and beneficial qualities, to name a few. But of course, always ask the individual if they want their interests included within support planning.

Highlighting strengths in an occupational therapy report has innumerable benefits. Using strengths-based wording in conversations and documentation positively affects the attitudes of peers and caregivers.[22] Also, when strengths are incorporated into therapeutic activities, improvements in client health and well-being, self-confidence, self-esteem, and sense of belonging are noted.[23] Honoring client strengths builds relational trust and safety. Finally, putting strengths front and center in report summaries makes it easier for caregivers, teachers, and other professionals to readily and easily incorporate strengths into their supports and interventions.

Component #11 – Accessibility of Reports

When writing reports, it's important for the practitioner to consider the impact and accessibility for the intended reader. While OTPs traditionally understand and prioritize the payer and setting requirements in reports, practitioners often forget to write to those whose words most meaningfully serve or harm: the client and/or their support system. Practicing both strengths-based and accessible language can ensure the report is meaningful and useful without further contributing to an ableist understanding of neurodivergence.

Ways to Promote Accessibility

1. **Plain Language**: Foregoing jargon, abbreviations, and academic-style writing for language that is clear, concise, and correct. Consider "Easy-Read" summaries for access to consumers of all literacy levels.

2. **Pronouns**: Ensuring pronouns match the client's preferred identity throughout.

3. **Layout**: Organizing reports in an intentional way, using colors, sans-serif size 12pt+ font, 1.5+ line spacing, bolding, and lists/bullets to promote readability.

4. **Audio/visual summaries**: Provide auditory or video recordings for clients who process information auditorily or visually better.

5. **Highlight key information**: Use text boxes or call-out sections to emphasize important findings or recommendations.

6. **Translating Reports**: Ensure your clients know they can access their reports in their ideal language.

Component #12 – Write Anti-Ableist and Empowering Goals

When conducting OT evaluations, practitioners must understand that sensory, motor, social, communication, and executive function abilities, and reactivity to demands, vary among neurotypes. Yet, within the dominant medical model of disability, the unique traits of Neurodivergent people are traditionally considered pathological and in need of "fixing" rather than simply a shift from the neurotypical standard. When goals and accommodations are written, outcome measures are created to assess the client's progress over time. Ne'eman[24] explains that carefully created goals, even with exacting outcome measures, may be morally biased, unethical, and fully inappropriate to use. Examples include goals that have outcome measures of reducing Neurodivergent characteristics. These might include measures of increased eye contact, reduced stimming, prioritizing one form of communication (such as speech) over other forms, or fostering turn-taking and small talk in conversations.

OT goals should prioritize enhancing participation in meaningful occupations while recognizing the role of underlying performance skills and client factors such as motor skills, coordination, organization, and social interactions as supportive elements. In traditional evaluations, standardized tests are used to identify "deficits" in either occupations or in underlying skills. Yet, when deficits are identified, the tendency is for deficit-based goals to be developed.[25]

Neurodiversity-affirming IEP advocate Lisa Baskin Wright discusses how goals are often written with the intention of "preparing" Neurodivergent people for future challenges in the areas of academics, work, or social situations. In fact, the thinking behind many ableist goals is to "develop stamina" for dealing with things that are uncomfortable.[26] Typically, these goals incorporate concepts of building tolerance, showing a willingness to engage with non-preferred interests, and camouflaging Neurodivergent traits. Yet, the negative impact of such goals is far-reaching and may foster distress and self-doubt in clients and set them up to fail now—and to fail later. Instead, Baskin Wright suggests that appropriate goals for a Neurodivergent person would be to develop the skills required to assess a situation and weigh their felt safety, determine their support needs in the moment, and demonstrate the agency and self-advocacy to participate or not participate in the situation. Rachel Dorsey, a speech and language pathologist and autism advocate, suggests that neurodiversity-affirming goals and accommodations focus on any of the five following important areas: self-advocacy, functional communication, sense of purpose and belonging, sensory and emotional regulation, and executive function supports.[27] The Autistic Self-Advocacy Network (ASAN), an Autistic-led organization, outlines in its white paper *For Whose Benefit* that ethical goals should focus on developing skills that are meaningful to the individual to promote autonomy and support self-determination.

Including Accommodations Within Goals

When writing neurodiversity-affirming goals, supports or accommodations must be written into the goals themselves to ensure that the expectations, contexts, and environments support the individual's function. Autism Level UP! recommends that goals are written "to include how partners will provide support and facilitate the person's attainment of their objectives."[28] For example, goals can be written with the objective of educating neurotypical populations about Neurodivergent social comfort, traits, and unique communication styles. Goals can be targeted toward parents or caregivers in areas of developing their advocacy skills to improve the quality of life, access to inclusion, and self-determination for their Neurodivergent loved ones. Furthermore, goals to adapt teaching modalities and to implement environmental changes over time would support Neurodivergent learning without specifically targeting the Neurodivergent person themselves. When applicable, writing a goal to directly address education and advocacy may be warranted.

Goal-Writing Template

Neurodiversity-affirming goals should incorporate the following qualities:

- The goal is meaningful to the client.
- The goal is not ableist or promotes neurotypicality.
- The goal presumes competence.
- The goal includes "built-in" accommodations written directly into the goal.
- The goal is measurable in ways that align with the client's neurodivergence.

An example of the final quality above is recognizing that a client's performance may vary from day to day due to many factors, such as environmental conditions, contextual elements, and interoception. Given neurodivergence can be a dynamic disability, it's important to take a range of performance measurements into account versus a single occurrence. For an example of a neurodiversity-affirming goal template, see Kids Master Skills' template in Figure 9.4.[29] For a more in-depth explanation of this goal template with examples, see Marnell.[30]

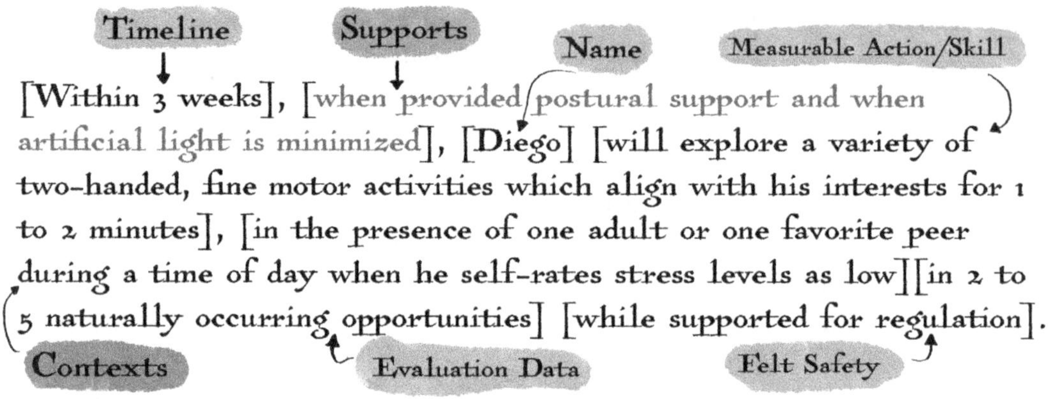

Figure 9.4—Kids Master Skills' Neurodiversity-Affirming Goal-Writing Template

It is important to remember that "measurable action/skill" within the goal-writing template should focus on measurable performance in an occupation. However, if you are targeting a performance component or an underlying skill, ensure it is a skill that is meaningful to the client, directly relates to the occupation, and adaptations and accommodations are incorporated. The goal should not be to make the client's performance in that particular skill more neurotypical, but rather to support the client's individual needs and preferences. Table 9.2 shows examples of ableist goals and their neurodiversity-affirming counterparts, with more examples contained within this chapter's Vault.

Table 9.2—Ableist Versus Neurodiversity-Affirming Occupational Therapy Goals

Ableist Goal	Explanation	Neurodiversity-Affirming Alternative
"Aqua will tolerate five minutes of messy hand play without refusal or minimal finger splaying." OR "Aqua will tolerate five minutes of sensory input and demonstrate decreased sensory sensitivity during sensory activities."	Sensory desensitization (without communicated approval by the learner) is not an affirming objective target. The goal teaches Aqua to ignore her sensory sensations and reduces her chances for self-advocacy, which ultimately leads to decreasing her safety. In other words: the OTP is teaching Aqua to dissociate from her bodily sensations to tolerate input that hurts or is aversive, which can have a catastrophic impact on her mental health.	"Aqua will self-advocate refusal using multimodal communication to express preference or disapproval..." As previously mentioned, sensory desensitization (without communicated approval by the learner) is not an affirming objective target. Additionally, the goal teaches the child to ignore their sensory sensations and reduces their chances for self-advocacy, which decreases their safety (you are teaching the child to dissociate from their bodily sensations to tolerate input that hurts or is aversive, leading to a catastrophic impact on their mental health). The updated goal teaches the specific skill of self-advocating, and self-determination is a health and well-being priority designated by the neurodiversity community. This goal also further protects the individual by teaching them to self-advocate for their needs instead of "accepting" things to happen to them, especially since Disabled individuals are much more likely to be abused or taken advantage of than non-disabled individuals.[31]
"When presented with a problem (e.g. non-preferred task, frustration), Roxas will accurately determine the size of the problem (little/big problem) and match their emotional response appropriately to the size of the problem."	"Size of problem" activities are problematic due to this goal teaching Roxas that their feelings are not valid and presumes that the OTP is more attuned to what Roxas is feeling more than Roxas themselves. Teaching Roxas to react to situations in the way the OTP would react or deem "appropriate" provides no functional skills nor realistically supports learners and their regulation.	"Roxas will describe their own bodily feelings/sensations and their associated feeling/emotion in a way that is meaningful to them in the presence of a safe co-regulation partner." Instead of focusing on the "size" of the problem, attempt to solve the "why" behind the emotional expression and teach Roxas how they can self-advocate for their regulation needs.[32]

cont.

Ableist Goal	Explanation	Neurodiversity-Affirming Alternative
"By October 14, client will demonstrate improved sustained attention for work task, as noted by supervisor feedback and increased productivity metric."	Prioritizing compliance and productivity over client's needs is problematic. Framing the goal around "improved sustained attention" assumes that the client's current attention patterns are deficient rather than different. "Increased productivity metric" focuses on external performance rather than the client's experience, well-being, or self-regulation strategies. This goal also lacks autonomy and self-determination. The goal is evaluated by "supervisor feedback," meaning the client's success is based on someone else's perception rather than their own experience. It does not consider what strategies the client finds helpful or how they define success. Finally, it does not account for accommodations or strategies. Instead of requiring the client to "sustain attention" in a neurotypical way, a neuro-affirming goal would focus on adapting the environment or using self-selected strategies to support engagement in a way that works for them.	"This period, client will report improved confidence initiating individualized sensory accommodations necessary to support just-right arousal for participation in work tasks as self-determined." This affirming iteration emphasizes the client's autonomy in identifying and utilizing accommodations that work best for them, rather than imposing a standardized approach. Instead of framing sensory differences as deficits, the goal highlights self-advocacy and confidence in meeting one's own needs. Rather than expecting the client to conform to neurotypical norms, it encourages them to engage in work tasks in a way that aligns with their sensory profile. Finally, words like "self-determined" and "confidence" shift the focus from external control to internal empowerment, reinforcing agency rather than deficit-based interventions.
"Ana will engage in non-preferred play activity for three minutes without signs of refusal and with minimal physical prompting within three months."	From a neurodiversity-affirming perspective, all play activities should bring enjoyment to the person performing them and should originate from the person's own curiosity. Creating a goal for a child to engage in a certain "type" of play, especially if not preferred by the person, is an example of the OTP imposing their own assumptions about what play should look like onto another person. Efforts to "expand" play skills should be abandoned and replaced by supporting the person to continue to explore their interests and experiences by providing opportunities and allowing the person to choose whether or not they are interested in engaging. Additionally, physical prompting violates the child's bodily autonomy and should not be used as a method to elicit a desired response, as it is not in the child's volition to do so.	The OTP will provide education to teachers and caregivers about how to identify signs that Ana is interested or not interested in various play activities (e.g. flapping, turning away, etc.) and how to support Ana by continuing those she is interested in and discontinuing those she is not. This new goal focuses on caregiver/teacher education in order to maximize Ana's ability to engage in her interests and meaningful play as it is self-determined. Doing so allows Ana to have the option of whether to explore other play options or continue with her current enjoyable activities. Maintaining Ana's intrinsic motivation to play across settings supports her ability to develop comfort and trust with the adults that she encounters as well as her sense of predictability in her experiences, both contributing to her ability to self-regulate and have positive experiences.

Summary of Components of Anti-Ableist Evaluations

The following list provides an overview of the key components discussed throughout this chapter, summarizing the core features of anti-ableist and neurodiversity-affirming occupational therapy evaluations.

- Utilization of assessment tools that focus on lived experiences, collaborative goal setting, hopes, and dreams (e.g. COPM, Visual Activity Sort, and the DASEL).

- OTP recognizes the client as the expert of their Neurodivergent experiences and emphasizes that their input is crucial to the evaluation.

- Encourage clients to choose how they want to celebrate and prioritize interdependence and independence within their lives.

- Outcome measures emphasize how well the environment has been modified, and the client's access to meaningful occupations within the environment.

- A focus of the evaluation is assessing environmental barriers, including attitudes of those within the client's life and overall accessibility (e.g. social, attitudinal, physical).

- Interests and strengths are evaluated and included as a critical part of the evaluation.

- The evaluation focuses on assessing occupational performance of meaningful activities, and contexts; performance components are assessed if they are integral to the client's desired occupation, the client wants to address them, and success isn't measured by how neurotypical they become.

- Goals are focused on how the individual can lead a self-determined life, such as increasing their self-advocacy skills, accessing robust communication, developing confidence in utilizing accommodations and supports in natural settings, and promoting positive disability identity.

- Cultural safety is emphasized, recognizing disability as its own culture with norms and this is promoted to both clients and caregivers throughout the evaluation.

- All occupations are equally valued, such as play and leisure being recognized just as important as ADLs, validating that clients may prioritize occupations over ADLs pending their unique preferences and circumstances.

- Strengths-based language and the language advocated for by the community (e.g. using identity-first language for Autistic individuals, and using person-first language for those with Down syndrome).

- Service plans do not attempt to change Neurodivergent characteristics to be more neurotypical (unless this is advocated for by the client).

Conclusion

Evaluations are a critical part of the occupational therapy process, not just for acquiring data to justify our services, but also for significantly influencing perceptions of the Neurodivergent individual. Referring physicians, teachers, administrators, caregivers and other family members, support workers, peers, interdisciplinary team members, and many others may all reference the evaluation and interact with the client accordingly. In occupational therapy, this initial understanding ultimately shapes and informs the client's treatment plan and subsequent support in participating in the occupations that are meaningful to them and improve their quality of life. Neurodiversity-affirming evaluations are not about analyzing deficits and administering norm-referenced assessments. They require OTPs to be curious about their client's interests, styles of communication and engagement, and sensory experiences, and to more deeply engage in conversations about their client's strengths, aspirations, and challenges to living a self-determined life. By considering the guiding principles and implementing the neurodiversity-affirming process laid out in this chapter, OTPs may begin to complete evaluations that truly support Neurodivergent participation as it is self-defined.

Endnotes

1 Patten, K. K. (2022). Finding our strengths: Recognizing professional bias and interrogating systems. *American Journal of Occupational Therapy, 76*(6), 7606150010. https://doi.org/10.5014/ajot.2022.076603, p. 1.

2 Hammell, K. W. (2015). Quality of life, participation and occupational rights: A capabilities perspective. *Australian Occupational Therapy Journal, 62*(2), 78–85. https://doi.org/10.1111/1440-1630.12183

3 Braun, M. J., Dunn, W., & Tomchek, S. D. (2017). A pilot study on professional documentation: Do we write from a strengths perspective? *American Journal of Speech-Language Pathology / American Speech-Language-Hearing Association, 26*(3), 972–981. https://doi.org/10.1044/2017_AJSLP-16-0117

4 Kelly, A., & Barnes-Holmes, D. (2013). Implicit attitudes toward children with autism versus normally developing children as predictors of professional burnout and psychopathology. *Research in Developmental Disabilities, 34*, 17–28. https://doi.org/10.1016/j.ridd.2012.07.018

5 Boheler, G., & Boheler, J. (n.d.). *Neurodivergent identity workbook.* Teachers Pay Teachers—OTs for Neurodiversity. www.teacherspayteachers.

com/Product/Neurodivergent-Identity-Workbook-6896772

6 Frolek Clark, G., & Rioux, J. E. (2019). Best practices in school-based occupational therapy evaluation and planning to support participation. In Frolek Clark, G., Rioux, J. E., & Chandler, B. E. (Eds.), *Best practices for occupational therapy in schools* (pp. 119–125). AOTA Press.

7 American Occupational Therapy Association (AOTA). (2022). *Occupational profile template.* www.aota.org/~/media/Corporate/Files/Practice/Manage/Documentation/AOTA-Occupational-Profile-Template.pdf

8 Hansell, C., Bissett, M., & Caine, A. (2022). The use of the term "occupational profile" in occupational therapy and occupational science literature: A scoping review. *British Journal of Occupational Therapy, 86*(1), 5–19. https://doi.org/10.1177/03080226221117461

9 Boheler, G., & Boheler, J. (n.d.). *Neurodivergent identity workbook.* Teachers Pay Teachers—OTs for Neurodiversity. www.teacherspayteachers.com/Product/Neurodivergent-Identity-Workbook-6896772

10 Cooper, K., Smith, L. G. E., & Russell, A. (2017). Social identity, self-esteem, and mental health in autism: Social identity, self-esteem, and mental health in autism. *European Journal of Social Psychology, 47*(7), 844–854. https://doi.org/10.1002/ejsp.2297

11 Roche, L., Adams, D., & Clark, M. (2020). Research priorities of the autism community: A systematic review of key stakeholder perspectives. *Autism, 25*(2), 336–348. https://doi.org/10.1177/1362361320967790

12 Autistic Self-Advocacy Network (ASAN). (n.d.). *For whose benefit? Evidence, ethics, and effectiveness of autism interventions.* Autistic Self Advocacy Network. https://Autisticadvocacy.org/wp-content/uploads/2021/12/ACES-Ethics-of-Intervention.pdf

13 Price, T., & Pride, T. (2023). The Canadian occupational performance measure (COPM): Critiquing its applicability with Indigenous peoples and communities. *The Open Journal of Occupational Therapy, 11*(3), 1–10. https://doi.org/10.15453/2168-6408.2085

14 Hunter, C., & Pride, T. (2021). Critiquing the Canadian Model of Client-Centered Enablement (CMCE) for Indigenous contexts. *Canadian Journal of Occupational Therapy, 88*(4), 329–339. https://doi.org/10.1177/00084174211042960

15 Novak, I., & Honan, I. (2019). Effectiveness of paediatric occupational therapy for children with disabilities: A systematic review. *Australian Occupational Therapy Journal, 66*(3), 258–273. https://doi.org/10.1111/1440-1630.12573

16 Dorsey, R., & Miles, J. (2022). *Goal writing for Autistic students.* Learn Play Thrive Continuing Education. https://learnplaythrive.com/goals

17 Braun, M. J., Dunn, W., & Tomchek, S. D. (2017). A pilot study on professional documentation: Do we write from a strengths perspective? *American Journal of Speech-Language Pathology / American Speech-Language-Hearing Association, 26*(3), 972–981. https://doi.org/10.1044/2017_AJSLP-16-0117

18 Proctor, M., Tomchek, S., & Dean, E. (Hosts). (2020). *Writing strengths-based goals and evaluations* (No. 12) [Audio podcast episode]. In Two Sides of the Spectrum. *Learn Play Thrive.* https://learnplaythrive.com/podcasts/writing-strengths-based-goals-evaluations

19 Braun, M. J., Dunn, W., & Tomchek, S. D. (2017). A pilot study on professional documentation: Do we write from a strengths perspective? *American Journal of Speech-Language Pathology / American Speech-Language-Hearing Association, 26*(3), 972–981. https://doi.org/10.1044/2017_AJSLP-16-0117

20 Proctor, M., Tomchek, S., & Dean, E. (Hosts). (2020). *Writing strengths-based goals and evaluations* (No. 12) [Audio podcast episode]. In Two Sides of the Spectrum. *Learn Play Thrive.* https://learnplaythrive.com/podcasts/writing-strengths-based-goals-evaluations

21 Marnell, L. (2025). *TAPP into strengths questionnaire.* Kids Master Skills. www.kidsmasterskills.com/tappintostrengthsquestionnaire

22 Braun, M. J., Dunn, W., & Tomchek, S. D. (2017). A pilot study on professional documentation: Do we write from a strengths perspective? *American Journal of Speech-Language Pathology / American Speech-Language-Hearing Association, 26*(3), 972–981. https://doi.org/10.1044/2017_AJSLP-16-0117

23 Lee, E. A. L., Scott, M., Black, M., D'Arcy, E., Tan, T., Sheehy, L., Bölte, S., & Girdler, S. (2022). "He sees his autism as a strength not a deficit now": A repeated cross-sectional study investigating the impact of strengths-based programs on Autistic adolescents. *Journal of Autism and Developmental Disorders, 54*(5), 1656–1671. https://doi.org/10.1007/s/0803-022

24 Ne'eman, A. (2021). When disability is defined by behavior, outcome measures should not promote passing. *AMA Journal of Ethics, 23*(7), 569–575. https://doi.org/10.1001/amajethics.2021.569

25 Wenger, C. (2024). *Neurodiversity-affirming IEP course* [Online Course]. www.speechdude.com/iepcourse

26 Autism Career Pathways. (2023, February 17). *Meaningful IEP goals* [Video]. YouTube. https://youtu.be/QLrKVYagWrw?si=oEiZhvX65lEhfV4B

27 SMIL Autism Resources. (2021, December 15). *Writing goals to foster Autistic identity* [Video]. YouTube. www.youtube.com/live/Zwj5io6-Lio?si=jlJWoFwl-oOwkira

28 Autism Level UP! (2022). *Individualized goals.* https://cdn.sanity.io/files/p6bm7moz/production/655952605356f5964e9a83e8bbe4b97887dda51c.pdf

29 Marnell, L. (2024). *Neurodiversity-affirming IEP goal bank and guidelines for OTs*. Kids Master Skills. www.kidsmasterskills.com/product-page/nd-affirming-ot-goal-bank

30 ibid.

31 Dorsey, R., & Miles, J. (2022). *Goal writing for Autistic students.* Learn Play Thrive Continuing Education. https://learnplaythrive.com/goals

32 Fede, J., & Laurent, A. (2020). *WHY's not size (It's not the size, it's how, and why!)*. Autism Level UP! https://cdn.sanity.io/files/p6bm7moz/production/5330d100030555fc4d1804ed555e949e4969de2e.pdf

CHAPTER 10

Neurodivergent Empowerment

Affirming Practices and Supportive Strategies

AMY LAURENT AND LISA MARNELL

Become an Affirming Occupational Therapy Practitioner

Therapists eager to embrace affirming occupational therapy (OT) practice would benefit from adopting certain intentional approaches. This journey represents a transformation, leading a professional away from providing OT that is strictly aligned with the medical model of disability, taught in most academic programs, to assuming a more thoughtful, neurodiversity-focused, and humble practice. Presently, we share several important ways for an occupational therapy practitioner (OTP) to consider novel perspectives and become the affirming ally they hope to be.

1. Notice and Address Internalized Ableism in Ourselves

Society exposes people to prevailing societal beliefs. OTPs may inadvertently adopt ableist thinking that is endemic to their worlds. This reflects internalized ableism and represents a challenge to our profession when it comes to working in an affirming manner with Neurodivergent (ND) clients. Questioning our assumptions is difficult but necessary. As mentioned in Chapter 8, critical reflexivity is crucial to enable OTPs to acknowledge their own thinking to shift to new and potentially uncomfortable ways to provide support to clients.

2. Humbly Seek Opportunities to Learn from Clients

While much of occupational therapy is deficit-based, neurodiversity-affirming practice requires us to stop viewing clients through an ableist lens. Embedded within this perspective is the medical model assumption that professionals are "experts" and that clients learn from us. Truthfully, the only expert in a specific neurodivergence is an ND person themselves. Even among people who share the same neurotype, their own personal experiences are unique. Accepting that "we don't know what we don't know" shows humility and openness to learning.

"Being" and not "doing" is a way of thinking that may serve us well as professionals. This means that OTPs must prioritize sharing space with their clients, cultivating felt safety for them, and learning from the clients in regard to their lived experiences. Rather than "doing" therapy with little humility or client understanding, an affirming OTP focuses on "being" with the client in ways that are meaningful and comfortable to the client.

Adopting a critically reflexive approach may look different from the OT you learned in school or what is common in practice. Yet, by *being* with a person, OTPs can learn so much about them, and in turn, understand and serve them better. "Being" with a client may look like sitting silently a few feet away from a preschooler who is building with Legos, perhaps helping them find pieces, reading their cues, leaving them alone, or simply sharing space. This approach entails humbly honoring and learning about an ND client's sensory, social, communication, and motor traits while witnessing first-hand how a person functions in a given setting.

3. Appreciate the Importance of Client Strengths

Typically, professionals use a deficit-based perspective when describing client characteristics and performance. As explored in the previous chapter, evaluation reports and intervention data rarely emphasize client strengths when compared to deficits.[1] Furthermore, when intervention is initiated, therapist-directed (rather than client-chosen) activities are typically considered to be "appropriate" therapeutic activities. Yet, embracing client strengths is associated with positive social engagement, learning, self-advocacy, and anxiety reduction.[2] Shifting perspectives from therapist-led to client-led, interest-focused support is illustrated in the example of a Dysgraphic college student excited to learn a new technology called SnapType. This program helps students complete simple university forms, and their motivation comes from a desire to achieve autonomy with their paperwork.

4. Use Affirming Language with Clients, Families, and Staff

The language that professionals use affects the perspectives and attitudes of both caregivers and clients. Yet typically clients and their families face deficit-based language in both spoken and written communication. Affirming OTPs can commit to substituting deficit-based language with strengths-based words, phrases, and concepts.

The language OTPs use may also affect a person's sense of self and confidence. Consider a young woman with Down syndrome who works at a YMCA. She loves greeting the "regulars" and is respected and well-liked by clientele. Although having Down syndrome is a part of who she is, she sees herself first as hard-working, organized, and kind. Because of this, she embraces person-first language, referring to herself as "a person with Down syndrome" to describe herself when considering her disability. She prefers others do the same.

5. Cultivate Client Autonomy Across All Settings

Supporting client self-awareness, self-understanding, advocacy, and self-determination ultimately leads to self-empowerment. Understanding one's needs is the first step to self-advocacy for Neurodivergent individuals. An example is a college graduate with dyslexia, excited to begin a teaching job. However, having several IEP meetings each week results in numerous lengthy reports to read and process. This situation could trigger stress, poor sleep, and diminished confidence. Yet, strategies they used in OT in high school enables them to understand their needs and advocate for options, such as requesting IEP drafts early, not being asked to read parts of the IEP aloud, and asking the team to write IEPs without long, unbroken passages of text.

6. Commit to Educate and Guide Caregivers, Teachers, and Support Personnel

"Kids do well if they can"[3] is an important mantra that has become popular in recent years. It highlights that Neurodivergent children and adults do not "choose" to act a certain way. Rather, neurobiological differences reflect different brain structures, functions, chemistry, and connectivity, which affect a person's match or mismatch with environments and activity contexts.

OTPs can support Neurodivergent clients by educating caregivers, teachers, and support personnel, reminding them that people "do well if they can." After a traumatic brain injury, a grocery store worker, back on the job, struggles with working memory. When the OTP visits his work site, she explains to management that despite "trying," the client struggles to remember several facts at once. She suggests they explore supports, such as making lists, providing frequent check-ins, and guiding the client to use simple memory strategies.

7. Hone Awareness and Sensitivity to Client Experiences

Throughout OT intervention, two questions should be asked of Neurodivergent participants: (1) what are your current goals for therapy? and (2) what treatment approaches and therapeutic activities feel comfortable to you?

Populations that OTPs support may have unique interoceptive awareness, motor skills, praxis, social traits, executive function, and sensory processing. Because of these differences, clients may struggle to identify what helps them feel regulated and/or how to communicate this to a practitioner. An older woman, post-stroke, may have minimal ability to communicate. An Autistic teenage girl may often find herself situationally mute after transitioning to high school, overwhelmed by sounds and noise in a crowded school. In both scenarios, client communication is limited, so therapists must proactively understand clients as best they can, notice either engagement or dysregulation, and propose adjustments to OT supports.

8. Honor Lived Experiences and Seek Neurodiversity-Informed Research

Relying on the lived experiences of the Neurodivergent populations we serve is imperative for affirming OT practice. We must be eager to listen and do our best to understand what our Neurodivergent clients are telling us. When an Autistic preschooler shows an aversion to joining circle time in the classroom, we must "listen" to them—perhaps the pitch of 20 tiny voices singing the *Good Morning* song is distressing to them. When a teenager with dyscalculia pushes away a worksheet, we must "listen" to their communication and perhaps consult with the teacher to rethink teaching strategies and regulatory supports.

In addition to committing to "listen" to Neurodivergent people, OTPs can "look" for neurodiversity-focused research. Research data that gathers the perspectives of Neurodivergent people represents a "gold mine" for affirming practitioners. For example, two recent studies interviewed Autistic participants to seek their perspectives on eye contact and potentially supportive social education.[4,5]

9. Select Professional Development Wisely

Taking part in neurodiversity-affirming continuing education is critical to an OTP's development. Yet, there is no standard that defines what is and what isn't affirming. In fact, the term "neurodiversity lite" or "performative neurodiversity" is used to describe "the appropriation and watering down of a human rights movement."[6] An educational course is considered "neurodiversity lite" when suggested interventions are clearly ableist and pathologizing or only tackle superficial concepts such as language changes. Yet, there are ways to discern whether a training or course is affirming. Seeking input from an occupational therapist who advocates for affirming OT practice may provide insight. Reading through the proposed course content is another approach. OTPs can ensure that ableist practices are not incorporated in the course outlines (e.g. traditional social skills training, exposure therapy, planned ignoring, or use of hand-over-hand teaching modalities). It is important to note that professional course approval from national or local state associations does not indicate that a professional course is affirming.

Neurodiversity-Affirming Supports

Affirming support starts with truly understanding the person you are seeking to support. Individualized support focuses on the whole person inclusive of all of their roles and identities. This is critical to recognize. As mentioned in previous chapters, people do not have a single identity, but many, and these identities intersect to provide unique constellations of priorities, strengths, and support needs. So, while this chapter seeks to provide general recommendations related to how to engage in the process of providing affirming support for ND individuals, these recommendations must always be considered in the broader understanding of all aspects of the client's life. In addition to seeking information from individual clients about their experiences and priorities to inform holistic and affirming practice, it is critical to look to members of the ND community at large for broader guidance about what constitutes affirming support for them. This guidance can be found in qualitative research and blogs, as well as online and in-person ND communities (see the Vault for a list of resources).

As shared in Chapter 1, neurodivergence reflects natural differences in neurocognitive performance. A neurodivergence or Neurodivergent identity influences every aspect of a person's life and occupational performance. When discussing Neurodivergent presentations it is critical to highlight the divergence as a difference, not as a deficit. OTPs must embrace this perspective as it is the foundation upon which affirming practice is built.

Differences inherent in ND influence a person's profile of performance components. Indeed, implications for various performance components are often associated with ND profiles. Knowledge of these is critical to help OTPs address the unique needs of their ND clients. One in particular that is critical to consider is a person's communication profile. Both receptive and expressive communication abilities play a significant role in an ND individual being able to actively engage in meaningful occupations and relationships, but are also critically linked to being able to participate in and access occupational therapy services.

In the context of an ND-affirming framework, we always work to both "presume competence and ensure understanding."[7] This seemingly simple phrase is important. It implies that we must consider our client's communication profile when planning and delivering supports. Table 10.1 offers a listing of a few common communication profiles and support strategies that are most accessible, as well as those that can help to scaffold further communication development.

Table 10.1—Exploration of Communication Profiles

Communication Profile	Accessible Ways of Taking in Information / Receptive Communication (Ensure Understanding)	Accessible Ways for the Client to Share Information / Expressive Communication (Ensure Access to and Respond to)	Scaffold Development (Presume Competence and Ability to Learn)	Example in Practice
Non-Verbal (individuals who have not yet developed a symbolic system for communication)	• Object-based communication • Routines • Simple/familiar phrases and words	• Gestures • Facial expressions • Proximity • Reenactment • Vocalizations	Model without expectation of use: • Spoken words and simple phrases tied to routines • Sign language • Photograph visuals • Picture symbols • Other AAC systems	OTP supporting child with non-verbal communication profile in school creates/uses object schedules to ensure the child comprehends and can actively engage in transitions. Objects are paired with spoken words and pictures.
Emerging Language (individuals who are at the early or emerging stages of symbolic communication development)	• Spoken words and simple sentences • Sign language • Picture symbols • Photograph visuals • Other AAC	• Spoken words and simple sentences • Sign language • Picture symbols • Photograph visuals • Other AAC systems • Gestures • Facial expressions • Proximity • Reenactment • Vocalizations	Model without expectation of use: • Increasingly complex sentence structures • Spoken words • Sign language • Picture symbols • Other AAC systems	OTP supporting early intervention client uses Autism Level UP! VIEW boards to support engagement in play, access to effective communication, and vocabulary development.[8]

Conversational Language (individuals who have robust symbolic communication abilities)	• Conversational speech • Sign language • Picture symbols • Other AAC	• Conversational speech • Spoken words • Sign language • Picture symbols • Other AAC • Gestures • Facial expressions • Proximity • Reenactment • Vocalizations	Model without expectation of use: • Multimodal communication • Increasingly complex sentence structures • Spoken words • Sign language • Picture symbols • Writing/spelling • Other AAC systems	OTP explores different ways to communicate with adult client to help them discover which communication methods are preferred, easily accessible, and energy-saving. OTP empowers client to use and advocate for those methods (e.g. writing/texting rather than speaking).
Nonspeaking (individuals who are symbolic communicators but do not use mouth words)	• Their preferred AAC system • Gestures • Facial expressions • Proximity • Reenactment • Vocalizations	• Conversational speech • Spoken words • Sign language • Picture symbols / their preferred AAC system • Gestures • Facial expressions • Proximity • Reenactment • Vocalizations	Model without expectation of use: • Multimodal communication • Increasingly complex sentence structures • Spoken words • Sign language • Picture symbols • Writing/spelling • Other AAC systems	OTP supporting client in transition to work program ensures that client ALWAYS has access to their AAC device and educates coworkers about the need to provide the young person time to formulate a response on their device when asking questions.
Gestalt Language (individuals who use/echo phrases, scripts, and sentences they have heard to convey their thoughts, ideas, and experiences)	• Multimodal communication • Spoken words and simple sentences • Sign language • Picture symbols • Other AAC • Known scripts with shared meaning	• Spoken phrases, scripts, sentences • Gestures • Facial expressions • Proximity • Reenactment • Vocalizations • Possibly picture-based communication	Model without expectation of use: • New functional gestalts • Multimodal communication (gestures, picture-based communication, AAC systems, writing, spelling) • Single words • Simple sentence structures	OTP providing clinic-based support researches client's favorite shows (e.g. watching them or talking to the client's family members about them) so that they understand their client's communicative intent and can respond to that intent (e.g. when a client exclaims "cinders and ashes cried Thomas" they know and acknowledge that their client is surprised).

It is important to recognize that communication profiles are not static. They are susceptible to the influence of regulation. In short, if someone is well regulated, meaning their energy and emotional state support their active engagement in the present moment, the information in Table 10.1 will provide useful guidelines to consider. However, if a Neurodivergent person is experiencing dysregulation, it is highly likely that their ability to both express themselves and comprehend information will be negatively impacted. This is to say that a person who typically has access to mouth words (aka speech) may not be able to access that capacity when they are dysregulated. This may also render them situationally mute and promote difficulties in processing conversational speech. Likewise, a Gestalt Language Processor who uses both Gestalt and creative language to connect and communicate with others may rely solely on familiar phrases and communication routines during times of stress.

In addition to influencing a client's communication profile, unique presentations of other performance components are often associated with specific neurodivergencies and contribute to support needs in areas of occupational performance. Table 10.2 illustrates considerations when planning affirming supports in collaboration with clients while respecting their Neurodivergent identities. These examples are by no means comprehensive (indeed complete volumes have been written about each of these topics) but they are included here in hopes of helping OTPs begin to think broadly about the Neurodivergent experience and implications for providing affirming and useful supports. The implications for support and recommendations will and should be differentiated based upon the occupation the client is engaging in or wishes to engage in.

Having knowledge of the common implications of ND on performance components and their impact on the occupational engagement of a client's particular neurodivergence is an important foundation for occupational therapy practice. Of course, individual clients are not textbook examples, and OTPs must consider unique presentations for a person accounting for all of their identities and intersectionality when planning support.

Above and beyond the implications of a unique ND identity that may help guide an OTP in determining areas where the provision of therapeutic intervention may facilitate meaningful engagement in roles and occupations, as well as the most effective and accessible ways to provide that support, it is critical to acknowledge that the ND client does not exist in a vacuum. Indeed, considering models such as the Transactional Model of Development[9] and the Person-Environment-Occupation-Performance Model,[10] as well as tools such as the Person in Context (PIC) Tool,[11] can help OTPs to provide holistic, affirming therapeutic support. They can help conceptualize affirming support in ways that ensure that the burden for change does not fall solely on the ND person. Indeed, these models and tools require us to assess the contexts in which the ND person exists and functions.

Included here for consideration is a practical tool that provides a framework for such exploration. The PIC Tool was developed by Autism Level UP! (See Figure 10.1.) This tool is structured to be completed in several steps:

1. Creating an individual profile and understanding the individual's experiences
   a. Seek input from the client and people who know the client well.
   b. Consider an individual's profile according to seven categories (i.e. physiological, interoception, sensory, motor, cognitive, communication, and social).
   c. Build and record the individual's profile in an attempt to capture how they experience the world.
   d. This profile should be free from judgment and simply reflect the person's experience.

2. Reflecting on contexts where a person engages with ease
   a. Again, seek input from the client and those who know the client well.
   b. Consider a range of environments and activities where the client engages and participates using the same framework of categories.
   c. Complete the activity and/or environment pages of the PIC for an activity that is likely to go well for a person (e.g. they reportedly can successfully engage in the activity in a way that they want to and do not regularly experience dysregulation).
   d. Consider the person's profile in the context of that activity or environment and to notice all the "matches" between the person's profile and the environment.

3. Reflecting on contexts where the person experiences difficulties with engagement
   a. Seek input from the client and those who know the client well.
   b. Complete the activity and/or environment pages of the PIC to consider an activity and/or environment where the client struggles to engage and/or experiences frequent dysregulation.
   c. Consider the person's profile in the context of that activity or environment and notice the "mismatches" by taking note of the domains where they occur. It is these mismatches that help us identify impacting factors in the environment that may be impacting engagement.
   d. Record the mismatches and use those as a base for planning accommodations, support, and intervention.

Table 10.2—General Recommendations for Neurotype Characteristics

Neurodivergent Characteristic	Difference That May Benefit from Support	General Affirming Recommendations
Differences in motor presentation (Common for those who are Autistic, Dyspraxic, or have acquired neurodivergence such as traumatic brain injury, long COVID, or multiple sclerosis)	Coordination Differences Motor Planning and Patterns	• Explore priorities for engagement in fine motor and gross motor activities deemed meaningful by the client (not the OTP). Structure sessions to build skills to support participation in those tasks and/or practice engaging in modified ways. • Don't attempt to change an individual's motor patterns simply because they deviate from the norm. In many ways, differences in motor patterns can increase engagement in occupations (e.g. increased skills in movement activities that require adaptive motor patterns, such as rock climbing or dance). • Collaborate with the individual to reconceptualize what meaningful occupational participation can look like. Support the client in being comfortable exploring accommodations and adaptations that align with their strengths and needs, empowering them to participate in occupations in ways that feel accessible and sustainable. • Consider motor differences' implications for a wide range of all roles and occupations.
Sensory processing differences in all internal and external sensory systems (vision, auditory, olfactory, gustatory, tactile, vestibular, proprioception, and interoception) (Common for those who have sensory processing differences, schizophrenia, are Autistic, ADHDers, or Dyspraxic)	Sensory Modulation Sensory Discrimination	• Support use of strategies to manage differences that impact function. Consider using Autism Level UP!'s "Heightened Perception: Challenge? Strength? Both!" to explore the individual's sensory processing differences from an affirming perspective (e.g. hypersensitivity to auditory input = hi-definition hearing).[12] • Help clients explore internal experiences and how these signals may impact engagement. Consider exploring Kelly Mahler's Interoception Curriculum. For an introduction, listen to this podcast on interoception.[13] • Do not employ therapies that work to increase tolerance to distressing input. • If a client advocates for exploring sensory input in support of a meaningful occupation, offer opportunities for client-led, joyful engagement without any expectation of changing or "normalizing" their sensory processing. For example, an individual who enjoys collecting stamps may wish to explore tactile discrimination to more easily peel stamps from envelopes while also considering adaptations.

Cognitive differences in areas of executive function, attention, logical thinking and reasoning, and regulatory gestalt patterns (Common for those who have intellectual and developmental disabilities [IDD], are Autistic, ADHDers, or have acquired neurodivergence)	Attention Executive Function Logical Thinking and Reasoning Regulatory Gestalt Patterns	• Provide support to help the individual regulate their attention through the use of sensory supports, cognitive strategies, and time management strategies such as chunking. Empower the ADHDer to understand that their attentional differences are not deficits but unique perceptions of time. When supported authentically, these differences can have significant positive impacts on academic and work-related tasks. Consider exploring resources offered by OT4ADHD, an ADHDer OT.[14] • Provide support to help the individual regulate their attention (in their way of attending, not neurotypical attention) through the use of sensory supports, cognitive strategies, and time management strategies such as chunking. • Focus on strengths and introduce accessible supports such as routines and visual organizers. Explore using tools such as the *Bullet Journal for Planning and Reflecting*.[15] • Validate and consider introducing tools such as Autism Level UP!'s Solve not Size of the Problem tools, "WHYs Not SIZE."[16] • Honor the need for and reliance on routine. Consider helping to create an occupational profile focusing on roles and routines making explicit connections to mental health.
Psychosocial differences (Common for those who have bipolar disorder, schizophrenia, depression, anxiety, an acquired neurodivergence, and are Autistic or an ADHDer)	Regulation Challenges Interaction Style Differences Mood	• Focus on providing accessible regulatory supports and scaffolding skill development through mutual/co-regulation. • Avoid neurotypical expectations for performative regulation. Consider exploring the Autism Level UP! Energy Regulation Framework. For an introduction read "Leveling Up Regulatory Support Through Community Collaboration."[17] • Validate Neurodivergent communication and interaction styles in the context of Double Empathy.[18] • Support the client in advocating for their interactive needs. Consider using the Person in Context (PIC) tool from Autism Level UP! to assist (Figure 10.1). • Utilize trauma-informed practice to explore mood and influences on occupational engagement (see Chapter 5). Support the client in the development of skills to help regulate attention, arousal, and mood on their terms. Empower the client to utilize those strategies and advocate for their needs when interacting with others. Consider working on increasing the individual's interoception awareness; you can't nurture self-understanding and self-advocacy without addressing interoception! • Consider exploring All the FeelZzz resources developed by Autism Level UP!, an alternative way to express pain, discomfort, and difference in the body and mind (a neurodiversity-affirming SEL curriculum).[19]

PIC - Person In Context | **Person Profile** | Part 1

	Factors to Consider	My Experience

Physiological	• Sleep
	• Nourishment
	  • Water, caloric intake
	  • Quantity, quality
	• Health
	  • Illness, allergy, injury	

Interoception	• Perception of Hunger • Perception of Pain • Perception of Arousal/Energy • Perception of Emotion • Perception of Needing to go to Bathroom	

Sensory	• Hypersensitivities / Hypo-sensitivities
	  • Sound, smell, taste, touch, visual, spatial, vestibular, proprioceptive
	• Preference for Seeking or Avoiding Sensory Input
	  • Frequency, intensity, time, type	

Motor	• Muscle Tone • Coordination/ Strength/ Endurance • Bodily / Spatial Awareness • Use of Mobility Support / Device • Preference for Movement	

Cognitive	• Executive Functioning Abilities
	  • Decision-making
	  • Processing and learning style
	• Prior Experience / Interests
	• Social Understanding
	• Reliance on Routine/ Predictability	

Communication	• Receptive Communication Abilities/Means
	  • Non-verbal, symbolic
	• Expressive Communication Abilities/Means
	  • Non-verbal, symbolic	

Social	• Social motivation • Preferred social partners (may be specific or general - e.g., sibling, older kids, younger kids, those with shared interests, etc.)	

Autism Level UP!

Figure 10.1—The Person in Context (PIC) Tool
Note. This is the first page of the 12-page resource.

With this lens, it is possible to work with clients, their families, and other partners in the community to determine if the appropriate course of action is making an environmental accommodation or creating an activity modification, thereby lessening the burden on the ND person and creating more welcoming and ND accessible spaces, environments, and activities. A logical extension of this process may also include the ND person learning to advocate for their right to accommodations. Learning to advocate for supportive and affirming accommodation may in turn become an important goal of OT services for ND clients (see Chapter 9 for more details).

In addition to acquiring advocacy skills to request reasonable accommodations, it may be that the ND person would benefit from therapy to help them develop skills needed to navigate environments, activities, relationships, and roles. In these instances, considering mismatches is critical, too. Such consideration helps us to determine which performance component(s) and skills are most critical to address and support to enhance engagement. This process of reflection also provides OTPs with a pathway to ensure that they are applying a critical lens when determining support. It ensures OTPs are not simply saying... "ohhhh there is a deficit in this thing... So, we must address it." Rather, OTPs are pausing to ask themselves, "is the occupation in question meaningful for the person? Is it a priority for them? Do they want to work toward being able to engage in it?" If the answer to these questions is yes, then OTPs can begin to create an affirming support plan that incorporates both goals for skill development for the ND person, as well as activity modifications and environmental accommodations.

Affirming OT practices must encompass a view that transcends addressing challenges to engagement arising from environmental mismatches and performance component differences. It must also help the ND person develop an integrated and positive ND identity. A primary goal of OTPs must be to support people in growing into themselves fully, and we can do this by supporting Neurodivergent participation. Indeed, it is critical that practitioners seek to understand, respect, and validate ND culture. We should strive for all therapeutic practices being designed in such a way that supports a person's authentic ways of being and engaging. Practitioners must guard against getting caught up in neurotypical ideals and practices, as these can lead to the ND client feeling as though they ought to live in such a way or perform to a standard that does not align with their neurology. In its extreme, such practices may encourage a person to mask. As explored in Chapter 5, masking is a trauma response that relies on the suppression of natural ways of being and calls forth an act to please others.

As OTPs move into affirming ways to provide support, there is a place to acknowledge that we are all learning and growing together. OTPs must look to learn from members of the community that they aim to support.

Likewise, it is important to acknowledge that our individual clients do not always know what they don't know, and at times we as therapists may be in a unique position to help them uncover knowledge about themselves and their ND identity. This should always be done from the perspective of curiosity—the discovery of knowledge leading to self-understanding that will empower the client to self-advocacy.[20]

With this information in mind, it is possible to start to compile a list of practices that align with the ND-affirming movement. These include practices that:

- challenge the assumption of independence as a primary target and embrace all humans as relational beings
- help a person grow into who they are embracing all of their identities; Neurodivergent individuals don't grow out of their neurodivergence... they grow into it
- presume competence—ND people have the ability to learn, change, and grow when supported in accessible ways
- prioritize the lived experience of the individual and the community for guidance in establishing priorities for support
- focus on ND-defined quality of life and promote living authentically, in alignment with their neurotype(s)
- prioritize self-determination, communication, and self-advocacy
- are trauma-informed
- insist on working toward cultural understanding—ensuring the therapeutic process is a two-way street. Change and growth are the expectations for the client *and* OTP[21]
- focus on strengths as defined by the person, acknowledging how those things can be leveraged to support meaningful engagement in different occupations and roles
- do not focus on control and compliance (i.e. behavioral modification techniques that encourage masking)
- are not reductionistic (focusing on single performance component), rather they embrace and support people in holistic ways
- do not target ND characteristics for intervention but rather understand and respect differences (e.g. sensory processing difference is supported rather than targeted for extinction or habituation).

For an additional extended list of affirming characteristics (practitioner and program) and a visual grading of popular OT techniques along the spectrum of having low-affirming qualities to having high-affirming qualities, see Carlson-Giving.[22] To support OTPs' ability to identify ableist practices across various occupations and explore neurodiversity-affirming alternatives, the co-authors developed Table 10.3. By examining these side-by-side comparisons, practitioners can reflect on their own approaches and consider more inclusive and affirming strategies in their work.

Table 10.3—Ableist Practices and Affirming Alternatives Across Occupations

Occupation/ Skill	Common Ableist Practices	Neurodiversity-Affirming Alternatives
Social Participation	• Neurotypical social skills training or neurotypical conformity • Promoting eye contact, the individual needing to learn neurotypical body language, getting better at small talk, sticking to the same topic for X minutes (unless client requested) • Prioritizing verbal language as if there is a hierarchy of communication	• Consider exploring social-emotional learning curriculums created by Neurodivergent individuals, such as Bridges Learning Systems, Social Cipher, Konfident Kidz, and Social Optics. • Facilitate coaching with the Neurodivergent client's loved ones/partners/caregivers on how Neurodivergent social participation looks different than neurotypical social participation and why this needs to be honored. • Help make sure the client can be their authentic selves in important contexts/environments by supporting neurodiversity-affirming environments (e.g. attitudinal barriers, sensory-inclusive). • Provide an environment where clients share what their communication styles are, and help advocate alongside them for others to honor their communication style; Steph of SGR OT has a fabulous guide to Neurodivergent social connection styles. • Utilize passions and monotropic interests and support the client (if they want) to pursue interest-based groups. Human beings thrive on connecting through shared interests or hobbies, and interest-based communities help to reduce pressure and create genuine connections. • Prior to meeting a client, reach out to them and/or caregivers to identify strengths and interests.[23] Be prepared to discuss or engage in client interests upon meeting them.

cont.

Occupation/ Skill	Common Ableist Practices	Neurodiversity-Affirming Alternatives
Sensory Processing	• Using deficit-based language ("sensory processing disorder") to describe unique Neurodivergent sensory processing • Presenting sensory modulation differences to client and family via a pathological lens (over-sensitivity to auditory and visual input) • Using exposure therapy or desensitization to attempt to lessen or "normalize" a person's responsiveness to sensory input while ignoring their distress • Using rewards to entice a person to "build tolerance" to uncomfortable and/or painful sensory input • Assuming that clients have volitional control over their responsiveness to sensory input • Not understanding or supporting a client's sensory discrimination differences (ability to interpret details and intensity of sensory information) • Providing services with the aim to make sensory processing differences "appropriate" or "adapting" them to be more neurotypical • Adopting a therapy practice based on the medical model of disability and an assumption that the focus of OT is to "fix" Neurodivergent students • Following the "lead" of behaviorists • Developing ableist IEP goals, therapeutic activities, and outcome measures • Discouraging student from talking about interests and passions	• Employ neutral language ("sensory processing difference") to describe the client's individualized presentation. • Seek to describe sensory modulation differences as natural variations of the human condition which often reflect enhanced perceptual abilities (greater awareness of the pitch/tone of human voices, increased visual perceptual ability to notice details). • Honor evidence in neuroscience that supports "gating theory" (Neurodivergent populations present with different abilities to inhibit or "tune out" sensory input).[24] • Never use rewards to entice clients to ignore their brain and body signals that function to warn them of dysregulating sensory input. • Intentionally cultivate clients' self-understanding of their own unique sensory processing; model, teach, and support self-advocacy efforts to communicate needs. • If clients are interested, provide no-demand opportunities within the environment for them to explore various sensory experiences and learn more about their sensory processing patterns. • Ensure that clients' sensory processing is understood and supported by caregivers; normalize sensory processing diversity. Consider having caregivers/support partners complete sensory assessments so they can learn about their own sensory processing experiences. • Promote sensory-inclusive environments and explore accommodation ideas in line with their sensory processing differences.[25] • Advocate for access to individualized fidgets, explicitly teach clients and partners how to use fidgets, and promote positive exploration of fidgets.[26] • Embody therapy practice based on the neurodiversity framework and consider the match or mismatch between a student and the environment and teaching modalities. • Become a school leader as an OTP, embracing leadership practices to teach others (formally via workshops and informally during daily interactions), model hands-on teaching modalities, challenge the status quo of behaviorist approaches, provide evidence that highlights lived experiences of Neurodivergent people,[27] neurodiversity-informed research,[28] and advocate for affirming IEP goals and accommodations.[29] • Focus on providing holistic support. Don't allow your practice to be restricted by others' perceptions. For example, advocating for and supporting regulation (a critical foundational skill for academic participation).

Academic Participation	• Expecting Neurodivergent students to work to understand and communicate better with neurotypical students • Sticking to a narrow and medical model of disability-based OT practice such as teaching handwriting or working on visual motor skill	• Use your knowledge base to foster development of sensory strategies, language-based strategies, and metacognitive strategies for regulation. Explore Autism Level UP! resources: The Regulator 2.0 and Bumper: A Whole Body Learner. • Help young students learn how they learn and support their ability to convey that information to others and advocate for their needs in the classroom environment. Explore Autism Level UP!'s Classroom Regulator. • Recommend neurodiversity-affirming accommodations.[30] • Advocate for sensory-inclusive classrooms.[31] • Use simple and valuable "mantras" to educate staff ("meet a student where they are," "kids do well if they can," "seek connection over compliance").[32] • Presume competence that a Neurodivergent student can understand your words and do not speak about them in front of them. • Teach staff to develop awareness of their energy levels and to be sensitive to how their presence affects student regulation. • Cultivate self-esteem, self-confidence, and a sense of social belonging through incorporating interests into schoolwork, projects, and social time, encouraging them to share their interests with their class. • Prioritize ensuring that students who are in programs (really, all students) away from their general education peers are included in general education as much as possible. Special education is a service, not a location, and Disabled students are general education students first no matter their support needs. It is our ethical responsibility to support and facilitate their inclusion to enable meaningful participation in the general education environment. • Explore resources by the Strengths-Based Collective, a neurodiversity-led organization that creates resources on how to be strengths-based throughout the entire IEP process (many of which are free!).[33] • Know and avoid ableist approaches such as requesting eye contact, using hand-over-hand instruction, planned ignoring, discouraging stimming, using sensory supports or sensory breaks as rewards, requiring compliance, dismissing strength and value of monotropic focus, and accepting labels of cognitive impairment based on testing standardized on neurotypical populations. • Learn how to avoid ableist language in the school setting and better understand the ableist and racist history of public education.[34] • For written expression, transform OT practice to shift away from handwriting (a neurotypical occupation) and visual motor skill development and toward embracing technology for written communication, implementing classroom accommodations, modifying teaching practices, exploring and developing sensory supports, educating staff on neurodiversity-affirming teaching practices, fostering self-empowerment, etc. • Know that any IEP team member can call an IEP meeting to discuss and alter student goals, accommodations, and service delivery at any time (also, an IEP can be amended through signed team approval at any point during the year and not just at an annual IEP team meeting).

cont.

Occupation/ Skill	Common Ableist Practices	Neurodiversity-Affirming Alternatives
Self-Advocacy	• Placing responsibility on a client to advocate for themselves effectively and independently every day • Normalizing and accepting that a Neurodivergent person may have no effective method of communication • Assuming it is the sole responsibility of the Neurodivergent client to advocate for their needs • Dismissing the need that a client communicates (such as when an OTP ignores a client's reluctance to take part in an activity)	• Understand that advocacy abilities vary and that one day a client may need supported advocacy (relying on a trusted person to advocate for their needs) but another day may use self-advocacy (relying on oneself to advocate for one's needs). • Provide education to ensure that caregivers, support personnel, and teachers can engage in productive two-way communication with a client to ensure their needs are understood. • Ensure the client has access to robust, multimodal, and accessible means of communication. Empower the client to utilize communication methods that are preferred and energy-saving. • Provide education to caregivers that a distressed individual needs time to decompress before being able to self-advocate or communicate about the experience. • Recognize accommodations are a human right, and ensure clients receive their accommodations as a standard practice. • Drop demands when a client expresses dissent and rethink therapeutic activities, teaching modalities, activity supports and accommodations, and even therapy goals (remember, being an ally is a lifelong journey).
Activities of Daily Living (ADLs)	• Making simplified assumptions about the reasons a client does not take part in ADLs when in reality other factors are at play • Providing rewards for participating in ADLs (ignoring sensory responsiveness to materials and environment) • Prioritizing client independence rather than interdependence with trusted caregivers	• Share that "Kids [and adults] do well when they can" with families and support personnel to remind them that "lagging skills" explain difficulties.[35] • Realize the many demands associated with ADLs (praxis, sensory factors, societal pressures, environmental demands, etc.). • Know that rewards do not build long-term skills, self-understanding, self-advocacy, or self-determination; prioritize understanding a client's strengths, challenges, and needs. • Accommodate materials to suit a client's sensory processing, praxis, and motor skill (use powdered soap, flavorless toothpaste, thick towels, etc.). • Accommodate the environment to support the client's sensory processing profile (e.g. block sensor on automatic toilet flusher in order to prevent flushing noise). To learn more about Neurodivergent perspectives on ADLs, review Morrison et al.[36] • Incorporate visual supports to support executive function demands of ADLs (use "to-do" checklists like a step-by-step guide for peri-care after toileting; provide "how-to" visuals such as pictures of different parts of the mouth for toothbrushing).[37] • Consider interdependence and ongoing support from caregivers to assist praxis, motor skill, emotional regulation, etc., ensuring it is welcomed by the client.

Feeding[38] *Given the complexities and considerations needed for feeding, feeding has its own row separate from ADLs. Additionally, there is an expanded resource on neurodiversity-affirming feeding approaches in the Vault if you would like more ideas.	• Systematic desensitization practices are used without client consent, assuming caregiver permission is sufficient • Recognize that many mainstream feeding programs or "picky eating support" often focus on making feeding easier on the caregiver versus supporting the client's relationship with food • Using behavioral approaches to feeding (e.g. rewards, compliance-infused, demand-based) • "Distraction-free" mealtime expectations may not be accessible and can heighten stress for Neurodivergent families • Promoting a strict "clean" or "healthy" diet and restricting access to preferred foods	• Only work on expanding a client's food repertoire if the client expresses a desire to do so. Make sure to educate the client that there is no such thing as an "ideal" number of foods for a client to be able to eat. That is a neurotypical way of perceiving feeding. • Focus on identifying the client's safe foods, help the client ensure they can access those safe foods across their environments, and provide supplements as needed. Help the client and their family to know that supplement use doesn't mean they are "failing" at eating, and help destigmatize the client's safe foods coupled with their supplements. • Even though many feeding programs incorporate food play, this approach does not eliminate the potential harm of feeding therapy for clients who have not consented or who do not wish to expand their food choices. Such a "playful" methodology can still lead to trauma. Repeated exposure to a new food can result in disembodiment, where the individual may feel disconnected from their body while eating, potentially causing them to mask their true feelings and dissociate to endure the experience.[39] • Create flexible mealtime environments that accommodate sensory needs and allow for comfort. • Explore interoceptive differences, recognizing that many Neurodivergent individuals may be hypo or hypersensitive to the sensation of hunger. Some clients may benefit from learning about "when to eat" and others may benefit from information about "how to eat" so that their nutritional needs are met, and their bodies are fueled adequately. • Recommended training opportunities to consider include the course offered by RDs for Neurodiversity, which is developed by Neurodivergent individuals. Additionally, the following trainings may align with the neurodiversity framework, though it is unclear if they have been informed by the insights of Neurodivergent individuals: responsive feeding therapy and Marsha Dunn Klein's Get Permission Approach. • Recognize that adults experience more barriers due to the reduced number of resources, and often have deeply engrained expectations and negative associations about food and mealtimes. Incorporate concepts of body and fat liberation.[40] • Help the individual unmask around nutrition and food by discussing with them ableist standards of health, and instead help them reconnect with their preferences. Help them reclaim their preferences, and combat ableist standards around variety and "proper" eating habits.

cont.

Occupation/ Skill	Common Ableist Practices	Neurodiversity-Affirming Alternatives
Work Settings	• Inadequate consideration of client's individualized needs and comfort with social interactions with both clients and co-workers • Ignoring the impact that environmental factors have on a person's regulation (lights, visual clutter, unexpected touch, messy/sticky tactile input, sudden/loud noises, sounds of talking, smells, etc.) • Assuming that work performance will be consistent day to day despite variability in fatigue due to sleep fluctuations, environmental stimuli, social work interactions, ability to access executive function skills; lack of clarity in directions or communication • Encouraging masking of one's unique Neurodivergent traits in order to appear more neurotypical • OTP provides limited education to company management regarding Neurodivergent clients' needs (e.g. benefiting from "heads-up knowledge of expected changes to the environment, work roles, co-workers, clientele, etc.) • Lack of proactive "heads-up" information from management when known changes are expected to happen (environment, work roles, co-workers, clientele, etc.) or lack of support when unexpected changes occur	• Avoid "pressuring" client to engage in neurotypical social engagement, which may cause anxiety/dysregulation, but rather encourage organic, interest-based opportunities for conversation and connection. • Ensure that either the client or a trusted co-worker/manager can recognize dysregulation within the Neurodivergent client and that effective strategies for emotional regulation have been proactively identified and practiced. • Fully analyze the match or mismatch between person factors, environment, and activity demands. • Consider using the Person in Context (PIC) resource which comprises a visual representation of elements such as person profile, activity, and environment which are then synthesized and analyzed to guide the development of supports, keeping in mind that supports include activity modifications and environmental accommodations, not just tools for the client to use in the work environment (Figure 10.1). • Confirm that principles of the double empathy problem are understood by co-workers and management and that everyone is encouraged to appreciate both Neurodivergent and neurotypical ways of being and to avoid mutual misunderstandings. • Collaborate with the employer to ensure the workplace offers robust, multimodal, and accessible ways for communication. Encourage the individual to use communication strategies that feel natural, sustainable, and supportive of their success at work. • Honor a client's choice to mask or not mask in work settings, allowing them the autonomy to choose if they feel safe to show up as their authentic selves. • Schedule individualized "check-ins" at the start of the workday or shift to share information the client has deemed important. • Put a familiar plan in place for times when unexpected and dysregulating events occur, using strategies such as providing co-regulation or allowing a break (screen time, movement, alone time, etc.).

Conclusion

Given the breadth of information contained within the chapter, it is clear that ND-affirming practice is not "a single thing," rather it is an all-encompassing mindset, one that touches upon every aspect of the therapeutic process. When preparing for and engaging in support with an ND client, the implications of the client's ND identity must always be at the forefront of consideration by the OTP, as there is no aspect of a client's life that neurodivergence does not influence. OTPs are in a unique position to empower their clients to embrace their neurodivergence while actively supporting their authentic engagement in the occupations, roles, and routines that make their lives meaningful. Likewise, the broad skillset of OTPs positions them to be leaders on teams and in the community, advocating for others to engage in ND-affirming care and relationships.

Some final thoughts: In order to confidently engage in person-centered, ND-affirming practice, OTPs must commit to continuous learning and reflective practice. Knowledge evolves, as do the implications of that knowledge. Embracing these facts is critical to provide the most current, innovative, and validating support. However, the commitment to continued professional growth by the OTP does not just ensure that their practices and supports change in meaningful ways, it also ensures OTPs maintain a focus on their own need to change and grow alongside their clients. At its very core ND's affirming practice is relational work. It values, honors, accommodates, supports, and celebrates all neurotypes.

Endnotes

1 Braun, M. J., Dunn, W., & Tomchek, S. D. (2017). A pilot study on professional documentation: Do we write from a strengths perspective? *American Journal of Speech-Language Pathology / American Speech-Language-Hearing Association, 26*(3), 972–981. https://doi.org/10.1044/2017_AJSLP-16-0117

2 Murthi, K., Chen, Y., Chore, S., & Patten, K. (2023). Strength-based practice to enhance mental health for Autistic people: A scoping review. *The American Journal of Occupational Therapy, 77*(2), 7702185060. https://doi.org/105014.ajot.2023.050074

3 Greene, R. (2021). *The explosive child: A new approach for understanding and parenting easily frustrated, chronically inflexible children* (6th ed.). Harper Collins Publishers.

4 Trevisan, D. A., Roberts, N., Lin, C., & Birmingham, E. (2017). How do adults and teens with self-declared autism spectrum disorder experience eye contact? A qualitative analysis of firsthand accounts. *PLoS One, 12*(11), e0188446. https://doi.org/10.1371/journal.pone.0188446

5 Holmes, L. G., Goebel, R. J., Hollingue, C., Zhu, S., Zhang, H., Shan, W., Wang, S., Caplan, R., Sanchez, A., Wharmby, P., Chiang, M., Person, M., & Rothman, E. F. (2023). Reductions in depression and anxiety among Autistic adults participating in an intervention to promote healthy relationships. *The American Journal of Occupational Therapy, 77*(2). https://doi.org/10.5014/ajot.2023.050108

6 Roberts, J. (2021, October 2). *Performative neurodiversity: The appropriation and watering down of a human rights movement for profit.* https://therapistndc.org/performative-neurodiversity-the-appropriation-and-watering-down-of-a-human-rights-movement-for-profit

7 Laurent, A. C., & Fede, J. H. (2024). *ENERGY: The framework, tools, strategies, & logic to support regulation.* Autism Level UP!

8 Laurent, A. C., & Fede, J. H. (2023). *Visual information engagement web.* Autism Level UP! https://cdn.sanity.io/files/p6bm7moz/production/988bef73b87d9133597bded-c7eaa14331dc61853.pdf

9 Sameroff, A. (Ed.). (2009). *The transactional model of development: How children and contexts shape each other*. American Psychological Association. www.jstor.org/stable/j.ctv1chs5hf

10 Bass, J. D., Baum, C. M., & Christiansen, C. H. (2015). Interventions and outcomes: The Person-Environment-Occupation-Performance (PEOP) occupational therapy process. In C. H. Christiansen, C. M. Baum, & J. D. Bass (Eds.), *Occupational therapy: Performance, participation and well-being* (4th ed., pp. 57–80). Routledge.

11 Laurent, A. C., & Fede, J. H. (2019). *The person in context*. Autism Level UP! https://cdn.sanity.io/files/p6bm7moz/production/a56067dcf8dd0b04f2bc6df7b1202ded49b5c8e9.pdf

12 Fede, J. H., & Laurent, A. C. (2020). *Heightened perception: Challenge? Strength? BOTH!* Autism Level UP! https://cdn.sanity.io/files/p6bm7moz/production/aa387214f174ba2a88e2e815eb214c27aef2d163.pdf

13 Farrell, M. (Host), & Mahler, K. (Guest). (2022, April 6). Autism and interoception (No. 44) [Audio podcast episode]. In *Two sides of the spectrum*. Learn Play Thrive. https://learnplaythrive.com/podcasts/44-autism-interoception-with-kelly-mahler

14 Flynn, L. (2024). *OT4ADHD*. OT4ADHD. https://ot4adhd.com

15 Laurent, A. C., & Fede, J. H. (2020). *Bullet journal for planning and reflecting*. Autism Level UP! https://cdn.sanity.io/files/p6bm7moz/production/4154cc5136a104e978d74644b8ab297e3a317bbd.pdf

16 Laurent, A. C., & Fede, J. H. (2020). *WHYs Not SIZE: Supports for problem solving informed by the Neurodivergent community*. Autism Level UP! https://cdn.sanity.io/files/p6bm7moz/production/9923ebd9e2b814e076cfadd63387f18e92fde4ff.pdf

17 Laurent, A. C., & Fede, J. (2021). Leveling up regulatory support through community collaboration. *Perspectives of the ASHA Special Interest Groups*, 1–18. https://doi.org/10.1044/2020persp-20-00197

18 Farrell, M. (Host), & Milton, D. (Guest). (2020, June 3). The Double Empathy Problem (No. 2) [Audio podcast episode]. In *Two sides of the spectrum*. Learn Play Thrive. https://learnplaythrive.com/podcasts/the-double-empathy-problem-2

19 Laurent, A. C., & Fede, J. H. (2021). *All the feelZzz: An alternative way for individuals to communicate pain, discomfort and perceived difference in their body*. Autism Level UP!

20 Laurent, A. C., & Fede, J. H. (2024). *ENERGY: The framework, tools, strategies, & logic to support regulation*. Autism Level UP!

21 Prizant, B. M., Wetherby, A. M., Rubin, E., Laurent, A. C., & Rydell, P. J. (2006). *The SCERTS Model: A comprehensive educational approach for children with autism spectrum disorders. Volume I: Assessment*. Paul H. Brookes Publishing Co.

22 Carlson-Giving, B. (2023). *Embracing Neurodivergent occupations and empowering disabled voices: A knowledge translation tool to support neurodiversity-affirming occupational therapy practice and challenge ableism within the profession* (Doctoral thesis). Boston University Research Repository. https://open.bu.edu/handle/2144/46622

23 Marnell, L. (2025). *TAPP into strengths questionnaire*. www.kidsmasterskills.com/tappintostrengthsquestionnaire

24 Schulz, S. E., Luszawski, M., Hannah, K. E., & Stevenson, R. A. (2023). Sensory gating in neurodevelopmental disorders: A scoping review. *Research on Child and Adolescent Psychopathology*, *51*, 1005–1019. https://doi.org/10.1007/s10802-023-01058-9

25 Seeberger, C. (2021, August 14). *What is a sensory-friendly environment?* Sensory Friendly Solutions. www.sensoryfriendly.net/what-is-a-sensory-friendly-environment

26 Laurent, A., & Fede, J. (2021). *Fidgets are tools*. Autism Level UP! https://cdn.sanity.io/files/p6bm7moz/production/f05844ee3e2bc6e127a39640d49b49e54330535f.pdf

27 Autistic Self-Advocacy Network (ASAN). (n.d.). *For whose benefit? Evidence, ethics, and effectiveness of autism interventions*. Autistic Self Advocacy Network. https://Autisticadvocacy.org/wp-content/uploads/2021/12/ACES-Ethics-of-Intervention.pdf

28 Sterman, J., Gustafson, E., Eisenmenger, L., Hamm, L., & Edwards, J. (2023). Autistic adult perspectives on occupational therapy for Autistic children and youth. *OTJR: Occupation, Participation and Health*, *43*(2), 237–244. https://doi.org/10.1177/15394492221103850

29 Marnell, L. (2024). *Neurodiversity-affirming IEP goal bank and guidelines for OTs*. Kids Master Skills. www.kidsmasterskills.com/product-page/nd-affirming-ot-goal-bank

30 Marnell, L. (2024). *Kids Master Skills' IEP accommodation bank and guidelines*. Kids Master Skills. www.kidsmasterskills.com/product-page/nd-affirming-iep-accommodations

31 Chaves, J., & Taylor, A. (2021). *Creating sensory smart classrooms*. Routledge.

32 Desautels, L. (2024). *Connection over compliance: Rewiring our perceptions of discipline*. Wyatt-MacKenzie Publishing.

33 Reed, K. (2025). *Strengths-based collective: Building resilience together*. Strengths-Based Collective. www.strengthbasedcollective.com

34 Bottema-Beutel, K., Sasson, N. J., McKinnon, R., Braun, C., Guo, R., Hand, B. N., Kapp, S. K., Espinas, D. R., Bailin, A., Lester, J. N., & Yu, B.

(2024). Recognizing and resisting ableist language in schools: Suggestions for school-based speech-language pathologists and related professionals. *Language, Speech, and Hearing Services in Schools*, 55(4), 1025–1038. https://doi.org/10.1044/2024_LSHSS-24-00036

35 Greene, R. (2021). *The explosive child: A new approach for understanding and parenting easily frustrated, chronically inflexible children* (6th ed.). Harper Collins Publishers.

36 Morrison, C., Cashin, A., & Foley, K.-R. (2024). Daily living skill support for Autistic people through a neurodiversity-affirming practice lens. *Australian Occupational Therapy Journal*, *72*(2), e13002. https://doi.org/10.1111/1440-1630.13002

37 Marnell, L. (2022, April 22). *Visual supports in Autism* [Video]. YouTube. https://youtu.be/FQvG1nwNX6g?si=hESxxxf7dSkCmLuR

38 Hunani, N. (2025). *Inclusive approaches to supporting Neurodivergent children with feeding challenges*. RDs for Neurodiversity. https://rdsforneurodiversitycourses.podia.com/inclusive-approaches-to-supporting-Neurodivergent-children-with-feeding-challenges-march-2025

39 Farrell, M. (Host), & Hunani, N. (Guest). (2022, August 17). Affirming approaches to picky eating: Moving beyond systematic desensitization (No. 53) [Audio podcast episode]. In *Two sides of the spectrum*. Learn Play Thrive. https://learnplaythrive.com/podcasts/53-affirming-approaches-to-picky-eating-moving-beyond-systematic-desensitization-with-naureen-hunani

40 Pratt Institute Libraries. (2024). *Fat studies: Introduction*. Pratt Institute Libraries. https://libguides.pratt.edu/fatstudies/introduction

CHAPTER 11

Advocacy

GREG BOHELER, JACKLYN BOHELER, AND ELIZABETH DUFFY

Introduction to Advocacy in Occupational Therapy Practice

What Is Advocacy? Why Is It a Part of the Occupational Therapy Process?

Advocacy is a fundamental, professional, and moral imperative for the profession of occupational therapy (OT).[1,2] Occupational therapy is rooted in advocacy, taking various forms across macro-, meso-, and micro- (contextual) levels. Since occupational therapy's inception, OT practitioners have leveraged advocacy as an essential tool and intervention for the promotion of client-centered, occupation-based outcomes and occupational justice.

Furthermore, OT has always emphasized occupational participation and performance which are closely linked to access and environmental situatedness. That is: a person's ever-changing relationship between the person, their contexts, and occupations affect participation and performance.[3,4] As explored in Chapter 2, practitioners have begun to look beyond individualistic factors or physical environments, toward social, economic, political, legal, or institutional elements of the environment.[5]

These structures and systems, through which people engage in meaningful occupations, provide the fertile ground for advocacy to take root. Just like roots grow within their soil, the foundation of advocacy is shaped by various systemic and institutional influences. As the roots adapt and grow, they may give birth to justice, access, and participation. Advocacy can be siloed or collective, like plants of different species (with distinct or even conflicting agendas) or the same species (synergy across efforts with shared goals). Some advocacy efforts thrive and lead to change, while others may stagnate because they lack the right conditions to grow. Like plants, all advocacy interacts with its environment, influencing and being influenced, and adapting over time.

However, these prevailing systems also harness power dynamics, along with social and cultural norms to promote an idealized way of being, thereby oppressing and marginalizing persons or groups that diverge. Even as increasing efforts have been made toward diversity, equity, and inclusion (DEI), disability is often overlooked. Ergo, Disabled people experience injustice as a Marginalized group without consideration and support from DEI efforts. Neglecting disability or accessibility in DEI represents a missed opportunity for justice.

So, how can occupational therapists be effective instigators of positive change, breaking down stigma and normalizing disability? Advocacy is a great start, as all DEIA (diversity, equity, inclusion, and accessibility) efforts inherently demand justice, and justice requires advocacy.[6] To become practitioners who are mindful of equity, inclusion, and justice, occupational therapy practitioners (OTPs) must navigate the waters of self-advocacy in collaboration with the people they serve. Many Disabled and Neurodivergent people have experienced services that strip away their autonomy or question their competence (e.g. hand-over-hand support without consent, non-robust communication supports, and making decisions for them). Occupational therapy practitioners can support self-advocacy for their clients by meeting them where they are, improving autonomy, and affirming their authentic ways of being. For example, if making choices or decisions is challenging for our clients, we can support self-advocacy by honoring "yes" and "no" responses, building toward making choices, and then supporting more complex decision-making.[7]

Specifically, as OTPs we are obligated to support Marginalized persons and communities to advocate for and obtain occupational justice. As occupational beings, humans derive meaning through doing, being, and belonging.[8] Increased barriers to access and participation exist for Marginalized groups or individuals, like those with disabilities. For Disabled adults, transportation barriers remain a significant impetus for access to employment, education, healthcare, and community participation. Data from the US Department of Transportation estimates that 15 million people have challenges related to transportation, with 40% of this number being Disabled people.[9] As noted in the Occupational Therapy Practice Framework, these barriers create an environment where advocacy is an essential mechanism for occupational justice in which people are empowered to "seek and obtain resources to support health, well-being, and occupational participation."[10] Examples of supporting advocacy in communities include advocating to a research journal to require any research about a Marginalized community to include a member from that community as a research team member and advocating to IEP teams and teachers about whole-classroom instruction on Neurodivergent and neurotypical communication skills to honor all communication styles.

Intersectionality, Interdependence, and Collective Access All Relate to Advocacy

As described throughout this book, intersectionality offers an indispensable lens for understanding how power intersects with the various identities that shape who we are. Systemic injustice manifests across social, cultural, political, and economic spheres, influencing and intersecting with individual traits. Consequently, effective advocacy and justice efforts must also address these systemic dimensions to foster meaningful, long-term change. Systemic advocacy is the force behind all major disability laws passed in the last half a century, but it doesn't always take the form of high-profile actions like sit-ins, protests, or social media movements. Sometimes, advocacy can be as simple as calling a local representative about Medicaid expansion, advocating for reimbursement for a neurodiversity-affirming intervention, or supporting and volunteering at justice-oriented non-profits. Justice-oriented practitioners must remain mindful of intersectionality, cultivating a humble understanding that allows them to effectively partner with diverse populations.

The collective, relational nature of advocacy echoes the interdependence that occurs in our daily lives. In addition to being a core construct of the disability justice framework, interdependence is a big part of disability culture.[11] It describes how, as relational beings, we are perpetually navigating varying levels of bi-directional dependence with or upon others.

> Complete independence is a myth; as relational beings we exist on a sliding scale of interdependence in nearly everything we do. When the faucet breaks, what do you do? Call a professional, text a friend or family member, search YouTube... all of these actions require a level of reliance upon other people. Next time you are making a sandwich, think about the number of people and systems involved in producing the materials you decide to use in creating your lunchtime masterpiece.

Interdependence directly contradicts aspirations toward independence that are upheld and promoted in many Eurocentric cultures.[12] The narrative of "independence" has permeated the field of occupational therapy. Consider traditional OT goals. How often have you encountered the phrase *the client will independently...?* (Fill in the blank.) Much of the language within the profession reinforces a narrow, single-minded focus on independence as the end goal. Clients in rehabilitation settings are pushed toward independent functioning; assist levels are used to determine a person's discharge from acute care; and school practitioners are funneled toward goals about decreasing interdependence upon others, whether it be self-regulation, executive functioning, or handwriting. Striving toward self-sufficiency is commendable, but the profession of OT needs to become more open to the reality of interdependence.

This is especially important for Disabled people, because if complete independence is unattainable for non-disabled persons, why do practitioners insist upon making it a goal for people who oftentimes benefit from accommodations and support? For example, a teen benefits from speech-to-text assistive technology at school, but the IEP team feels he is capable of doing the work without it, so they propose to remove this accommodation from their IEP. Across practice settings, reducing or fading supports is viewed as progress. Embracing interdependence requires confronting the idea that independence is the outcome and normalizing accommodations that benefit everyone. Likewise, advocacy infers interdependence; even self-advocacy doesn't occur in a vacuum, devoid of others' influence. Problems require people. Having more than one person or group leverage their experience, strengths, and positionality is ultimately what brings about systemic change. Therefore, collective advocacy and collaboration are foundational tools in an occupational therapist's toolbox.

Advocacy and the Neurodiversity Community

Appreciating the Diverse Ways in Which Disability Groups Advocate

Advocacy can be overt or subtle; it can be big or small; and it can be both methodical and messy. Disability represents just one facet of the beautiful diversity that is humankind. Advocacy, as an essential tool for the disability experience, is equally diverse in how it is employed, acted upon, and leveraged to create positive change. Neurodivergence itself represents a large umbrella of human brain differences that can contribute to disability due to the person–environment transaction. Therefore, neurodiversity-affirming advocacy reflects a broad scope of ways Neurodivergent people and groups advocate. Historically, disability advocacy has leaned toward justice for people with physical disabilities, which reflects the human tendency to address that which is visible.[13] This bias is mirrored within neurodiversity-centered advocacy efforts as certain more visible people and/or disability communities are typically prioritized over others.

Examples of this include people with more complex or observable manifestations of disability versus more "invisible" presentations. People with "invisible" disabilities are often overlooked within advocacy efforts, and many times their concerns are dismissed because their challenges are less apparent. The Inaccessibility Cycle by Pacing Pixie underlies how inaccessible spaces lead to society believing Disabled people do not exist, and therefore justifies the lack of accommodations to persist.[14] In short, if people are not visible in the community due to barriers to participation, they are less likely to be included in advocacy efforts.

Likewise, racial, cultural, and socioeconomic factors play into advocacy efficacy and even prioritization. Many Marginalized populations are disempowered from advocacy efforts, including BIPOC people, women, or people who are within lower socioeconomic brackets. A common critique of the Neurodiversity movement is that it ignores Nonspeaking and those with intellectual disabilities from advocacy efforts. Misconceptions and miscommunication often impact advocacy efforts, as they alienate different shareholders. Jules Edwards and Meghan Ashburn's book, *I Will Die on This Hill: Autistic Adults, Autism Parents, and the Children Who Deserve a Better World*, gives practical solutions and advice on how to bridge these differences to foster more inclusive advocacy.[15]

When advocacy efforts do not center or give leadership to those who are most impacted, advocacy can cause harm. For example, many white Neurodivergent advocates advocate for the abolishment of applied behavioral analysis (ABA). However, ABA is often the only "childcare" that is available for Neurodivergent children with support needs, and this trauma is even further compounded for BIPOC Neurodivergent children (who are often kicked out of traditional daycare centers due to "behaviors"). This demonstrates the nuance that exists within advocacy, and how imperative it is to center multiply Marginalized advocates to ensure harm reduction in our advocacy efforts.

Access to formalized services and support is often gate-kept by an official diagnosis. With autism, the diagnostic criteria were developed based on research primarily involving white male children, which ignores the potential for different presentations among undiagnosed Autistic females, people of color, or adults.[16] In this growing area of advocacy, Neurodivergent people are fighting for the right to services that are withheld because they don't meet every criterion. Additionally, many people feel excluded from embracing a disability identity, which can help reduce shame about the challenges one experiences.[17] Disability identity not only provides a framework for understanding one's own experiences but also fosters connection to disability culture and community—where solidarity and support may be found.[18] This is why within many Neurodivergent spaces (including the Autism and Attention Deficit/Hyperactivity Disorder [AuADHDer] communities), self-diagnosis has become a widely accepted norm.[19] This practice serves as a form of collective advocacy, challenging a flawed system and affirming people's right to self-recognition and a sense of belonging.

Subcommunity Advocacy

While some Disabled people have multiple disabilities, there is a strong presence of disability subgroups within the advocacy space. Disability-specific advocacy is a bit of a misnomer, as all disability advocacy overlaps in the pursuit of collective access; but here are some beautiful examples of how particular disability groups advocate.

Visibility is a key component of disability advocacy and justice, and no group is more experienced with this than those with physical disabilities. Historically, Americans with physical disabilities have been at the forefront of the disability rights movement. From Title 19 to the Rehabilitation Act of 1973, the Americans with Disabilities Act (ADA), or the Individuals with Disabilities Education Act (IDEA), people with physical disabilities have played their part in changing the laws and culture of the United States. Perhaps the biggest ongoing culture shift initiated by people with physical disabilities is the normalization of accommodations in everyday life. Automatic doors, closed captioning, ergonomic equipment, and assistive tech are everyday accommodations that benefit all. The concept of universal design stems from advocacy efforts that led to the passing of the Americans with Disabilities Act (ADA). Additionally, Universal Design for Learning (UDL) is becoming common practice in school and employment settings, because accommodations offer equitable access for the benefit of all. The Universal Design for Learning guidelines align incredibly with neurodiversity-affirming practice, in the way in which they encourage autonomy, authenticity, and diversity in learning.[20]

That which benefits all is a common theme with disability advocacy, but there is often a need to recognize the diverse ways different disability subcultures advocate for their own visibility and rights. The Down syndrome community is known for its tight-knit network of national and local community organizations focused on their specific advocacy priorities like early intervention, mainstreaming in schools, and addressing early onset Alzheimer's. Socialization and positive self-esteem are strengths often associated with Down syndrome, which may contribute to the approach toward advocacy for the Down syndrome community.[21] Down syndrome organizations are highly effective in using media—such as reality TV shows, billboards in Times Square, or viral social media campaigns—to raise awareness about key advocacy issues. Members of this community also engage in collective efforts through community organizations, reinforcing their presence within the broader public sphere. Similarly, the deaf community advocates through Deaf culture-centered events, creating a sense of solidarity and visibility that directly challenges the marginalization they face.

Sustainability for Advocates

All neurodiversity advocacy efforts must be led by and accomplished in collaboration with Neurodivergent persons with lived experience of disability. Change doesn't happen overnight, and advocacy efforts are often draining. Sustainability is another disability justice principle that describes the need for collective and individual pacing to ensure steady, cohesive, advocacy efforts. Energy regulation is a consideration among Neurodivergent advocates who may have challenges related to monitoring, sustaining, and prioritizing energy levels.

One popular approach to support sustainability is the utilization of energy strategies. For example, spoon theory is a commonly used tool that Neurodivergent people utilize to monitor and regulate their energy levels.[22] "Spoons" represent a mechanism for measuring the energy required per task; each task subtracts from the total amount of spoons one has allotted for a given period of time. People can gain more spoons by engaging in occupations or interests that help reset their energy meter. Other energy regulation strategies might include the use of adaptive equipment, task simplification and pacing, mindfulness and grounding exercises, and boundary-setting to prevent burnout. As occupational therapy practitioners, it is within our domain to support people in learning and employing a variety of helpful energy strategies tailored to their unique needs.

Another way to support energy conservation for advocacy is through collaboration and load sharing. As discussed, interdependence is an essential element in obtaining collective access and liberation. All people involved in disability advocacy must share responsibility in the way that best suits their strengths and contexts. Communication across neurotypes is essential for this work, as individual strengths are strategically leveraged and power is shifted via allyship. Occupational therapy practitioners should embrace allyship as an ongoing process toward community and justice. As such, several important considerations must be acknowledged. Communication across neurotypes should take into consideration the double empathy problem, which describes challenges across neurotypes rather than problematizing Neurodivergent communication styles.[23] For example, Autistic to Autistic communication often flows easier than Autistic to neurotypical communication. In order to break through communication barriers, neurotypical allies must meet in the middle and embrace cultural humility. Cultural humility is as much a foundational tool within the ally's toolbox as it is for OTPs. It involves adopting a learner's mindset which honors others' lived experience. In this way, allies can learn from those they support to co-facilitate the communication needed for advocacy and justice-seeking. Communication established on trust encourages the sharing of responsibility and power and invites honest conversations. Conversations about injustice can often lead to frustration and conflict, but this is okay. In fact, Neurodivergent people may be more expressive the more supported or safe they feel. So, instead of becoming offended by criticism, neurotypical allies should invite these potentially uncomfortable conversations as opportunities for growth.

Disability Allyship and Accompliceship

There is no one way to allyship, just like there is no single avenue for advocacy. Allyship is an ongoing journey, with each individual taking a different path. However, there are similar steps that all people can take toward allyship and accompliceship. To illustrate some of these essential steps, refer to the Disability Allyship Framework (see Figure 11.1).

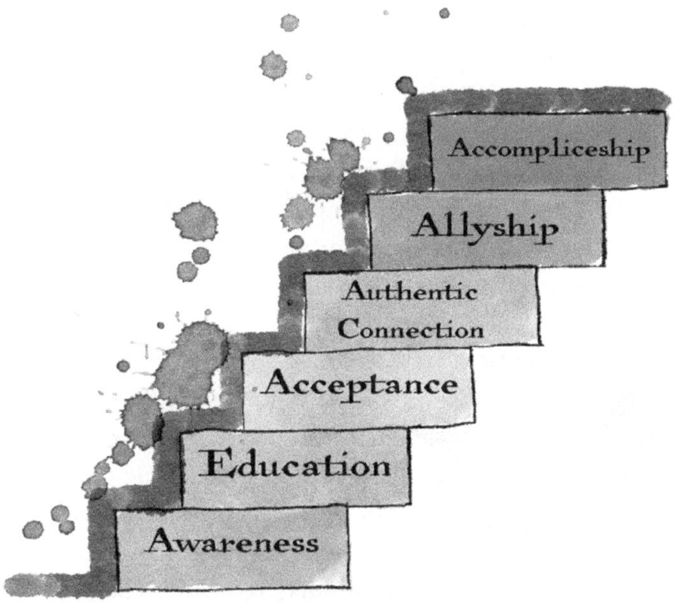

Figure 11.1—The Disability Allyship Framework
Note. Created by Greg Boheler.

Step One: Awareness

The different steps of the framework represent different stages toward allyship, although it is worth noting that allyship can be context-dependent, and one's allyship journey is rarely unidirectional. The first step is simple, awareness. This is a stage characterized by curiosity and a budding willingness to understand the nuances of disability as natural variations of what it means to be human. Oftentimes advocacy efforts spend a lot of time and money focusing on awareness (i.e. breast cancer awareness, autism awareness). And while this is a necessary first step, it is the action that follows awareness which really matters.

Example: A neurotypical OTP is challenged on Facebook for promoting training on standardized assessment tools that Neurodivergent OTPs argue are not inclusive. Initially unaware, the OTP listens to the feedback and begins to research more neurodiversity-affirming assessment tools.

Step Two: Education

The education stage is where the real work begins. During this part of the journey, individuals start to engage deeply with disability-related concepts—such as terminology, etiquette, and culture—through various sources, including media, texts, and discussions. As with all forms of allyship, a key component of disability education is to learn directly from those with lived experience of disability. The voices of Disabled individuals, along with their families, provide the context and understanding necessary for collaborative action.

Example: An OTP has an Autistic client who has demand avoidance traits, something the OTP has not yet encountered. To be proactive, the neurotypical OTP seeks out resources on Pathological Demand Avoidance (also known as Pervasive Drive for Autonomy) and consults neurodiversity-affirming OTP groups to gather strategies for promoting autonomy and meaningful engagement during sessions. The OTP learns the PDA community has created a screening tool, called the Extreme Demand Avoidance Questionnaire (EDAq).[24] The onus of education should not rest on the Neurodivergent client, but the OTP.

Step Three: Acceptance

Acceptance is a precursor for action; at least, an action that is respectful of disability culture, and implemented in partnership with Disabled individuals. Acceptance can be uncomfortable because it requires acknowledgment of one's own position of power and ableism. In short, acceptance is where people begin to embody cultural humility, which is a process of self-reflection in which individuals challenge themselves to remain open-minded to others' experience, acknowledge and address power imbalance, and critically reflect on their own beliefs and values (sort of like what is explored in Chapter 8).

Example: An OTP working with a client with ADHD notices the client struggles to stay on task, frequently getting distracted. Rather than seeing this as a lack of motivation, the OTP reflects on their own assumptions and acknowledges how they may have unintentionally viewed productivity through an ableist lens. After learning from ADHD advocates, the OTP accepts that ADHD is a natural variation in attention and executive functioning. They take the time to learn more about ADHD and consult with the client to understand their preferences. This self-reflection leads to a shift in approach, incorporating strategies like task breakdowns and movement breaks while honoring the client's experience and adjusting productivity demands accordingly.

Step Four: Authentic Connection

Authenticity is one of the core values of disability culture for two key reasons, both of which are related to choice and autonomy. Within Neurodivergent communities, authenticity is prized because so much of a Neurodivergent person's life is spent masking their true identity to fit in with neurotypical norms. Among Neurodivergent people, masking holds value as a self-preservation mechanism because it enables them to camouflage their true nature, thereby avoiding stigmatization. However, masking comes at a cost to one's mental health, which can ultimately lead to burnout.[25]

Additionally, a universal component of the Disabled experience is vulnerability. Because Disabled individuals live in a world not designed for them, they are compelled to embody vulnerability to receive support. Mia Mingus calls this "forced intimacy," one of the cornerstones of ableism, as Disabled people are forced to be vulnerable to receive basic access or support.[26] The pervasive nature of inaccessibility colors the lives of Disabled persons every day in a variety of ways. Socioculturally constructed barriers to access and participation are most often overcome by seeking social support such as becoming vulnerable and asking for help. Vulnerability is a powerful mode of expression that can lead to strong human connection; however, non-disabled individuals have more choice about when and where they are vulnerable in comparison to their Disabled peers. Everyday actions like opening a (non-automatic) door can be a challenge for some individuals, and they must become vulnerable (often toward strangers) to ask for assistance.

On the journey of allyship, modeling vulnerability and authenticity is imperative for building honest relationships with Disabled people, especially Neurodivergent adults. Finally, it's important to remain unafraid to ask questions. When approached from a place of authenticity, people are more willing to share their truths, thereby increasing shared understanding and trust.

Example: An OTP is supporting a young adult with an intellectual disability who seems disengaged during a cooking activity at his day program. In an effort to connect, the OTP playfully cracks a few jokes that match the individual's sense of humor: "I see you over there, slacking off and leaving all the work to me!" By tapping into shared humor and authenticity, the OTP helps break the ice, creating a more relaxed and engaging environment that encourages the individual to participate more actively.

Step Five: Allyship

Allyship is not an identity; it's a practice—rooted in action, support, and service. It involves actively challenging oppressive power structures and addressing inequities and ideologies that perpetuate discrimination and harm toward Marginalized groups. Allyship can serve both reactive and proactive roles: it can respond to oppression, helping to heal the wounds of injustice, or it can be used proactively to build equitable systems and structures.[27] Regardless of when or how it is applied, allyship is rooted in mutual trust and respect between allies and the individuals or groups with whom they partner.

Traditionally, allies are conceived as "dominant group members who work to end prejudice in their personal and professional lives, and relinquish social privileges conferred by their group status through their support of nondominant groups."[28] Research indicates that social justice movements are more impactful when allies from dominant groups collaborate in advocacy efforts.[29] However, allyship efforts are also undertaken by individuals with shared social status or identities—often referred to as "solidarity" in literature. Cross-disability solidarity is foundational to disability allyship and advocacy. Despite differences, creating a unified front is essential for achieving collective access.

A focus on access and equitable participation is just one way OTPs are uniquely positioned to engage in allyship alongside disability communities. With their expertise in context, environment, and social determinants of health and well-being, OTPs are encouraged to be mindful of these factors and actively support inclusion.

Disability allyship begins with:

1. **Self-awareness and acknowledging one's privilege**: Recognizing the ways in which privilege shapes our perspectives and actions.
2. **Embracing accessibility**: Actively advocating for environments that are inclusive and equitable. Advocating for things like closed captioning, flexibility in scheduling, or sensory-friendly environments supports Disabled populations.
3. **Doing with, not for**: Supporting empowerment by working alongside Marginalized communities rather than acting as saviors. *Nothing about us without us* is a core sentiment of the disability justice movement.[30]
4. **Centering Disabled voices**: Prioritizing the voices and leadership of those who are most affected by exclusion. Inviting Disabled speakers to your workplace, resharing Disabled social media advocates, or prioritizing and compensating Disabled creators for their work.

Allyship is a lifelong commitment—a continuous process of building relationships based on trust, consistency, and accountability with Marginalized individuals and/or groups of people.

Example: An OTP working at an assisted living facility notices that the local public library lacks wayfinding signs, creating confusion and potentially limiting access to its full range of amenities. Aspiring to support the library in improving accessibility, the OTP arranges a meeting with the library director to offer consultation. Recognizing the importance of centering the Disabled perspective in any accessibility improvements, they develop a plan to invite residents from the OTP's facility to visit the library and provide feedback on their experience.

Step Six: Accompliceship

Every accomplice is an ally, but not all allies are accomplices. Accompliceship is an extension of allyship in which a person leverages their privilege and power to take risks on behalf and in collaboration with Marginalized people. An accomplice is putting themselves at risk, such as their social capital, job security, or financial resources. An individual may be empowered to serve as an accomplice in one setting but as an ally in another, making accompliceship context-dependent. The key to accompliceship is a stance of humility. It is critical to establish trust and open communication with Disabled people before stepping into the role of accomplice. Positioning Disabled people to lead and stepping in when called upon is a balancing act.

Example: A Disabled coworker faces discrimination as their accommodation requests are ignored. An ally might act as a sounding board, helping the coworker develop a plan to advocate for their needs. An accomplice, however, takes a more active role—approaching the manager with or on behalf of the coworker (with their permission) to leverage their own standing and push for change, regardless of potential repercussions.

Application of Disability Justice Principles to Everyday Advocacy

As OTPs, we advocate for our clients every day. It is not just part of what we do: for most of us, it is part of who we are. However, in the last few years, my (Elizabeth's) advocacy has changed significantly. "We're missing something," I said in a team meeting, as experienced SLPs and OTPs discussed clients who had made minimal "progress" despite years of therapy. Some strategies we used worked for many clients. Some techniques didn't make sense, and still others raised significant red flags in my mind. "But this is evidence-based practice" and "the gold standard" of treatment, I was told.

My son received an autism diagnosis at age three, shortly after this conversation with the therapy team, and questions continued circulating in my mind. My older sister (who also has an Autistic child) told me she learned the most from Autistic adults. This started my journey of unlearning and relearning how to be an advocate (and OT in many ways). One of the first neurodiversity panels I attended had Jules Edwards, Cole Sorensen, and Donnie Denome as panelists (all Autistic advocates). It was the first time I had heard about disability justice, the dignity of risk, and many other concepts, despite more than ten years of experience as an OTP. Many of the ideas I embraced with ease, and some I sat with in discomfort—from guilt, disagreement, and defensiveness. This discomfort urged me to dig deeper. As my understanding grew from seeking and listening to other perspectives (especially from multiply Marginalized groups and other Neurodivergent professionals and researchers), I saw how many needs are unaddressed or harmfully addressed by those who are supposed to be "experts." So began my formal advocacy journey.

I had many more questions than answers and gaps in knowledge than I was aware of, but I knew that advocacy did not require one person with all the answers. Advocacy requires community, humility, and curiosity. Advocacy evolves and grows as we listen, understand, self-reflect, and apply the disability justice principles (not just in our practice but within a community of others). Table 11.1 includes examples of how to practically apply the disability justice principles to advocacy.[31] Beyond using the disability justice principles to guide our advocacy, I recommend exploring how disability justice, transformative justice, and restorative justice work together to ensure harm reduction and repair within our advocacy.

Table 11.1—Applying Disability Justice Principles to Advocacy

Disability Justice Principle	Application to Analyzing Resources and Research	Application for Neurodivergent Advocates	Application for Neurotypical Allies
Intersectionality Amplify and center voices of those with lived experience, honoring how intersectionality provides valuable and unique perspectives. This is a vital part of harm reduction and providing affirming services.	Does this work include multiple perspectives and intersectionality? If not, is it clear why they did not? Example: Work about autism is written by white neurotypical OTs in Maine. Autistic people with IDD or Nonspeaking Autistics aren't included.	Affirming crisis support may be different for BIPOC or LGBTQIA2S+ communities; before advocating for specific services make sure the lived experiences of Marginalized groups are emphasized.	The following limit diversity within OT: degree inflation; cost of education that exceeds reimbursement rates; inflexibility of programs, including fieldwork requirements. Advocate flexibility and cost-effectiveness in academics and better reimbursement rates.
Leadership of Those Most Impacted Presume competence. Lived experience is the cornerstone of evidence-based practice. Support leadership of those most impacted. Intentionally center Nonspeaking, intellectual disability (IDD), and those with multiple intersectionality in our advocacy efforts.	In reviewing a research study examining the effectiveness of a service for IDD, are they included in the study's creation? Are their lived experiences highlighted and referenced? If not, take the article with a grain of salt.	While advocates promote the abolition of ABA, many Marginalized communities rely on ABA centers as their primary form of childcare, often because traditional options exclude or are inaccessible to their children's needs. Advocacy efforts should prioritize creating reliable, neurodiversity-affirming childcare alternatives that serve these communities' needs.	ASHA is against facilitated communication techniques. Many Nonspeaking advocates support these methods since traditional AAC did not work for them. ASHA fails to modify its stance despite significant lived experience evidence that demonstrates efficacy.
Anti-Capitalist Politic Prioritize mental health, rest, and leisure as human needs that deserve insurance reimbursement (redefine medical necessity); support social justice initiatives; resist internalized ableism and capitalistic expectations.	The work emphasizes treatments that are costly or that target neurotypical ideals. For organizations: how much money goes back into supporting the community versus marketing, excessive salaries of leadership.	You are constantly feeling overwhelmed by various tasks such as responding to emails. You discuss this with your team and form emails are developed to reduce email demands.	Many disability waivers will not cover services or items that are for "comfort and convenience." Use your expertise to demonstrate the service is necessary and disability-related.

Commitment to Cross-Movement Organizing Continue to reflect on your biases and how they impact your work. Actively explore other social justice movements.	Is there evidence of ableism, racism, sexism, ageism, classism, genderism? Example: A work discussing the impact of ableism in school systems ignores how racism intersects and magnifies the ableism experienced by BIPOC students.	You attend networking events to meet with other advocates in different movements/ fields to see how you can support one another.	You develop a resource list of services and supports that are led by those with lived experience. Network with other professions to ensure a broader lens of understanding the needs within different movements.
Recognizing Wholeness Recognize the rich layers of yourself and how you are worthy despite your productivity. Have flexible expectations for yourself and others.	Does this work promote the idea that there is a "normal" way of being/ existing? Example: The work focuses on addressing deficits within a person versus identifying and addressing barriers in the environmental contexts of the person.	Ensure your schedule has planned regulation breaks for yourself and your colleagues. If you work in a setting where you don't build your own schedule (e.g. outpatient), engage in micro-breaks through brief regulation activities (e.g. deep breathing, stretching) when the workload allows, even if it is only for a few minutes.	Advocate against productivity as a measure of worth/ value in our field or your company by engaging in your National/State OT organizations or sharing research about the negative impacts of high productivity on care.
Sustainability Build a community to ensure each member can take breaks and find balance.	Does this work promote unrealistic expectations? "Treatments" that do not consider barriers to participation (financial, time, mobility, transportation, energy, etc.). Example: ABA that requires 20–40 hours of "treatment" per week.	Prevent burnout: take breaks before you need them; be intentional about boundaries and expectations. Engage frequently in activities that bring you joy / fill your cup. Intentionally connect with other local organizations to prevent duplication of work.	Promote universal accommodations and flexibility within your circles. Prevent compassion fatigue. "Look at where your influence is going to maximize impact. Plan for how you're going to respond. Create your infrastructure."—Oswin Latimer
Commitment to Cross-Disability Solidarity Who is missing from our circles and why? Be intentional with building relationships or listening more to those missing perspectives.	Does the work represent diverse perspectives, i.e. BIPOC, IDD, and Nonspeaking/ minimally speaking, those with diagnoses beyond ADHD and autism?	Facilitate or support online forums/ social groups where Neurodivergent individuals can share strategies, challenges, and insights (e.g. DisabilOT, Occupational Therapy and Disability Studies Network).	Familiarize yourself with a variety of disability movements: Mad liberation, Neurodiversity, DEAF/BLIND, Health at Every Size, etc.

cont.

Disability Justice Principle	Application to Analyzing Resources and Research	Application for Neurodivergent Advocates	Application for Neurotypical Allies
Interdependence Advocate for change within our profession to shift from independence as the goal toward interdependence as a beautiful reality.	A work only mentions independence as a goal and does not mention the concepts of autonomy or interdependence. Therefore, this source likely is not using a neurodiversity-affirming lens.	Confront the ideal of independence that is ingrained in our culture. Learn to ask for help—start with something small and build from there.	Don't presume independence as the goal. Normalize supports, accommodations, modifications, and services. Model interdependence in your own life.
Collective Access Embrace nuance and flexibility within your community. Navigate differences of opinion with curiosity and humility to foster an authentic community. Ensurc accessibility of services.	The work understands that cultures view disability in different ways, and thus, priorities may be different depending on the culture.	Avoid getting into debates over language use that distracts or prevents people from feeling included. Meet people where they are.	Your clinic only accepts private pay. You research how to contract with insurance, especially Medicaid, and schedule a meeting to discuss with management.
Collective Liberation Continue working on building a more inclusive community where you and others can show up authentically.	Does this work exclude anyone? If so, is it clear why? Does the work build community? Or is it divisive?	You are aware of a public listening session the state has scheduled to discuss a proposed change to a disability service. You collect testimony and collaborate with a local organizer to share at the public listening session.	Your client's application for disability has been denied. You connect them with a pro-bono disability law service. The client reports the service was helpful, and you share this resource with your team and other clients.

Advocacy in Practice: B3 Coffee

B3 Coffee* is a disability-justice-focused non-profit organization based in Chapel Hill, North Carolina, founded by two Neurodivergent occupational therapists: Greg and Jacklyn Boheler. B3 is premised upon the way coffee brings people together, facilitating connections across populations that may not otherwise interact. These connections play a vital role in breaking down stigma and increasing the visibility of the disability community.

* https://b3coffee.org | @b3coffee on Instagram/Facebook

Inspired by Anne Wilcock's *Doing, Being, Belonging, Becoming Framework*, B3 stands for the organization's core values: being, belonging, and becoming better together.[32] B3 adheres to a "no-hierarchy" model between people with and without disabilities, meaning that Disabled people hold leadership roles at all levels of the organization, and everyone involved is considered a "B3 member," whether identifying as an ally or a person with lived experience.

B3 Coffee aims to combat the systemic "drop off" in support experienced by many adults with disabilities following their exit from high school, contributing to social and economic marginalization. While coffee is B3's primary medium for interfacing with the public, B3 has developed a wide range of social and vocational offerings to address the multidimensional needs of its members—alluded to within the examples below.

Disability justice principles are intentionally woven into B3 Coffee's daily practices and advocacy efforts. For example...

- *Interdependence* is a disability justice principle that is consistently reinforced within B3's community programs. While the concept is challenging for some B3 members, our community program facilitators (usually OTPs) find ways to teach its sentiments in plain language, through interactive, occupation-based instruction. B3 members often engage in role plays or community outings in which they may need to ask for help or provide help (i.e. getting lost on public transit or finding an item at the grocery store). To support recall of help-seeking skills, we use the term "get help power," which goes along with a corresponding hand signal. This shared terminology/gesture has become a familiar part of B3's culture, across social and vocational settings. Independence is never the intended outcome of B3's programming; rather, an atmosphere of collective care and supported self-advocacy positions B3 members to thrive.

- *Recognizing Wholeness* is a disability justice principle incorporated into the admissions process for B3's paid internship program, designed as a transitional employment model. Whereas many employers choose candidates based on skills or competency, the B3 admissions process seeks to establish balanced and diverse cohorts, representing a wide range of support needs and intersectional identities. Aiming to connect interns with employment post-internship, B3 consults with employers to advocate for accommodations, assistive technology, and/or customized employment options for their members.

- *Leadership of Those Most Impacted* is a disability justice principle that is critical to the enactment of B3's mission. B3 hosts a weekly Zoom call as a casual opportunity for members to socialize around structured conversation topics ("weekly challenges"): enabling self-determination, members are tasked with coming up with these topics. These calls are also used as an opportunity to seek member feedback on B3's current/future offerings (i.e. "What kinds of socials should we do this summer?") and promote opportunities for leadership within the organization (i.e. "Who would like to be a speaker at the disability pride parade?").

B3's disability-justice-informed approach to advocacy is often described as "revolutionary" by onlookers, as unfortunately, the vast majority of comparable organizations are *not* Disabled-led and fall into a charity model of disability to drive their advocacy. Importantly, B3 places a strong emphasis on allyship education in order to prevent ableism from seeping into the organization—each non-disabled member of B3 is expected to complete allyship trainings, covering disability etiquette, language considerations, the history of the disability rights movement, and more. A takeaway for occupational therapy practitioners: advocacy must start from within—a tremendous amount of internal work is required to unlearn ableism and embody the principles of disability justice.

Disability Advocacy Across Practice Settings

We have examined many of the practical strategies OTPs can use in their commitment to disability justice, but each practice setting has its own unique features that add nuance to advocacy efforts. The following lists include just some of the tips and strategies for common practice settings.

Outpatient Pediatrics

- Encourage the development of advocacy related to regulation strategies (i.e. "when I feel ___, I can use these strategies").
- Seek advice on creating a sensory-friendly environment from Neurodivergent adults (i.e. colleagues, self-advocates, and professionals who specialize in sensory).
- Focus on how your interventions translate to the client's more natural environments (e.g. home, school, daycare setting).
- Educate families on neurodiversity and help them feel confident and comfortable in educating others about neurodiversity. Check out the Autism Self Advocacy Network and Playspark for helpful handouts.

Inpatient Acute

- Use affirming language which presumes competence in documentation and interaction with patients (i.e. "Brie benefits from... supports" versus "Brie requires... supports").
- Normalize accessibility features during all team meetings.
- Familiarize yourself with local neurodiversity-affirming groups, services, and resources to share with clients.
- Consider facilitative disability justice peer support groups where patients can interact and be in solidarity with each other.
- Identify and address access barriers across roles and settings.
- Support patients in creating a personalized regulation plan.
- Advocate for trauma-informed training for your staff.

Outpatient Rehabilitation

- Focus on identifying and addressing barriers for your clients with supports, services, and accommodations across settings and roles.
- Advocate for all occupations to be considered "medically necessary" that can be addressed by occupational therapy.
- Consider executive functioning differences when designing home programming.
- Familiarize yourself with local neurodiversity-affirming groups, services, and resources to share with clients.

School-Based

- Use language that presumes competence in documentation and IEPs (i.e. "Joe will continue to develop" versus "Joe will develop"). Think about how strengths-based documentation can be a "quiet" form of advocacy (see Chapter 9 for strengths-based documentation guidelines).

- Avoid ableist language in documentation (i.e. "Kai uses unique communication strategies" versus "Kai interacts atypically").

- Encourage the development of advocacy related to regulation strategies (i.e. "when I feel ___, I can use these strategies"). Support students in creating personalized self-regulation plans and teach paraprofessionals how to assist students in implementing these strategies.

- Encourage or aid families to invite neurodiversity-affirming advocates to all IEP meetings (self-advocates and/or non-disabled allies).

- Advocate for the school districts to replace Functional Behavioral Assessments (FBAs) and Positive Behavior Support Plans (PBSPs) with the Why Toolkit,[33] a neurodiversity-affirming and trauma-informed replacement. A Vault item exists that shares strategies for how OTPs can infiltrate the FBA process and minimize their harm.

- Collaborate with teachers to educate on sensory processing differences, and how they can promote sensory health in their classrooms by implementing universal design concepts from a sensory perspective. Feel free to download a presentation educating general education staff on sensory processing health and how to make their classrooms more sensory inclusive from the Vault .

- Make sure self-advocacy goals are included within IEPs.

- Train paraprofessionals on neurodiversity-affirming and trauma-informed alternatives to behavioral approaches for supporting regulation.[34] A presentation for this training exists within the Vault .

- Collaborate with counselors and teachers to integrate neurodiversity-affirming social participation and SEL curriculums to replace neurotypical SEL and social skill training programs.[35] Examples are shared in Chapter 10.

Community-Based

- Promote and disseminate the voices of Disabled advocates (i.e. social media influencers, Neurodivergent practitioners, educators, or speakers).

- Implement Neurodivergent-led and allyship training for local organizations or businesses.

- Normalize accessibility at community-based events or meetings (i.e. are the client's favorite community spaces accessible to them, such as automatic door openers if they are a wheelchair user?).

- Support access to regulation spaces and tools in the community and at any events (i.e. enclosed calming tent, cooler/fans, fidgets, headphones/ear plugs, quiet activities, and reading materials).

- Connect Disabled persons with affirming support services, non-profits, local agencies, advocacy groups, etc. Network within your community to ensure these recommendations are affirming.

- Understand state and national disability systems and find loopholes to ensure access to services and supports.

- Write accommodation letters, letters of medical necessity, etc.

- Develop a network of contacts who may be able to serve as resources for Disabled clients (connect your clients to these allies).

- Connect clients with neurodiversity-affirming organizations (particularly those that focus on supporting foundational outcomes like mental health, community participation, and belonging).

- Support clients through the process of obtaining disability-related support and services.

- Advocate for OTPs to be recognized as mental health providers.
  - Support state and national initiatives/organizations that advocate for OT practice and inform them of the benefits of OTPs being mental health providers.

Higher Education

- Advocate for the inclusion of Neurodivergent and Disabled people in higher education via Neurodivergent/disability support or meet-up groups, inclusive post-secondary education programs, and certificate-based community college programs for people with intellectual and developmental disabilities.

- Educate Disabled college students on their right to accommodations and help them navigate disability services effectively.

- Encourage open communication and advocacy between students and professors to ensure accessibility needs are understood and met.

- Coach peer support on how to affirmatively engage with and understand Neurodivergent communication styles and support needs.

- Join advocacy efforts for on-campus Disability Cultural Centers, Neurodiversity Hubs, or other "safe spaces" for Disabled students.
- Advocate for the "dignity of risk" of students with intellectual disabilities, ensuring they have the opportunity to experience the fullness of college life without over-protection.
- Check out the resource in the Vault created by Christopher Edwards and Lori Vaughn that dives into how higher education can better support Neurodivergent students.

Conclusion

In the realm of occupational therapy, advocacy is not just a supplementary task but a foundational and ethical practice that upholds the values of justice, equity, and access. Advocacy is a mechanism through which we can support people to navigate barriers to participation in meaningful occupation. Remaining mindful of complex relationships between the person and their contexts enables OTPs to facilitate advocacy at the micro-, meso-, and macro-levels, ensuring that Marginalized communities—particularly those with disabilities—are empowered to achieve greater autonomy, inclusion, and participation.

The principles of disability justice are vital components in the advocacy process. We must recognize that all people, regardless of their abilities or identities, are interconnected and dependent on one another. Advocacy in OT, therefore, must not only address the needs of the individual but also challenge and change systems that perpetuate oppression, inequality, and exclusion. Furthermore, the journey toward allyship and accompliceship is integral to fostering real and sustained change. As professionals dedicated to occupational justice and empowerment, OTPs must ally themselves with Disabled people, using their privileged positions to take risks and leverage their resources to dismantle barriers for those they serve.

Ultimately, disability advocacy is a collaborative process that requires humility, awareness, and a deep commitment to justice. It is through our collective efforts—honoring self-advocacy, supporting self-determination, and promoting systems change—that we can foster a world where all people, regardless of ability, have equal opportunities to thrive and be authentic in the occupations that matter most to them.

Endnotes

1 American Occupational Therapy Association. (2020). Occupational therapy practice framework: Domain and process (4th ed.). *American Journal of Occupational Therapy, 74*(2). https://doi.org/10.5014/ajot.2020.74S2001

2 Kirsh, B. H. (2015). Transforming values into action: Advocacy as a professional imperative. *Canadian Journal of Occupational Therapy (1939), 82*(4), 212–223. https://doi.org/10.1177/0008417415601395

3 American Occupational Therapy Association. (2020). Occupational therapy practice framework: Domain and process (4th ed.). *American Journal of Occupational Therapy, 74*(2). https://doi.org/10.5014/ajot.2020.74S2001

4 Dickie, V., Cutchin, M. P., & Humphry, R. (2006). Occupation as transactional experience: A critique of individualism in occupational science. *Journal of Occupational Science, 13*(1), 83–93. https://doi.org/10.1080/14427591.2006.9686573

5 Smith, D. L. (2023). Social and environmental determinants of occupation: An intersectional concept focused on occupational justice and participation. *Journal of Occupational Science, 31*(2), 209–215. https://doi.org/10.1080/14427591.2023.2212676

6 Malcom, S. (2024). Strengthening the case for DEI. *Science, 383*, 1395–1395. https://doi.org/10.1126/science.adp4397

7 Shogren, K., Wehmeyer, M., Palmer, S., Forber-Pratt, A. J., Little, T. J., & Lopez, S. (2015). Causal agency theory: Reconceptualizing a functional model of self-determination. *Education and Training in Autism and Developmental Disabilities, 50*(3), 251–263. www.jstor.org/stable/24827508

8 Bailliard, A. L., Dallman, A. R., Carroll, A., Lee, B. D., & Szendrey, S. (2020). Doing occupational justice: A central dimension of everyday occupational therapy practice. *Canadian Journal of Occupational Therapy (1939), 87*(2), 144–152. https://doi.org/10.1177/0008417419898930

9 Bezyak, J. L., Sabella, S., Hammel, J., McDonald, K., Jones, R. A., & Barton, D. (2020). Community participation and public transportation barriers experienced by people with disabilities. *Disability and Rehabilitation, 42*(23), 3275–3283. https://doi.org/10.1080/09638288.2019.1590469

10 American Occupational Therapy Association. (2020). Occupational therapy practice framework: Domain and process (4th ed.). *American Journal of Occupational Therapy, 74*(2). https://doi.org/10.5014/ajot.2020.74S2001, p. 61.

11 Bettin, J. (2019). The myth of independence: How the social model of disability exposes society's double standards. *NeuroClastic*. https://neuroclastic.com/celebration-of-interdependence

12 Jackson, J. C., & Medvedev, D. (2024). Worldwide divergence of values. *Nature Communications, 15*(1), 2650. https://doi.org/10.1038/s41467-024-46581-5

13 Temple University Institute on Disabilities. (2019). *Disability rights timeline*. https://disabilities.temple.edu/resources/disability-rights-timeline

14 Pacing Pixie. (2023). Disability awareness by a proudly disabled educator. www.pacingpixie.com/disability-awareness

15 Edwards, J., & Ashburn, M. (2023). *I will die on this hill: Autistic adults, autism parents, and the children who deserve a better world*. Jessica Kingsley Publishers.

16 Williams, Z. J. (2022). Race and sex bias in the Autism Diagnostic Observation Schedule (ADOS-2) and disparities in autism diagnoses. *JAMA Network Open, 5*(4), e229503. https://doi.org/10.1001/jamanetworkopen.2022.9503

17 Lewis, L. F. (2016). Exploring the experience of self-diagnosis of autism spectrum disorder in adults. *Archives of Psychiatric Nursing, 30*(5), 575–580. https://doi.org/10.1016/j.apnu.2016.03.009

18 ibid.

19 Newberry, L. (2023, May 2). *Why so many people are diagnosing themselves with autism and ADHD*. Los Angeles Times. www.latimes.com/california/newsletter/2023-05-02/self-diagnosis-autism-adhd-group-therapy

20 CAST. (n.d.). *The universal design for learning guidelines*. https://udlguidelines.cast.org

21 Skotko, B. G., Levine, S. P., & Goldstein, R. (2011). Self-perceptions from people with Down syndrome. *American Journal of Medical Genetics. Part A, 155A*(10), 2360–2369. https://doi.org/10.1002/ajmg.a.34235

22 Miserandino, C. (2003, May 21). *The spoon theory*. But You Don't Look Sick. https://butyoudontlooksick.com/articles/written-by-christine/the-spoon-theory

23 Milton, D., Gurbuz, E., & López, B. (2022). The "double empathy problem": Ten years on. *Autism: The International Journal of Research and Practice, 26*(8), 1901–1903. https://doi.org/10.1177/13623613221129123

24 PDA Society. (n.d.). *The Extreme Demand Avoidance Questionnaire (EDAq)*. PDA Society. www.pdasociety.org.uk/resources/information-on-the-eda-q

25 Miller, D., Rees, J., & Pearson, A. (2021). "Masking is life": Experiences of masking in Autistic and nonAutistic adults. *Autism in Adulthood, 3*(4), 330–338. https://doi.org/10.1089/aut.2020.0083

26 Mingus, M. (n.d.). *Forced intimacy: An ableist norm*. Leaving Evidence. https://leavingevidence.wordpress.com/2017/08/06/forced-intimacy-an-ableist-norm
27 De Souza, L., & Schmader, T. (2025). When people do allyship: A typology of allyship action. *Personality and Social Psychology Review, 29*(1), 3–31. https://doi.org/10.1177/10888683241232732
28 Brown, K. T., & Ostrove, J. M. (2013). What does it mean to be an ally? The perception of allies from the perspective of people of color. *Journal of Applied Social Psychology, 43*(11), 2211–2222. https://doi.org/10.1111/jasp.12172, p. 2211.
29 Ganegoda, D. B., Shukla, J., & Shapiro, D. L. (2024). Garnering support for social justice: When and why is "yes" likelier for "allies" versus "disadvantaged group advocates"? *Organizational Behavior and Human Decision Processes, 182*, 104332. https://doi.org/10.1016/j.obhdp.2024.104332
30 Sins Invalid. (2019). *Skin, tooth, and bone: The basis of movement is our people* (2nd ed.). [Digital version]. www.sinsinvalid.org
31 ibid.
32 Wilcock, A. A. (1998). Reflections on doing, being, and becoming. *Canadian Journal of Occupational Therapy, 65*(5), 248–256. https://doi.org/10.1177/000841749806500501
33 Persike, C. (2022). *The why toolkit: A guide to building more accessible communities*. Supportive Solutions. https://supportablesolutions.com/thewhytoolkit
34 Laurent, A., & Fede, J. (2020). When words fail: Leveling up language to improve experience. *Autism Level UP*. https://cdn.sanity.io/files/p6bm7moz/production/2461a458fc602cd4563c0ec828a10aa0bcc5414c.pdf
35 Bridges Learning System. (2025). *Bridges Learning System*. https://bridgeslearningsystem.com

SPOTLIGHT

Sass Meets Advocacy: Wit and Wisdom from a Nonspeaking Advocate

BRI GUERRA AND BRYDEN CARLSON-GIVING

I was introduced to Bri's work by my dear friend Sarah, the Autistic OT. And wow, I am so thankful Sarah led me to Bri. Bri is a Nonspeaking Autistic, and they are equally tenacious as they are witty and unapologetically bold. Often underestimated, their voice cuts through ableism with a clarity and conviction that compels occupational therapy to rise and meet the challenge. Below is a collection of reflections by Bri, adapted from their social media pages coupled with our conversations. As you will read, Bri has an unmatched ability to turn absurd assumptions that are deeply ingrained within our profession into insightful commentary.

Navigating ableism in the schools:

> "Looking back on my time in schools before typing, I need to make one thing clear. The percentage of times adults accurately identified why I was upset was in the single digits. Lol. Oh how many times did I hear the word antecedent. I was a lab rat, with some pretty poor scientists. Data collection on complicated humans is foolish. The egregious oversimplifying or failure to see how their actions impacted me hurts to this day.
>
> Of all the many lies I've heard spoken about me, one that truly infuriates me is the baloney that I lack the ability to relate. My desire for human connection is profound. Having motor planning difficulties makes it nearly impossible to respond quickly in ways neuronormative expectations dictate. And my ways of relating are constantly pathologized as nonfunctional or somehow impaired. I'm always astounded by people's inability or unwillingness to see my humanity. Isn't

that what it means to relate? I'm lol'ing at how absurd it all is when I'm so often surrounded by neurotypicals with their noses in their phones. So tired of certain people making up all the nonsensical rules and insisting there's one right way to be human.

Teachers say all students must have good listening skills. Listening can look different for students like me. I'm more apt to follow a lesson if I'm not distracted by cascading images my mind must process or intrusive thoughts about a teacher's mannerisms and style. I have so many thoughts at once at times I need to manage stimuli. What may appear to some as disinterest or disrespect is the exact opposite. My ways of being a scholar must be accepted if I am to be included and valued."

On the importance of learning from Disabled voices:

"It disappoints and depresses me when adults prioritize protecting their feelings over learning from Autistic and Disabled people. Decentering oneself is a necessary practice if one wishes to do less harm and be a good human. Don't reject opportunities to grow and be informed by Disabled people. Dimensions of allyship include being ok with making mistakes and not feeling your character or heart is being called into question.

I am not a bitter person. Ableism finds a path into my hopeful days regularly. It is delivered via sunny faces and good intentions as often as it is due to an intolerant mind and fear of other. I am yearning for inclusion in every aspect of life. I'm tired of messages that only certain spaces can accommodate me, that I'll have to be outside the system to be successful, to be accepted, to find friends. I have learned many attempts to help me leave me in the same position as in when I have been rejected. Isolated. I have learned recurring attempts to try to make me mirror others' enthusiasm feels typically similar to attempts to control me and my authentic expression. I have learned dreams are reserved for those who society currently makes room for and that I am considered overly ambitious."

Engagement on Disabled terms:

"When you expect me to look you in the eye you are prioritizing Western, neurotypical standards and your own comfort. My youth was spent being manipulated to please others. Looking into a person's eyes is a deeply personal and moving experience. That engagement level so often feels inappropriate to the moment or task at hand. Having people demand my connection in situations where I don't authentically feel such regard makes me uncomfortable and distracted by how I feel about the demand or the person. It would be wonderful if everyone allowed individuals the right to engage in ways authentic to them."

Embracing belonging (with some humor):

> "My belief is that I belong everywhere. People need to realize the full motivations and mindset behind their interactions with Disabled folk, be it an attempt to help or control or exclude. My hope is the Disabled perspective is increasingly centered and drives action. I'll never get tired of little moments of agency.
>
> Last weekend I saw the Broadway tour of *Mean Girls The Musical*. It was amazing. Hilarious if not terrifying look at high school culture. I do love when the neurotypicals poke fun at themselves."

Practical implications for occupational therapy practitioners:

- Reflect on how you can embrace the culture of Nonspeaking individuals. Nonspeaking individuals often form their own communities where their unique forms of expression, communication, and shared experiences create a distinct cultural identity. Review these fabulous blog posts by NeuroClastic to learn more about Nonspeaking perspectives and culture.[1,2]

- Don't assume that verbal speech is the most important way of communicating with clients. Place equal value on all forms of communication (e.g. AAC, gestures, sign language), and do not place verbal speech at the top. All communication is valid; there is no hierarchy of how human beings communicate. Occupational therapy practitioners should explore the repository of resources by xMinds to learn more about how to support Nonspeaking individuals (though initially made for Nonspeaking students, most resources can be generalized across settings).[3]

- Practice engaging in ethical listening, which is when a person pays attention to all of the ways an individual is communicating, including Nonspeaking and speaking forms of communication. You are authentically attending to the various forms of the human communication experience. To challenge your assumptions about communication and learn more about ethical listening, see Lebenhagen.[4]

- Bri helped create the free resource, The Nora Project's Standards for Inclusive Schools, a roadmap for building inclusive schools so Disabled students can be their authentic selves. Standards are written for the educator and the student across three domains (diversity, community, and advocacy), and relationships are at the core of these standards.[5]

Where to Follow Bri

Facebook: www.facebook.com/SabrinaGuerraNonspeakingAdvocate

Instagram: www.instagram.com/brinonspeakingadvocate

Endnotes

1 NeuroClastic. (2021, August 14). *On using nonspeaking, minimally speaking, or unreliably speaking over "non-verbal": Nonspeakers weigh in*. NeuroClastic. https://neuroclastic.com/on-using-nonspeaking-minimally-speaking-or-unreliably-speaking-over-non-verbal-nonspeakers-weigh-in

2 NeuroClastic. (2021, February 21). *Nonspeaker perspectives on representation*. NeuroClastic. https://neuroclastic.com/nonspeaker-perspectives-on-representation

3 Partnership for Extraordinary Minds. (2025). *Nonspeaking Autistic students resources*. xMinds. https://xminds.org/Nonspeaking-Autistics

4 Lebenhagen, C. (2020). Including speaking and nonspeaking Autistic voice in research. *Autism in Adulthood Knowledge Practice and Policy*, *2*(2), 128–131. https://doi.org/10.1089/aut.2019.0002

5 Zimmerman, J., Schrero, L., & Newton, J. (2025). *Standards for inclusive schools*. The Nora Project. https://thenoraproject.ngo/standards-for-inclusive-schools

CHAPTER 12

The Empowering Neurodivergent Occupational Participation and Well-Being (EMPOWER) Model

BRYDEN CARLSON-GIVING

Consider the occupation of eating. When you think of this activity, does your mind immediately go to eating at a dining table or grabbing fast food on the go? Our society and profession often highlight particular methods of eating (usually Eurocentric ways). However, the experience of eating is shaped by preferences, culture, time, and circumstances, revealing that our understanding of any occupation is reduced to the narrow confines of our experiences and (sometimes limited) imagination.[1] The different ways human beings engage in the occupation of eating are as varied as the countless asteroids floating through our galaxy. Now, apply this idea to other types of occupations, such as play, work, and leisure. It's sort of mind-blowing isn't it, trying to conceptualize all of the ways we could engage in these occupations. Reflect on your personal approach to addressing these occupations; do you prioritize certain ways of engagement over others? Do you have a preconceived idea of what participation "should" look like, and how much does this preconceived idea influence our clients' identities, hopes, and dreams? The only way you can expand your reality and imagination of how others engage in meaningful activities is by letting go of how you think engagement "should" look like, and toward the lens of what engagement *can* look like. You can do this by fostering courage, asking questions through genuine curiosity, and embracing a mindset of open-hearted exploration with your client guiding the process.

Introduction

As we arrive at this chapter, the co-authors and I want to take a moment to recognize the commitment it's taken to get here. By engaging deeply with these topics, you've already taken significant steps toward becoming a practitioner who not only understands these principles but is ready to put them into action. We're proud of the progress you've made, and now, it's time to bring it all together.

Throughout this book, we've journeyed together through the most vital principles that can reshape occupational therapy into a more equitable, inclusive, and justice-infused practice. We've explored strengths-based approaches, trauma-informed care, antiracism, disability justice, Neurodivergent perspectives on occupation, and we have illustrated many ways to translate neurodiversity-affirming concepts into practice. These concepts are more than just theories; they are the foundation of a practice that seeks to empower those we serve.

In this chapter, I introduce the Empowering Neurodivergent Occupational Participation and Well-Being (EMPOWER) model.[2] The EMPOWER model is a practical approach to weave together everything we've discussed so far, guiding you in applying these concepts within your occupational therapy practice. It's designed not only to foster Neurodivergent participation and well-being but also to dismantle the deeply rooted ableist systems within occupational therapy (it's possible!). We can pave the way for the profession to reconnect with its origins as an authentically just and equitable field! The EMPOWER model is not just a framework—it's a call to action and a guide for reimagining how we, as occupational therapy practitioners (OTPs), can support Neurodivergent clients in ways that are both deeply affirming and rooted in justice.

The EMPOWER Model

It has been advocated within our profession that occupation-based models should guide our practice,[3,4] though there remains no occupational therapy model centering Neurodivergent lived experiences. There also isn't an occupational therapy framework that requires OTPs to reflect on their ableism, conceptualizes Neurodivergent ways of living, or provides a practical framework for how OTPs can implement neurodiversity-affirming principles in practice. Additionally, there is no current occupational therapy model and framework that authentically validates and empowers my perceptions of my disabilities. For example with my ADHD, ADHD is often seen as a deficit of attention, whereas in reality it is a wonderfully complex neurological variation that changes the brain's processing of time and information. It's not that ADHDers struggle to pay attention but rather we experience the world through a unique lens that alters our perception of time. For tasks I adore, three hours feels like a quick slip of time such as five minutes. Though for activities that feel like a complete bore but they need to be done, five minutes elongates and stretches to feel like three hours. This difference in experiencing time influences every aspect of our lives (and maybe this example even resonated with you). Now, don't get me wrong, this characteristic comes with its challenges, but I also can do many tasks far more efficiently and perform better than my neurotypical peers. There is no occupational therapy (OT) framework that truly captures and supports this richness of ADHDer ways of living, let alone other Neurodivergent neurotypes, which led to the EMPOWER model.

> Instead of expecting Neurodivergent individuals to engage in neurotypical ways of living and our definitions of what is considered meaningful participation, we need to strive for a society that actively empowers these vibrant expressions of occupational engagement. Not doing so is a denial of humanity.

As previously mentioned in Chapter 2, the medical model of disability is the primary lens the profession provides services, leaving significant gaps when it comes to promoting anti-ableist practices, and in some cases, perpetuating ableist views of occupational participation. Throughout my research conducted for my doctoral project *Embracing Neurodivergent Occupations*,[5] I synthesized common themes found in disability activism and neurodiversity-affirming literature and resources. The EMPOWER model emerged from a conscientious effort and as a direct response to these gaps, with the goal of honoring the beautiful and complex lives of Neurodivergent individuals. The EMPOWER model seeks to expand on how we view occupation, inform how OTPs can challenge ableism, using a new occupational therapy process, and ultimately support authentic Neurodivergent occupational participation. I was really inspired by Taylor's work in her 2022 article "Beyond 'Bad' Behaviors: A Call for Occupational Scientists to Rethink Autism".[6] In this article, Taylor beautifully illustrates how Autistic ways of doing, such as Autistic play or stimming, are Autistic occupations. I absolutely loved this, and her work influenced how I began to think about how other disability communities have their own culture and valued ways of participation. Culture informs occupation and, just as many disability communities have shared practices, these cultures give rise to distinct occupations. Just like how disability communities have distinct characteristics and practices, we must also recognize that these cultures give rise to distinct occupations (Neurodivergent occupations).

The EMPOWER model was designed and illustrated by me, with the model depiction (see Figure 12.1) inspired by my love for science and fantasy video games (I wear my nerd hat with pride, thank you).

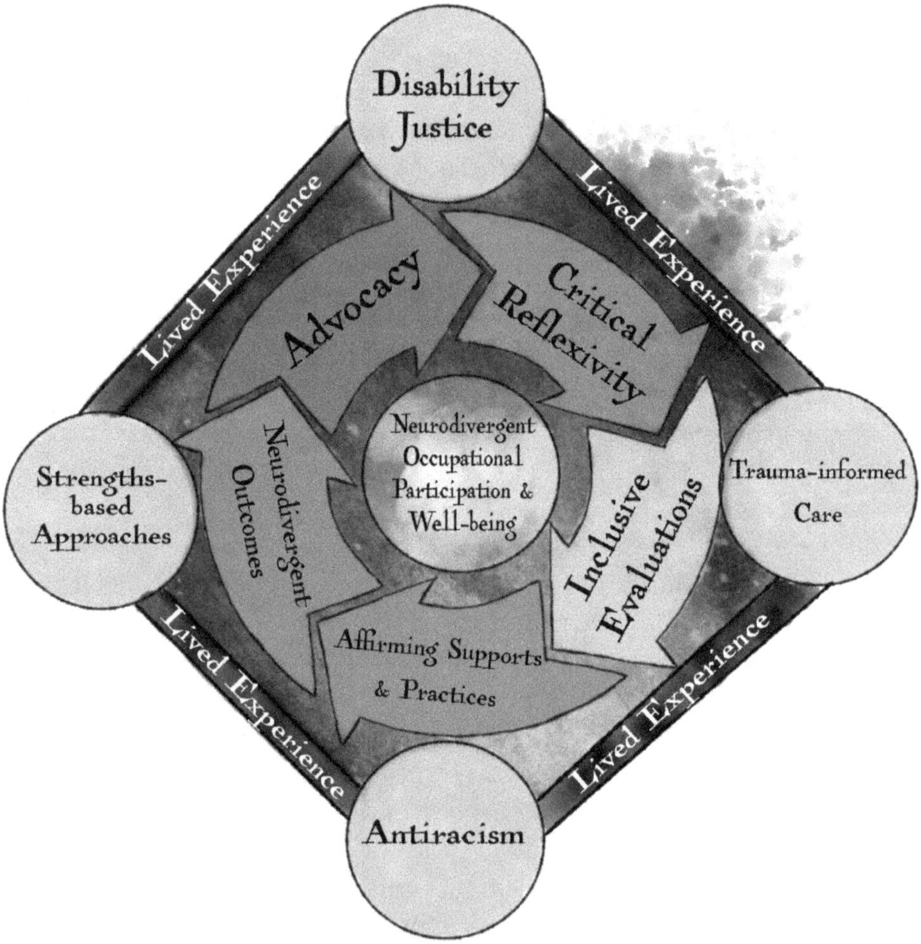

Figure 12.1—The EMPOWER Model

The EMPOWER model is grounded in four key frameworks essential for neurodiversity-affirming practices: disability justice, trauma-informed care, antiracism, and strengths-based approaches. All four foundations are bonded and connected by lived experience; I've always thought of lived experience as the "mortar" that binds the foundations together because lived experience is everything when it comes to neurodiversity-affirming practice. Central to the model is an anti-ableist occupational therapy process that includes five steps: (1) critical reflexivity, (2) inclusive evaluations, (3) affirming supports and practices, (4) Neurodivergent outcomes, and (5) advocacy. The anti-ableist occupational therapy process within the model is an infinite cycle, highlighting the work that is ongoing within continuous self-reflection as we work to ensure our practices remain neurodiversity-affirming. By integrating these foundations with the anti-ableist OT process, I am hopeful that OTPs are more likely to support Neurodivergent occupational participation, Neurodivergent well-being, and authentic Neurodivergent flourishing in life (Table 12.1 describes the main ideas for each component of the EMPOWER model). Although the EMPOWER model is designed to guide OTPs when supporting clients, the model can also help guide practice when supporting groups, communities, and populations. The chapters in this book highlight many ideas that resonate with the EMPOWER model, and in these next few sections, I want to show you how these ideas intersect and how the EMPOWER model can be one way to bring them into practice.

Table 12.1—Core Principles and Concepts of the EMPOWER Model Components

Component	Principles + Main Ideas
Disability Justice (Chapter 4)	• Disability justice centers the voices of Disabled individuals and emphasizes disability as its own culture. • Embrace disability justice principles as outlined by Sins Invalid:[7] (1) intersectionality, (2) leadership of the most impacted (the movement must be led by those who are the most impacted by the oppressive systems), (3) anti-capitalist politics, (4) commitment to cross-movement organizing (social justice must contextualize disability), (5) recognizing wholeness (disabled individuals have inherent worth, and are full of vivid life experiences; this must be explicit secondary to our capitalist society), (6) sustainability, (7) commitment to cross-disability solidarity, (8) interdependence, (9) collective access, and (10) collective liberation.
Component	**Principles + Main Ideas**
Trauma-Informed Care (Chapter 5)	• Principles are (1) safety; (2) trustworthiness and transparency; (3) peer support; (4) collaboration and mutuality; (5) empowerment, voice, and choice; and (6) cultural, historical, and gender sensitivity.[8] • Neurodivergent individuals are coming into a world that was not made for us, isn't safe for us, and we experience trauma everyday secondary to ableism that compounds over time.
Antiracism (Chapter 6)	• Antiracism recognizes and challenges systemic racism that heavily perpetuates our society, including occupational therapy. • Antiracism necessitates self-reflection of biases and requires intentional actions to dismantle racism. OTPs cannot be neurodiversity-affirming without being antiracist.

cont.

Component	Principles + Main Ideas
Strengths-Based Approaches **(Chapter 7)**	• Principles include (1) presuming competence of Neurodivergent individuals, (2) including Neurodivergent individuals as collaborators in research and the therapeutic process, (3) building authentic partnerships, and (4) creating high-functioning and supportive environments.[9] *It is important to note that being strengths-based does not ignore the challenges experienced by Disabled individuals. It means we frame the individual's disability in a way that honors who they are, and our practices focus on the supports they need.[10]
Critical Reflexivity **(Chapter 8)**	• One essential aspect missing from most mainstream occupational therapy models is the requirement of the practitioner to engage in critical reflexivity. • Critical reflexivity is the process where practitioners examine their own beliefs, biases, and the socio-political contexts that influence their practice.
Inclusive Evaluations **(Chapter 9)**	• Aspects of neurodiversity-affirming evaluations include: (1) centering the client's lived experiences, (2) affirming assessment tools, (3) strengths-based documentation and report writing, (4) empowering goals, (5) observing meaningful activities in natural environments, and (6) analyzing environmental supports and barriers.
Affirming Supports and Practices **(Chapter 10)**	• Neurodiversity-affirming supports and services focus on enhancing clients' quality of life by supporting self-determination and promoting positive disability self-identity. Strategies prioritize connection and relationship-building, respecting personal interests, and addressing environmental contexts impacting clients' participation.
Neurodivergent Outcomes **(Chapter 3)**	• OTPs must move beyond neuronormative standards of health and well-being, recognizing that there is no single "right" way to engage in occupations. When viewing occupations through the neurodiversity framework, Neurodivergent ways of living—what we can call Neurodivergent occupations—are recognized as legitimate and valid forms of being and doing.
Advocacy **(Chapter 11)**	• Advocacy requires OTPs to acknowledge the inequities present within the profession and society, and that it is a moral imperative to confront such inequities. Advocacy isn't just the large demonstrations (like walking down the street during a protest), but can be the most brief, everyday moments. It's the conversation you had with a teacher about Autistic perspectives, or it's discussing the oppression of BIPOC individuals in healthcare with your therapy colleagues. Though these moments may seem small, they are vital and often far more impactful than we realize!

Note. This table highlights how the EMPOWER model's concepts connect to chapters throughout this book.

If interested, there is a download available in the Vault that includes the EMPOWER model as an application template to help you implement the model within practice in addition to an in-depth case study showcasing how to apply the EMPOWER model. The next sections of this chapter illustrate how the EMPOWER model exemplifies five primary neurodiversity-affirming occupational therapy principles, including how the model: (1) prioritizes lived experience as evidence, (2) promotes anti-ableism, (3) supports Neurodivergent development, (4) fosters client-centered practice, and (5) endorses occupation-based practice. Table 12.2 showcases how the EMPOWER model demonstrates these principles in occupational therapy practice.

The EMPOWER Model Prioritizes Lived Experiences as Evidence

Lived experience absolutely must be the foundation for all decisions made when providing OT services with Neurodivergent individuals. Given how our profession has been missing the mark when attempting to support Neurodivergent individuals, believing and honoring Neurodivergent experiences is the only way to provide equitable services. When attempting to bring research to the decision-making table, this leads to a necessary discussion on evidence-based practice.

Inequity and Evidence-Based Practice

Evidence-based practice (EBP) has been an essential component of OT practice for the past few decades, with EBP often described as applying the best research evidence combined with clinical experience and the client's circumstances and values within OT service decision-making. Now, don't get me wrong, we want to provide the highest-quality care possible for our clients. It's an ethical responsibility, and it is what our clients deserve! That being said, we must discuss the shortcomings of EBP and how EBP doesn't often account for or represent the lived experiences of the Marginalized communities we intend to serve.[11,12]

Much of EBP does not include the voices of Marginalized clients within healthcare service decision-making and research-creation, a critical concern raised by the Neurodiversity community. Think about the last few peer-reviewed published papers you have read about supporting Neurodivergent individuals, whether it is about individuals with sensory processing differences, those with intellectual developmental disabilities, or ADHDers. That article you read about how a particular intervention supports a student's sensory processing differences and their regulation at school—were members of this community involved in the writing of the article? The article about ADHDer children and attention—did ADHDers help decide what was important to measure or help guide the study's outcomes? Historical trends of research expand beyond ableism; BIPOC individuals are not adequately included as subjects or asked to participate in the design of health services research.[13,14]

Most EBPs and published research were not designed or developed with input from BIPOC, Disabled, or Queer individuals, resulting in our approaches perpetuating biases, reinforcing systemic inequalities, and causing harm to Marginalized communities. It's a reality we cannot ignore and the clock is ticking.

When an intervention is determined to be effective, who is the intervention actually effective for? Is it effective for the Neurodivergent individual based on their hopes, dreams, and input, or is it deemed effective by the non-disabled researcher or practitioner based on what they assume to be important for the Disabled individual? What are the outcomes listed within the article, and who exactly is defining those outcomes?

An example of this could be an OTP working with a Dyslexic late-elementary student having a hard time with reading. Because ableism and neurotypicality influence our clinical reasoning, the OTP's first ideas for how to support the student might have the student focus on improving their reading speed and accuracy through traditional reading methods. The therapist's clinical expertise and perceptions, shaped by an ableist perspective, may lead them to emphasize interventions that aim to "correct" the client's reading difficulties, such as intensive phonics training, retention, and recall, exercises designed to improve reading fluency.

However, this approach may not align with the student's needs or values. The student might instead want to practice using alternative strategies, such as using assistive technology (e.g. speech-to-text software combined with the Dyslexie font), audiobooks, and teaching the student how to self-advocate for these accommodations. If the OTP instead focused on remediating or "correcting" the student's reading challenges, the OTP may inadvertently reinforce the idea that the student must conform to neurotypical standards of what reading a book "must look like." By incorporating the student's interests in technology and focusing on accommodation, the OTP supports the student in a strengths-based way that aligns with their goals, their Neurodivergent learning style, and emphasizes empowerment. Given many of our practices have ableist biases or exclude Neurodivergent individuals from the research process, we must critically question the meaningfulness of our published research and the extent to which ableism influences our work, and critically reflect on how we practice as OTPs.

If you are interested in exploring alternatives to EBP, I highly encourage you to explore Lived Experience Informed Practice (LEIP)[15] and Community-Defined Evidence Practice (CDEP).[16] LEIP, conceptualized by the Queer and Disabled advocate Sonny Jane Wise, emphasizes that lived experience must be the foundation for practice. Research can still be a component, though only utilized when the research validates Neurodivergent lived experiences. CDEP, conceptualized by the National Latinx Network, was created to bridge the gap between peer-reviewed published research and community-relevant practices. CDEP emphasizes that communities are the experts on what is meaningful and important to them, not what outsiders determine to believe what is best for the community. As you will learn throughout the exploration of the model, the EMPOWER model resonates with LEIP and CDEP. The EMPOWER model prioritizes the voices and perspectives of communities, valuing lived experiences above research evidence. The EMPOWER model acknowledges the systemic biases within research (e.g. racism and ableism), prioritizing the voices that are often marginalized in traditional research methods. The EMPOWER model attempts to provide space for these voices to be heard so we can better understand and support the complex realities of Neurodivergent individuals. If you would like to dive deeper into the hidden inequities of evidence-based practice and even access a checklist for helping to examine ableism in peer-reviewed articles, consider checking out my website.[17]

The EMPOWER Model Promotes Anti-Ableism

Ableism is so ingrained in our practice that discriminatory attitudes and beliefs about Disabled people have become normalized; it's so common practice that you don't even notice that what you are doing could be potentially ableist! For example, many health professionals practice under the ableist assumption that disability inherently diminishes an individual's quality of life. These assumptions conflict with what many Disabled individuals are saying, who describe their disability in a positive light, and their disability has positively impacted their identity as a human being, well-being, and life satisfaction.[18,19,20] These biases stem from ableism, stigma, and ignorance, making it essential for us as OTPs to adopt an anti-ableist approach to challenge and dismantle these harmful assumptions.[21,22,23]

As previously mentioned in Chapter 2, anti-ableism is taking action against ableism, including but not limited to inequalities, prejudices, and discrimination based on physical disabilities. Ableism also affects individuals with developmental, executive functioning, emotional, psychiatric, and Neurodivergent disabilities; ableism does not differentiate between any difference in the human experience. Anti-ableism requires intentional action; as OTPs, committing to anti-ableism means being conscious of disability and ableism and taking steps to eliminate disability inequality within society.

The EMPOWER model is meant to be a practical guide for OTPs to implement these strategies, all the while emphasizing the importance of viewing the individual, occupation, and environment as constantly being interconnected. You cannot separate the individual, the environment, and the occupation as separate entities. By adopting an inclusive and intertwined perspective, you can better understand the experiences of Disabled individuals within the context of an ableist society and take concrete steps to challenge and change these inequities in your daily practice.

The EMPOWER Model Supports Development of Neurodivergent Identity

Neurodivergent individuals have the right to engage in occupations that affirm who they are, occupations that foster a sense of belonging within their culture, and validate ways of living that may even be performed differently when compared to neurotypical occupations. OTPs play a critical role in supporting this by promoting and facilitating Neurodivergent occupations that are reflective of the individual's unique neurotype and lived experience. Supporting OTPs and their ability to promote Neurodivergent participation and well-being are emphasized throughout the model. When you authentically enhance participation in Neurodivergent occupations, you are not just providing a service—you are actualizing occupational justice by upholding the dignity and autonomy of Neurodivergent individuals. The EMPOWER model serves as a guide for OTPs to ensure their practices are supporting Neurodivergent engagement and supporting Neurodivergent occupational participation.

The EMPOWER Model Fosters Client-Centered Practice

Client-centered practice requires the incorporation of the client's perspectives throughout the entire service provision process and has been an essential component of occupational therapy practice since the origins of the profession.[24] Client-centered occupational therapy is a collaborative approach *with* the client, a strong semantic difference to the term *patient* secondary to Neurodivergent individuals feeling like services are being provided *to* versus *with*, especially in a system that marginalizes Neurodivergent perspectives. Client-centered services prioritize the client's voice, fostering respect and shared decision-making. As brilliantly stated by Bailliard et al.,[25] client-centered services are narrative-centered, meaning we can "enable clients to be and do what they find personally meaningful... and co-create therapeutic processes and ongoing, socio-culturally congruent narratives of 'healing' towards clients' ideal futures and occupations." By actively incorporating the lived experiences of Neurodivergent individuals into every step of the occupational therapy process, we not only support their healing from the impacts of ableism but also promote their participation in meaningful occupations as acts of social and occupational justice.

Throughout the EMPOWER model, client-centered practice is exemplified throughout every stage of the anti-ableist occupational therapy process. The EMPOWER model demands active and thoughtful collaboration with the client.

For example, when working with a Neurodivergent student struggling with sensory overload in a classroom, the OTP might first listen to the student's own description of what aspects of their day or their environment feel uncomfortable. By including these insights, the OTP can recommend specific accommodations, educate the student's team on their sensory processing patterns, and help the student feel more understood and supported within the school. The narratives and stories of Neurodivergent individuals are the most valuable sources of information, and OTPs can tailor services to better address the client's environmental factors and the broader context of their hopes and dreams within an ableist society. This approach not only supports the client in navigating an ableist world but also fosters a positive Neurodivergent identity.

When I am working with my Neurodivergent students and their families, and affirm that "yes, requiring your student to sit still at their desk goes completely against what their body needs" or "yes, the behavior management plan doesn't even begin to touch the surface of what your student truly needs and in fact causes more harm," I am validating their stories. I am telling them "I believe you, and it needs to change." And let me tell you, having someone share that they believe you when practically nobody else does is powerful. Almost like reaching a life raft in a raging, stormy sea, a small but crucial lifeline that emphasizes the safety, security, and peace that comes with being believed. It is such an exhale.

The EMPOWER Model Endorses Occupation-Based Practice

Since our profession began the return journey to occupation-based practice, it's been considered best practice for OTPs to be occupation-centered in our work, including evaluation and therapeutic supports.[26] Occupation-centered practice is also known as a top-down approach; you are always beginning with the client's participation in that occupation. Using an occupation-centered approach, you are focusing on activities that are meaningful to the client while also recognizing the intersection of their broader life context with that occupation, such as social roles, cultural background, and environmental factors. Occupation-centered practices recognize we are all occupational beings, and that participating in meaningful activities is central to our health, well-being, and identity. Because it prioritizes what is meaningful to the client, occupation-based practice naturally aligns with neurodiversity-affirming frameworks and supports the health and well-being priorities of Neurodivergent individuals.

The opposite of occupation-based practice is impairment-based practice, aligning with a bottom-up approach. Impairment-based practice has the OTP begin with identifying and having services focus on treating specific impairments (hence the name), such as functions of the body or physiological structures (e.g.

muscle weakness, cognition, sensory processing). Impairment-based practice does not require OTPs to reconcile or consider how the environment impacts that individual's participation in occupations (it is impossible to be neurodiversity-affirming while also implementing deficit-based practice). The idea is focusing on body structural components and that performance factors are prerequisites for supporting occupational performance, with the assumption that treating the body structural components leads to an upstream gain in occupational participation. However, this upstream gain assumption is not supported by research.[27]

In impairment-based practice, goals are typically set by the therapist and focus on addressing impairments without connecting them to meaningful occupations. This might look like an OTP working on sensory tolerance to shaving cream because the individual is hypersensitive to tactile input (this is also really ableist; never work on sensory tolerance unless the client advocates for it!). This approach overlooks the crucial contextual factors that must be considered, and services provided do not directly involve activities that actually matter to the client (working on cutting even though the student isn't passionate about arts and crafts). Impairment-based approaches are closely tied to the medical model of disability given their focus on remediating identified deficits, and influence the OTP to incorporate ableist practices. Despite the profession's push toward occupation-based practice, research indicates that impairment-based and bottom-up approaches are still the primary approaches to therapy in various settings within occupational therapy[28,29,30]; they are still the norm and this needs to change.

Using an occupation-based practice is critical when working with Neurodivergent clients, and is a necessary component of neurodiversity-affirming practice. With the EMPOWER model, you start by focusing on the client's participation in activities that matter to them. As you work together, you assess their needs and preferences through evaluation and intervention. If you and the client find that addressing specific impairments is necessary to help the client reach their goals, absolutely integrate this into your approach! There are definitely times where using a bottom-up framework or theory can help understand a specific performance challenge. That being said, I always encourage my students to begin viewing the client and their needs through an occupation-based lens, and then use the bottom-up framework as a secondary lens to inform (not define) their understanding of the client and their needs. The important thing here is you are empowering the client's autonomy; you are providing them the choice to choose. You are allowing the client to advocate for their needs by allowing them to be a collaborator in how their services will be provided. However, the primary focus should always be on using occupation as both a means and an end, ensuring that your therapy's goal is helping the individual participate in activities that are meaningful to them (not to us) rather than solely targeting impairments.

Table 12.2—The EMPOWER Model and Neurodiversity-Affirming Therapeutic Principles

NA Therapeutic Principle	EMPOWER Model Examples
Prioritizing Lived Experience	• **Inclusive Evaluations** (*Chapter 9*): OTPs can start the assessment process by asking clients to share their stories and experiences, supporting them to be in the "driver's seat" when it comes to shaping goals. An example for a client with schizophrenia, an OTP might ask them to describe what a typical day looks like, inquiring in a non-judgmental way about how their hearing of voices inhibits and promotes their ability to function throughout the day rather than relying on data from standardized assessments (or even viewing their hearing of voices immediately as a bad thing). • **Disability Justice and Antiracism** (*Chapters 4, 6*): OTPs must apply an intersectional lens to understand how a client's various identities (e.g. race, gender, disability) interact and are impacted by the environment to even begin to have an understanding of their occupational performance and participation. For instance, an OTP working with a Black, Disabled woman may consider how racism, sexism, and ableism affect her access to healthcare and employment opportunities and tailor supports accordingly, such as providing her strategies and resources to advocate for herself during medical appointments, positive identity development, resource mapping (helping the client in locating culturally safe resources), exploring job opportunities that align with her strengths and interests, and accommodate her disability(ies). The OTP would pursue ongoing education and resources to learn about antiracism and reflect on their presumptions of what occupation looks like (think about: when someone asks you to envision someone participating in dancing, how often do you picture an Indigenous person enacting the Eagle or Grass Dance instead of a white person engaging in ballet or modern dancing?).
Promotes Anti-Ableism	The EMPOWER model includes an anti-ableist occupational therapy process, with anti-ableist examples including: • **Critical Reflexivity** (*Chapter 8*): Regularly reflect on your views of disability and how having a neurotypical (and Neurodivergent) identity may influence your assumptions and practice. Consider how these biases might affect your work. • **Inclusive Evaluations** (*Chapter 9*): Shift to a neurodiversity-affirming approach by using assessment tools that validate Neurodivergent lived experiences (most often not standardized), writing strengths-based reports, and prioritizing the Disabled individual's experience as the primary source of information. This step also includes developing goals that empower clients and recognize the diversity of occupations, particularly those that may differ from neurotypical norms.

cont.

NA Therapeutic Principle	EMPOWER Model Examples
Promotes Anti-Ableism *cont.*	• **Affirming Supports and Practices** *(Chapter 10)*: Integrate neurodiversity-affirming components into every step of your therapy process. Ensure that you are promoting inclusivity and belonging, and tailor supports to meet the unique needs of Neurodivergent clients without assuming what you think they should be! • **Neurodivergent Occupations and Outcomes** *(Chapter 3)*: Ensure that you are supporting Neurodivergent individuals in participating in occupations that are meaningful to them, and not how you think participation should look. It's okay if we participate in meaningful activities that are different from how most people perform them! Challenge and dismantle preconceived notions about what constitutes an occupation. Reflect on the example shared by Dr. Dallman in Chapter 3: Why do we consider it "socially appropriate" or "normal" to listen to folks walking along the street or entering a grocery humming their favorite songs as we pass them by but not the person with schizophrenia interacting or responding to their voices? *This* is Neurodivergent occupational participation! • **Advocacy** *(Chapter 11)*: Engage in advocacy efforts at all levels—micro, meso, and macro—to promote neurodiversity and combat ableism within your practice, workplace, and the broader community.
Supports Neurodivergent Development	• **Disability Justice** *(Chapter 4)*: The EMPOWER model emphasizes the importance of recognizing and addressing the systemic barriers that Neurodivergent individuals face; you cannot avoid this and be neurodiversity-affirming! For example, functional behavior assessments (FBA) have been advocated against by Neurodivergent individuals secondary to the FBA and followed with a positive-behavior support plan (PBSP) relying mostly on superficial expressions of emotional expression, with limited inclusion of the student's internal states, voice, and contexts. An OTP can advocate for the inclusion of the Why Toolkit, which is a (truly a rad resource) trauma-informed and neurodiversity-affirming alternative to support the team in better understanding the Neurodivergent student and the adaptations and education that must occur. • **Strengths-Based Practice** *(Chapter 7)*: The EMPOWER model focuses on amplifying the strengths and capabilities of Neurodivergent individuals while creating supports that honor who they are and how they see themselves. • **Affirming Practices and Supports** *(Chapter 10)*: Affirming supports and practices involve providing services that validate and celebrate Neurodivergent identities. OTPs need to modify services to align with the individual's neurotype and preferences; it takes practice, but I promise it gets easier over time. For example, if a client uses stimming as a form of self-regulation, a practice that supports a positive Neurodivergent identity would involve supporting this rather than discouraging it, and providing education to their families on how to support stimming within their natural environments.

Fosters Client-Centered Practice	• **Trauma-Informed Care** (*Chapter 5*): Let's say an OTP is working with a Neurodivergent client who has experienced trauma from previous therapy sessions. The practitioner OTP should create a safe and predictable environment by allowing the client to set the pace for therapy and choose activities that feel safe to them. Even though we are often dictated to be as productive as possible, challenge capitalist culture, and take your time with the client. It's absolutely possible with some wordsmithing, and ensure you are relating your work to function! • **Antiracism** (*Chapter 6*): An OTP is working with a Black Neurodivergent student who struggles with sensory overload at their predominantly white school. The OTP collaborates with the school to implement environmental changes. This may be advocating for culturally inclusive, sensory-friendly spaces within the school for which the adolescent can retreat for breaks and feel more comfortable (access to culturally relevant music, culturally significant textiles on the walls, essential oils with scents tied to various cultures, such as sage and sweetgrass for some Indigenous communities).[31] Ideally, the OTP would collaborate with teachers on ways to implement more culturally relevant materials and activities within the classroom to minimize triggers and maximize an atmosphere of acceptance that is welcoming and affirming of the student so we can reduce the potential need for the student to feel like they need to leave the classroom. • **Critical Reflexivity** (*Chapter 8*): OTPs should regularly reflect on their own biases and assumptions about neurodivergence and ableism. When we discover a new therapeutic technique or program, we must engage in reflection to ensure the program is accepted by the community we are attempting to support. Exploring Facebook groups led by Neurodivergent individuals is a great start! You can search the group to see if the community has shared their feedback on that technique or whether or not the theory guiding the program is validating Neurodivergent experiences.
Endorses Occupation-Based Practice	• **Critical Reflexivity** (*Chapter 8*): An OTP working with an Autistic adult who struggles with neurotypical social norms in the workplace might initially think that the goal should be to help the client "fit in" better with neurotypical colleagues. Through critical reflexivity, the OTP examines their own biases and the ableist assumptions that equate success with conforming to neurotypical social behaviors. This reflection leads the OTP to shift their approach, focusing instead on how the work environment can be adapted to support the client's Autistic communication style, such as through written communication or structured meetings with clear agendas. With their Autistic client's permission, the OTP works with the Autistic adult on leading training for their workplace discussing the double empathy problem and Autistic communication styles to promote acceptance and understanding within the workplace.

cont.

NA Therapeutic Principle	EMPOWER Model Examples
Endorses Occupation-Based Practice *cont.*	• **Inclusive Evaluations** *(Chapter 9)*: Prioritizing naturalistic observations, the client's lived experiences, and using assessment tools that focus on the client's interests, participation in occupations, and consideration of contextual factors instead of the evaluation prioritizing standardized assessments and locating deficits. Evaluations should be respectful and tailored to the Neurodivergent individual's occupational identity. • **Affirming Supports and Practices** *(Chapter 10)*: Occupation-based interventions are designed around activities that are empowering and meaningful for the client. For example, a teenager with depression who loves digital art might work with the therapist to develop a routine that incorporates digital art-making as a form of self-expression and stress management. The OTP could even explore ways to adapt the activity to accommodate executive functioning and sensory processing differences.

Future Directions

Acknowledging that the EMPOWER model is still in its early stages and hasn't yet been formally tested or vetted, there's much room for growth and refinement, and I have two prioritized next steps. If you would like more practical ideas on how to implement the EMPOWER model in practice, including the EMPOWER model action plan, a case study, and more, please visit the Vault ! The first step is to publish the model as a theoretical paper in a peer-reviewed journal. I am honored to share that the article has been accepted for publication and is scheduled for release in fall 2026. The article will be a fabulous supplement to this chapter, offering a deep examination of the research informing the model and providing many practical examples of how to implement aspects of the model in practice. My hope is that publishing the model will help it gain recognition, enter academic conversations, and ultimately support the model's general visibility. At the time of this writing, the article was accepted for publication and I hope it's published soon![32]

One of my dreams is to conduct a qualitative study inviting Neurodivergent OTPs to critically examine the model—tearing it apart, providing feedback, and sharing insights on what resonates and what's missing. As a Neurodivergent individual myself, I recognize that my perspective is shaped by layers of privileged intersectional identities, and I want the model to reflect the diverse and complex experiences of Neurodivergent ways of living. Once I receive this feedback, I plan on expanding the EMPOWER model and how it can go beyond micro-level practices (e.g. one-on-one with the client), and support population and community-level Neurodivergent occupational participation. I also would like to collaborate with Indigenous OTPs and modify the model to better resonate with Indigenous occupations and contexts.

Conclusion

The EMPOWER model stands as a transformative approach in occupational therapy, challenging us to rethink everything we have known about occupation and what ways of living can look like, especially with Neurodivergent individuals. By grounding our practice in disability justice, trauma-informed care, antiracism, and strengths-based approaches, coupled with an anti-ableist OT process, we can begin to dismantle the deeply rooted ableism that pervades our work, mainstream approaches, evidence-based practices, and within our profession. It is about occupational therapy services that give value to lived experiences, help build positive Neurodivergent identity with our clients, and make sure our practice really is client-led and occupation-based.

But embarking on this journey is not easy; I know because I am still on this journey myself! Becoming anti-ableist goes against much of what we've been taught, and it requires an ongoing and intentional effort to unlearn and relearn. Creating and facilitating change requires discomfort and that is okay! We need to build our resiliency (myself included) around being able to have the necessary tough conversations because from these conversations, so much personal, community, and societal growth comes from this discomfort.

As you apply concepts from this book to your work as an OTP, remember that this is a lifelong journey; you don't take one neurodiversity workshop or read a book and think "okay I am now neurodiversity-affirming, no more reflection for me!" Give yourself permission to stumble and make mistakes along the way. It's important to approach this process with patience, reflection, and kindness toward yourself. Even for those of us who have been deeply engaged in this work, navigating the complexities of ableism is still a (very frustrating) learning experience. As we move forward, we must remember that every new insight we gain or even the smallest of actions are significant and beautiful strides toward making our profession (and world) more validating and affirming for all human beings. I believe in you, and you got this!

Endnotes

1 Talero, P. (2020). Diverse perspectives of health and disability through an occupational lens. In K. Barrett, S. Coppola, & L. A. Jaramillo (Eds.), *International occupational therapy: Strategies for working and learning abroad* (pp. 57–72). American Occupational Therapy Association.

2 Carlson-Giving, B. (in press). The EMPOWER model: A framework for fostering neurodivergent occupational participation and supporting neurodiversity-affirming occupational therapy practice. *Open Journal of Occupational Therapy*.

3 Grief, A., & Stoffel, A. (2019, April 5). *Using participation and occupation to guide the pediatric occupational therapy process* [Conference session]. American Occupational Therapy Conference, New Orleans, LA, United States.

4 Skuthan, A., & Stav, W. (2024). Occupation-based assessments in pediatric occupational therapy practice. *OTJR: Occupation, Participation and Health*, *44*(2), 159–167. https://doi.org/10.1177/15394492231188315

5 Carlson-Giving, B. (2023). *Embracing Neurodivergent occupations and empowering disabled*

voices: A knowledge translation tool to support neurodiversity-affirming occupational therapy practice and challenge ableism within the profession [Doctoral dissertation, Boston University]. ProQuest Dissertations and Theses Global. https://hdl.handle.net/2144/46622

6 Taylor, E. (2022). Beyond "bad" behaviors: A call for occupational scientists to rethink autism. *Journal of Occupational Science*, 1–16. https://doi.org/10.1080/14427591.2022.2136231

7 Sins Invalid. (2019). *Skin, tooth, and bone: The basis of movement is our people* (2nd ed.). [Digital version]. www.sinsinvalid.org

8 Substance Abuse and Mental Health Services Administration (SAMHSA). (2014). *SAMHSA's concepts of trauma and guidance for a trauma-informed approach*. Substance Abuse and Mental Health Services Administration. https://store.samhsa.gov/sites/default/files/sma14-4884.pdf

9 Patten, K. K. (2022). Finding our strengths: Recognizing professional bias and interrogating systems. *The American Journal of Occupational Therapy: Official Publication of the American Occupational Therapy Association*, *76*(6). https://doi.org/10.5014/ajot.2022.076603

10 Reed, K. (2024). *Strengths-based collective*. www.strengthbasedcollective.com

11 Tawa, K. (2020). *Redefining evidence-based practices: Expanding our view of evidence*. www.clasp.org/wp-content/uploads/2022/01/Evidence-Based-Practice-Brief_05152020.pdf

12 Taylor, E. (2022). Beyond "bad" behaviors: A call for occupational scientists to rethink autism. *Journal of Occupational Science*. https://doi.org/10.1080/14427591.2022.2136231

13 Tawa, K. (2020). *Redefining evidence-based practices: Expanding our view of evidence*. www.clasp.org/wp-content/uploads/2022/01/Evidence-Based-Practice-Brief_05152020.pdf

14 Martinez, K., Callejas, L., & Hernandez, M. (2010). Community-defined evidence: A bottom-up behavioral health approach to measure what works in communities of color. *Emotional & Behavioral Disorders in Youth*, *11–16*. www.engagelivinglab.org/wp-content/uploads/2021/04/Community-Defined-Evidence-Martinez-et-al-2010.pdf

15 Wise, S. J. (2023). Lived experience informed practice: An alternative to evidence-based practice. *Medium*. https://medium.com/@livedexperienceeducator/lived-experience-informed-practice-an-alternative-to-evidence-based-practice-23a60e35602f

16 Community-Defined Evidence Practice (CDEP) Integration Advisory Group. (2021). *Concept paper: Policy options for community-defined evidence practices (CDEPS)*. California Pan-Ethnic Health Network. https://cpehn.org/publications/concept-paper-policy-options-for-community-defined-evidence-practices-cdeps

17 Carlson-Giving, B. (2025). *How current mainstream EBP approaches perpetuate inequity and injustice*. Neurodivergent Nexus. https://neurodivergentnexus.com/ebpandableism

18 Kafai, S. (2022). *Crip kinship*. Arsenal Pulp Press.

19 Napoli, S. (2023). *The disabled mindset: Embracing my disability identity*. Disability & Philanthropy Forum. https://disabilityphilanthropy.org/resource/the-disabled-mindset-embracing-my-disability-identity

20 Vine, G. (2024). *Occupational therapy, disability activism, and me: Challenging ableism in healthcare*. Jessica Kingsley Publishers.

21 Andrews, E. E., Ayers, K. B., Brown, K. S., Dunn, D. S., & Pilarski, C. R. (2021). No body is expendable: Medical rationing and disability justice during the COVID-19 pandemic. *The American Psychologist*, *76*(3), 451–461. https://doi.org/10.1037/amp0000709

22 Doebrich, A., Quirici, M., & Lunsford, C. (2020). COVID-19 and the need for disability conscious medical education, training, and practice. *Journal of Pediatric Rehabilitation Medicine*, *13*(3), 393–404. https://doi.org/10.3233/PRM-200763

23 Kennedy Krieger Institute. (2022). *Becoming anti-ableist: A disability justice informed approach to supporting the disability community*. www.kennedykrieger.org/sites/default/files/library/documents/community/maryland-center-for-developmental-disabilities-mcdd/Anti-Ableist%20and%20Inclusive%20Practice%20Resource%20Guide%20FINAL2.pdf

24 Mroz, T. M., Pitonyak, J. S., Fogelberg, D., & Leland, N. E. (2015). Client centeredness and health reform: Key issues for occupational therapy. *The American Journal of Occupational Therapy*, *69*(5), 6905090010. https://doi.org/10.5014/ajot.2015.695001

25 Bailliard, A. L., Dallman, A. R., Carroll, A., Lee, B. D., & Szendrey, S. (2020). Doing occupational justice: A central dimension of everyday occupational therapy practice. *Canadian Journal of Occupational Therapy. Revue Canadienne D'ergotherapie*, *87*(2), 144–152. https://doi.org/10.1177/0008417419898930, p. 147.

26 Skuthan, A., & Stav, W. (2024). Occupation-based assessments in pediatric occupational therapy practice. *OTJR: Occupation, Participation and Health*, *44*(2), 159–167. https://doi.org/10.1177/15394492231188315

27 Novak, I., & Honan, I. (2019). Effectiveness of paediatric occupational therapy for children with disabilities: A systematic review. *Australian Occupational Therapy Journal*, *66*(3), 258–273. https://doi.org/10.1111/1440-1630.12573

28 Skuthan, A., & Stav, W. (2024). Occupation-based assessments in pediatric occupational therapy practice. *OTJR: Occupation, Participation and Health*, *44*(2), 159–167. https://doi.org/10.1177/15394492231188315

29 Burley, S., Di Tommaso, A., Cox, R., & Molineux, M. (2018). An occupational perspective in hand therapy: A scoping review. *The British Journal of Occupational Therapy*, *81*(6), 299–318. https://doi.org/10.1177/0308022617752110

30 Holler, R., Chemla, I., & Maeir, A. (2021). Disability orientation of occupational therapy practitioners in physical rehabilitation settings: Tension between medical and social models in theory and practice. *The American Journal of Occupational Therapy*, *75*(4), 7504180010. https://doi.org/10.5014/ajot.2021.042986

31 Sequoia Proudly Indigenous. (2025). *Sequoia proudly indigenous: Home*. Sequoia Proudly Indigenous. https://sequoiasoaps.com

32 Carlson-Giving, B. (in press). The EMPOWER model: A framework for fostering neurodivergent occupational participation and supporting neurodiversity-affirming occupational therapy practice. *Open Journal of Occupational Therapy*

Acknowledgements

To the co-authors and contributors—this remarkable journey of words and dreams would not be possible without the nearly 50 co-authors and contributors who have embraced this vision. Thank you for sharing your heart, soul, and experiences with this book, and thank you for your trust and patience as we navigated this adventure together. Embarking on the role of an editor (let alone writing a book) was new to me; I hope my efforts were worthy of your brilliance. Your community is the greatest a smalltown Disabled Queer boy can hope for. This book isn't mine; it's ours.

To Lori—this book never would have existed if it were not for your support of my outlandish ideas during my doctoral work years ago, and thank you for being patient with my incessant emails looking for comfort, guidance, and feedback. You are the epitome of an extraordinary occupational therapy practitioner, and I am eternally grateful for our friendship (thank you, Karen Jacobs, for connecting us!).

To Jessica Kingsley Publishers—when you initially reached out about my writing a book because you'd heard a few of my podcasts... I thought your email was spam (sorry). Thank you for not only believing in this idea, but holding space for us to unapologetically call out occupational injustice and hopefully inspire others.

To my family—your warmth knows no bounds. Mom, thank you for your endless encouragement, and your tenderness really is infinite. Marcus, thank you for teaching me the strength of resilience and to face life's challenges head-on. Tay Tay and Aerica, thank you for reminding me to not "sweat the small stuff" and being a wellspring of humor and light.

And last but certainly not least, to Zack—thank you for being the tether to my kite. You have a gift to see beauty in the chaos. Thank you for reminding me that I don't need to earn rest, and even when this project quickly became all-consuming, you were a comforting barrier during my frequent "zooming ins." I love you, and your warmth shines brighter than ten thousand suns.

Appendix A – Reflections for Change

This tool has been designed to be reused after each chapter.

Reflections for Change

What new insights have you gained that challenge your previous understanding and assumptions of occupational therapy?	What actionable steps or ideas can you implement based on your new learning to promote inclusivity and empowerment in your practice?
What challenges do you foresee in applying the principles from this chapter, and how might you overcome them?	What new questions or curiosities have emerged for you as a result of this chapter that you would like to further explore?

Appendix B – Matrices for Action

BRYDEN CARLSON-GIVING, MUSHARRAT J. AHMED-LANDERYOU, AMY COOPERSMITH, MEG FERRELL, RYAN LAVALLEY, AMY K. LYNCH, DEVLYNN NEU, AND TONI SAIA

When I (BCG) first envisioned this book, I knew I wanted a resource that had practical strategies on how to apply some of the foundations of the book (disability justice, trauma-informed care, antiracism, and strengths-based approaches) to the five steps of the anti-ableist occupational therapy process (critical reflexivity, inclusive evaluations, affirming services and supports, Neurodivergent outcomes, and advocacy). I encourage you to use this resource as a supplementary tool alongside their corresponding chapters to support your journey in being a neurodiversity-affirming and justice-focused practitioner. An expanded version is available for download within the Vault. I would like to extend a heartfelt thank you to the contributors who helped shape this resource.

Critical Reflexivity	
Disability Justice	• Take self-assessments, such as the Assessment of Individual Ableism,[1] the Symbolic Ableism Scale,[2] and the Neurodiversity Attitudes Scale,[3] to examine your implicit biases and how they influence your work with Disabled individuals. • Respect and learn about the language choices of the individual. Identity-first language (i.e. Autistic) and person-first language (person with autism) are both valid options.[4] • Review common ways ableism appears in therapy spaces; use this resource as a "checklist" of sorts as a regular check-in.[5]

cont.

Critical Reflexivity	
Trauma-Informed Care	• Recognize Neurodivergent individuals have a higher chance of experiencing trauma secondary to living within an ableist world, and experiencing ableism every day. One big area of microaggression occurs when neurotypical individuals presume Neurodivergent individuals do not have or understand emotions (double empathy problem). • Neurodivergent individuals often have how they feel or their emotions misunderstood or mislabeled by neurotypical individuals (e.g. don't presume how someone is feeling based on what you think those feelings look like). It is vital that providers reflect on their own mannerisms in therapeutic alliance and ensure they do not contribute to this presumption. Different Neurodivergent cultures have their own norms for expressing emotions. Providers need to expand cultural humility concepts to understand and respond to the emotional perspectives of Neurodivergent individuals.
Antiracism	• Learn and unlearn—interrogate how you have been recycling the status quo of racism, discrimination, and disadvantage through self-beliefs, own values, existing knowledge, and world views; apply Otto Scharmer's[6] four levels of better listening, especially when having conversations about inequities. • Embrace the concept of Two-Eyed Seeing. With each knowledge representing an eye, you combine the perspectives and strengths of Indigenous knowledge with the perspectives of Eurocentric knowledge, and you utilize both eyes together in order to benefit all.[7]
Strengths-Based Approaches	• Read "Strengths-based approaches: What if even the 'bad' things are good things?" as an introductory article on the importance of why the profession must shift to a strengths-based mindset and how this paradigm shift can transform occupational therapy: "how powerful will occupational therapy be for everyone when we bring those strengths into the light, celebrate them, embrace them as essential to each of our identities?"[8] • Patten[9] highlights the following reflective questions to ask yourself regarding strengths-based practice: – Am I focusing on weaknesses in the absence of strengths? – Am I offering activities and choices that are related to interests? – Am I viewing Neurodivergent interests as strengths versus motivators or worse yet suppressing them as maladaptive behaviors? – Am I combining a strengths perspective with the challenges that are being addressed? The first place to find the answers to those questions is to examine our evaluations, goals, individual educational plans, and interventions. If the answer is a one-line response for "strengths," it is time to see the biased perspective and make the shift to an authentic strengths-based practice. • Recognize Neurodivergent individuals have interests, strengths, and abilities that often surpass their neurotypical peers, especially when in the right contexts.[10]

Inclusive Evaluations	
Disability Justice	• Consider evaluating the intensity of masking experienced by the individual, such as the Camouflaging Autistic Traits Questionnaire for young adults and above (CAT-Q) and the Masking Regulator for adolescents.[11] • Set goals with the Neurodivergent individual and do not assume the family's priorities align with the individual's hopes, dreams, and identity. While the family's/caregiver's experience is valuable, ensure that the individual's perspective and needs remain the primary focus.
Trauma-Informed Care	• How can you modify assessment tools that require touch (e.g. manual muscle testing, range of motion) to support the individual's regulation? Always ask for consent, take extra time to explain why, or gather this data by observing the client participating in an activity.[12] • Reflect on the need to utilize assessments that require gender norms, as this may inflict harm on Transgender and Gender-Expansive individuals. Is there a need to use an assessment that requires comparison to gender norms? Do the norms apply to your client? What other assessment options could you select that are Neurodivergent and gender accessible?
Antiracism	• Standardized assessments are not suitable for use with any population that is not represented in the data on which the norms were developed (e.g. cultural bias of aiming for Eurocentric developmental milestones, lack of linguistic diversity); these assessments do not consider the historical and socio-cultural contexts that Marginalized individuals experience, including the impact of trauma, and ongoing systemic inequalities. Traditional standardized norms centered on white experiences may lead to pathologizing cultural differences (e.g. family structures, communication styles, expectations around independence).[13] • Utilize assessment tools that focus on cultural identity and/or cultural well-being, such as the Cultural Identity Assessment (within the Vault), the Ethno Cultural Assessment,[14] or the Multicultural Mental Health Outcomes and Assessment Tools.[15] • Consider prioritizing observation of culturally relevant tasks over norm-referenced assessment tools.[16]
Strengths-Based Approaches	• Ask the client/caregivers to provide a list of the individual's passions and interests prior to evaluation.[17] Neurodivergent individuals report a greater ability to communicate, regulate themselves, and overall well-being when provided with unrestricted access to interests;[18] if evaluation activities incorporate the individual's interests the OTP can get a more realistic and accurate idea of the individual's skills when engagement and interest is maximized. • Review Chapter 9 for resources on formulating neurodiversity-affirming goals, recommended assessment tools across the life-span, and how to write strengths-based evaluation reports.

cont.

Affirming Services and Supports	
Disability Justice	• Before suggesting changes, assess whether the client perceives a need for them. Actively listen to their goals and priorities, ensuring interventions align with their lived experience rather than assumptions about what needs to be fixed (e.g. if your client has a functional technique for dressing that works for them, trust their expertise in their own body and routine. Focus on their stated goals rather than making unnecessary changes). • Consider having a goal of services be the individual's ability to access a safe space for rest and recovery within their important, natural environments.
Trauma-Informed Care	• **Beauty of Co-Regulation**: When an individual is experiencing dysregulation, telling them to "use the tools you were taught" is too late. In that moment, the prompts you are providing require the cortex for reasoning. When an individual is not regulated, the cortex is unavailable due to a highly activated nervous system. Expectations of self-regulation are both unkind and unreasonable, and risk triggering old or creating new relational trauma. Instead, invite the individual to co-regulation. Share with them choices of tasks or activities to do together which could be regulating, and let the individual decide which to do. Then, be a safe regulatory partner without expecting the individual to regulate on their own.[19] • **Normalize responses to trauma**: Use empathetic language when discussing behaviors or how a client responds (especially within documentation), acknowledging how trauma is expressed differently, and all of these responses are valid.
Antiracism	• Integrate racial healing frameworks, such as the Truth, Racial Healing and Transformation (TRHT) model, to support clients and communities in processing racial trauma and rebuilding agency.[20] • Challenge cultural assumptions in intervention—OTPs may make assumptions about what is considered to be a meaningful activity based on the dominating Eurocentric cultural framework. Collaborate with clients to identify meaningful activities that align with their cultural practices, and not necessarily the dominating norms of what participation in those activities is "supposed" to look like. • Challenge how behaviorism and behaviorist models are used in OT practice, not only due to many frameworks of behaviorism causing harm to Neurodivergent individuals, but how the harm disproportionately impacts BIPOC Neurodivergent individuals.[21]
Strengths-Based Approaches	• **Supporting an authentic partnership**: In today's fast-paced world, teachers, families, and caregivers may want to complete the task for the client instead of providing the client the chance to complete the task on their own terms. Instead of going along with urgency culture, take the time to engage authentically with clients and facilitate environments that highlight their strengths. Though society and insurance companies may pressure you, this isn't a sprint. Skill development for these skills are lifelong journeys that require patience and a focus on sustainable growth.[22]

	• **Learn deeply about the Neurodivergent neurotype you are supporting**: The descriptions of Neurodivergent neurotypes in the Diagnostic and Statistical Manual often do not align with the lived experiences of Neurodivergent individuals. Get curious: what does it feel like to navigate the world with a Neurodivergent brain? Explore trainings, blogs, and social media accounts from Neurodivergent individuals with different intersectional identities. The experience of a white, Queer, Autistic woman may be quite different from that of a Black, straight, Autistic man. Recognize there is more than one way to experience that neurotype (e.g. there isn't one way to be Autistic, an ADHDer, or a voice-hearer). From understanding the double empathy problem, we have learned that without intentional learning and curiosity, we are likely going to misunderstand our Neurodivergent colleagues. Learn more about action steps for strengths-based treatment planning at Ferrell et al.[23]

Neurodivergent Outcomes	
Disability Justice	• Support participation in occupations related to activism, such as protesting, community organizing, crisis response, and reducing activist burnout. • **Acknowledge crip time**: *Crip* is a reclaimed slur by Disabled individuals. Disabled individuals benefit from extra time and effort secondary to the plethora of barriers that exist within an ableist world. Crip time is a concept that recognizes and embraces that Disabled individuals benefit from more flexibility, time, and accommodations. Crip time also signifies liberation, such that the Disabled individual reclaims their time and experience and celebrates how time is experienced differently by Disabled individuals compared to non-disabled individuals (and that is beautiful and okay).[24]
Trauma-Informed Care	• Prioritize activities that align with the individual's interests, gender identity, gender expression, sensory processing patterns, and strengths to promote safety, engagement, and well-being. While these activities promote trust and relationship building between the individual and the OTP, they also support the individual in identifying powerful coping mechanisms and support their healing.
Antiracism	• Regularly challenge expected or assumed outcomes and measures provided by health care systems (e.g. push back against prioritizing outcomes like productivity or conformity over quality of life and self-acceptance, engage in systems advocacy by being at the table and promoting change in how outcomes and success are defined). • Listen for occupations that you may not be aware of or familiar with due to your own positionality and racialization (e.g. be mindful of how Eurocentric norms and racialization shape what you consider to be "valid" or "valuable" occupations and work to dismantle those assumptions in your practice). • Support clients in reclaiming ancestral occupations that may have been historically erased or devalued secondary to colonialism and racism.

cont.

Neurodivergent Outcomes	
Strengths-Based Approaches	• Challenge the idea that Neurodivergent occupations need to be "fixed." For example, ableist views of Neurodivergent performances and occupations include: non-functional play, inflexible, limited eye contact, disordered sensory processing, and decreased attention spans. Strengths-based and neurodiversity-affirming viewpoints would highlight these characteristics instead as what they are: Neurodivergent play, social participation differences, unique sensory processing, and love for sameness.[25] • Explore Autism Level UP!'s resource on sensory processing differences, "Heightened Perception," which discusses how sensory processing differences can pose challenges depending on the context, but also that heightened perceptions can also create remarkable strengths. Use this resource with your clients and support their exploration of their sensory processing patterns in meaningful activities and environments.[26]

Advocacy	
Disability Justice	• Review *Becoming Anti-Ableist: A Disability Justice Informed Approach to Supporting the Disability Community*; it's a fabulous and free 20-page resource that serves as an introduction to how to modify your approaches to be more anti-ableist.[27] • Research must not exploit participants for profit—whether academic (papers, presentations, grants) or otherwise—without ensuring they receive meaningful and equitable compensation. Historically, Disabled people, especially those from Marginalized communities, have been coerced or expected to share their stories and bodies for research, often to their detriment, reinforcing harmful practices like eugenics; therefore, fair compensation that aligns with non-disabled participant standards is essential for equity.[28]
Trauma-Informed Care	• To embrace intersectionality from a trauma-informed perspective, it is essential OTPs learn about the complex layers of trauma experienced by Marginalized individuals specific to their community. Examples include: - For learning about LGBTQIA+ considerations, review Neumann et al.[29] - For recognizing and addressing the impacts of racism on trauma, review Williams et al.[30] and Abou-Arab.[31] - To understand the impacts of colonial trauma and considerations when supporting Indigenous individuals from a trauma-informed perspective, review Smallwood et al.[32] and Gone.[33]
Antiracism	• Recognize where you are at in your allyship journey, and learn how to enact occupational therapy practice that embodies an authentic antiracist stance from an allyship perspective. Remember that learning and progress in becoming an ally isn't linear. We are human beings, and making mistakes is inevitable. "Failing forward" is often a necessary part of learning how to progress as an ally to antiracist work. When you receive feedback of harm you have caused, resist the urge to be defensive or retreat from the work. Taking accountability and committing to do better going forward are vital aspects to be an ally.[34]

	• Consider exploring the *White Ally Toolkit Workbook*[35] and the *Antiracism Toolkit for Allies*,[36] both free resources to harness your ability to be an ally to antiracism work. • For OT educators, consider including the Culturally Responsive Care in Occupational Therapy embedded in Service-Learning (CRCOT-SL), which guides OT educators on how to teach students to support occupational participation and social justice within a local and global context.[37]
Strengths-Based Approaches	• Instead of describing an individual as "low-" or "high-functioning," shift the language to describe environments. Chapter 7 provides practical ideas for making the shift from low/high-functioning individuals to low/high-functioning environments. • If you are involved in research, consider incorporating the Strengths, Skills, and Goals Matrix (SSGM) to promote community-based participatory action research. The SSGM is a tool originally developed to support the participation of Neurodivergent adolescents and young adults as partners in research. The SSGM has a step-by-step guide with examples on how to apply the tool in practice.[38]

Endnotes

1 Bridges Learning System. (2021). *Assessment of individual ableism*. Bridges Learning System. https://bridgeslearningsystem.com/wp-content/uploads/2021/12/SEA-Bridge_Assessment-of-Individual-Ableism.pdf

2 Friedman, C., & Awsumb, J. (2019). The symbolic ableism scale. *Review of Disability Studies: An International Journal, 15*(1). https://rdsjournal.org/index.php/journal/article/view/814

3 Schuck, R. K., Choi, S., Baiden, K. M., Dwyer, P., & Uljarević, M. (2024). The Neurodiversity Attitudes Questionnaire: Development and initial validation. *Autism: The International Journal of Research and Practice, 28*(11), 2821–2833. https://doi.org/10.1177/13623613241245756

4 Saia, T. (n.d.). *The shift to identity-first language*. Anti Ableist Teaching. www.antiableistteaching.com/modules/theshifttoidentity-firstlanguage

5 Turner, I. (2023). *Ableism in the therapy room*. KDH Counseling. www.kdholmeslpc.com/isla-turner-ms-lpc/ableism-in-the-therapy-room

6 Scharmer, O. (n.d.). *Mindful listening and speaking: 4 levels of listening*. Team Change. www.teamchange.nl/wp-content/uploads/Mindful-communication_handout.pdf

7 Martin, D. H. (2012). Two-eyed seeing: A framework for understanding Indigenous and non-Indigenous approaches to Indigenous health research. *Revue Canadienne de Recherche En Sciences Infirmieres [The Canadian Journal of Nursing Research], 44*(2), 20–42. https://pubmed.ncbi.nlm.nih.gov/22894005

8 Dunn, W. (2017). Strengths-based approaches: What if even the "bad" things are good things? *British Journal of Occupational Therapy, 80*(7), 395–396. https://doi.org/10.1177/0308022617702660

9 Patten, K. K. (2022). Finding our strengths: Recognizing professional bias and interrogating systems. *The American Journal of Occupational Therapy, 76*(6). https://doi.org/10.5014/ajot.2022.076603

10 Nash, J. (2024). *Neurodiversity in the workplace: A strengths-based approach*. PositivePsychology. https://positivepsychology.com/neurodiversity-in-the-workplace

11 Fede, J., & Laurent, A. (2023). *The masking regulator*. Autism Level UP! https://cdn.sanity.io/files/p6bm7moz/production/4de925ca8a61578a68a0a9bc506484fbdf1f9e27.pdf

12 Clairy, K., Ochsenbein, M., & Spielmann, V. (2021). Trauma in Neurodivergent participations. In A. Lynch, R. Ashcraft, & L. Tekell (Eds.), *Trauma, occupation, and participation: Foundations and population considerations in occupational therapy* (pp. 345–366). AOTA Press.

13 White, T., & Beagan, B. L. (2020). Occupational therapy roles in an Indigenous context: An integrative review. *Canadian Journal of Occupational Therapy. Revue Canadienne d'ergotherapie, 87*(3), 200–210. https://doi.org/10.1177/0008417420924933

14 Finley, L. Y. (1990). *Ethno cultural assessment*. PRIME Institute. www.psychrehabassociation.org/sites/default/files/series-documents/ho_3_multicultural_assessment_guide.pdf

15 Transcultural Mental Health Centre. (n.d.). *Multicultural mental health outcomes and assessment tools*. www.dhi.health.nsw.gov.au/transcultural-mental-health-centre-tmhc/resources/multicultural-mental-health-outcomes-and-assessment-tools

16 Pidgeon, F. (2015). Occupational therapy: What does this look like practised in very remote Indigenous areas? *Rural and Remote Health, 15*(2), 3002. www.ncbi.nlm.nih.gov/pubmed/25912169

17 Marnell, L. (2023, April 18). *An end to ableism: Adopting neurodiversity-affirming and strengths-based approaches for pediatric Autistic clients* [Conference session]. American Occupational Therapy Association Conference, Kansas City, MO.

18 Patten, K. K. (2022). Finding our strengths: Recognizing professional bias and interrogating systems. *The American Journal of Occupational Therapy, 76*(6). https://doi.org/10.5014/ajot.2022.076603

19 Lynch, A., & Mahler, K. (2021). Trauma effects on neurobiological, social, emotional, and motor function: Considerations for occupation. In A. Lynch, R. Ashcraft, & L. Tekell (Eds.), *Trauma, occupation, and participation: Foundations and population considerations in occupational therapy* (pp. 19–39). AOTA Press.

20 W. K. Kellogg Foundation. (n.d.). *Truth, racial healing, and transformation*. Heal Our Communities. https://healourcommunities.org

21 Seiger, M. (2022). Disparities in behavior interventions for Black, Indigenous, and people of color in schools. *Culminating Projects in Special Education*, 123. https://repository.stcloudstate.edu/sped_etds/123

22 Ziviani, J. (2015). Occupational performance: A case for self-determination. *Australian Occupational Therapy Journal, 62*(6), 393–400. https://doi.org/10.1111/1440-1630.12250

23 Ferrell, M., Dorsey, R., & Selvaggi-Hernandez, S. (2023). *A strengths-based approach to supporting Autistic kids* [Online Course]. Learn Play Thrive. https://learnplaythrive.com/strengths-replay

24 Yao, D. P., Sy, M. P., Martinez, P. G., & Laboy, E. C. (2022). Is occupational therapy an ableist health profession? A critical reflection on ableism and occupational therapy. *Cadernos Brasileiros de Terapia Ocupacional, 30*. https://doi.org/10.1590/2526-8910.ctore252733032

25 Marnell, L. (2023, April 18). *An end to ableism: Adopting neurodiversity-affirming and strengths-based approaches for pediatric Autistic clients* [Conference session]. American Occupational Therapy Association Conference, Kansas City, MO.

26 Fede, J. H., & Laurent, A. C. (2020). *Heightened perception: Challenge? Strength? BOTH!* Autism Level UP! https://cdn.sanity.io/files/p6bm7moz/production/aa387214f174ba2a88e2e815eb214c27aef2d163.pdf

27 Kennedy Krieger Institute. (2022). *Becoming anti-ableist: A disability justice informed approach to supporting the disability community*. Kennedy Krieger Institute. www.kennedykrieger.org/sites/default/files/library/documents/community/maryland-center-for-developmental-disabilities-mcdd/Anti-Ableist%20and%20Inclusive%20Practice%20Resource%20Guide%20FINAL2.pdf

28 Saia, T., Yaghmaian, R., Cuesta, R., Mueller, C., & Pebdani, R. N. (2024). A call to action for disability and rehabilitation research using a DisCrit and Disability Justice framework. *Disability and Rehabilitation, 46*(14), 3189–3195. https://doi.org/10.1080/09638288.2023.2242780

29 Neumann, N., Neu, D., & Ungco, J. C. (2021). Addressing LGBTQIA+ trauma: Your role and your responsibility. In A. Lynch, R. Ashcraft, & L. Tekell (Eds.), *Trauma, occupation, and participation: Foundations and population considerations in occupational therapy* (pp. 195–223). AOTA Press.

30 Williams, M. T., Holmes, S., Zare, M., Haeny, A., & Faber, S. (2023). An evidence-based approach for treating stress and trauma due to racism. *Cognitive and Behavioral Practice, 30*(4), 565–588. https://doi.org/10.1016/j.cbpra.2022.07.001

31 Abou-Arab, A. (2021). Trauma-informed care: Historical and modern implications of racism and the engagement in meaningful activities. In A. Lynch, R. Ashcraft, & L. Tekell (Eds.), *Trauma, occupation, and participation: Foundations and population considerations in occupational therapy* (pp. 223–245). AOTA Press.

32 Smallwood, R., Woods, C., Power, T., & Usher, K. (2021). Understanding the impact of historical trauma due to colonization on the health and well-being of Indigenous young peoples: A systematic scoping review. *Journal of Transcultural Nursing, 32*(1), 59–68. https://doi.org/10.1177/1043659620935955

33 Gone, J. P. (2023). Indigenous historical trauma: Alter-native explanations for mental health inequities. *Daedalus, 152*(4), 130–150. www.amacad.org/publication/daedalus/Indigenous-historical-trauma-alter-native-explanations-mental-health-inequities

34 Lavalley, R., Grenier, M. L., Stanley, K., & Marsden, D. (2024). Active antiracist allyship in occupational therapy practice. In M.

J. Ahmed-Landeryou (Ed.), *Antiracist occupational therapy* (pp. 137–155). Jessica Kingsley Publishers.

35 Campt, D. W. (2018). *The white ally toolkit workbook: Using active listening, empathy, and personal storytelling to promote racial equity.* I AM Publications.

36 Toolkits for Equity. (2020). *Antiracism toolkit for allies.* Duke University Press.

37 Talero, P., Kern, S. B., & Tupé, D. A. (2015). Culturally responsive care in occupational therapy: An entry-level educational model embedded in service-learning. *Scandinavian Journal of Occupational Therapy, 22*(2), 95–102. https://doi.org/10.3109/11038128.2014.997287

38 Allemang, B., Patton, M., Greer, K., Pintson, K., Farias, M., Schofield, K., Samuel, S., Patten, S. B., Sitter, K. C., & Dimitropoulos, G. (2023). Development of the strengths, skills, and goals matrix: A tool for facilitating strengths-based adolescent and young adult engagement in research. *Research Involvement and Engagement, 9*(1), 89. https://doi.org/10.1186/s40900-023-00502-w

Appendix C – List of Supplemental Downloads and Resources in the Vault

The Vault can be reached at:
https://neurodivergentnexus.com/neurodiversityaffirmingotbook.
Password: Neurodiversityot123.

General

- Plain-text of all figures
- Case studies on applying the neurodiversity framework into OT practice by Elizabeth Duffy, Kelsie Olds, Stephanie Olszewski, Robert Pereira, and Rachel Robertson
- List of advocacy organizations and social media accounts to follow
- Expanded applying the foundations to the anti-ableist OT process resource
- Reflections for Change PDF
- An extended resource with ideas on how higher education can support Neurodivergent students (e.g. accommodations, curriculum and assessment, universal design learning, and more) written by Lori Vaughn and Christopher Edwards
- A handout of the co-authors and contributors with their bios
- A Vault item exists that provides resources and strategies to promote neurodiversity-affirming practice in early intervention

Chapter 1 – Introduction to Neurodiversity

- A glossary of terms specific to this chapter

Chapter 5 – Trauma, Interoception, and Occupational Therapy

- A resource describing the ACE study in more detail, with a table of implications for each key finding from the ACE study
- A resource describing how OTPs can address and support each trauma emotional expression (fight, flight, freeze, fawn, hyperarousal, and hypoarousal)
- Case studies

Chapter 6 – Antiracism Occupational Therapy Practice: Why, What, How?

- A glossary of terms specific to this chapter
- A resource that describes how to support antiracism at the macro-level (e.g. leadership, management)

Chapter 9 – Inclusive Evaluations

- The co-authors' version of an occupational profile focused on supporting Neurodivergent clients
- A resource describing the health and well-being priorities of Neurodivergent individuals found within the literature
- A template guiding OTPs throughout the evaluation process with a built-in checklist to support neurodiversity-affirming evaluations
- A template of a letter to be sent to health reimbursement agencies to help advocate for service coverage when they require norm-referenced assessments
- Information on each of the recommended assessment tools, including a description, pricing, website location, and additional notes
- Neurodiversity-affirming goal checklist
- Expanded Table 9.1 (ableist reasons for referral) with more examples
- Expanded Table 9.2 (ableist goals versus neurodiversity-affirming goals) with more examples

- The Cultural Identity Assessment, including the provider guide and a sample case vignette

Chapter 10 – Neurodivergent Empowerment: Affirming Practices and Supportive Strategies

- Resource highlighting more recommendations for OTPs wanting to implement neurodiversity-affirming feeding therapy

Chapter 12 – The Empowering Neurodivergent Occupational Participation and Well-Being (EMPOWER) Model

- EMPOWER model application template with a filled-out version as an example
- Supporting literature for each component of the EMPOWER model
- A case study applying the EMPOWER model in OT practice

...and more! By the time this book is published, there will likely be more resources that have been created and are available to download than are listed in this appendix. Explore the Vault and see what's there!

Index

RAISING READERS
Books Build Bright Futures

Dear Reader,

We'd love your attention for one more page to tell you about the crisis in children's reading, and what we can all do.

Studies have shown that reading for fun is the **single biggest predictor of a child's future life chances** – more than family circumstance, parents' educational background or income. It improves academic results, mental health, wealth, communication skills, ambition and happiness.[1]

The number of children reading for fun is in rapid decline. Young people have a lot of competition for their time. In 2024, 1 in 10 children and young people in the UK aged 5 to 18 did not own a single book at home.[2]

Hachette works extensively with schools, libraries and literacy charities, but here are some ways we can all raise more readers:

- Reading to children for just 10 minutes a day makes a difference
- Don't give up if children aren't regular readers – there will be books for them!
- Visit bookshops and libraries to get recommendations
- Encourage them to listen to audiobooks
- Support school libraries
- Give books as gifts

There's a lot more information about how to encourage children to read on our website: **www.RaisingReaders.co.uk**

Thank you for reading.

hachette UK

1 OECD, '21st-Century Readers: Developing Literacy Skills in a Digital World', 2021, https://www.oecd.org/en/publications/21st-century-readers_a83d84cb-en.html

2 National Literacy Trust, 'Book Ownership in 2024', November 2024, https://literacytrust.org.uk/research-services/research-reports/book-ownership-in-2024